A Year in Command
in Afghanistan

ALSO BY MICHAEL J. FORSYTH
AND FROM MCFARLAND

*The Great Missouri Raid: Sterling Price and
the Last Major Confederate Campaign in
Northern Territory* (2015)

*The Camden Expedition of 1864 and the Opportunity
Lost by the Confederacy to Change the Civil War*
(2003; softcover 2008)

*The Red River Campaign of 1864 and the Loss by the
Confederacy of the Civil War* (2002; softcover 2010)

A Year in Command in Afghanistan

Journal of a United States Army Battalion Commander, 2009–2010

MICHAEL J. FORSYTH

McFarland & Company, Inc., Publishers
Jefferson, North Carolina

The thoughts expressed in this book are the author's only and do not reflect the official policy of the United States Department of Defense.

LIBRARY OF CONGRESS CATALOGUING-IN-PUBLICATION DATA

Names: Forsyth, Michael J., 1966– author.
Title: A year in command in Afghanistan : journal of a United States Army battalion commander, 2009/2010 / Michael J. Forsyth.
Description: Jefferson, North Carolina : McFarland & Company, Inc., Publishers, 2017 | Includes bibliographical references and index.
Identifiers: LCCN 2016046066 | ISBN 9780786472871 (softcover : acid free paper) ∞
Subjects: LCSH: Forsyth, Michael J., 1966– | Afghan War, 2001– —Personal narratives, American. | United States. Army—History—Afghan War, 2001– | Command of troops.
Classification: LCC DS371.413 .F67 2016 | DDC 958.104/742092 [B] —dc23
LC record available at https://lccn.loc.gov/2016046066

BRITISH LIBRARY CATALOGUING DATA ARE AVAILABLE

ISBN (print) 978-0-7864-7287-1
ISBN (ebook) 978-1-4766-0109-0

© 2017 Michael J. Forsyth. All rights reserved

No part of this book may be reproduced or transmitted in any form or by any means, electronic or mechanical, including photocopying or recording, or by any information storage and retrieval system, without permission in writing from the publisher.

Front cover: The author on patrol overlooking Forward Operating Base Kalagush in Afghanistan (U.S. Army)

Printed in the United States of America

McFarland & Company, Inc., Publishers
  Box 611, Jefferson, North Carolina 28640
  www.mcfarlandpub.com

To the memory of Sergeant Elijah John-Miles Rao,
killed in action on 5 December 2009.

A fine soldier, man, husband and father.

Contents

Acknowledgments	ix
Preface	1
Abbreviations and Definitions	5
Introduction	17
I. Preparations and Perceptions, 4 April 2008 to 1 June 2009	25
II. Execution: The Reality from Arrival through the Afghan Presidential Election, 2 June 2009 to 23 August 2009	77
III. Execution: Mounting Frustrations and a Change in Outlook, 24 August 2009 to 6 December 2009	150
IV. Sustaining the Fight and Making a Difference, 7 December 2009 to 3 April 2010	225
V. Change of Mission: Pressing to the Finish Line, 4 April 2010 to 31 May 2010	286
VI. Possibilities	334
Chapter Notes	343
Index	345

Acknowledgments

When engaging in writing of any significance, there are inevitably numerous people who provide invaluable support. As I worked on recording my thoughts and editing my Afghan journal, several trusted associates and family members were of enormous assistance. I would like to take this opportunity to express my appreciation for helping me to tell a better story.

First, I would like to thank Dr. Dorrie Karolick from the U.S. Air Force Academy's Department of Military and Strategic Studies. Upon my arrival at the academy to take up my teaching position, Dr. Karolick made me feel at home and helped me to become an effective instructor. When I mentioned that I was preparing my journal for publication, she graciously consented to read the manuscript. She made a great many suggestions to improve the organization, flow, and diction of the text that I incorporated throughout. Her advice enabled me to make a better product that I hope the reader will find informative and enjoyable.

Several other colleagues here at the Air Force Academy provided advice, support and input as I continued with the book. Lieutenant Colonel Patrick Donley provided me with several unpublished papers that he produced while working as an advisor in the Ministry of Rural Rehabilitation and Development. I drew ideas from these documents as I formulated ways in which we could achieve better results with development in Afghanistan. Drs. John Farquhar and Jim Titus engaged me in many discussions about the situation in Afghanistan, allowing me to crystallize many of my ideas about how diplomatic solutions might alleviate some of the regional tensions associated with the situation in Afghanistan. Our department head, permanent professor and U.S. Air Force Colonel Thomas Drohan, encouraged me to get the "story" out, and his support facilitated the endeavor.

Next, I would like to thank Captain Matthew Frye, who served as one of my staff officers during our time in Afghanistan. He compiled a pictorial history of the deployment that records what happened in Afghanistan. Most of the photos used in this book are drawn from the archive that he assembled, and therefore I am much indebted to his work in bringing together the pictures.

I would like to thank all of the soldiers and officers of 2nd Battalion, 77th Field Artillery Regiment, along with the members of the regimental association who are veterans of service with the battalion. This book is about the battalion's service in Afghanistan, and without the soldiers' outstanding performance in training and later in combat there would not be much of a story to tell. All of the soldiers made great contributions for their country that deserve our full recognition.

I could not have accomplished any of this without the support of my wife and children. As hard as deployments to combat are on soldiers, they are infinitely tougher on the families left behind because of the unknowns. Families do not know what is happening on a daily basis in a combat zone and therefore always have nagging anxiety as to what is happening to their soldier, whether parent, child, or spouse. Further, families have to continue with the daily grind of living, which includes managing a household, going to school, working, and caring for children. This is a difficult task, and my family has always handled my deployments readily and with dignity. My wife Maryellen has stood by me for 23 years, providing continuous, faithful support regardless of the challenges associated with being married to a soldier. She has been, and always will be, my stability through all that life brings our way. My son Andrew is now a lieutenant in the Air Force and did a great deal to help my wife during my absence. He is a fine young man and is always there for his mother. Without his stoic sense of responsibility, going to Afghanistan three times would have been far more difficult on my wife and I; his dependability made things infinitely easier. My daughter Ashley was a junior in high school when I deployed. She continued to do well in school and sports and is now headed off to college to swim for Western Kentucky University. Her experience as the child of a deployed soldier has left her with the desire to work with wounded veterans, which she recently did in supporting the Wounded Warrior Games here in Colorado Springs. I am thankful for my family and their continued love and support as I served in Afghanistan and later completed this project.

Finally, I must thank God for looking after our battalion in Afghanistan along with the families of the soldiers. Nothing is possible without Him, and I must note that He is the reason that I am able to accomplish anything.

Preface

I began writing this book in 2008 when I started a journal to record my experiences as a U.S. Army battalion commander. Our Army was (and still is) at war and had been for seven years at that point. The organization was under pressure due to being required to fight on two fronts over an extended period of time. The operational tempo for troops was staggering as they rotated in and out of the combat zone every other year. This practice placed great stress on a small number of American citizens who had volunteered to serve in the military, as well as on their families. My purpose in writing this book was to chronicle the experiences of a fairly typical unit in the U.S. Army from my perspective as a battalion commander. I wrote about the unit and my experiences starting at Fort Carson, Colorado—our home station—as the battalion began to train for deployment to Afghanistan and followed it through our time there and then back home two years later. This volume is a portrait of what the unit had to do to prepare for combat and how the soldiers handled the experience when they were in the crucible. It is also a self-portrait of my thoughts and actions over the course of my command. I do not intend to portray my own experience as anything more than that of a soldier and officer who was determined to do his duty for his country.

I had intended to publish this book much sooner, but I ran into significant difficulties as I sought to get it into print. The journal ended in the summer of 2010, and I finished editing the manuscript in 2011. That year I sent the completed document to the Department of the Army for review to obtain permission to publish. In accordance with Department of Defense regulations, I must receive permission to publish any work that is based upon my personal experience of service. The reasons for this regulation are fairly obvious: the department wants to ensure that prospective authors are not revealing secrets or sensitive information or taking a position that is overly critical of national leadership, all of which could have detrimental effects on the nation. Therefore, in compliance with the regulation, I submitted my manuscript to the appropriate authority. After several months I received a letter from the department informing me that the manuscript was disapproved for release, barring me from publishing my work. I was stunned by this development. I could not understand why the department had denied permission to publish the manuscript. There was nothing in the document that could possibly bring disrepute upon the organization or nation; frankly, it is a story that takes a positive view of soldiers and what they have done to make Afghanistan safe for its people. Therefore, I sought answers as to why the department had arrived at its decision.

The point of contact working with me at the Department of Defense pointed out that the process was not over just because permission was denied. The department has an appeals process available to obtain a reversal of such decisions. Thus, in mid–2012 I filed a formal appeal with a rebuttal of the decision. After several more months the gentleman at the Department of Defense called and told me that I had won my appeal and sent a letter stating this fact. However, this was not the end of the story. The same letter informed me that a new concern had arisen and the department had decided to classify the manuscript, which again would prevent its public release. As before, I was dismayed by this surprising result. At this point I began to think that I would never have the opportunity to tell my story. Yet it was still not over. My point of contact at the department went to bat on my behalf to dispute an outcome that he deemed unfair. This man informed me that the classification of a document like mine can be challenged and downgraded. Once briefed on the process, I filed a challenge to the classification in early 2013.

Finally, at the end of 2015, I received word that the Department of Defense had decided to remove the classification and, further, I would receive permission to publish the manuscript provided that I redact certain passages that the department deemed sensitive (which I have done). On receiving this news, I was both astonished and relieved. After four years of trying to tell a story about one small part of the Army's experience in Afghanistan, I at last had the opportunity to move forward. Even now, I do not understand why my manuscript was so heavily scrutinized or what issues almost derailed the publication process. Honestly, the story is a simple one of the resilience and special qualities of the American soldier. There are many other works by soldiers and civilian leaders who served in Iraq and Afghanistan that contain explosive content and politically sensitive material designed to create buzz and sell books. I have to assume that these works went through the same approval process to which mine was subjected. Yet my book, containing benign subject matter, was scrutinized as if I were attempting to publish the *Pentagon Papers* in the early 1970s. I was more than a little irritated by the process. Nevertheless, I am happy to finally present this material for anyone who might find it interesting.

My concern at this point is: Will the reader find the content relevant? Since I finished the manuscript in 2011, the entire character of the conflict in Afghanistan has changed. The surge in Afghanistan is over, and the whole operation has transitioned to a new phase of the long war known as Operation Freedom's Sentinel. Our troop strength has dropped below 10,000 personnel, a level not seen since 2003. Further, responsibility for the fighting now rests with the Afghan security forces, and it is an open question as to whether the Afghans can win the war and secure the future for their people. Against this backdrop, this book will hit the street.

There are three things I hope to achieve through publishing my story. First, I want to draw attention to the selfless service of the American soldier during a time of war. Although our country has done much to stand by its service members with a great outpouring of gratitude, few understand the full extent of their sacrifices, particularly when they are "at home" preparing for the next deployment. Second, as a historian, I would like to make my own personal contribution to history as a primary source from today's conflict. I have written three books and several articles about the Civil War; yet, before now, I had not composed anything of a contemporary nature based on personal observation. Finally, I would like to provide a small glimpse into my own personality and experiences as a man, husband, father, soldier, officer, and mid-level leader in the U.S. Army. I hope that my family, friends, and readers will appreciate this viewpoint after I am gone. As one who loves the study of history, I understand the critical importance of primary sources, and I hope this book fulfills some small need.

In my original introduction, written more than four years ago, I thanked a number of people to whom I owed a great debt in getting through this project. To that list I must add two more names: Mr. James Hill and Mr. Bert Haggett proved of great assistance to me in ushering the manuscript through the Department of Defense review process. Without their help and persistence—which they certainly were under no obligation to provide—my pursuit of approval for publication would doubtless have languished within the huge bureaucracy of the Pentagon. Thus, I would be remiss and unappreciative if I did not show gratitude to these men for their dogged assistance in my quest. To both of you, thank you again.

Finally, a thread running throughout this manuscript and a sustaining element for my life is my faith in God. The ultimate foundation for any successful endeavor in my life is the grace given to me every day. This faith was critical during our time in Afghanistan, for the human spirit needs something above itself to believe in, especially when we observe our world mired in seemingly endless chaos. God supplies this need in abundance in my life, and it is my hope that this is a central part of the story for those who might read these pages.

Abbreviations and Definitions

1SG: First sergeant—the senior noncommissioned officer of a battery or company. On average, he or she has between 18 and 22 years of service and is from 36 to 42 years of age. This leader works directly for the battery commander and implements all policies and directives in the unit.

13B: The alphanumeric designator for a cannoneer. These designators signify the military occupational specialty of a soldier.

6400 mils: A circle. Just as a compass uses 360 degrees to form a circle, artillery uses 6400 mils to form a circle, which provides more precision in gunnery.

AAR: After action review—an open discussion of actions conducted in an operation. As part of the review, the unit personnel critique the action to determine ways to improve or what to sustain in order to develop greater proficiency in mission tasks.

AASLT: An air assault operation by helicopter.

AFG: An abbreviation for Afghanistan.

ANA: Afghan National Army.

ANP: Afghan National Police.

ANSF: Afghan National Security Forces, consisting of all entities of the Afghan security apparatus such as the police, army, and border guards.

AO: Area of operation—an area assigned to a unit in which it is responsible for security. In counter-insurgency a unit works directly with the local leaders in this area to build the capabilities of the indigenous security forces and capacity of the government. Further, security operations are designed to facilitate progressive development of all organs of the government and its economy. Everything positive flows from security operations.

ASG: Afghan Security Guards—locally hired Afghans who, under the supervision of a contractor, provide local security for coalition bases.

Abbreviations and Definitions

BC: Battery commander—a captain in command of an artillery battery. A battery comprises approximately 100 soldiers and is armed with 6–8 howitzers. The commander is a leader with 4–8 years of service in the Army and is from 26 to 32 years of age on average.

BCT: Brigade Combat Team—a brigade consisting of maneuver (infantry or armor), artillery, logistics, and specialized units. This is the basic unit that the Army employs to fight and win at the tactical level in battle.

BDA: Battle damage assessment—after any engagement with the enemy, a battle damage assessment is estimated for intelligence purposes. The assessment includes such items as damage to equipment, enemy equipment captured, and enemy killed, wounded, or captured.

Bde: Brigade.

Bn: Battalion.

Btry: Battery—the basic artillery unit, with 6–8 guns.

C2: Command and control—a term used when discussing the transmission of orders, movement of units around the battlefield, and maintaining awareness of the current situation.

C&S: Command and staff—a meeting of the commanders and staff officers within the unit to provide an update on unit status to the battalion commander.

CA: Civil Affairs—a critical component of conducting counter-insurgency that involves development of infrastructure and government capacity.

CG: Commanding general.

CI: Counter-intelligence.

CJTF—Combined Joint Task Force: a headquarters organized for a specific mission. In Afghanistan these task forces comprise a division or corps headquarters with all other services contributing experts to the staff to augment the capability of the unit.

CMD: Command.

COA: Course of action.

CoC: Change of command, in which one officer turns over command of the unit to another officer.

COIN: Counter-insurgency.

COL: Colonel—a senior officer just below the rank of brigadier general. He or she has served 20–30 years in the Army and is from 42 to 52 years of age.

COMEX: Communications exercise, designed to test communication systems to ensure that they are in proper working order. These exercises are conducted before training or operations to guarantee systems readiness.

CoP: Chief of police.
CPT: Captain—an officer who serves as a battery or company commander or as a staff officer on a battalion or brigade staff. He or she has 3–9 years of service and is from 26 to 34 years of age, on average.
CPX: Command post exercise—an exercise focused on training the staff in the command and control of a unit while it interfaces with other units in the area, including the higher headquarters.
CQ: Charge of quarters—the sergeant on duty in the barracks. His or her duty is to ensure that there is order in the single soldier housing units and that the area remains clean.
"Crew-served" (weapons): Weapons that require more than one person to operate—thus a crew of two or more. These include machine guns and howitzers, among other systems.
CSM: Command sergeant major—the senior enlisted soldier in any unit, including battalions, brigades and divisions. Most CSMs are over 40 years of age and have served more than 20 years in the Army.
D-30: A 122mm howitzer of Soviet origin. This is the primary weapon system of the Afghan artillery.
DC: District center—the seat of an Afghan district government. It is similar to a county courthouse in the United States.
DFC: District field coordinator—an Afghan election official assigned at the district level.
"Distro": The distribution platoon in the logistics company. This platoon is responsible for the delivery of all supplies—including ammunition, food, and fuel—to the units within a battalion.
DOL: Directorate of logistics—every Army post has this agency, which manages property and logistical support for all the units located on that installation.
"Dry": An exercise conducted with weapons, but without the use of live ammunition.
EOD: Explosive ordnance disposal—a team of soldiers whose job is to defuse and/or dispose of bombs and explosives such as mines and IEDs.
ETT: Embedded training team—a small team of American military trainers attached to an Afghan army unit to provide training, advice, and mentorship to the unit's leaders and soldiers.
FA: Field artillery—one of the 16 branches of the Army. The Army manages the careers of its personnel according to the branch to which they are assigned.
FAR: Field artillery regiment.
FB: Firebase—a position used by artillery to deliver fire in all directions to

support maneuver troops. It is a hardened, static defensive position from which to offer protection to the gunners.

FDC: Fire direction center—the hub of any artillery unit, which conducts mathematical computations to ensure that the guns will hit their target. It also determines the proper ammunition to engage the target.

FDNCO: Fire direction noncommissioned officer—the NCO in the artillery fire direction center of a battery or battalion. He works directly for the fire direction officer and is the expert on artillery gunnery in the section.

FDO: Fire direction officer—the officer in an artillery fire direction center who directs the fire of a battery or battalion.

FECC: Fires and effects coordination cell—a staff section on the brigade staff made up of artillerymen that acts as a liaison between the field artillery battalion and the brigade headquarters. It plans, coordinates and executes fires from artillery, aviation, and other platforms in support of brigade operations.

FIST: Fire Support Team—a team of forward observers (usually about 10 personnel) under the leadership of an artillery lieutenant. The team supports an infantry company and provides coordination of artillery fires in support of that unit.

FO: Forward observer—a junior enlisted soldier or sergeant who serves with an infantry platoon coordinating artillery fire for that unit. This soldier has 1–4 years of service and ranges from 18 to 24 years of age, on average.

FOB: Forward operating base—a location that is usually the base of a battalion headquarters or a larger unit headquarters. It is a hub for logistics and operations in a specific area, with several satellite combat outposts extending farther into that area.

FRAGO: Fragmentary order—an operation order that addresses only critical information needed to execute the operation.

FRG: Family readiness group—every unit in the Army has a family readiness group, and its purpose is to facilitate family communication within the unit and enable families to cope with the challenges of life in the military.

FRSA—Family readiness support assistant: a civilian assistant to the commander who provides administrative support for family programs and acts as a liaison between the military command and the families of the soldiers.

FSCX—Fire support coordination exercise: a training exercise in which all weapon systems are brought to bear in a coordinated manner to overwhelm the enemy in the target area, facilitating maneuvering of the ground forces.

FSE—Fire support element: the artillery liaison element of a maneuver/infantry battalion that plans, prepares, and coordinates the use of artillery fire for that unit.

FSO—Fire support officer: a field artillery officer who serves as the artillery battalion's liaison to the infantry maneuver unit. He is responsible for the coordination of artillery fire in support of the maneuver unit.

GEN—General (4 stars): this is currently the highest rank that a serving officer can hold.

GoA: Government of Afghanistan.

HCT—Human intelligence collection team: a small team of soldiers whose military occupational specialty is collecting and analyzing intelligence gathered from human sources.

HE—High explosive: the primary shell used for artillery fires.

HHB/HHC—Headquarters and headquarters battery or company: the headquarters unit of a battalion or brigade. It has all the command and control elements to facilitate the commander's ability to make decisions and implement orders.

HTT—Human terrain team: a team of civilians employed by the Department of Defense that maps population demographics to provide situational awareness to commanders.

IED—Improvised explosive device: the weapon of choice among our enemy in Afghanistan. An IED is any explosive that is rigged to explode in a manner other than its intended use. For example, in Afghanistan the enemy will pack a pressure cooker with explosives and place it on a timer or some other device that will cause it to explode, inflicting maximum damage and casualties on U.S. forces.

Illum—Illumination: an artillery shell used for lighting up the night sky or marking targets.

IN: Infantry.

IO—Information operation: an operation designed to deliver a focused message to a specific audience.

J-bad: Jalalabad.

JFO—Joint fires observer: an artillery forward observer who has attended the Joint Fires Observer School at Fort Sill, Oklahoma. The school trains the observer to provide terminal control of aerial assets on targets in support of maneuver units.

JRTC: Joint Readiness Training Center, located at Fort Polk, Louisiana, and one of the Army's training centers where entire brigade combat teams can train together in a large exercise utilizing all assets available to the unit. Such exercises incorporate a "live" enemy to challenge the brigade in its conduct of "combat" operations.

LeT: Lashkar-e-Tayibba—an Islamic fundamentalist organization dedicated to the separation of the province of Kashmir from India. This group sends members into Afghanistan to gain combat experience before going back to the Kashmir to fight for their cause.

LFX: Live fire exercise—a unit exercise in which a series of weapon systems are employed in coordination with a scheme of maneuver. Such exercises are very dangerous because of the use of live ammunition combined with the movement of many units. These exercises are necessary to hone teamwork to a sharp edge in preparation for combat.

LPD: Leader professional development, similar to officer professional development. However, leader professional development is expanded to include senior noncommissioned officers in the program for specific military subjects.

LT: Lieutenants (either second or first lieutenants). These are the junior officers in the Army and the first line of officer leadership. In an artillery battalion lieutenants serve primarily as platoon leaders, fire direction officers, or fire support officers with the infantry. They have 1–3 years of service and are generally 22–25 years of age, although the current war has seen an influx of older officers who have served as noncommissioned officers before going to officer candidate school. Our battalion had two lieutenants who were over 40 years of age.

M203: A 40mm grenade launcher mounted under a M16 or M4 rifle.

Maneuver units (platoons, companies, battalions): Any mounted element whose purpose is to find, fight and defeat the enemy through the use of maneuver and firepower. These can be infantry, armor, or mechanized units.

MEDCAP: Medical civil assistance program—an operation in which unit medical personnel provide assistance to a local community.

MET: Meteorological data—weather data used by an artillery unit to predict the fall of an artillery shell. The unit calculates elements such as wind direction, air pressure, air density, and so on, in order to ensure accuracy of firing. Proper prediction and calculation is a critical artillery gunnery skill.

METL: Mission essential task list—every unit in the Army has a list of tasks considered essential in order for it to accomplish its wartime mission. These tasks are the focus of training for the unit, and achieving a high state of proficiency is critical to success in combat. The commander continually assesses unit proficiency in these tasks.

MoI: Ministry of the Interior—the Afghan ministry responsible for internal security. It is the executive authority for the Afghan National Police and the Afghan Border Police.

MRAP: Mine-resistant ambush protected vehicle—a wheeled vehicle that has a V-shaped bottom and light armor to shield personnel inside the vehicle. It was developed during the course of the Global War on Terror to offer better protection to the crews in the event of an IED explosion than that afforded by the "Hummer," which is the primary utility vehicle used by the Army.

MRE: Mission rehearsal exercise—the final exercise that a brigade combat team conducts at Army training centers such as JRTC, in which the unit is placed in simulated conditions of the deployment theater to test its ability to accomplish the mission.

N2KL: Nuristan, Nangarhar, Konar, Laghman (the four eastern provinces of Afghanistan).

NCO: Noncommissioned officers—enlisted leaders in the rank of sergeant through command sergeant major.

NDS: National Directorate of Security—the Afghan intelligence agency.

NGO: Nongovernmental organization—groups that are not affiliated with any government and proliferate throughout Afghanistan. They are generally charitable organizations such as Doctors Without Borders.

O/C: Observer/Controller—an instructor at a training center who facilitates a major training exercise and provides feedback to enable the commander to evaluate the readiness of the unit.

OCC-P: Operation coordination center–provincial—these are coordination centers manned by all elements of the Afghan National Security Forces located generally at the provincial capital. Their purpose is to coordinate security operations across their respective provinces.

OEF X: Operation Enduring Freedom—tenth rotation of American troops to Afghanistan.

OIC: Officer-in-charge—an officer assigned as the leader of a special task such as a funeral or running a rifle range.

OP: Observation post—a position forward of a main defensive position that provides observation of a specific area for early warning of enemy movement.

OPD: Officer professional development—a program within a unit intended to build the professional knowledge of the leaders to enhance unit effectiveness and proficiency.

OPs SGT: Operations sergeant—the senior noncommissioned officer in the battalion or brigade operations center. He is usually a master sergeant who has served between 18 and 20 years in the Army and ranges in age from 36 to 40, on average.

Abbreviations and Definitions

Out-of-Traverse: A target of a howitzer that is outside of the left or right limits of the cannon (which has a finite ability to move left or right from the direction it is aimed). Whenever a target is "out-of-traverse," the gun crew must lift the trails of the howitzer to point it at the target.

PCC: Pre-command course—a seminar for lieutenant colonels and colonels preparing to take command of battalions and brigades in the Army.

PDSS: Pre-deployment site survey—reconnaissance of a location in the combat theater by the commanders, command sergeants major, and select staff officers prior to deployment to that location.

PEO: Provincial election officer—an Afghan election official who oversees the conduct of elections at the provincial level. He supervises the district field coordinators within the province.

PL: Platoon leader—a lieutenant in command of 25–40 soldiers.

Platoon plus—vernacular for more than a platoon. Example: A platoon of 36 soldiers reinforced to 50.

PLT: Platoon—a small unit of 25–40 soldiers.

PRT: Provincial reconstruction team—a military organization associated with a specific province of Afghanistan whose mission is to facilitate development of infrastructure and government administration.

PT: Physical training—every unit in the Army conducts physical training each day in order to maintain proper fitness so the soldiers can endure the physical stresses of combat.

QRF: Quick reaction force—a specially designated force of varying size whose mission is to respond to emergencies or other immediate needs.

Ramadan: An annual Islamic religious celebration that lasts for a month. It is a period of fasting and reflection through which the individual draws closer to Allah by surrendering to his will. Ramadan occurs at a different time each year based on lunar cycles.

Rear d.: Rear detachment—the element that remains at home station when a unit deploys into the combat theater. The purpose of the rear detachment is to serve as a liaison between the unit forward and the families at home. This detachment also cares for wounded warriors and facilitates processing of un-deployable soldiers out of the Army.

Recon: Reconnaissance.

RPG: Rocket-propelled grenade—a common weapon favored by the Taliban in Afghanistan, originally developed by the Soviet Union as an anti-tank weapon. It is used by the Taliban to initiate ambushes, attack vehicle convoys, and strike against troops.

S1: The personnel officer of a battalion or brigade, usually a lieutenant or captain. His/her responsibility is to manage the personnel administration for the battalion based on the guidance of the commander. This individual normally has 1–6 years of Army service, and the average age is 24–30 years old.

S2: The intelligence officer of a battalion or brigade, generally a captain or major. His/her responsibility is to gather and assess intelligence about enemy activity for the commander. Depending upon the unit headquarters, this individual has 4–8 years of service if a captain in a battalion, or 10–14 years of service if a major at brigade level.

S3: The operations officer of a battalion or brigade, often a major. His/her responsibility is to provide oversight for daily activities and plan future operations. This individual normally has 12–14 years of Army service, and the average age is 34–38 years old.

S4: The logistics officer of a battalion or brigade—a captain or major. He/she is responsible for managing the supply operations for the unit. Depending upon the unit headquarters, this individual has 4–8 years of service if a captain in a battalion, or 10–14 years of service if a major at brigade level.

SFC: Sergeant first class—a mid-level noncommissioned who serves as a platoon sergeant and the right hand of a lieutenant platoon leader.

SGT: Sergeant—the first noncommissioned officer in the chain of command. A sergeant is normally in charge of between 4 and 9 soldiers and averages 21–25 years of age. In an artillery battalion he serves as the gunner of an artillery piece.

"shura": Pashto term for a meeting of elders or local Afghan leaders formed into a council.

SOP: Standing operating procedures—the standards according to which a unit functions on a daily basis for routine operations. Standardization allows all personnel to understand what has to be done in a given situation so that the task is always performed correctly.

SPC: Specialist—an enlisted soldier below the rank of sergeant. The average age of a specialist is between 19 and 23 years old.

SRP: Small rewards program—a weapon turn-in program that provides a small monetary incentive to Afghans for the purpose of removing dangerous weapons and ammunition from a select area.

SSG: Staff sergeant—serves as a section chief or squad leader of 7–12 soldiers. Staff sergeants have about 6–8 years of service and are between 25 and 30 years of age. In an artillery battalion a section chief is the commander of one artillery piece.

TAC: Tactical command post—a forward command post detached from the battalion or brigade tactical operations center to provide command and control closer to the scene of action. It is a very small element that includes the commander and operations officer, with 3–5 additional personnel, depending on the situation and mission.

TB: Taliban.

TGT: Target.

TIC: Troops in contact—friendly soldiers in contact with the enemy in combat.

TNG: Training.

TOA: Transition of authority—a hand-off of responsibility for an area between two units.

TOC: Tactical operations center—the main command post of a battalion or brigade. It is the hub of command and control from which the unit staff monitors and controls actions on the battlefield.

WP: White phosphorous—an artillery shell used for the purpose of providing smoke screens. It is also incendiary; when activated upon impact, the payload burns at temperatures approaching 2,000 degrees.

XO: Executive officer of a battalion or brigade. This is either a major or a lieutenant colonel who serves as the second in command, with direct oversight of administration and logistics. He or she usually has 13–17 years of service and is 36–39 years of age.

N2KL—Nangarhar, Nuristan, Konar and Laghman Region. Highlighted is the Battalion Area of Operation. Our firing batteries were scattered around the entire N2KL region providing artillery support to the brigade's maneuver units.

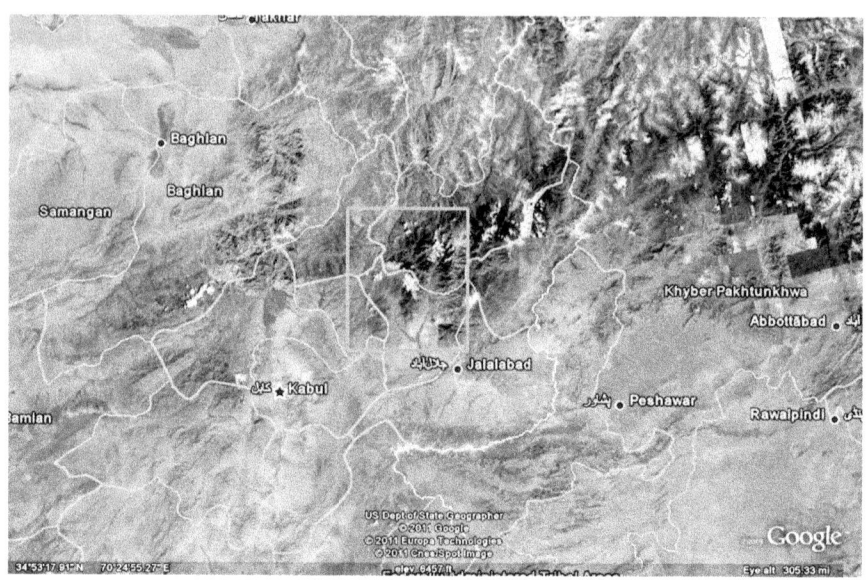

N2KL Region. Again highlighted is the Battalion AO.

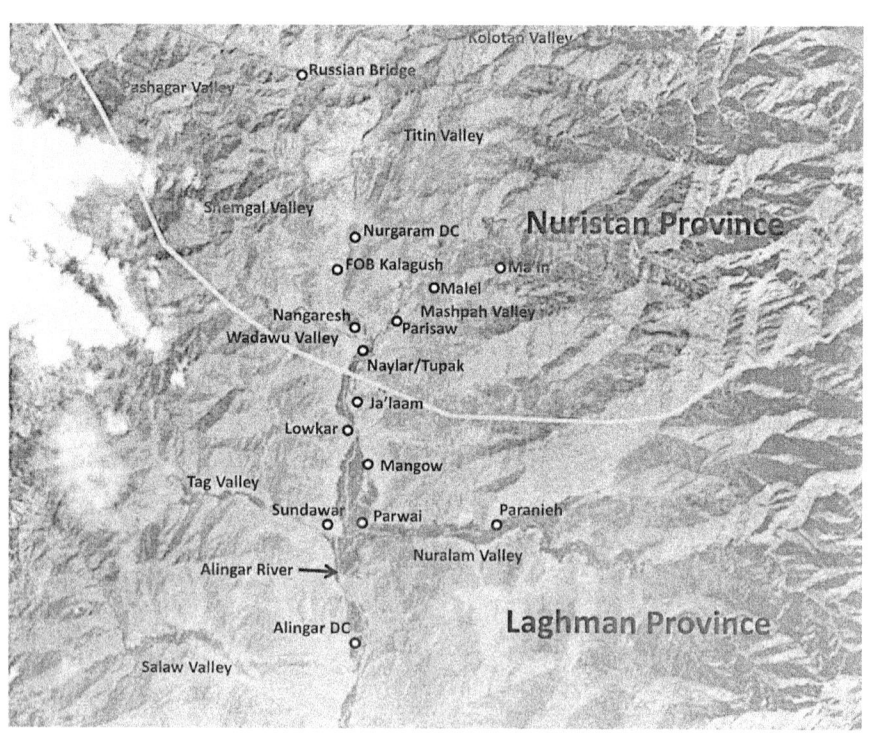

The Central Valley—AO Steel.

Introduction

At the time of this writing (2011), our nation has been at war in Afghanistan for more than nine years. It is the longest-running war in the history of the United States. Unless one's head has been in the sand during that time, readers will know that our involvement in Afghanistan resulted from the shocking events that took place on 11 September 2001. On that day nearly 3,000 Americans were killed by Al Qaeda terrorists who had trained in Afghanistan. The government of Afghanistan, led by the extremist Taliban, provided sanctuary to the organization, enabling Al Qaeda to plan, prepare, and execute operations against Americans projected from Afghan soil.

The war that ensued following that fateful day has impacted upon me to an extent that is difficult to put into words. On 11 September 2001, I was sitting in a classroom at the Command and General Staff College in Fort Leavenworth, Kansas. This is the school that Army majors attend to prepare them for future assignments to higher command and general staff positions. It is for the up-and-coming leaders of our Army. As I sat in the classroom listening to a mundane presentation about joint operations, an instructor from the section next door burst into our room and told our instructor to turn on the television immediately. It was about 8:00 AM Central Standard Time. As our instructor turned on the set, we saw an image of the New York City skyline with the World Trade Center towers prominent in the picture. One of the towers was emitting a heavy smoke two thirds of the way up the structure. In the distance an aircraft made its way across that forest of skyscrapers at an altitude altogether too low for the safety of passengers or occupants of nearby buildings. The morning was crystal clear and the sun shone on a beautiful early autumn day in New York. In my mind I thought I was watching a movie—it did not seem real. Then, moments later, the plane banked hard, angling toward the second tower. At 8:03 AM (CST) it impacted with a fireball. I thought, "What the hell is this?" It was all surreal, as if watching a dream in slow motion. It took me a few minutes to realize what had happened: The shadowy terrorist organization Al Qaeda had just launched a surprise attack on U.S. soil, killing more Americans than the attack on Pearl Harbor. It shook our nation to the core—and it changed my life forever.

Over the past nine years I have served three combat tours in Afghanistan. I have seen the mission in Afghanistan evolve from early 2003 until 2011 firsthand. I believe in the mission and know that we must win in Afghanistan. However, my thinking about what we must do and the expectations of what we can accomplish have changed drastically. That is the subject of this book, which is my journal from my third and most recent tour. The intent is to share with you, the reader, my thinking about the conflict and how it evolved when tempered by experience as a commander in combat. I have the greatest respect for the Afghan people and their resilience after enduring so many years of conflict. While I still believe that victory is necessary for our nation and the people of Afghanistan, the solution does not rest solely with the United States and our military. Victory is up to the Afghan people, whom we must wean off reliance on our largesse after almost ten years of American presence in their country. I learned this lesson during my third tour in Afghanistan after daily interactions with the Afghan government, people, and security forces, as well as intermittent contact with the enemy. It was an eye-opening and critical lesson.

* * *

I was commissioned in the U.S. Army as a field artillery officer in 1988 from the Murray State University ROTC in Kentucky. I got married that same year, and within four years my wife and I had two children. Our journey through the Army took us to multiple assignments across the United States, including Fort Bragg, North Carolina; Fort Campbell, Kentucky; Fort Polk, Louisiana; Fort Sill, Oklahoma; Fort Leavenworth, Kansas; and Fort Drum, New York. Along the way I deployed to combat in the Persian Gulf War in 1990–1991 and spent a year unaccompanied in Korea. Our experience prior to September 2001 prepared the family for the challenges that awaited in the new century.

During my time at the Command and General Staff College I competed for, and was selected to attend, the School of Advanced Military Studies (SAMS), also located at Fort Leavenworth. This gave me the opportunity to further my education and equipped me with the tools to work as a plans officer on a general staff. The school educates field-grade officers (majors and lieutenant colonels) in military theory, history, planning, and practical decision-making. While I was attending SAMS in 2003, the nation initiated the war in Iraq that removed Saddam Hussein and quickly degenerated into an unexpected insurgency. The Iraq theater forced our effort in Afghanistan to a backseat in the minds of the public. In fact, when close relatives learned that I had been assigned to a unit deploying to Afghanistan, they were relieved. In a startling moment, they said they were happy I was headed to Afghanistan, as opposed to Iraq, because "there is nothing going on over there." I knew better than this, but I let their misperception stand. Following graduation from SAMS, I reported for duty as a plans officer in the 10th Mountain Division at Fort Drum, New York, in June 2003. The unit was already in the process of deploying, and I had to prepare myself to leave shortly after arrival. Thus began my first of three tours in Afghanistan.

I arrived in Afghanistan in July 2003. When I stepped off the C-130 that transported us from Manas, Kyrgyzstan, I remember a hot blast of wind hitting me in the face. It was well over 100 degrees, with a south wind blowing hard at more than 20 knots. Afghanistan was in the midst of a period known to Afghans as the "100 days of wind." I spent the next nine months of this tour working as a plans officer on the Combined Joint Task Force 180 staff manned by personnel from the 10th Mountain Division.

It was about 20 months after the ouster of the Taliban. There were a little more than 9,000[1] American soldiers in Afghanistan at that time. At this fairly early point in the war it was believed that a small U.S. force would be sufficient to hunt down Taliban and Al Qaeda as required, provide security, and enable the fledgling government of Afghanistan to build capacity while developing infrastructure. The hope was that this approach would project an image that the Americans were not there to occupy or disturb the Afghan culture. Instead, we were there simply to assist Afghanistan to its feet in a nonintrusive way. The memory of the recent Russian occupation was fresh in the minds of Afghans and our leaders, and it was believed that a small U.S. footprint would block the perception that we were in any way like the Russians in the 1980s.

The problem with this strategy was that without adequate boots on the ground, security was a chimera. The lack of American or Afghan security forces in a nation as large as the southeastern United States, and with a population estimated at more than 30 million, created a vacuum in the hinterland where our forces were not located. The Taliban and Al Qaeda had been soundly defeated on the battlefield in Afghanistan, but they left the country for sanctuaries in Pakistan. Here, they consolidated their strength and took time to motivate the faithful for an insurgent campaign to retake Afghanistan. Unharassed across the border, the Taliban leaders recognized the vacuum created by insufficient security forces, and they sought to fill it with their brand.

During my first tour I noted many positives in Afghanistan. First, the people were (and for the most part remain) very supportive of U.S. efforts in their country.[2] Driving out the Taliban was viewed as salvation by the myriad ethnic groups in Afghanistan, including the Pashtun people who had originally produced the Taliban movement. This enthusiasm provided the impetus for the people to establish a new government. Hamid Karzai, the provisional president at that time, was a popular figure, and he played an integral role in bringing delegates together in Kabul to write a constitution in a *jirga*[3] session. The constitution established the Afghans' form of government and the procedures by which they would appoint and elect officials to sustain a republic. The *Constitutional Jirga*, as it became known, generated great excitement and optimism among the people. Finally, there was a flurry of reconstruction—or I should say *construction* activity—throughout the country. People could see firsthand, through the construction of the ring road and other projects, that progress had gained momentum and better days were ahead. However, lurking in the shadows were elements that would undermine the progress and enthusiasm.

* * *

At the end of my first tour in Afghanistan in May 2004 I believed that the United States would ultimately win a significant victory. Lieutenant General David Barno, the overall commander in Afghanistan at the time, had introduced a sound counter-insurgency strategy in the country in which units would work with the population owning their respective areas of operation. Each unit would provide security in its area in order to enable the government of Afghanistan to build capacity, continue construction projects, and partner with Afghan National Security Forces. The problem with the implementation of this strategy was the paucity of U.S. forces, which represented a mismatch among ends, ways and means. Although the strength of our forces increased over time,[4] the ratio to the relative population forced our units to focus on a small number of targeted areas. Therefore, instead of providing true population security, these units pressed the Taliban away from the populated areas into the hinterland and trackless mountains. The Taliban, using these sanctuary areas created by avoiding contact with our scarce forces, began to build strength for a comeback.

I arrived in Afghanistan for my second tour in February 2006, this time with the new 3rd Brigade, 10th Mountain Division, which was one of the Army modular brigades created in 2004. I deployed to Afghanistan as the brigade effects officer[5] for this tour, making me an integral part of the planning and execution of all unit operations. With an outstanding command team that understood counter-insurgency, we deployed full of confidence that our unit could finally tip the balance to victory. There was still a great force deficit in Afghanistan, but when the 10th Mountain returned in 2006, the division had over 22,000 troops and the Afghan National Army had built to a strength approaching 30,000.

With these available troops, the division headquarters, as the Combined Joint Task Force, planned to build on the foundation established by the previous rotations from the past few years. We started by launching an all-out effort to push the Taliban out of the populated areas, fighting and isolating them in the remote mountains. Our leaders believed that keeping the enemy away from critical areas would provide the breathing space necessary for the government of Afghanistan to train and deploy its security forces and build the bureaucratic machinery required to run a country. Then we would turn responsibility of our areas back over to the Afghans to enable our eventual withdrawal. The strategy was to clear the enemy out of an area and hold them back so as to allow the government to grow in capacity and build the infrastructure free of enemy incursions. This would have been a sound plan if the Afghan government had held up its end of the bargain. It did not.

When I came back to Afghanistan I noted several things that began to shake my confidence. First, the government led by Karzai had made little progress in capacity building since my last tour. Instead of grasping the opportunity to build competent leadership, the officials, from district through national levels, engaged in graft and corruption, weakening the people's support for their government. This, along with the thin troop levels, provided the Taliban with an opportunity to launch its resurgence with a vengeance, thus filling the aforementioned vacuum.

Simultaneously, I noted that casualties were rising to levels much higher than I had seen during my first tour. While our troops followed through in our initial action (Operation Mountain Lion in the Korengal Valley), the government engaged in underhanded schemes to line the pockets of the local officials. The result was that the government failed to build capacity and left our troops out in the wilderness fighting on its behalf. The Taliban took full advantage of the situation by tying down our troops in remote places like the Korengal, Kamdesh, and Waigul valleys while at the same time disrupting life in the populated areas. Yet the feckless and incompetent Afghan officials were able to retain our commitment to their cause by telling us our efforts were working even as these same leaders did little to take charge of their own destiny.

Once my second tour ended, I left Afghanistan to take charge of our brigade rear detachment at home. I arrived back at Fort Drum in June 2006 as a new lieutenant colonel charged with taking care of our brigade's wounded warriors and acting as a liaison between the unit members who were still deployed and the families left at home. While my confidence in what U.S. forces could accomplish was somewhat shaken, I still believed we could fulfill the mission of building a stable, friendly Afghanistan that rejected terrorism on its soil. I naively believed that the Afghan officials just needed more time and security forces to bring about mission success.

* * *

In April 2008 I assumed command of the 2nd Battalion, 77th Field Artillery Regiment, in the 4th Brigade, 4th Infantry Division. Known as the Steel Warrior battalion, this unit comprises two gun batteries of eight howitzers each, a headquarters battery, and a support company providing logistics. There were 400 soldiers who had just redeployed from Iraq, where they had served as an infantry battalion. The unit had great esprit de corps, solid junior leadership, and combat experience. However, they lacked two things critical to success in Afghanistan: knowledge of their jobs as artillerymen and familiarity with the culture, people and nature of the insurgency in Afghanistan, which is different from that of Iraq. The first factor is fundamental, but the second is more subtle. On the surface, it might have seemed easy to transfer the knowledge gained from combat experience in Iraq to Afghanistan, but this is a fallacy. Afghanistan is a significantly different environment. Therefore, among my most important tasks as a new commander was educating the leaders regarding the reality of the challenges in Afghanistan. Here my experience in two previous tours came to the forefront.

As I prepared to deploy to Afghanistan, this time as a battalion commander, I remained confident that our nation could facilitate the emergence of an Afghan nation and defeat the Taliban. My mission was to establish the direction for the battalion to support our brigade and contribute in a small way to what I believed was possible. Based on my previous experience, I laid out the following list as guidance for the year we would spend training in Afghanistan. It consisted of a training component and an education aspect. The training vision was to achieve excellence in what was called the "Big 5":

- Artillery Gunnery
- Physical Training
- Marksmanship
- Medical Skills
- Battle Drills

Based on our anticipated mission and my experience in Operation Enduring Freedom IV and VII, I believed that these five areas represented the critical skills required for success, with emphasis on artillery gunnery. The rural nature of the insurgency and frequency of remote engagements by the maneuver forces facilitates the employment of indirect fire. Given the unit's lack of proficiency in this area, our training had to bear down on precision gunnery. Additionally, our brigade had its training vision with a dozen tasks noted as essential, and we combined the vision of the brigade commander with my own to develop the way forward in training the unit.

To educate the officers and senior noncommissioned officers, I introduced a professional reading program and intelligence briefings to develop a common understanding of the Afghan environment and the core problems. The purpose of this program was to compress the time needed to become effective upon arrival in theater. A common rule of thumb is that it takes 90 days for a unit to develop a good situational understanding so that it can operate efficiently. I wanted to bring the number down from 90 to 45 days. We read a range of books, from novels to historical surveys, including *The Kite Runner, Ghost Wars, Charlie Wilson's War, The Great Game*, and Rudyard Kipling's *The Man Who Would Be King*. If we were going to make a difference and provide a solid contribution to victory in Afghanistan, I wanted everyone on the same page to ensure that we were ready.

The leaders and soldiers of the 2–77th Field Artillery were a very highly motivated group of professionals. Most of the leaders had a great deal of combat experience, especially the noncommissioned officers. While few of my lieutenants had deployed, they were among the most intelligent set of young leaders I had seen assembled in one unit during my entire career. The battery commanders were all new to their commands but committed to their jobs and taking care of their people. The fine first sergeants teamed with them would ensure that our training kept on pace and was performed to standard. My field grade officers were loyal and extremely hard-working and talented; these individuals would run the unit and sustain it on a daily basis. Finally, the battalion command sergeant major was my right-hand man; I called him my "scout dog." He was a strict disciplinarian, driven to make the unit succeed, and supremely competent. With his taciturn demeanor and high standards, at times he clashed with junior leaders in the unit. However, one thing is certain: his efforts and devotion to the unit elevated its performance and paid great dividends during the stress of combat. Overall, we had excellent material to begin the journey toward deployment to combat in Afghanistan for Operation Enduring Freedom X (OEF X).

* * *

This book covers the three phases of our unit's Afghanistan experience. It begins with our preparations—including my perceptions—for the deployment to OEF X; execution and encountering reality during the first six months in Afghanistan; and sustaining the fight to make a difference during the final half of the deployment before coming home. As stated previously, this volume will chronicle how my perceptions of what was possible changed over the years of my command and our year in Afghanistan. There is a "crisis of leadership" in Afghanistan that is working against the success of our mission in the country due to the corruption and incompetence of the Afghan leaders. The journal records my day-to-day interaction with those leaders, my frustrations, and my realization of what it would take to achieve victory in Afghanistan. It also demonstrates how the soldiers of 2-77th Field Artillery, who are representative of our nation, provided selfless service to not only the United States but also Afghanistan. In addition to my thoughts as recorded in the journal, I provide clarifying information—written in *italics*—to enhance readers' understanding of events. I will at times use the names of the people discussed in the journal. However, there are times when I might have been quite angry with certain individuals, and in an effort to save anyone embarrassment and preserve the dignity of all, I have eliminated most references to the names of these people. I name Afghans only through pseudonyms that stand in for the true names of the individuals, so as to protect the identities of friendly Afghans and safeguard classified information regarding enemy commanders. My hope is that this book will provide the reader with an appreciation of our nation's soldiers and a glimpse of what our Army is doing to make Afghanistan a better place. The narrative and opinions presented are my own and do not represent any official policies of the Department of Defense.

I
Preparations and Perceptions, 4 April 2008 to 1 June 2009

I learned that I would command a battalion in early 2007 and that I would take the Steel Warrior battalion in 2008. The brigade was slated for deployment to Afghanistan in May 2009 as part of OEF X (the tenth rotation of U.S. troops to Afghanistan). This would be my third trip to Afghanistan, and I was excited about the opportunity to again serve there. I still believed that our forces could deliver a clear-cut victory with the right resources and commitment. During my second tour I had seen things that caused me to question some of my assumptions; yet I continued to believe that we could make the ultimate difference. Consequently, I set about establishing the vision for the battalion as it prepared for deployment.

Throughout 2008 the insurgency in Afghanistan had gained steam. Consistent reports filtered in regarding deepening graft and corruption in the Afghan government. This, combined with increasing Taliban aggressiveness, drove support among the American people for the war effort downward. Of all the issues in Afghanistan, the lack of altruistic leadership from government and security officials (and their desire to enrich themselves) is central to the slow pace of progress. The failure of Afghan officials to consider the welfare of their people first created a wedge between the population and the government, causing the people to feel disconnected from the government because the self-interest of the officials overrode the needs of the many. The Taliban is well attuned to this gap and fills the vacuum with its brand of control in places where the reach of the government is limited. The failure of the Karzai administration in the previous five years to develop a relative competence forfeited the goodwill and support of the people. This gave the Taliban the opportunity to compete for that support and made the insurgency a legitimate force. It would take time for these facts to sink into my mind. In the meantime, the focus for 2–77th Field Artillery was preparation for the mission.

The Army has settled into a cycle of training and deployment throughout the course of the Global War on Terror. A typical Army brigade has now deployed three to four times (or more in some cases) to Iraq and or Afghanistan. The deployments have run from 12 to 15 months in duration for combat operations. Units then return home for a period averaging 12–18 months that is characterized by regeneration of combat power through intense training and reequipping.

A garden variety unit will spend the first 90–180 days "resetting." This means that the soldiers will take 30 days' leave upon return, receive replacements for those individuals leaving the unit, requisition equipment, and begin small unit training. This sets the stage for 90 days of intense training that includes a rotation to one of the training centers in California or Louisiana. The focus of this intense training is larger unit exercises, staff training, and replication of theater conditions. This represents the capstone of the twelve-month cycle as the unit develops the cohesion required to achieve effectiveness in combat. The final 90–120 days before deployment consist of low-level training of individuals and reemphasis on specific skills, plus loading and shipping of equipment to the theater and a final opportunity for leave. What should jump out at the reader is this: between deployments the soldier spends most of the time "at home" preparing to return to combat. The dedication of these soldiers is a source of pride for Americans and a measure of the sacrifice they make even when at home. The families who support them deserve honor for accepting deployments and the accompanying preparation time as a way of life so that Americans at home do not have to worry about future 9/11s.

The 2-77th Field Artillery returned from Iraq in January 2008 after fifteen months of participation in what became known as the "surge." The battalion served as an infantry unit in Baghdad and had provided security for the population in a notoriously violent Shiite neighborhood in Sadr City. The experience had hardened the soldiers to the reality of combat, but many important artillery skills had atrophied. When I took command in April 2008, the battalion had thirteen months to prepare for the next deployment to Afghanistan.

I assumed command of 2-77th Field Artillery, the organic[1] artillery battalion for the 4th Infantry Brigade Combat Team of the 4th Infantry Division, on 29 April 2008. The tradition of the Army change-of-command ceremony has a long history. It is representative of the transfer of responsibility between the outgoing and the incoming commanders. The central part of the ceremony is the passing of the unit colors. On that beautiful sunny day, with Pike's Peak as a backdrop and my family there at my side, I accepted the flag of the battalion. Thus, responsibility for more than 400 soldiers, in excess of $60 million worth of equipment, and a tough mission in Afghanistan passed to me. The journey began that day.

I. Preparations and Perceptions, 4 April 2008 to 1 June 2009

Ahead of us were thirteen months of preparation before flying to Afghanistan. The battalion had little equipment when I took command, so the first priority was to draw items we would need to begin training. Second, the unit was hemorrhaging personnel at a high rate as soldiers went to new assignments and schools. Drawing replacements was critical to begin building teams and make them cohesive in order to function well in combat. Setting teams early would facilitate effective training. Finally, we had to set the vision in motion by ensuring that all the leaders internalized my intent as the common path we would follow. My vision was that we would, as a team, become the best gunners in the U.S. Army, maintain the capability to act as an infantry unit if called upon to do so, learn the Afghan environment in order to function at a high level within 45 days of deployment, and take care of each other as a family in all that we did. If we could do these basic things, I believed we would go to Afghanistan ready and able to carry out our mission while at the same time making a positive impact on the Afghan people. With the challenges in mind, we embarked on the preparation phase of our deployment.

The journal begins now. In the first part of the journal the focus is on the training and prep work that we did for the deployment. I made weekly entries in the journal for the first year based on the pace we set out of the gate. Each entry summarizes my assessment of the unit, the people,[2] the effectiveness of training, my frustrations, and personal observations. The entries also contain comments about family events and other things that occurred with my wife and children during that time. Finally, my perceptions of Afghanistan at that time and my confidence in our ability to make a difference come through in each entry. This section sets up the contrast for where I was mentally as I approached my third deployment to Afghanistan and how those preconceptions would change as I felt the weight of responsibility bearing down on me in theater.

Daily Prayer (at the end of every day I concluded with a prayer that followed this outline):

I—Thanks and Praise
II—Forgiveness
III—Immediate Requests
IV—Standing Requests and Intercession
    a. Family
    b. Unit
    c. Those who have lost in war
    d. Those in need
    e. Salvation

V—Blessings
  a. Nation
  b. Soldiers
  c. Those less fortunate
  d. A strong marriage
VI—Strength
  a. To do the right thing
  b. To make right decisions
  c. When I am tired
VII—Conclusion, in the Lord's Name

4 April 2008

I am now at the Pre-Command Course at Fort Leavenworth. I will assume command of 2-77th FAR (Field Artillery Regiment) later this month, and as I contemplate the responsibilities it entails I am humbled by the immense range of concerns I will have every day.

I am starting this journal to record the events that occur during my command for my own future remembrance and for posterity. I hope that it may be of some interest to my family in the future.

It is my prayer as I assume this responsibility that God will provide me with His love, wisdom, and guidance. I will do my best to execute my duty as a servant-leader, setting the proper example for my soldiers and their families daily. I hope in doing so that I might have a positive influence on them as they assume positions as future leaders of our nation.

Finally, I pray that our Lord will bless my beautiful wife Maryellen and our kids as they make this journey with me. Lieutenant Colonel Michael Forsyth.

The Pre-Command Course, known as PCC, is a short school for future battalion and brigade commanders from across the Army. The three-week course provides an orientation to command; depending on the type of command, officers study tactical scenarios and conduct decision-making exercises to hone their skills. A servant-leader is one who seeks to meet the needs of the led rather than self. I required all of my officers and senior noncommissioned officers to read The Servant *by James C. Hunter, which develops the concept of the servant-leader.*

22 April 2008

Arrived at Fort Carson today and signed in. Since PCC I spent the week with Mare and Ash for spring break in Ohio. It was nice to relax prior to taking command. I drove over 1,900 miles to get here, and thankfully there were no issues along the way. I am happy to be here and anxious to take command. I will begin in-processing tomorrow morning and later start getting to know the battalion. Although I am ready to begin, I just wish Mare and Ash were here with me so we could do it together.

My family did not initially accompany me to Fort Carson, Colorado. My daughter Ashley was a freshman in high school at the time, and rather than disrupt her school year in northern New York, I left my wife and daughter at Fort Drum to allow Ashley to finish out the term.

24 April 2008

I have now met several of the unit leaders and am beginning to get a sense of the state of the unit. There is a great deal of animosity between the CMD (command) group and staff/units. The Bn (battalion) gunnery skills are seriously eroded, and Ldr (leader) experience is almost exclusively Iraq. So, I am going to have to work hard to repair the animosity and rebuild morale. The key is to generate a "team" mentality instead of "us" vs. "them." Then we will have to work hard to relearn core FA (field artillery) competencies. Finally, our LDP (leader development program) will focus on Afghanistan to change the mentality from Iraq focus to OEF (Operation Enduring Freedom). I met the CSM (command sergeant major), and I think we will complement each other nicely. Much work to be done in the FRG (family readiness group), apparently, and I will work with Mare to establish a good FRG before deployment. Many challenges, but I am ready to get started.

Before I took command, I made it a point to get out and meet all the leaders to gauge where the unit was in terms of training, morale, family readiness, and attitudes, and to understand the mix of personalities. I discovered that while there was great material, there was much work to do in order to ensure that we were ready for Afghanistan.

25 April 2008

I completed in-processing today and met the battery commanders. Overall, a quiet day, and I just continued getting familiar with my surroundings. Mare will be here tomorrow, and I am certainly ready for her to be here. Can't wait to finally take the reins and start preparations to go to Afghanistan.

28 April 2008

We conducted 5 rehearsals today in preparation for the CoC (change of command ceremony). It should be a nice ceremony. I am very glad that

Maryellen and Ash are here. I only wish they were staying, but Ash has to go back to finish the school year.

I got some interesting feedback on the morale of the unit from an interesting source. Ms. Tai runs the sew and dry cleaning shop off-post. She told me that she loves the brigade except for the current command team of 2–77. She told me she felt this way because the outgoing commander and CSM never thanked her for sewing all the SPC (specialist) and below equipment for free. She also said that the NCOs do not like them because they don't believe they care about the soldiers. They want a change, and I hope I can provide it. The key is that I must remember that I exist to serve, not to be served.

29 April 2008

Assumed command today. The weather was beautiful and the troops looked great. It is humbling to look out over the formation and realize that I am responsible for these young Americans. I was very happy to have the family all with me, and now I am ready to take charge.

I will do my best and work to embody the Servant-Leader.

30 April–6 May 2008

I have spent the past week familiarizing myself with the Bn and counseling my field grades (majors) and Cdrs. The Bn has some excellent leaders and motivated soldiers, and I feel blessed to have a group of good folks.

I observed FDC (fire direction center) training today, and our FDO (fire direction officer) and chief are actively involved in training and laid out a good plan for prep of the FDCs. I am having them focus on standards of precision, standardization of the FDCs in the Bn, and operations in mountainous terrain (intervening crest issues).

The S3, CSM, and XO laid out our plan for section certification yesterday in a logical sequence. Key is leaders prepared and ready to train the sections. As I speak to the staff, I am stressing the importance of establishing systems for routine business to ensure efficiency. Without systems, we will spin our wheels unnecessarily and cause our soldiers to question the competence of their leaders.

The key to a competent field artillery battalion is the accuracy of the fires it provides, and that begins with good fire direction centers. Therefore, my priority for gunnery started with the fire direction centers. Mountainous terrain increases the complexity of the artillery mathematical solution by an order of magnitude. If artillerymen miss the target, they can cause serious damage to the confidence of the people engaged in a counter-insurgency effort. Since our entire effort in Afghanistan is about the people, we could not miss— thus, my emphasis on precision gunnery.

7 May 2008

Today was a good day as I continue to meet my people and learn about the battalion. I am favorably impressed with all of my people. They are motivated and combat experienced. The only area of disappointment so far is in PT (physical training). These folks have got to get in a better state of conditioning for Afghanistan. I expressed my dissatisfaction at the training meeting and set some goals for the group. I want the Bn average at 250[3] in 90 days.

I did my first legal action today on a kid who did cocaine. Hopefully, he will recover, but if not, we will chapter him. The Army is no place for drugs. People have to depend on each other, and a druggie can't be depended on.

I was very surprised at the poor state of physical conditioning within the battalion. In combat your ability to stay alive is directly proportional to what kind of shape you are in. Further, a person who is in better shape handles stress with greater resilience. I could not allow our soldiers to accept a poor state of fitness because their lives depended on it. As a result, I clamped down immediately on physical training.

Commanders in the Army have legal authority over their soldiers and the responsibility to use that authority to impose appropriate discipline for the good of the unit. The Army in 2008 had serious issues with drug and alcohol abuse. Much of this problem stemmed from soldiers blowing off steam after surviving a combat tour or using these substances as a coping mechanism. Nevertheless, it is unacceptable and puts people in danger, including the user; plus it breaks down trust among soldiers that they need when putting their lives on the line. This problem, as I would soon realize, was more endemic than I had anticipated, and it took time to clean it out of the unit to prevent it from having a corrosive effect on cohesion.

8 May 2008

I continued with counseling today and have now spoken with all the battery commanders. I am pleased with all of them. They are motivated, but young and in need of guidance. So, I will do my best to mentor them through the day-to-day business of their training plans in prep for Afghanistan.

The staff sections also have many good young officers. However, one issue pointed out to me today is the fact that these FA officers feel shortchanged in professional development. All the LTs (lieutenants) held the same job for 2½ years without rotating duty positions. To be a solid FA officer, you have to hold jobs as FSO (fire support officer) and PL/FDO (platoon leader/fire direction officer). So, my challenge here will be to develop a sound rotation plan to develop well-rounded officers without upsetting the cohesion of the maneuver units and FA batteries. For the future of the FA, I have to do it.

9 May 2008

Walked through the barracks today. I was impressed with the facility and the state of police (cleanliness of the area). You never know if soldiers are living clean or if their leaders are checking unless you walk through their living areas. They all looked very good and I am pleased. The only thing that concerns me is the fact that there is not a central corridor that the CQ (charge of quarters) can control. Therefore, visitors can enter from the outside with no one knowing. It will require vigilant checks by the leaders, and my CSM is energizing the effort. I also pray that the Lord will help these soldiers to think before they act and always do the right thing.

10 May 2008

We have a tasking for the salute battery today at the Sky Sox game. A Btry is shooting, and I will take Andy (my son) to the game later today.

All went well at the game and the salute went well. After the game I got a call that PVT Forester was injured when one of the guns was dropped on his foot during unloading of the piece. He has four broken toes. This proves the old adage that you can do 1,000 things right, but one bad thing zeros it out.

It is traditional for an artillery battalion to fire salutes for special occasions, and the battalion got a tasking from higher headquarters to provide a battery for several weeks to cover such events. The first one that A Battery did was for Military Appreciation Night at the stadium of the Colorado Springs Triple-A affiliate baseball team, the Sky Sox. That night one of the best soldiers in the battalion was injured when taking a howitzer off a flatbed truck following the salute. For a time it was thought that this fine young man might lose a couple of his toes, but thankfully he healed completely. This was the first safety mishap during my command. We did many things well during my tenure of command, but, as I state in the entry, it only takes one bad event to make everyone forget the good things you do on a daily basis.

12 May 2008

Command maintenance went well, and the leaders were engaged in teaching their soldiers how to perform maintenance. I also spent the afternoon counseling the LTs and learning about them and their viewpoint concerning the unit and FA branch. Across the board they felt that:

- the FA Bn did not manage their development
- they wanted guidance and mentorship
- modular organizations are detrimental to the training of fire supporters and their growth and professional development

I agree with all, and in this brigade I will do everything to reverse this in our unit.

Only bad news today was that Forester may lose a toe. Surgery is tomorrow and I will be praying for him tonight. More to follow.

Among the many issues the Army has been dealing with since the beginning of the war is professional development of junior officers. The field artillery has struggled to produce competent officers well versed in core FA skills. Because of accelerated promotions as a result of the war and the need for unit cohesion, field artillery lieutenants have found themselves serving in only one duty position for their entire time as lieutenants. This is detrimental to the branch in the long run because these officers will not have seen how the overall system works if they have only served in one duty position. They need to have at least two jobs, preferably three, for the good of the branch and the individual. At my level as a battalion commander, my aim was to remedy this problem by shifting lieutenants from fire support to gunline for the purpose of providing a well-rounded start to their career and developing their competence as well as personal confidence. Winning support of the infantry battalion commanders in moving these lieutenants and the brigade commander is key. To their credit, they were enthusiastic supporters of this objective.

13 May 2008—Andy's Birthday

I visited Forester after the surgery today, and he did not lose the toe. Also, the Dr. told him it was "miraculous" how the middle toe has recovered. I was so glad to hear that and I know that God answers prayer. He has one toe that is still an issue, but things are looking better and I will keep praying.

I did my first USR (unit status brief), and overall the battalion is looking better than 4–25 FA looked before I left Fort Drum. (4–25th FA was my previous unit.) We are short a few 13Bs (cannoneers) and will lose some section chiefs. We are looking good equipment-wise, too, and will likely get the M198s by 1 June. This will enable A Btry to start training sooner on the 155mm rather than later.

I had a heart-to-heart with the Cdrs today. My assessment is that the unit is still in relaxation mode 120 days after redeployment (from Iraq). I told them it has to change now, so that they get in the correct frame of mind to prepare for the future in Afghanistan.

Every battalion, brigade and division in the Army produces and briefs a unit status report that goes all the way up the chain of command to the senior leaders of the Army. The return of a unit from a deployment is a time of upheaval with the loss of personnel and the need to draw equipment. Four months after returning from Iraq, 2-77th FA was not in bad shape, but my initial assessment would change, as it took much longer to get replacements than we originally anticipated. This would cause issues with our execution of training and building of cohesion in the subordinate units, but it was a challenge that we had to deal with and overcome to prepare for the mission.

Based on what I knew of our mission in Afghanistan, we had to convert one of our batteries from a M119A2, 105mm battery to a M198, 155mm battery. This meant that we would have to train the units in separate systems with the accompanying logistic challenges. Although it was not easy, I found it exciting to have the opportunity to command a composite unit with two different weapon systems. It gave us tremendous flexibility and increased capability.

Finally, as noted in the entry, I could see that four months after the unit had returned from Iraq an air of relaxation continued to hold sway. The troops were still in "I just got home mode," and this attitude would prove detrimental to preparation for Afghanistan if I did not put a stop to it immediately. That day I huddled with the commanders in my office and told them that preparation for Afghanistan began with them. They had to instill an air of seriousness in order to get the most out of our training. If they did not, it would mean an untrained unit, which would in turn result in unnecessary casualties. This I would not allow. Shortly after this talk, things turned around for the better.

13 May was also my son's 20th birthday. As he was a cadet in the U.S. Air Force Academy, all I could do was speak to him by phone, which was fine because he had begun his journey in the service and this is all part of the dynamic of serving the country.

14 May 2008

We did METL (mission essential task list) task refinement at the training meeting today to ensure that we have the right focus for our training plan. The units did a lot of good work, and we have all the major tasks set and will refine the sub-tasks this week. Then we will schedule a brief to the BCT (brigade combat team) Cdr to gain approval.

I counseled 6 LTs today and tomorrow will complete all initial counselings. I think I have a great group of officers and want to give them the direction they need to succeed and let them run. If I can establish the right command climate, I think that the Bn can accomplish anything that gets thrown our way.

Finally, Forester got out of the hospital today, foot intact. He will get all bones reset next week and then rehab. I will keep praying.

All Army units use mission essential task lists to focus training. These are fairly standard based on the type of unit. However, with the ongoing war, units must modify these objectives according to the situation, location, and mission they will encounter upon deployment. Therefore, we spent a good deal of time early in my command refining these task lists to make sure we had the right vision to accomplish our mission in Afghanistan.

15 May 2008—Mare's Birthday

Today was a good training day, with all the leaders working on their FA safety skills through a practice test. We are going to certify all the leaders next week in artillery safety before we proceed to gunner's testing followed by section certification. We should then be ready for PLT TNG (platoon training) by Aug.

I counseled my radar technician and chemo (chemical officer) today; only stragglers left now. I want all the officers to have a common frame of reference as leaders in the battalion. I told all of them that they have to be servant-leaders and team players. A common vision for all leaders will help us get where we need to be and succeed in our mission in Afghanistan.

The good day was ruined by the fact that one of my soldiers was beaten up last night. If guys would not put themselves in bad situations, they wouldn't have so many issues.

It's Mare's birthday today and I miss her, but we will finally be back together next week after being separated for weeks by the move and Ashley having to finish school in NY.

Before any artillery unit proceeds with training, it is necessary to ensure through a safety test that all leaders know their tasks. The test consists of ques-

tions that require the taker to demonstrate knowledge of the features of the weapon system, proper procedures for mitigating unsafe acts on the system, and mathematical calculations necessary for safe gunnery. If leaders do not pass, they don't take up a position on a gunline. Everyone from commander down to gunner must demonstrate their skills, with a minimum passing score of 90%. Once this certification of leaders is complete, we proceed to training sections and platoons. It is a long and regimented process, but necessary to prevent missing the target with a 95-pound TNT projectile.

16 May 2008

Today I did a foot march with the staff to Waldo Canyon (in sight of Pike's Peak). It is absolutely beautiful here in Colorado, and there are so many things to see and do. I sure was blessed to get command here.

We also had our routine EO (equal opportunity) training today, followed by sensing sessions (which are meetings with the soldiers to gauge attitudes within the unit). There is always interesting feedback from soldiers in sensing sessions. I will review the results on Monday.

Finally, tonight was my first hail and farewell (these are social functions at which units welcome new leaders and say farewell to those going to new assignments or leaving the Army). Most of the staff is changing out, but the one that hurts the most is the XO. He is an outstanding officer who was clearly the guy holding things together in the unit. He will be missed, but he has to move on for his own professional education at JAWS (Joint Advanced Warfare Studies School at Norfolk, VA).

17 May 2008

I served as OIC of a funeral team today for a World War II veteran, a retired COL (colonel). The COL died two weeks after his wife, and they had an amazing story. He was a volunteer at age 17 and became a P-51 pilot. She was in the British Army in the Royal Artillery. They got engaged before D-Day and married right after V-E Day. After the war he went into the Arkansas National Guard and was activated for Korea as an artillery officer. He stayed on active duty until the 1970s, when he retired after having commanded 6–37th FA. The son, an AF (Air Force) COL, spoke with me and I told him about Andy. He told me to have him call after giving me his card. He said he would give Andy the skinny on becoming a fighter pilot.

A Btry had two incidents last night. That is my trouble unit so far. They have a good BC (battery commander) now, but apparently the last one was a dirtbag. As a result, discipline has been lax. With persistence we will turn it around.

19 May 2008

More counselings today, but the most enlightening thing was review of the surveys from last Friday's sensing sessions.
Here is what I got from them:

- Most soldiers want harder PT
- Concerned about training and preparing for Afghanistan
- Feel they are not ready as artillerymen
- Confidence is low in the NCO corps at SGT/SSG (probably because they are being promoted too soon, having never really done their jobs)
- Time with families
- They want leadership by example
- Concern about cohesion in the unit

Based on these comments, we have a lot of work to do. The proper balance between TNG and time with families is going to be difficult to achieve, but we have to get it right for their sake.

As I came into command I wanted to get not only my own impressions of the unit but also a feel for what the soldiers had to say about their unit. There are always the usual complaints about silly things, but the feedback in this entry demonstrates the maturity and true concerns of these young folks. They wanted to be challenged and train hard. The NCOs surprised me because they saw, as I did, that their state of competence was not what they would like, since most of their time in the Army was served as infantrymen and not artillerymen. As a result of the survey, many of my own observations were confirmed. Further, I had to figure out how to ensure that while we trained hard, we allowed the soldiers opportunities to spend time with their families. They needed the balance of time with families because this is what sustains them and why they serve. Striking the correct balance was an important issue requiring command interest.

20 May 2008

I led a staff OPD (officer professional development) this afternoon on the recognition-primed decision-making process. I want the staff all on board so that we have the fastest possible process for developing orders. This will enable us to act faster than the enemy and retain the initiative so we can win. The process is cdr-driven (by experience) and the staff fleshes out the plan. We did it in 4–25th FA (my previous unit) when I was the XO and S3, and it works. We will have to train with it, but once everyone is comfortable we will be much more efficient in orders production.

I also interviewed four ladies for my FRSA (family readiness support assistant, a civilian on the staff) opening today. All are well qualified, so it comes down to finding a team player and matching the personality to the unit. My FRSA will have to work well with others, have compassion, and be capable of organizing training, meetings, and documents. Ultimately, the personality compatibility will be the deciding factor.

The production of plans and orders by a staff is a critical task in combat. The best staffs do this quickly and with clarity. To make my staff more efficient, I introduced them to the recognition-primed decision-making process developed by Gary Klein—author of Sources of Power: How People Make Decisions—*and a team of researchers. It enables a staff to cut the time required to produce an order by about one-third. Because counter-insurgency is time sensitive and requires a great deal of initiative, I implemented this planning process as our primary tool for order production. Speed is critical in combat, and I didn't want my staff to add friction through a cumbersome planning process. The FRSA is a critical individual on a unit staff. This individual is the interface between the unit, the commander's spouse, and family organizations. When the unit is deployed, the FRSA is the "go-to" individual for families in need and for the transfer of information back and forth from theater to home station. My main criterion for selection was compassion and team attitude. I found the right person in the interview process, and she was indispensable when we deployed to Afghanistan.*

21 May 2008

Bn safety day today. Our effort to reduce safety incidents (especially relating to alcohol) rolled into this training. We are having continuing issues with alcohol abuse. It all comes down to guys thinking of themselves over others. If we can get folks to think of others before they act, we can reduce the number of incidents.

I have decided to offer Mrs. Amanda Waterman the FRSA position. I called her references today and they gushed about her. She is calm, compassionate, and takes initiative, and that is what I need.

Had lunch today with Andy, his buddies (from the Air Force Academy), and their girlfriends. It was good to see him. I wish we had our house so he could come over, but that is still a month away.

The CSM and I also walked through the Btry orderly rooms (these are the office areas of the batteries) today to check the flow of information and release times based on the soldier surveys. There are problems and the CSM is going to start working with the 1SGs to fix it. We will cover in C&S (command and staff meeting) tomorrow.

Of all the problems affecting the Army today, substance abuse tops the list. Just a few years ago it was taboo to drink and drive or use hard drugs. Today it seems that some troops simply don't care. This is a readiness issue because a soldier dismissed due to substance abuse is someone you have to replace. More important, it is a moral issue. Drinking and getting behind the wheel of a car puts others' lives in danger. This is a selfish act. My aim in holding Safety Day was to make the soldiers think not only of the legal consequences but also about others who are affected by one dumb decision in a bar.

22 May 2008

A very full day today. I met with the FECC (brigade fires and effects coordination cell) today to map out our training plan. I don't own the fire support elements, but, as the senior fire supporter in the brigade, it is my responsibility to provide the direction so that the FOs (forward observers) can call for all types of fire. The modular brigade organization has been detrimental to the training of fire support teams, so I will interject myself with the maneuver commanders to reverse the trend for the benefit of the whole brigade. Step 1 is to consolidate the fire support elements in the HHC (headquarters company) of each Bn. Then, having consolidated them, we will be able to train to an endstate: trained teams able to integrate all fires into maneuver operations. Training will consist of certification, JFO (joint fires observer school) at Fort Sill, FSCX (fire support coordination exercises) with the company commanders and their fire support elements echeloning all fires, and the MRE (mission rehearsal exercise) at JRTC (the Joint Readiness Training Center at Fort Polk, Louisiana). I will work to convince the new brigade commander to adopt this plan (although all the battalions had new commanders, we still did not at this point have our brigade commander on board). I think he will support it.

I go on leave tomorrow to pick up Mare and Ash. I will pick up again on 6 June when I arrive back here.

6–13 June 2008

We got in from Fort Drum on the evening of the 6th. It is good to have the family here finally. I took most of the week to get myself reoriented. Over the past couple of weeks our adverse incident rate went down significantly. The CSM has every NCO in the chain of command coming in on Saturdays to do PT with the offenders from previous incidents. This method seems to be driving down the incidents, as the leaders are getting more involved in keeping their people under control.

Maryellen met the FRSA this week, and I think they will have a good working relationship. PT seems to have made some progress after my rantings, as averages have gone up fairly noticeably. We culminated the week with a Bn 12-mile road march. I came in fourth out of the Bn. It is important for a leader to show his mettle by pushing himself. If I rant about PT, then I have to show that I can do it too.

16–20 June 2008

We had a great week of training this week. We had artillery skill proficiency training for our 13Bs (cannoneers) and our young guys are learning a great deal. The FDCs all practiced fire mission processing (the calculation of data to accurately engage a target with cannon fire) and what I observed was outstanding. We have a good core of NCOs who know gunnery, and the young soldiers are steadily picking up sound skills. The Bn also did its first ever AASLT (air assault) training on Tuesday, with G Co working with a marine aviation unit. Finally, we conducted marksmanship training at the simulation facility. We should have over 80 firers next week on our first live fire range. I took all the leaders up Barr Trail (to Pike's Peak) on Friday and gave them a Bn coin at the top. It was a tough climb, but that is what I wanted. A tough shared experience will bring them all closer and build confidence as we ready for combat. The Spartans of old did this, and we will too in order to build a strong team.

23 June–4 July 2008

Since I have been trying to settle into our new house, I had not had a great opportunity to write down my thoughts in the last couple of weeks. The past two weeks were highlighted by the brigade CoC on 2 July and having to pull together three 20-man fire-fighting teams to go to California for a month. Due to this latest tasking, I believe it is unlikely that we can get the Bn fully trained for JRTC in January 2009 if we have to execute the mission. My training plan is now pushed back 30 days, meaning I cannot certify the sections until the end of September and will not be able to shoot by PLT until November. The post is not judicious about taskings as we approach the collective training period. We are getting no relief from taskings because training management at garrison level is not prioritized. A division headquarters here locally could fix that.

On the bright side, it looks like we will have some needed changes in the brigade start to take effect. Here are some of the things the new boss is concerned about:

- Will bring a "light" mentality into the BCT, something we really need
- Emphasis on PT—Co Avgs of 270 and up
- 12-mile (road march) monthly with 25-miler semi-annual
- Wants to get the BCT staff functioning more smoothly and more in the manner it should
- Other concerns:
  - Jr. leader involvement with soldiers
  - Soldiers knowing the TNG schedule
  - Soldiers knowing the PT plan
  - Leaders planning TNG and PT by task, condition, standard
  - Will ask soldiers questions about their perception of unit and training
  - Do we have a brigade motto?
  - Focus on MOS (military occupational specialty) TNG (for us, this is the "Big 5")
  - PLs (platoon leaders) and PSGs (platoon sergeants) preparing PLT training plans
  - Pull-up and dip bars outside each Bn headquarters for strength and conditioning

The arrival of a new commander, as can already be seen through my arrival in the battalion, is a time of change. When our new brigade commander arrived, it was refreshing because his focus was on hardening the unit to prepare it for Afghanistan. This made my job easier because the emphasis now spread throughout the brigade and my rantings about physical training were backed up at all levels. Mental and physical toughness are critical to accomplishing the mission and, more important, to preserving the most precious resource of any unit—the soldiers.

5–13 July 2008—Brigade block leave period

Spent the week getting the house in order, not much else. Good news is that the tasking to fight fires in California is now dropped. This will allow us to focus on our training once leave is over.

14–18 July 2008

This week we started working in earnest on section certification. The FDCs are ready to complete Table VII (artillery training is divided into tables, or steps, that progress from the simplest tasks to the most difficult), as their training program has been thorough and detailed through the diligence of my FDO and FDNCO. The guns are a little behind because they lacked weapons for so long. We had only four training guns. Now we are up to eight, four for each battery. Spent a lot of time with the radar this week. We just got it back from reset and they started their training program this week. They are the best-trained section in the battalion and retain most of the personnel from the last deployment. I sure need an S3. Lack of one is hurting the unit because I don't have an experienced field grade in the shop providing daily guidance. I guess that is my own fault because I hand-picked one who is currently deployed based on his experience vs. taking a guy readily available now who would not be a good fit for the unit. But, by doing so, it means that I have to wait for a couple of months before he comes on board. Only time will tell if I made the right decision in waiting for the guy I picked. I still think I did the right thing.

During this short week a number of things occurred, including pressing on with our section certification training. The training is broken down into tables that progressively build on skills until the section is ready to function together as a team. Table VII is the "dry" fire table in which the sections conduct fire missions without ammunition. This step is the final one before going into the field and firing live artillery on the range. As noted in the entry, we were short on howitzers for a number of months. It takes time to draw all the necessary equipment after returning from deployment, and delays impact the progression of training. The battalion was supposed to have 16 guns; however, more than six months after returning from Iraq we still only had half our authorization. It forced the unit to get creative with our training to ensure that all soldiers could practice their skills. Finally, I had only one major in the battalion for a period of three months. As noted above, this was a self-inflicted shortfall. I could have had a major who was available in the brigade immediately to fill the position of operations officer (known in units as the S3). However, this officer did not have the skill sets required for the job or, in my opinion, the leadership traits it would take to push our unit to achieve a high state of readiness. I heard through Army personnel channels that there was a guy with the experience and leadership ability that I was looking for on a deployment to Iraq. I made an immediate request to get him, but the catch was that I had to wait until late summer. I questioned myself for making this decision, but it turned out that my future S3 was an outstanding artillery officer who proved to be the key to our future success. As I look back now, I know I made the right choice, as painful as it may have been at the time.

Intense Training Period Begins

This marks the point at which we had most of our unit equipment, and the battalion transitioned from a relatively slow pace to rising intensity in training in preparation for the next deployment.

21–25 July 2008

This was a very busy week but extremely productive training in several areas. I also had a tough decision to make: A young captain in the FECC had been designated as my incoming B Btry Cdr before I took command. However, I learned last Friday that he was having issues with PT—the run. I brought him in and questioned him on Monday morning to see if this was true, and he confirmed the issue to me. I told him that I was not inclined to place a guy in command who could not lead, especially at PT. I have been harping on improving PT for weeks, and it would weaken my credibility to place a guy in command who could not run. Therefore, I recommended to the brigade commander that the captain not take command and instead bring over one of the infantry battalion fire support officers to take B Btry. He accepted my recommendation, and that is what we are doing. I like this kid, but the team and B Btry need a commander who can lead. The decision came down to what was good for an individual vs. what was good for the team. I picked the team.

The week demonstrated great advances in training. ASPT (artillery skills proficiency testing) is complete and we started gunner's training. I ran the battalion 5.2 miles on Friday and 27 fell out, which is far fewer than our last unit run. So, we are getting better every day, as I knew we would. These young folks just have to believe they can do anything and they will.

Next week we start gunner's testing and go on the staff ride to Little Bighorn—an insurgency on American soil. I want the officers and NCOs to think critically so they have minds flexible enough to solve complex problems. If they inculcate this thinking, we will win in Afghanistan.

Ash had a good swim meet this week, placing in the top eight in 6 of 7 races. She is very good and I am proud of her. I hate waiting around at swim meets to watch her swim, but I do it because it is important and I care.

Staff rides are a leader's training exercises to study historical battles and walk the ground to glean lessons that can be useful in the future. As part of my leader development program, we studied and went to Little Bighorn. It proved a good learning experience and was beneficial for building our team into a cohesive set of leaders.

28 July–1 August 2008

We got all of our gunners tested this week and will do "Big 3" (leaders of the gun lines) testing next week. The big event for the week, though, was our leader training to Little Bighorn Battlefield. I am a true believer in staff rides, and this one was very good. I wanted my leaders (master sergeant and above) to get three things out of it:

1. Critical thinking about our jobs
2. Examining the tactical decisions
3. Team-building

It is impossible to know/quantify what the effect of such a training event is, but I believe that all of the leaders will get much from it. They will be better leaders and gain more trust in each other. We have a good team and I think this adds to the cohesion of the team.

4–8 August 2008

An excellent week of training. Since the BCT began protecting us from taskings, we have been able to accomplish a lot. This week we got all leaders certified for cannon live fire, 26 soldiers through combat lifesaver (medical training), 2 FDCs certified, the howitzer sections continued their training for certification, and we formed the maneuver platoon so that they can begin working together. Also, we did a machine gun range. Not bad, but still a long way to go to be prepared for Afghanistan next year. We will get there.

We also did a change of command this week. B Btry got a new commander, and he is a good young man. He appears a little timid, but he will settle in, and I know B Btry will remain a great battery. It is our 105mm battery and charged with the air assault mission.

By August the pace of our training began to build steam, and we would run fast right up to the time of deployment. Out of the many important tasks from this entry, perhaps the most important was the formation of our infantry maneuver platoon. The mission in Afghanistan would require us to provide population security and patrols in a fairly large area. The battalion would not receive any infantry to accomplish this mission. Therefore, we had to form our own infantry platoon. To make sure this unit was ready and could perform as a cohesive team, I knew we had to form it early and make the members train, live, eat, and sleep together. So, I tasked my CSM with pulling together the leaders and soldiers who would man the unit from all of our batteries. The result was a hodgepodge of the different career fields in the battalion—from cooks and mechanics to weathermen and surveyors—all put together to perform an infantry maneuver mission. The brigade gave me a cavalry officer for a platoon leader, and starting in early August these young men became a band of brothers that would do more and go further than any other soldiers in the battalion. Much more information regarding their accomplishments will come out over the course of this journal.

11–15 August 2008

Focus for the week was the TLP (troop leading procedures) to prepare for our first FTX (field training exercise). I want all of our jr. leaders to make it a habit to conduct good TLPs for each operation, including a good 5-paragraph field order and rehearsals. In this all of the units did very well. We did our QTB (quarterly training brief) this week, which went well, but I was shocked to learn that our Bn has the reputation of whining. One of my explicit goals was to have a unit whose reputation was quiet competence. After seeing other units in my career that became known as whiners, I aimed not to allow this to be the case in 2–77. My books[4] are both about teamwork and the failure of leaders to get along because of self-centered behavior that led to failure in the Red River Campaign. The thought that anyone at the brigade thinks we are like this pains me, and I aim to change that interpretation.

Following the Quarterly Training Brief (QTB), my brigade commander pulled me into my office and informed me of this perception. As time went on I learned that the source of this friction was a long-running dispute between one of my field grade officers and the brigade executive and operations officers. It took me a while to figure this out, but once I determined the source I worked to quell the problem and perceptions. When one senior officer in a unit demonstrates an attitude that is one of non-cooperation with higher headquarters, two things tend to happen: first, his subordinates will reflect the same attitude to higher headquarters; second, the higher headquarters will believe that this problem permeates the whole unit, which in some cases it does. The overall effect of such a situation is that the subordinate unit will find it harder to accomplish tasks because others will view the unit as detrimental to the mission. One of the most important aspects of military operations is teamwork, and I could not let our unit suffer because the leaders were having issues figuring out how to work together for the benefit of the entire brigade. Following this revelation, I spent the rest of my command establishing the proper working relationship with higher headquarters as well as adjacent units.

18–22 August 2008

Outstanding week of training as we completed dry fire (meaning without live ammunition) certification. It was a tough event for our section chiefs, and they realize now that we will not pencil whip this critical hurdle in our training progression. Only half of the guns got first-time gos (in other words, passed the test on the first try). That's OK because, whether the NCOs realize it or not, they and the unit will be more competent and confident in the delivery of fires. I wanted a high standard, and thanks to the CSM and my Ops SGT (operations sergeant) I got it. We will shoot for the first time next week, and all are excited to make it happen. Also did leader training today with LTs and SFCs (sergeant first class) on the guns. Point was to get them hands-on with the guns so that they know how to better check them for safe operation and can QC (quality control) gunnery precision. It was well worth it, as our leaders were still talking about it this evening. We have a leaders' marriage retreat this weekend, and I hope that it will be a good event for my subordinate leaders and Mare and I.

The dry fire certification is the necessary last step in certifying gun sections in order to confirm that they can safely fire artillery and hit the target. We made it difficult to pass the first time in order to drive home the importance of safety and hitting the target. Shooting artillery is serious business and missing can cause civilian casualties, which we do not want because this will lead to the loss of support from the civilian population in Afghanistan. Therefore, we made it tough so that the leaders would internalize the fact that what we do in Afghanistan is critical and lack of precision is unacceptable. I also made it a point to conduct a series of marriage retreats in the battalion for soldiers and leaders. With the pace of deployments and training, the first thing that gets lost in the shuffle is relationships. I wanted all of my subordinates to have an opportunity to build on their relationships and used part of my battalion budget to pay for these retreats. Led by my chaplain, these retreats took place at a nice hotel where couples could relax and spend time with each other. The chaplain took a short amount of the time to conduct workshops on sustaining a relationship and resolving the conflicts that every marriage inevitably encounters.

25–28 August 2008

Although a short week, it was very productive. The battalion shot (live artillery ammunition) for the first time in two years this week. We put over

1,000 rounds down range safely. The accuracy was also a nice surprise. The very first round was within 50 meters of the target.[5] FA units struggle at times with the gunnery solution, but I am proud that our guys did well. We also calibrated a base lot of ammo so that we can maintain good muzzle velocities for our pieces.

The only hiccup was on Wednesday morning when the batteries deviated from the plan without my approval. Every gun had certified on Table VIII (live fire) on Tuesday, so we developed a plan to shoot PLT missions the next day before going in. However, the guns decided to blast rounds down range without regard for the training plan in an effort to get in (from the field) quicker. When I saw what was happening I put a stop to it and ripped the BCs' heads off. They have to learn to conserve training resources and always maintain good gunnery data. I hope the butt chewing worked and they get it straight.

1–5 September 2008

This week was used to recover from our FTX last week. Our motor pool and equipment is starting to look real good, and the line was in great condition during my inspection yesterday. In addition to recovery, I conducted 3 OPDs One was for the LTs on managing their careers and what jobs they need to become better future senior officers. Then I did one for our CPTs on training management. There is a gap among our company grade officers in their ability to manage and conduct training that was not present when I was a CPT. Finally, I did another in our series on prep for Afghanistan by discussing *Charlie Wilson's War*. I want all of our leaders to understand the environment in Afghanistan, think critically, and see what is important to win there and why they have to fight it with a sound counter-insurgency strategy of clear and hold. I preach the 85/15 rule to them. 85% of our job is nonlethal. The 15% of combat-related tasks establish the security conditions to conduct the other 85%, consisting of assistance and mentorship of the government.

8–12 September 2008

Another good week of training, with the maintenance team arriving to work M198 (155mm howitzers) training with A Btry and our first slingload (transporting a load via helicopter through the use of slings) of a howitzer. The week culminated in Organization Day, and the 2–77 Vietnam veterans participated.

Our rigging training (training in the configuration of slingloads) was outstanding this week, and the culminating event was the first lift of a 2-77 howitzer by a helicopter since the Vietnam War. 2-77 after that war was a heavy (or armored) unit for 3½ decades. The recent activation as a light (a unit without armor) unit enabled us to begin working on our AASLT mission, one we will have to be proficient at in Afghanistan. It was appropriate that the Vietnam vets were on hand to witness it.

On 11 September I hosted a 9/11 memorial prayer breakfast with our Vietnam vets in attendance. It was good to have the previous generation of 2-77 soldiers there because those men passed their knowledge on to the current generation in this war. I hope that our legacy for them and us will be victory in Afghanistan.

Each year units in the Army conduct an Organization Day. This is a day for the unit to celebrate its history through competitions, give awards to outstanding performers, and have a unit social function. In 2008 our Organization Day coincided with a reunion of the 77th FA Association. The association today consists of Vietnam veterans and those from this generation who choose to participate in the preservation of the regimental history and share in the camaraderie of veterans. We incorporated them into our celebration, and they added a nice dimension to our reflection of the history of our unit. These vets earned the Presidential Unit Citation in Vietnam for their defense of a firebase at Soui Tre. This is the highest honor bestowed on a unit for actions in combat and is similar to the Medal of Honor for actions by an individual in combat. Preserving the history of our unit and having these "old-timers" around to bond with our younger soldiers was an important aspect of unit cohesion, which I encouraged throughout my two and a half years of command. The Vietnam veterans supported us in tangible and intangible ways before, during and after our deployment to Afghanistan, and I owe a personal debt of gratitude to them for their support of this new generation of soldiers. They gave us the moral support that they never got in the dark days of Vietnam.

15–19 September 2008

I made a trip to Fort Sill to learn more about the new 155mm ammo (ammunition) and to talk to the incoming LTs with orders to our battalion. It was a very productive trip, and I learned much about advances that are being made in FA ammo and accuracy. Too bad it has taken so long to make these needed improvements. The FA branch for too long has dawdled in improving our systems and evolving to meet the changing way of warfare. And although I don't think these changes are radical enough (as I have stated in articles I have written), at least things are moving in the right direction.

In training we had a significant range week, but still a long way to go for our guys to improve their marksmanship. Next week we will do a convoy LFX (live fire exercise) and certify B Btry to fire by platoon. A Btry will start dry certification with the M198s (this is the battery that had to convert from our fielded weapon system to the 155mm howitzer to meet the demands of the mission in Afghanistan).

I had the commanders and staff over on Friday evening for a BBQ and was happy to have them over to relax.

22–26 September 2008

Very good convoy LFX, but unit needs a lot of work on marksmanship. B Btry is now section and platoon certified and can shoot in support of maneuver. The BC is doing a great job and getting better every day. A Btry did their M198 dry certification and will live fire next week.

Overall the unit continues to make great progress in training and preparing for JRTC and deployment. I project now that we will be a "T" (trained in a task) in all of our tasks after JRTC. However, marksmanship and PT are big concerns, along with staff development. These are going to continue getting great emphasis until we get it right. Enforcement of standards at NCO level is also somewhat lacking, but the CSM is attacking that one and I think we will be OK.

29 September–3 October 2008

We fired our 155mm howitzers this week and certified A Btry with the M198s. While they were in the field the Army did shots for a future commercial. It seemed like an entire platoon of civilians arrived out there to shoot the commercial.

The certification went well, but I continue to be very dissatisfied with the FOs (forward observers). Since the FA does not own them anymore, I can't dictate the training plan. As a result, the training is haphazard and uneven between the three maneuver units. Further, the brigade FECC is poorly led. Therefore, my recommendations on training the FOs only receive the attention that the maneuver commander chooses to place on them, some better than others.

The Army needs to fix this and bring the FIST (fire support elements) back under the FA Bn. Then the most senior fire supporter can oversee FO training. Until that happens FIST training will be overwatched by infantry, and they will tend to task them for other needs and spread their equipment across their units instead of with the FIST teams for their intended purpose. This is a must fix for the Army.

Beginning of Unit Collective Training

At this point we transitioned from small element [section] training to platoon and higher-level unit training; this is a significant step in the training preparation for deployment because it involves a great deal of staff coordination to develop cohesion across the battalion.

6–9 October 2008

Our maneuver platoon conducted team live fires this week. This little platoon of mechanics, surveyors, MET (meteorological), cooks and gunners is doing well as an infantry platoon. We have paired them up with 1-12 Infantry to work their training plan. They are coming together, and I feel they will have success in Afghanistan securing our AO. We completed the battalion PT test, and since I took command the batteries' averages have risen by about 20 points and G Company raised their average by 31. Still, we have work to do to reach 270 averages.

We finally made some traction on ranges this week, with almost all the soldiers now qualified, and we had a rise in scores. Eventually, we will get a good portion of the Bn to expert status.

Four-day weekend this weekend and thank God. I am beat.

A team live fire exercise is one in which a team of four soldiers is presented with a scenario, and during the course of the exercise a series of targets present themselves for engagement. The four-man team must then engage the target with fires and maneuver to defeat the threat. Therefore, the four soldiers must maneuver together and coordinate their fire to accomplish the mission. When four individuals with loaded weapons are firing live ammunition, it requires a great deal of skill and leadership to engage the target safely. This exercise, conducted on foot, is a necessary building block before advancing to squad (nine soldiers) and platoon (36 soldiers) live fire exercises. I was very happy with the performance that I observed, particularly for soldiers whose primary jobs were not infantry oriented. As stated previously, the average PT scores for our units upon my taking command were very low, in my opinion. However, within 120 days all had made significant improvement toward reaching our unit goal of 270 for each battery/company. Our young folks could improve and achieve; all they needed to do was believe they could do it.

13–17 October 2008

Warrior Strike Exercise Prep—We did some rehearsals for the exercise this week and I don't think we will have any issue with our ability to provide fires in support of the exercise. The FIST does concern me, especially at the brigade. If I owned them in the FA Bn, I would have a lot more confidence that they were actually training up to what they need. Unfortunately, the Army reorganized them with maneuver and I can't guarantee their skills. I just have to try to influence their training as best I can.

I counseled all the BCs, field grades and CSM. Right now B Btry is looking very good and they have excellent NCOs. All need work, though. The war has produced a different type of BC these days from the ones I knew and was 10 years ago. They have combat experience—as maneuver—but they don't understand training or even artillery. A big challenge. My S3 is a future Bn commander, and there is little I need to tell him. My XO is a good man but doesn't communicate clearly or organize well. He's got to work on that. The CSM is very good but sometimes so negative that he is killing initiative. Tough to convince him of that, but I laid it out there.

Warrior Strike was a brigade exercise controlled by the brigade headquarters in the field to train and develop our collective skills at battalion level and below. Brigades conduct large exercises like this to orchestrate training and also to hone the ability of brigade and battalion headquarters to command and control their units when widely distributed across the field. This is a way that units prepare for combat missions through practice in a field environment.

20–24 October 2008

Warrior Strike A (first iteration of the exercise) went very well, concluding with massing the battalion (firing all the guns simultaneously on one target from different firing positions) on Friday. We still have a lot of work to do before Afghanistan, but we have made great progress with gunnery and collective skills since I took command. When we go to the field in November we will do platoon evaluations to give the platoon leaders and BCs an idea of where the units stand on proficiency of their collective tasks. We will start timing fire missions to see if they are starting to meet the standard for firing within the set times laid out in the manuals. My A Btry has got a lot of potential, but in 2nd platoon they suffer from poor NCO execution. One of the biggest challenges of command is fitting the right people in the right job. I am going to shuffle some in that unit soon so that we can start getting them to reach their full potential. The CSM will make the changes.

1–7 November 2008

The staff conducted its first planning exercises with LTP (the leadership training program from Fort Polk, LA). I had already given two LPDs (leadership professional development) to prepare the staff to do the recognition-primed decision-making process, but this was the first time we had actually gone through the order-producing process as a team. I was pleasantly surprised at how well they did. Specifically, my assistant S3 and FDO. My S3 did very well guiding them, and I have to say that my confidence in the battalion's ability to do its job continues to rise with every exercise. We did two orders, including the actual tactical order for JRTC. Additionally, I had the BCs come in to the exercise to receive the orders and provide feedback. They did a nice job, giving the staff some good pointers. Overall, a very good week for the battalion.

The Joint Readiness Training Center at Fort Polk, Louisiana, sends a team of trainers to each unit before their exercise at the center. The team conducts what is called the leadership training program at the unit station, working with battalion and brigade staffs on planning and preparing orders using the military decision-making process (MDMP). The MDMP is a four-letter word in the Army, as most staff officers view it as a tedious, cumbersome process. These young officers would prefer to be in leadership positions in the batteries rather than on staff. However, the process provides a system to enable logical planning of military actions. Using a method that I learned at Fort Leavenworth, I truncated the process of military planning for our battalion, using the recognition-primed decision-making process, which makes the development of plans more commander-driven. This process is just what I wanted to enable us to become more nimble on the battlefield. The staff impressed me with their ability to pick it up and run quickly.

10–14 November 2008

The week started off well, with final planning and rehearsals for our platoon evaluations during Warrior Strike B. Then plummeted when the BCT Cdr again accused me of not being a team player. I did a bone-headed thing by leaving a COMEX (communications exercise) he stated that he wanted me at. I had a scheduling conflict involving my FRG and had my meeting on the calendar for a long time. However, I was wrong about that. But the other things he identified were so ridiculous.

1. My email signature block
2. Our slides for presentations do not say "Warriors"
3. Missing a beer call, and he knows how I *abhor* drinking
4. Two of my guys were talking in the back of the room at a rehearsal
5. Our invitations for the battalion St. Barbara's Day Ball did not go through the brigade personnel officer

I. Preparations and Perceptions, 4 April 2008 to 1 June 2009

There is nothing I want more than for this brigade to be successful. That is why I am working so hard to get the battalion ready, since it supports the whole unit. Yet he believes that I just do my own thing. He has assaulted my dignity because everything I exist for is to serve this country of which the brigade and the battalion are part. I have always worked hard for my unit and country, and the implication that I am not a team player hurts and could not be further from the truth. I don't know how to change that perception and now worry that the battalion will suffer because he thinks I am only about me. I would rather be dead than have that stick to the battalion. Maybe that is what will have to happen, my death in combat, to prove otherwise.

As happy as I am with the progress of the battalion and to be here, I am now saddened to be perceived in this manner. Especially when the impression is wrong. I love the Army and will do anything for my unit.

As anyone will note from the entry above, the commander's accusation hurt me beyond description. The Army is all about teamwork, and in my whole career I had never been accused of anything approaching selfishness. It cut me to the very core. To me selfishness is the root of all wrongful acts and the worst form of human sin. What worried me at this point was that such a perception would affect the battalion negatively. Perceptions of units are based on the personalities of their commanders, and any inkling of selfishness would hurt the unit in many tangible and intangible ways. I would have to work hard for the rest of my command to dispel this notion.

17–21 November 2008

Another very good training week in field. We conducted PLT evaluations for all the firing platoons combined with situational training exercises in accordance with the mission in Afghanistan. Every platoon leader was challenged. They all know that there is more to their jobs than just firing. They also have to survive, report, and see the big picture. This exercise helped them understand that.

We also fired a platoon sergeant who was all talk and no action in A Btry. One of the jobs of a commander is to place the right people in the right jobs—in other words, build a team. When one individual is counter to the ability to accomplish the mission, you have to get rid of him, and that is what we did. Since we already decided to remove the A Btry 1SG, that unit will get a new PSG and 1SG next week. I think they will soon be the best battery since the NCO leadership down there has been the biggest stumbling block to success. Concluded week with direct fire (meaning the howitzers fire at close targets that the crews can see). No better way to finish a good week.

I was very happy with the performance of the platoons during this exercise. The way they accomplished the mission set before them gave me great confidence that we could provide fires in support of the brigade and that we would be successful in Afghanistan. The firing[6] of the platoon sergeant was fortuitous since the CSM and I had considered making some changes down in A Battery anyway. The sergeant in question was hindering A Battery from reaching its full potential. The 1SG was also weak, and when the platoon sergeant became insubordinate in the field, it gave us the opportunity to make the needed changes. We replaced them with a couple of very good NCOs, and from that time on A Battery began to operate on the level that I always knew they were capable of achieving. It is always tough to fire someone, but you have to think of the unit above the individual, and in this case we made the right move.

1–12 December 2008—PDSS to Afghanistan (Pre-deployment site survey)

All the commanders traveled to Afghanistan on 1 December. The flight was the usual pain, with 24 hours on an airplane. Then, when we got to Kyrgyzstan, the weather and aircraft problems prevented us from getting into AFG (Afghanistan) until the 5th. Once we landed in Bagram we immediately caught a helicopter to Jalalabad. Afghanistan has changed a lot since my first time there in 2003. Bagram has swelled to over triple the size it was when we were there (in the 10th Mountain Division). Also, J-bad (Jalalabad) is a sprawling FOB (forward operating base) where there was once only a minor presence.

For so long the U.S. relegated Afghanistan to an economy of force theater (meaning that Afghanistan was a lower priority for resources) compared to Iraq, but that is all changing. When we arrive there will be three other brigades on the ground, plus two more coming soon thereafter. The only issue will be how to sustain it all logistically. Since Afghanistan is a landlocked country, bringing in supplies for six brigades and two division headquarters (approximately 60,000 personnel) is difficult. It is not as easy to "surge" there as the politicians seem to think.

I made it out to several firebases while I was there, including where the Bn HQ will be at Kalagush in Nuristan. Kalagush is in a beautiful valley with snow-covered mountains and a river just below the base.

From my time there during this short visit, I believe I know what we have to do in Western Nuristan to achieve solid progress.

1. Push road construction north to connect all districts and open the economy.

2. Establish presence in Dow Ab district to cut northern infiltration routes leading to the capital region.
3. Train the ANP (Afghan National Police) to eventually take over the districts in W. Nuristan.
4. Maintain disciplined batteries to support our infantry for the year.

If we can do this, we will be a success. However, we may not go into W. Nuristan. The brigade commander is considering another mission for us, possibly in Nangarhar. I have spent time there before and have engaged the governor before (Shirzai). Our mission would then be completely different, and I would have to revamp our objectives for the year. After getting stuck in Turkey for a day, we finally made it back to U.S. on the 12th and Colorado on the 13th. But no rest. We have to load out for JRTC next week and the Ball.

All battalions and brigades in the Army conduct pre-deployment site surveys (PDSS) as a part of their preparation for combat missions in theater. It provides the unit commanders and staff with an opportunity to gain situational understanding through standing on the ground and meeting with the command team conducting the mission in real time. This was an excellent trip for me, as it confirmed that our training plan was on track and gave me an idea of what we had to accomplish when we arrived in Afghanistan. The items noted in the journal entry were my "going-in assumptions." However, my vision of what we had to do changed as we moved closer to deployment. Our most important task was providing population security in order to allow the government of Afghanistan at the district and provincial levels to build capacity and competence. To achieve this, I had to modify what I believed was true when I made the trip to Afghanistan. I noted that I originally believed that we had to establish a presence in Dow Ab District in order to cut infiltration that flowed toward Kabul. This was an erroneous assessment. The bulk of the population of W. Nuristan and northern Laghman lay to the south of Kalagush, while Dow Ab is situated to the north (see map). Providing security to that population so as to enable the government to expand capacity required our presence to the south as opposed to the north. Had we moved north to establish presence, we would have spread our already meager forces far too thin to provide security anywhere. Therefore, as we moved closer to the deployment, my thinking evolved to focus our efforts where the population existed, which was south. The other items that I identified during the PDSS remained true (with some modifications) as we went along. The bottom line is that successful counter-insurgency requires a population that feels secure and a government with security forces that can perform in a relatively competent manner. This was our central goal as we approached deployment.

14–19 December 2008—St. Barbara's Day Ball on the 18th

This was another extremely hectic week as we conducted rail outload (loading the train for shipment) and made final preparations for the St. Barb's Day Ball. We did three rehearsals of the event to ensure that we had it right. General Vessey arrived on the afternoon of the 17th, and he is certainly a character. He was at Anzio in World War II; commanded the battalion in Vietnam, earning the Presidential Unit Citation; and finished his career as Chairman of the Joint Chiefs during the Reagan administration. We had him speak to our officers and soldiers during the day on the 18th, and all found him very entertaining.

The ball was an outstanding event and great fun for all. The GEN gave a memorable speech (most speeches at balls are forgettable), and the Bn built a great deal of camaraderie from the event. Best of all, no one got into any trouble that night. Andy came with us and sat with Maryellen and me. The ball is definitely one of the highlights of my command, and I enjoyed it thoroughly with our guests and family.

Load out for JRTC went well, and now all of our equipment is on its way to Louisiana for the exercise down there in January.

General John W. Vessey commanded 2nd Battalion, 77th Field Artillery Regiment, in Vietnam. When it came time to choose a guest speaker, I did not hesitate to send an invitation to the general to speak to his old battalion. He is a man of integrity and still very energetic in spite of his 87 years at that time. I was able to strike up a great friendship with him as a result, and throughout the remainder of my command I kept him informed of how his old unit was doing. St. Barbara's Day is a tradition in the field artillery branch, and every year around the world FA units celebrate the occasion with a military ball, a formal event at which the guests wear the civilian equivalent of a tuxedo and the ladies wear ball gowns. St. Barbara is known as the patron saint of the artillery and, according to legend, provides protection to all field artillerymen. The St. Barb's Day balls can range from "stuffed shirt" affairs to great fun. It is an opportunity to relax and remember the heritage of our branch of the Army, and I am happy to say that the one ball we were able to conduct during my command was a great success.

Capstone Training Exercise in Preparation for Deployment Begins

At the start of the new year we traveled to Fort Polk, Louisiana, for the concluding exercise in our preparation for Afghanistan; this event marked the first of two final events in our training before we deployed.

5–9 January 2009

Following two weeks for block leave for Xmas, we immediately jumped into action at JRTC. I arrived at Fort Polk on 7 January after being up all night waiting to load the plane at Fort Carson. Ridiculous. The first few days were spent getting everybody down to JRTC and drawing our equipment. My XO has disappointed me because he does not have a good plan for the draw or checking to make sure it is done right. I had to remind him of this, and he is getting out and doing more now.

Met with the O/Cs (observer controllers who facilitate the exercise and evaluate the readiness of the unit) on the 9th. I know many of them from past assignments. The lead O/C I have known since I was a 2LT, and his operations officer I served with in the 10th Mountain Division as the XO/S3 team for our battalion there. I have reminded the commanders and staff that JRTC is a learning experience and not a test. Our objective is collective learning so that we will be ready for Afghanistan. I do want to validate that all the training we have done to this point was on the money and that we are headed in the right direction. I believe we are, but I asked the O/Cs to confirm this for me.

The exercise at the Joint Readiness Training Center would confirm whether we were ready for Afghanistan and validate the training we had conducted at Fort Carson. I was confident going in that we were on track, but a different set of eyes providing an assessment would find things that I could not. The exercise was based on a scenario similar to our actual mission in Afghanistan and would not only test our readiness but also place a great deal of stress on the leaders, giving me a good idea of who was up to the challenge. I identified a couple of leaders whom I did not deem suitable for our upcoming mission. I then had to make plans for moving them[7] in order to get the right people in position for the deployment. I could not take a chance on any leader whom I did not have full confidence would do the right thing in combat and take care of our soldiers in the manner they deserved.

10–17 January 2009

Following our prep for the rotation, we have now commenced a tough training regimen before the force-on-force phase of the rotation. Each firing platoon will shoot 400 rounds in live fire to support the infantry in their ranges just beyond danger close (600 meters from the maneuver forces). This will be a good opportunity to validate that our platoons are ready and that our training plan to this point was effective.

Also, all of our platoons are going to do situational training lanes to train our ability to react to contact, interact with local nationals, and work with Afghan forces. While this is good for the firing platoons, it is especially good for our maneuver platoon and distro (distribution logistics) platoon.

I will try to see as many of these training events as possible, but I have several that I have to participate in myself. I have to do a key leader engagement and do staff training. I knew coming in that the weakest element of our battalion from a training standpoint was the staff. Our focus up to JRTC was on building good platoons, and we did that. But I assumed risk with the staff, knowing that some of their best training would come at JRTC. I did teach them the recognition-primed decision-making model, and we used it during LTP, but we still had not conducted full command and control of units in an exercise. We have very good people, and I believed I could assume some risk here because I thought they would pick it up quickly. I believe my decision to assume that training risk will be borne out, but we will see.

My biggest challenge down here will be with my CSM. While he is very capable, he still can't see that running a Bn is different from being a 1SG. He gets into everything, and when he starts inserting himself into the staff he causes friction. One thing I specifically asked the O/Cs to do for me was help settle the CSM down—help him stay in his lane (upholding standards and being my scout dog) and learn to trust the good people we have. However, I can tell by his first 24 hours down here that he is going to drive me crazy with negativity and friction.

Our live fire exercises kicked off on the 15th, and we are off to a good start. I was able to visit 2/B Btry when they got started up at Peason Ridge, and they were right on target after calibration of the powder lot. The GLPS (Gun Laying Positioning System—a laser locating device) in the platoon did not work and the second aiming circle would not declinate, leaving only one aiming circle. So, the platoon laid by compass. Some of the leaders were wary of using the compass, but I intervened and verified that it was safe. This gave the unit confidence in an alternative—and old-fashioned—method of lay, something most of the young leaders have never done. Once the rounds hit the target, their confidence soared. Good day at the range.

On the 16th the staff started the CPX (command post exercise) to practice targeting, planning, and C2 (command and control). After a shaky start with our info flow and systems, the staff began to come into its own by setting some SOPs in place to govern routine actions. By the end of the day on the 17th the staff was starting to fire on all cylinders. One reason was my outstanding young assistant S3, who is doing a fine job planning, and the other is our new targeting officer. We made him a battle captain, and he was the key to success in current operations. Our decision-making/planning process is also a huge success, and the staff believes in it. Plus, the O/Cs are impressed with our process for planning.

18–22 January 2009

The CPX ended on the 19th, and we began to make the transition to the force-on-force portion of the exercise. By the end of the CPX the staff was really beginning to work like a well-oiled machine. The big area that they will need to improve upon is follow through. From the targeting meeting we were able to generate good TGTs and plans to service them. However, we do not have a good system for following through on requests for assets that are generated from the targeting process. Requests for recon or attack are not "fire and forget." You have to have a system for getting requests in early and then checking on them.

Also, we need to improve conveying information to me and running estimates. I solved this by having the staff put together a briefing book to keep me updated and also forcing the staff to provide the latest info to the book—thus an updated estimate. This killed two birds with one stone. One of the things I am considering is moving my HHB Cdr and getting a hard charger in the job. While my HHB Cdr is a nice guy and I like him personally, he is not a high-energy, motivating individual and not above average. He is middle of the road. To do all that I am going to ask HHB to do, I need a highly motivated, inspiring leader. Plus, the current commander is so lackadaisical with his own property I wonder if he will take care of his people. I think a change is in order.

B Btry finished the live fire on the 18th, and A Btry will move up there to shoot. We are getting the new MACS (modular artillery charge system—improved gunpowder for cannons) charges to shoot. This is great, so that our guys will see the latest in ammo and practice with what we will have in Afghanistan. The winds were blowing in such a way that we could hear the LFX 40 km away. A Btry got off to a fast start, picking up right where B Btry left off. Overall, good shooting.

On the 21st I got to meet the "Afghan" counterparts. Since I have so few combat forces for securing my AO, the focus has got to be on the non-lethal side of business. So, my main effort in securing Dagari (the village name at the training center) will be using CA (civil affairs), information operations, and cooperation with ANSF (Afghan National Security Forces) to win/secure the area.

The scenario started on the 22nd and, like any JRTC rotation, it quickly became overwhelming with all the events that get thrown at you. We took indirect fire, conducted our first patrols, and the remote firebases began supporting their infantry Bns with 6400 mil fires (meaning indirect fires in all directions). We are a little weak in out-of-traverse missions, and I can tell that we will have to work on this when we get back to Fort Carson in our next section certification. However, that said, we are actually off to a fast start in the force-on-force portion of the rotation. Tomorrow we have a mission to capture a TB (Taliban) operator that is supposed to arrive in Dagari to smuggle IED parts.

As stated before, the rotations to the Joint Readiness Training Center are meant to simulate combat conditions in the theater. The entry above provides an idea of the vast number and complexity of tasks that modern soldiers must demonstrate proficiency in to survive and become successful in combat. The soldiers of our battalion had to show that they could perform multiple missions in a stressful environment safely in order to accomplish our mission. They did this with quiet competence, and I was very proud of them. Today's U.S. soldier is a smart operator who has assimilated and adapted to the challenges of modern combat with little complaint. All Americans should be in awe of what they have accomplished for the nation in the past 10 years in training and in combat, protecting the people of the United States as well as Afghanistan.

23–26 January 2009

We launched Operation Steel Balls on the night of the 23rd. We used our maneuver platoon and the ANA (Afghan National Army) company we now have. We put the Bn headquarters (TAC—tactical) forward to C2, and within an hour of launching the operation we had "killed" the bodyguard of the target and captured the guy we wanted. All with no friendly casualties. Not a bad operation overall. Earlier in the day our ANA contingent finally arrived. I had been clamoring for two days to get a credible indigenous force down with us to enable us to do combined patrols so that we can better work with the locals. In response the "governor" sent the ANA colonel down to provide us with a company to patrol our district.

Also, I have now met with the "mayor" twice, and he has given me a long list of issues and is reluctant to trust me, so I will have to work hard to earn it. I have invited him to our base tomorrow for a dinner along with the governor to start building the relationships that will enable us to win. Our CA team is working on plans for a clinic survey, school ribbon cutting, and delivering a generator to the village as our first steps of goodwill.

On the 24th we set up checkpoints on either side of the town to start doing a biometric survey of the population. This is very much in line with what Galula (counter-insurgency theorist David Galula) recommends from

I. Preparations and Perceptions, 4 April 2008 to 1 June 2009 61

his experience combating the Algerian separatists in the 1950s. I hosted the dinner tonight and the governor did come with the ANA Cdr. I had the "press" there, and at the conclusion of the event I delivered the generator. The mayor seems to be coming around now. We will conduct the clinic site survey tomorrow, and I will discuss the plan for the school opening when I visit the village.

Early morning on the 25th the ANA colonel came to visit me, saying he had a source that said an AQ (Al Qaeda) operative would be in Dagari tonight. So, we started planning with the ANA a way to capture this guy. We fully integrated them into the planning and rehearsals and placed them in the lead to capture the TGT. We gave the operation the code name Operation Steel Valkyrie. Meanwhile, I conducted my visit with the mayor while the CA team did the site survey and the medics conducted a MEDCAP (medical civic assistance program) in the village. The mayor is coming around now and is beginning to trust us. He even invited me to lunch with him, which was pretty funny. The role players served me BBQ chicken. Not bad and better than an MRE (meal ready to eat).

When I got back to the TOC (tactical operations center), we did the rehearsal for Valkyrie and it went really well. We launched a combined TAC (tactical center forward) that evening once the Afghan source reported the target's arrival in the village. All went smoothly until one of the ANP (Afghan National Police) turned on us and shot a U.S. soldier. The ANA managed to capture the TGT, but we did not get a thorough site exploitation because the maneuver platoon pulled out too early and our medical platoon did not respond quickly enough to our casualty, resulting in a died of wounds. We have to work on this for future missions. We conducted an AAR (after action review) of the mission that night to capture the lessons.

The 26th was scheduled for the school opening. That day we conducted the school ribbon cutting, and it was not without some drama. We had a very good security plan and laid everything on with attention to detail. However, during the ceremony an individual who did not want to see it take place threw acid in the face of a female onlooker. The ANP arrested him. We allowed them to handle the situation. Sometimes in an insurgency it is best if we do nothing and allow the locals to handle things, and that is what we did.

That evening the perimeter of the FOB was attacked, and while we had good security some things did not go well. The maneuver platoon all focused on a single sniper in Dagari, and security at the gate forward was allowed to weaken. I went out with the S3 to see what was going on when I found this lapse in 360-degree security. With the help of the S3 we got it straightened out, but not before a fratricide occurred. We still have to drill into people's heads to watch their sectors of fire so we don't lose all-around coverage. The FSCX (fire support coordination exercise) in February should help reinforce this.

In only a few days of the exercise we had an enormous number of events thrown at us. This was great training because it prepared us for what we would encounter in Afghanistan. It is hard sometimes not to laugh during the scenario because of the role player factor. But the Army does an outstanding job of bringing together resources to make the scenario as real as possible. As we will see, many of the situations presented above became reality in Afghanistan. One in particular was an attack on our forward operating base that occurred in November 2009.

27 January 2009

We ENDEX'd (ended the exercise) last night at around 2200 (10 PM), and after clearing all weapons and checking for brass (ammunition that could still be in the chamber of a weapon) we played "The Yanks Are Comin'" over the loudspeaker system. Tomorrow is the FA AAR, and over the next couple of days we will wrap everything up so that we can fly home.

Went to the fire support AAR today. While there were many good things that came out of it, there are still several troubling issues. First, too many company commanders don't properly employ their FO teams. Then when "xxxx hits the fan" it is too late. Second, there is clearly a difference in competence between the three Bn FSEs and the way they are trained and employed. 1–12 (Infantry) is in good shape because their command has placed heavy emphasis and reliance on fires, and it shows. 3–61 Cavalry is doing well, but just not as solid as 1–12. 2–12 Infantry is by far the worst because they have relegated their FSO (fire support officer) to nonlethal operations. So, when they need solid lethal fire planning, the FSO was not able to do it. They belatedly realized the need in the final two days at JRTC, but it was the B Btry, 1st Platoon FDO (fire direction officer, and one of my officers) who controlled all the fires and later received an award from the training center called "the hero of the battle." The FDO was LT Tatford. (**I wish the fire supporters belonged to the FA Bn. Then I could train them.) While we were down here he finally made weight, allowing me to promote him. Good young man, but being a linebacker at West Point made it difficult for him to make the Army weight standards.

Following the exercise at JRTC there is a series of after-action reviews. The purpose of these meetings is to thoroughly critique the exercise and performance of the unit. This allows the unit to identify what it is doing well and what tasks still require work. I had to attend three of these reviews. The first one was for the fire support system. As stated several times throughout the journal, I wished that I had full control of the fire support soldiers assigned to the three maneuver battalions. Prior to 2004, all fire support soldiers were assigned to the field artillery battalions for training and then attached to the maneuver battalions for exercises and combat operations. As the senior fire support officer in the brigade, it is my responsibility to ensure the system works in the brigade. However, without command authority, I cannot dictate the training priorities; I can only recommend training priorities to the maneuver commanders as the field artillery battalion commander. Therefore, there is always an uneven level of training across the fire support elements based on the priorities of the maneuver commanders. I was able to work well with my counterparts, but they set the priorities for their battalions, and at times these came into conflict with what I believed was critical for the fire support system. One of the few people whom I name in the journal is noted in this entry, 1LT Reagan Tatford, better known as Willie in the battalion. He demonstrated outstanding leadership at JRTC and carried this competence into Afghanistan. He has since come home, having resigned from the Army to pursue other interests in his home state of Louisiana.

28 January 2009

The FA battalion AAR was today, and overall the performance was outstanding by the Bn. Everyone really came through during the exercise, with a couple of exceptions. Things we still need to work on:

- 6400 mil firing capability (I knew this coming down to JRTC)
- Air assault tasks (never had a chance to really practice the collective tasks like slingloading or helicopter pickup ops)
- Staff follow through after orders are issued (learned this during the rotation)
- Need to work with XO and replace the HHB Cdr

I was disappointed with my XO on two counts at the end of the rotation. First, he was manifested to go out on the first flight back home. XOs push logistics, and he can't do that if he is already home. Second, the poor supervision of logistics coming down to JRTC has led to the loss of 4 sets of MILES (multi-integrated laser engagement system—for laser "tag" during force-on-force with rifles) gear priced at $50,000. I have had a talk with him about it, but now I have to put it in a written counseling. He does not communicate well, and this confuses everyone and frustrates those who have to accomplish the required tasks. To be a successful senior leader, one must communicate, and he simply does not.

The other disappointment is our HHB Cdr. He is a mediocre leader at best, and I have made the final decision to recommend a new Cdr take over at the one-year mark (of the outgoing Cdr's tenure). HHB's supply accountability is poor, they are disorganized as a unit, and every order is met with excuses for why things cannot be done. Plus, the lackadaisical attitude of the Cdr and his sarcasm have worn me down. I need a good guy to take the unit into combat, and I have decided that that person is the fire support officer in 1-12 Infantry. I will recommend to the Bde Cdr that we bring him over for an April change of command.

29-31 January 2009

The unit has wrapped up the final logistic pieces, and we are now ready to move back home. On the 30th I took all the officers who remained on the ground up to Mansfield and conducted a staff ride based on the major battle that I wrote about in my book on the Red River Campaign. I focused the staff ride on teamwork and leadership.

Flew out on the 31st, but not before we had a scare with the CSM. We thought he had a heart attack, which wouldn't surprise me with the way he is most of the time. Turns out he has a muscle strain in his chest.

The CSM got a little better as the rotation went along, but he still wants to get into everything and at times drives me crazy with his negativity and micromanagement. For all his good qualities, these two things are the cause of a good deal of friction in the Bn, and if he could solve this, he would be the best CSM in the Army. I am not sure with his personality he can change, though.

Got home at 2200 Saturday night, and it is good to be back.

2-6 February 2009

Spent this week getting things back in order at Fort Carson and pulling our equipment off the train. We also have laid out the plan for the fire support coordination exercise at the end of the month called Operation Gunsmoke. We will combine the exercise with our final section certification. The exercise is a defensive scenario, and we will support it with 2 155mm and 2 105mm howitzers (see photos of these howitzers), plus a 105mm direct firing in the firebase. Simultaneously, we will rotate all sections through section certification focused on 6400 mil ops (our gunnery weakness from JRTC).

I got very angry with the CSM in the coordination meeting because as we were laying all this out he sat shaking his head and complaining about too much to do. Well, I blew my stack for the first time with him, and he finally got the message that I don't want the negativity anymore, I want solutions.

Lesson: An important thing that a Cdr must do is *push his people*. They can always do more than they think they can, and the commander has to show them this. They can do more than one thing at a time if organized and planned properly.

9–13 February 2009

Overall this was a fairly quiet week, and I concentrated on catching up with my counselings. Most were fairly easy, but of course the tough ones were the two I conducted with my XO and HHB Cdr. My XO is a hard worker and loyal to a fault, but his inability to communicate and organize the staff/synchronize for mission accomplishment is a drag on unit efficiency. The ability to communicate clearly and effectively run a staff are the essence of what a field grade officer is supposed to do. It is because of this that I don't believe he can be a battalion commander. I told him that this week, difficult as it was to do, because I like him. But a commander must have courage and tell people the truth, however tough it might be.

I also told the HHB commander that his performance led me to recommend his early exit and the brigade commander agreed. If he can't manage his supply room or plan simple things, then he can't keep troops alive in combat. He didn't take it well, but my concern is not an individual; it is the unit. The battery deserves the best possible leadership, and I have to find it and get it in place regardless of hurt feelings. My wife was mad at me too because the BC's wife has the best family readiness group. I had to explain to my own wife that the unit needs the best and he ain't it. She was still mad, so I picked up a picture of Andy in his uniform and asked her what she expected of his leaders. I told her that it was my job to make sure that kids like him had the best, even if that means hurting an individual. It was tough to tell it to him, but, again, failure to do so would be a professional failure on my part to take care of the unit.

17–20 February 2009—Short Week

We were off on Monday and came back to work on Tuesday. Most of the week was spent preparing for Gunsmoke. We did a walk-through at the range on Wednesday and then on Friday the Bn ran the brigade fire support rehearsal. I took the opportunity to make it into an OPD (officer professional development) and push my influence on the young fire supporters.

I told them my tenet of "no maneuver soldier conducts an operation without a fire plan." And that every plan consists of a fires paragraph, target list, and fire support execution matrix (these items explain how the plan works so that the maneuver folks understand how artillery, air support and mortars will support their plan). Finally, they have to rehearse every plan. Then I talked them through prepping an engagement area for fires. I believe we will have a good exercise, and I am going to spend the whole week with the fire supporters and let the CSM and BCs handle the section certification.

The week was capped off by a visit from a soldier's spouse. She married a young soldier whom I was court-martialing two weeks before he pleaded guilty in trial to barracks theft, drugs, conspiracy, etc. She and her mother came into my office to basically accuse the unit of mistreating him. I politely listened and tried to answer her questions, but all she really wants is the conviction overturned and his benefits. I was angry because the guy she married is the lowest of the low in the Army. Anyone who steals from another soldier is a man of no honor and should be treated accordingly. Further, this girl is in for a shocker when he gets out and he shows his true colors. Finally, what mother allows their child to marry a felon and then acts like it is "the system's fault"? This soldier was no victim; he, along with his wife, is not willing to accept responsibility for his actions or see things for what they are. These people are typical of a trend in our country to refuse responsibility for actions taken, and it makes me sick. I am sure this won't be the last we hear from this spouse.

23-27 February 2009—Operation Gunsmoke (Final Training Exercise)

This was the last major exercise of our prep for deployment and will bring together direct, indirect, and air in a fire plan for base defense as we might encounter in Afghanistan. The expected frictions occurred each day with communications, MET (weather data), and safety data. But each day the exercise came off and gave each FSO a chance to execute fires with his commander. We have some standouts among the lieutenants. LTs Dearman, Shrobe, Shrode, and Wasilewski are going to be good ones, and those units are in good shape.

The main lessons from the exercise across the board were:

1. FO employment (centralized or decentralized)
2. Use of attack guidance
3. Target location error and using the tools to eliminate the error (their laser equipment)

The guns fully supported and the maneuver folks were impressed with the effects, especially the direct fire gun at the firebase. We blew the crap out of the targets. It culminated with our own maneuver platoon, and they did outstanding. I personally did the AAR and the guys enjoyed shooting it up. Next week we will start loading up the equipment for Afghanistan. Finally.

Ready for Afghanistan

From this point we begin carrying out final tasks to deploy to Afghanistan, representing the final phase of our preparation.

2–6 March 2009

Very hectic week. We had to recover equipment from the field, turn in equipment to DOL (Directorate of Logistics) to leave behind, and load everything else in containers for shipment to AFG. Everybody has pitched in to get it done, and it has gone well this week in spite of the wide-ranging tasks.

The one part of the week that was extremely irritating was the fact that the spouse of the court-martialed soldier filed a complaint with the CG's (commanding general's) office in reference to her husband. As I have already written, she asked many questions about her husband and others involved in the case. I could not discuss the others because it is not releasable to her. I tried to help her with answers about her husband and to get his uniforms, but that was not enough. The only thing that would satisfy her is his release from jail and an honorable discharge, and that will never happen. So, I spent several hours writing a six-page rebuttal to her accusations of his mistreatment. (The old adage that you spend 90% of your time with 10% of your unit [the dirtbags] is so true.) I tried to be nice and not disparage her husband when she visited me, but now that she has pulled this I laid out every rotten thing he ever did over the past several months in the document. I hope she realizes what she married.

The soldier mentioned above was convicted in court-martial by a jury of his peers of theft from another soldier, breaking and entering, selling the stolen goods in conspiracy, using the money to buy drugs, and drug use. This young man received a two-year sentence, reduced to one to serve at a military jail. He and his co-conspirators were a cancer in the unit, as they were all involved in the buying, selling and use of drugs. Such things only serve to weaken units and in combat make them vulnerable to enemy action. Once we cleared out this drug ring, the unit gained a great deal of cohesion and stability. Our disciplinary issues dropped significantly after this point and just in time for our deployment to Afghanistan, where we needed everyone's full attention on their jobs.

9–13 March 2009

This week was consumed with our outload for Afghanistan. I spent some time every day in the motor pool with the CSM checking on progress and on what equipment was going. The last thing I want is to get over to Afghanistan and not have everything we need. We did have a couple of situations that did not make me happy. Folks started cutting corners in maintaining discipline, and we had to tighten it up. Specifically, down in HHB there were all kinds of accountable equipment laying out unsecured in a pile of stuff that was obviously earmarked for the trash. (Yet another reason why we need to move the HHB Cdr.) We had a Bn formation to show people that throwing away good equipment is unacceptable. Then I caught several people driving their cars in the motor pool and had to put a stop to that. Bottom line is that when a lot of things are going on and time is short, people start cutting corners. Leaders have to be on the spot to prevent lax discipline, and that is why I was down there a lot this week. By Thursday afternoon all containers (89 shipping vans) were gone and all the rolling stock was prepared to move. I asked the COL to give my movement officers and NCOs brigade coins for the job they did in moving the battalion equipment.

16–20 March 2009

We did our personnel checks for deployment this week. These checks have gotten progressively more stringent since I first came in the Army. Any little "ailment," real or imagined, makes a soldier non-deployable. When I was in 1–39th FAR (Airborne) during the Gulf War (1990–1991) there were a total of 10 non-deployables in a Bn of over 600 men. 2–77th has 428 soldiers, and I am carrying about 60. That number will come down to about 25 after we get them all cleared, but the point is that this represents 15% of our strength vs. 2% when I was stationed at Fort Bragg. It is all because of the political environment in our country. The people who are against the war will grasp anything to make the military look bad, and one of the things they latch onto is how the war is destroying soldiers' lives. All crap. Leaders in the military bend over backward to help soldiers and spend most of their time doing it. Yet we get excoriated by people who have never served for not doing enough for their own political agenda and advancement.

On the positive side, we had a good range and I got to qualify too. I got expert. Our new scopes tripled the number of experts in the Bn. On Friday we did safety day before block leave starts. I am glad we are getting a break. It has been a long haul with the training we have been doing since last June, and, looking back, we have accomplished so much. We will do fine in Afghanistan.

Every unit that deploys to combat goes through a very rigorous screening to ensure the readiness of all soldiers physically and mentally. It takes several days to complete the screening, and those soldiers identified as not ready ("non-deployable") receive immediate medical attention to fix the issue. Those who require long-term treatment remain back from the deployment, which affects the strength of any unit. Some will fully recover from their ailments, while others have chronic issues that require separation from the Army. It is sometimes frustrating to a commander because inevitably there are a number of soldiers who come up with issues who had never had any problems before. The strength of a unit is a primary concern for a commander, and maintaining physically and mentally ready soldiers is the essence of the job.

23 March–5 April 2009

Block leave went well, with only two calls about misconduct. Both were domestic squabbles that are always difficult to determine who is at fault. Both were dealt with by the rear detachment, and everything was pretty quiet.

We went to the Grand Canyon during the first week and had a good time hiking the rim and going down into the canyon. It is amazing how big that thing is. How folks can look at something like that and deny there is a God is beyond me. The weather was horrid on the drive home. We hit a blizzard at the Colorado/New Mexico line and ended up spending the night at a truck stop in Walsenberg, CO, sleeping in the car. Another "memory" made. Ha. The second week was good, and we just did a few things around Colorado Springs. Good break before we hit the home stretch to deployment.

6–10 April 2009

It was a pretty good week and fairly smooth coming out of block leave, giving us time to get back into the swing of things. The big event for the week was the HHB change of command. I am glad we made the switch. As I have said before, I hated to do it as much as I liked the outgoing commander and his wife, but I know that deep down I am doing the right thing for the battery and battalion. He just didn't have the drive and determination that I want in a BC. The new HHB commander, I believe, does have that drive, and I am looking forward to having him turn that unit around as we get ready for our final training days before combat in Afghanistan. I am confident he will do well and the Bn will only get better.

13–17 April 2009

Other than our ranges, this was a fairly uneventful week. We did get about half the Bn qualified and shot our machine guns. However, too many of our people do not achieve expert. And many of the NCOs do not know how to teach shooting skills. It is very sad. I shoot very well, and it is hard for me to understand what is so difficult. Nevertheless, I will keep pressing to improve marksmanship. Every soldier should be proficient on their weapon and know how to use all other weapons in the unit.

Over the weekend Maryellen's nephew was shot in a random incident in Denver. She is a nervous wreck now and spent most of the weekend at the hospital in Denver. It angers me when people complain of the human cost of the war when the idiotic violence in our own country likely exceeds the cost in Iraq and Afghanistan combined. People need to wake up to the violence that exists here in America.

20–24 April 2009

We had a busy week culminating with an exercise we called Steel Challenge. I got the idea last week while doing PT with the CSM. We had been trying to figure out a way to evaluate where we were on the Warrior 12 Tasks (the brigade top twelve combat tasks for Afghanistan), but we had simply not had the time to work it into our schedule. While we were doing PT last Friday the CSM off-handedly said that we should do some tasks as a part of PT after we saw a unit doing litter carries. I got with the S3 and we sketched out a concept consisting of a road march; along the route the platoons, which we organized by their firebase location, with their PLs and PSGs leading, would react to situations that tested their knowledge of the tasks. The CSM did not want to go that elaborate because it might conflict with our motor pool equipment turn-in. But I forced it, and it was a great training event. Bottom line, we need more crew-served weapon training, but our medical skills are very good. The firing units are in great shape, but G Co needs work. I gave awards to first, second, and third places. Here is who won the awards:

- Maneuver Platoon took first, having the best scores in almost every task
- 1st Platoon, A Btry took second
- 3rd Platoon, B Btry tied for third with, surprisingly enough, the S1 (personnel shop)

I. Preparations and Perceptions, 4 April 2008 to 1 June 2009

This again proves that our maneuver platoon is well trained and came a long way in the nine months since their formation and training. LT Great did a fine job with his platoon, along with LTs Dinnen and Nerdalen in A Btry, and Tatford in B Btry. Their platoons are ready for Afghanistan.

We also did deployment briefings. I briefed all the families on our deployment and what they could expect. If soldiers and families will just do what was briefed and access the available resources, all will run pretty smooth. But my experience as a rear d. (detachment) tells me that about 10% of our families will have serious but preventable issues. Oh, well, you can give people the tools, but if they don't use them, then they (the tools) are paper weights.

I believe that competition makes everyone better, and whenever we had the opportunity we introduced an element of competitiveness to training to make it more interesting than it otherwise would have been. A commander has to be careful with the use of competition, however, because animosities can sometimes crop up between units when there is a perception that certain units are treated better than others. To prevent this, the key is fair evaluation and remembering good sportsmanship, as all are taught at a young age. This is also commander's business. When competition is introduced in a healthy manner, it can really enhance training and enable growth across the board.

27 April–1 May 2009

This week we cased the colors, signifying that we are ready for deployment. A year ago, when we started training, I knew that it would be a long uphill climb to get where we needed to be. Overall, I think we got there. We were untrained in shooting artillery and needed work on a host of other skills. But, little by little, we got there by focusing on the "Big 5." From now until we deploy I am going to have the soldiers shoot rifles, hone medical skills, and spend time with their families.

We also had A Btry get "Warrior Shocked," which is when the brigade does a surprise check of a unit to test PT and Warrior 12 Tasks. A Btry did well on the tasks, but I was kind of let down by their performance on the PT test. I had expected them to average around 260, but they only got a 248. It is better than where we started last year. However, I really thought they would have finally built up some stamina. They will take another PT test in two weeks.

Casing of colors is a solemn ceremony that marks the start of the deployment phase of the unit's life cycle. In the ceremony all commanders, with their command sergeants major, case the unit colors, meaning that they put them away until they reach the theater. The colors will not go on display again until the unit reaches its destination. It officially marks the end of training and signifies that the unit is ready for combat.

4–8 May 2009

We are getting our final touches on training. We had 5 ranges this week and are down to one guy in the unit who is not qualified. Plus, we have 80 experts in the unit. Before this round of ranges we had only 12, so we now have six times the number of expert riflemen that we had last year. I am pretty happy with this improvement. Also, our sharpshooters more than doubled. This will serve us well in Afghanistan.

I did shura training (a shura is a meeting in Pashto) on Wednesday, and all the BCs conducted practice key leader engagements. Using an interpreter is a skill that is tough to learn, and maintaining what we learned at JRTC is important. Overall, the feedback is that everyone did well.

Finally, we did the Bn PT test. Once we tabulate the results, I will give unit and individual awards for those who meet the standards in my PT policy.

I did a final FRG steering meeting and focused on casualties and how it affects individuals and units. All of the training the ladies have done to this point has focused on process. But I wanted to drive home the point that they have to be prepared to deal with the emotional effects of casualties in units. It could either bring people together or divide them. So, they have to prepare for this and how they would react. They also have to understand how it could affect them personally and that compassion "fatigue" can set in. Family readiness is critical to a unit's readiness, and I wanted to make sure they had given thought to the emotional aspects of suffering casualties before we leave so they are mentally prepared.

Even though we were within three weeks of deploying, training did not stop, nor would it stop after we were in theater. These final weeks focused on individual readiness in terms of marksmanship, physical fitness, and medical skills. Additionally, we had to use the remaining time to focus on the families. As a rear detachment commander in another unit, I saw firsthand what can happen to a unit when it suffers casualties. The family members will either come together to support the ailing member or they will divide up into groups. The latter reaction can be very detrimental to the unit and families. Therefore, as we prepared to fly out at the end of May 2009, I met with the family members to impress upon them the need for unity no matter what happened and to prepare in their minds how to deal with a casualty situation. Suffering casualties is the reality of war, and ignoring it would have been dishonest to our families.

11–15 May 2009

Training is now complete until we arrive in theater. The last of the ranges are done and all the required pre-deployment tasks are done too. On Monday the first of our soldiers flew out. We now have 12 guys in Afghanistan ready to receive our equipment and start pushing it out to the firebases. It's amazing. We have been talking about this for a year, and now we have pushed out the first package of soldiers to begin the mission. I think at this point everyone is tired of talking about the mission and we all just want to get over there and get the job done. I feel the same way.

It was Andy and Maryellen's birthdays this week. Andy is now 20 and Mare is 44. Unbelievable. He is halfway through college; it is just so strange that Andy is that old now. Soon he will have his own career. I got him an autographed baseball from Curt Schilling, and we went to the ballpark for the weekend to catch the minor league Cubs.

18–22 May 2009

We sent the advanced party out on the 19th led by the XO. We have at least one guy going to all 10 locations where we will have either a firebase or a logistics node. Everyone is anxious to just get over to Afghanistan and get the job done. We trained a solid year for this, and now it is time to do what we trained for.

I put the Bn on half days this week so everyone could maximize their time with family. Hopefully, we won't have a lot of dumb incidents from soldiers with time on their hands. It is very important to spend time with family before departure. I have been in units where you worked late every day until the deployment. I was determined that such a morale-killing policy would not occur on my watch, and I have been successful with it.

I wanted to do a softball tournament to build morale, but the weather has not cooperated, so I postponed it until next week. I promoted a couple of LTs to CPT on Monday. They are both on advanced party, so I wanted to promote them before they left.

24–29 May 2009

Final week before we all leave. The highlight of this week is a softball tournament. Everyone took this week to relax, spend time with family, and prepare to leave. I wanted to do the softball tourney as a way to come together as a unit before we deploy. I spoke to everyone for the last time in one place. After Saturday everyone will scatter to the four winds, and we won't be in one spot again until we return to Fort Carson. We will be scattered around NE Afghanistan at over 10 different bases providing fires for the brigade. I just pray that our training and efforts in preparing for the mission pay off with accurate fires on every fire mission for our maneuver units. Also, at the softball tournament I promoted several LTs to CPT and 1LT at home plate. I am very pleased with the overall quality of the young officers in the Bn. They are good young people, and the Bn has done well with them as our jr. leaders.

The first main body went out on Saturday, 30 May. It is always a sad day to see, with families upset over the soldiers leaving for combat. Some are stoic, some cry, others have to be sent home early because they can't handle seeing their loved ones boarding the bus to the airfield. My hope and prayer is that every single soldier will come back safe to their loved ones.

From 29 May 2009 until June 2010 the battalion was never again in one place at one time. Supporting our brigade and securing the area of operations assigned to us required the unit to spread out over 10,000 square miles in 14 different locations. To see my unit, I would have to travel frequently to check on how everyone was doing in Afghanistan. It is always tough to see the reaction of families when their soldiers leave for deployment. It is quite a sacrifice on the part of these young people to leave home for a year to go into a hostile environment. I had hoped that I would be able to bring everyone home, as stated in the journal entry. Unfortunately, that did not happen.

1 June 2009

My last day at home. Maryellen and I went to the promotion ceremony for one of my officer's spouses in another battalion. Then we went to the commissary to pick up some things. After dropping the stuff off at the house, we went to old Colorado City and had lunch at one of the outdoor eateries. We had a very nice day together. We have always been fairly close, and after 21 years of marriage we are still blessed. I always hate to leave, but it is my job and duty. Ashley made a bunch of cookies to bring up to the Bn tomorrow so that there would be goodies for the soldiers. I ate some at home, and she did a really good job baking.

I am very ready to finally get to Afghanistan. I have been talking about it for a year to the Bn. Now I am ready for us to show what we can do and get it over with. I do want to make sure that during our year we make a positive impact toward progress in Afghanistan. Based on what the advanced party is telling us, the unit we are replacing has done little to advance progress over there and their staff is leaving theater before we even arrive.

To me this is very unprofessional and poor form, but we will deal with it, and, as I said, our effort will go toward helping Afghanistan get a step closer to full sovereignty.

Preparation Phase Ends

By 2 June 2009 most of the battalion had departed for Afghanistan, except a small number of soldiers who would deploy later. Based on two previous tours to Afghanistan and full faith in our nation's Army, I fully believed that we as Americans could achieve victory. Therefore, our unit's training focused on what we could do to bring about a victorious result. As the reader can see from the entries in the journal, the battalion and our brigade worked extremely hard during the year at home to prepare for the mission to Afghanistan. A year that is supposed to provide time with family and a respite from previous deployments to combat is, in reality, a busy period devoted to getting ready for the new challenge. The performance and motivation displayed by the soldiers, in spite of adversity, bolstered my confidence. However, what I encountered in Afghanistan on my third tour would shake my belief that we alone could achieve victory. The things that would change my opinion included Afghan governmental incompetence, overly centralized leadership and structures, and the unadulterated corruption of so many officials. Dealing with these problems daily gradually wore down my confidence and preconceptions, leading to a change in what I believed was possible.

The reason I was so confident going into my third tour in Afghanistan was my own previous experience and the success of the so-called "surge" in Iraq.[8] In 2003–2004, and again in 2006, my discussions with and observations of the Afghan people led me to believe that the Afghans were anxious for the opportunity to finally join the family of nations and that they hated the Taliban. Much polling data supported this belief. All the Afghans needed (or so the thinking ran) was support from us to keep the enemy at bay, enabling them to get on their feet and take charge of their own affairs. Furthermore, the magnificent job that our troops did during the "surge" in Iraq bolstered this belief in our ability to bring about victory. The 2–77th Field Artillery had participated in the "surge," and there was a great deal of combat and counter-insurgency experience resident in the battalion. The effort in Afghanistan had for so long suffered from a distinct lack of resources. As we headed to the theater in mid–2009, resources of all kinds were beginning to pour into the country. I was certain that this would tip the scales in a manner similar to what had happened in Iraq.

The battalion and the brigade as a whole made a valiant effort to prepare for this tour, and all indications pointed to the fact that we could finally turn the corner to victory. Any soldiers as committed as ours were could surely defeat any enemy. The soldiers, their leaders, and I all shared a confidence that we were the key to victory. They had been part of the successful Iraq surge and were now on the cusp of another that would show their mettle and win the war. But what I learned over the course of the next six months was that victory was not up to us; the vision had to be shared by our Afghan counterparts.

Shortly after arrival in Afghanistan my confidence began to erode. In my dealings with Afghan government officials I began to encounter disturbing signs of weakness on their part that they did not care to resolve. None of the district or provincial officials could competently administer their areas. Simple tasks such as prioritizing security measures for elections seemed beyond their ability to plan for. Further, the overly centralized nature of the Afghan government paralyzed local officials to the point that they would not (or could not) make decisions without consulting the national government in Kabul. Finally, rampant corruption at all levels, from district to national, worked against implementation of policies beneficial to the people. The constant struggle on our part to develop competence, facilitate decision-making, and demand transparency wore down my confidence over time. By the mid-point of the deployment my ideas had begun to change with reference to what we as Americans could do to achieve victory. I realized that the Afghans themselves were the true key to victory. But what were they willing to do to achieve it?

I departed for Afghanistan on 2 June 2009, ready and anxious to make a difference, and I believe that we did make a difference in our time there. The battalion got off to a fast start, and our efforts were not without positive results in many areas. But the behavior of the Afghans that I observed began to change my perceptions. A tragedy on 5 December 2009 was my personal turning point, and my expectations of what was possible for us to achieve were tempered by firsthand experience.

II

Execution: The Reality from Arrival through the Afghan Presidential Election, 2 June 2009 to 23 August 2009

Upon our arrival in Afghanistan, arrangements were made to push the battalion out to the various firebases. The firing batteries were scattered in two-gun packages to austere locations to support maneuver forces across the region known as N2KL (Nangarhar, Nuristan, Konar, Laghman). The battalion headquarters would occupy FOB Kalagush in western Nuristan with our maneuver platoon, plus two guns. We also had a squad of military police attached to the battalion and a provincial reconstruction team (PRT) co-located at Kalagush. The battalion would have the dual mission of providing fires for the far-flung maneuver units and acting as a maneuver unit in our area of operation, providing security across 1,200 square miles. By 6 June our units were set in their locations.

The first order of business upon arrival was to begin conducting a relief-in-place (RIP in military parlance) with the unit we were replacing. A relief-in-place requires both units to cooperate in facilitating a smooth transition of responsibility from outgoing to incoming unit. Over a short two- to three-week period the units have to share and absorb knowledge that took over a year to build. The better the collaboration between the units, the faster start the incoming unit can achieve as it assumes responsibility.

Many challenges awaited our battalion as we began the acclimatization process. First, there was the enemy. The Taliban operating in our area was a tenacious and wily foe and would constantly disrupt our efforts to assist the Afghans. Second, there were the Afghan government and security officials we would have to deal with on a daily basis. Third, we had to work with the Afghan people in the districts. The Afghans are not monolithic but a mix of many different ethnic groups, tribes, and clans. Grasping the diverse divisions and fissures of Afghan society would prove a tough proposition. Finally, there was the terrain of eastern Afghanistan, a combination of mountains, desert, and farmland baked under searing heat in the summer and wrapped in snow in the winter. Together these factors made the year in Afghanistan memorable, to say the least.

The enemy in our area organized around local cells coordinated by leaders living in Pakistan. These individuals provided the case and direction to the resident leaders who actually lived in the area conducting the day-to-day operations. Each cell worked a specific location within our area of responsibility, primarily where their families lived. The various cells rarely cooperated on anything and were a loose, decentralized patchwork. The enemy's primary mode of operation was the use of IEDs (improvised explosive devices), but they also conducted small arms ambushes and rocket attacks. The cells also used criminal activity, similar to mafia groups in the United States. They engaged in smuggling gems and timber as well as selling drugs and demanding "protection" money from local villages, which both financed their operations and enriched the cell leaders. Understanding the nature of the enemy's operations was critical to devising tactics to counter their intent. Working much like police in the local area would prove the best approach to defeating the enemy in western Nuristan and northern Laghman.

The government officials we partnered with were no less frustrating than the enemy. In fact, one could say that their actions were as much of a bar to success as the Taliban. Each province contains a number of districts within its boundaries. For ease of comparison, the provinces are similar to states in America, while the districts are like counties. Each entity has its own echelon of government, including a governor, police chief, intelligence chief, tribal affairs director, and so forth. Our battalion—and myself specifically—was charged with establishing a partnership with these officials to mentor them in security planning, budgeting procedures, and administration. Considering the low education levels and primitive nature of the area, this was a huge challenge. It was an even greater problem due to the fact that, without exception, those officials used their positions for self-enrichment. Of all the challenges I encountered in Afghanistan, dealing with these selfish officials was the most irritating and frustrating endeavor. If I had detected any sense of altruism or care for the people whom the district and provincial leaders were charged with governing, I would have found the job far more gratifying. Unfortunately, I did not find any officials of this nature.

The people of western Nuristan and northern Laghman were quite a disparate lot. The major ethnic groups resident in the area were the Nuristani and Pashtuns. These groups were sub-divided into several tribes, including the Pashai, Wamai, Gajur, and Alkozai. They further divide into clans, and many of the people are identified by the valley where they live, which have their own unique customs and dialects. The area is completely rural, dotted by small villages and farms located next to the rivers and streams. The livelihood of the people is derived from the land, as the economy is based on subsistence farming. Visiting a typical valley in western Nuristan and northern Laghman is like stepping back in time. The houses are made of mud brick and walled like a medieval castle for protection. The farming methods are primitive, and much of the work is performed by women. Oxen pull plows, seed is sown by hand, and harvesting and threshing follow methods hundreds of years old. Electricity is a luxury, and at night total darkness envelops the valleys, creating a brilliant night sky.

This rural society, in its isolation, creates people who are naturally suspicious of outsiders. In the 1980s the Soviets attempted to penetrate the valleys of Nuristan and Laghman, setting up district capitals in the villages of Nangaresh and Alingar. However, Mujahideen fighters drove them out in a series of vicious fights, including one in Alingar in which the rebels defeated a DRA (Democratic Republic of Afghanistan Army) infantry battalion with its Soviet advisors. The Mujahideen then set up a liberated zone that they controlled for the rest of the Soviet-Afghan war.[1] Because of this, our battalion would have to work hard to gain the trust of our neighbors. Following the Soviet invasion, the civil war, and the Taliban government, the people would naturally fear anyone from the outside. The people of this area had two simple needs: security and liberty. At the heart of our varied tasks, the primary mission of the battalion was to provide security to facilitate a normal life. This would remain the focus of our efforts in Afghanistan from start to finish.

Afghanistan, and particularly the eastern part of the country, is very beautiful. Western Nuristan has mountains that rise up to 15,000 feet, providing a tremendous backdrop for our operations. These mountains are heavily forested with pine, cedar, and hardwoods that produce high-quality wood. The mountainous nature of the terrain leaves very little arable land; therefore, any agriculture performed in Nuristan is done in hardscrabble, terraced plots on the slopes. By contrast, Laghman is a breadbasket. The mountains, while still impressive, are much lower in elevation as compared to Nuristan. The Alingar River is a whitewater river fed by snow melt from the Nuristani mountains to the north. The runoff provides the water that has turned the Alingar River Valley into a vast green zone. The district of Alingar is dominated by the river that allows rice, corn, wheat, fruits of all kinds, vegetables, and livestock to thrive in abundance. Contrary to popular depictions of Afghanistan as a barren, remote desert, this part of Afghanistan is a jewel. The irony of the area's beauty lies in the fact that a war is ongoing. Many times during my year as a battalion commander, I lamented that war was despoiling such a gorgeous place. In the absence of war, this part of Afghanistan would be an outdoorsman's dream. This, however, is wishful thinking. There is a war on, and we had to accomplish our mission to win it.

As I would learn over the course of our first six months, victory was not up to us. Although we had several successes, such as the Afghan national election, it seemed that some Afghan officials were actually working against our efforts. Our forces set the security conditions to enable the Afghans to win the war. They will win with sound governance, sufficient security forces, and reintegration of moderate Taliban members back into society. In essence, victory depends on the political competence of the Afghan government. We provide the breathing space to make this goal possible. The problem is that the Afghans have yet to grasp the opportunity we have offered them. This is the great lesson that hard experience drilled into my head. The 2-77th Field Artillery and our brigade, the 4th Infantry Brigade Combat Team, 4th Infantry Division, valiantly plowed forward and put

An excellent view of the Alingar River Valley looking south. This valley cut through the center of our operational area, and the white water river that runs through it is the critical economic engine for the agrarian population. This panorama provides an outstanding perspective of the beauty of Afghanistan (photograph by the 2-77th Field Artillery Public Affairs Officer, Captain Matthew Frye).

everything we had into accomplishing the mission. For us, it started in June 2009.

Friday,[2] 2 June 2009—Departure

I will attempt to record what happens every day in Afghanistan from now on. Today was the day that the rest of the battalion deployed, minus a rear party. Maryellen and Ashley came in with me (Andy is in Alaska doing his summer training with an AF [air force] squadron; we said bye to him on Saturday). They stayed with me until the buses came. Mare is a pretty strong woman and has always handled these things well. I do hate to leave her and Ashley home by themselves for a year. I guess Trigger will have to guard them. After another long wait at the airfield, we finally took off around 2000 (8:00 PM). We flew to Bangor, Maine, and then to Leipzig, Germany (site of the Napoleonic Battle of the Nations). We will arrive in Kyrgyzstan some time on the 4th. It sure is a long flight.

The day you leave on a deployment is always the worst time because you hate to leave your family. While a soldier is anxious to get moving, there is always the corresponding dread that comes with deployment day. I hated leaving my wife and daughter alone for a year. Sometimes a soldier worries for the safety of his family while deployed. As noted in the entry, I depended on my dog Trigger, a seven-year-old male yellow lab, to take care of them while I was gone.

3–4 June 2009

We arrived at about 0500 in Kyrgyzstan, and it was a beautiful, cool morning, with the Pamirs off to the south capped in snow. It always amazes me coming to the war zone because Kyrgyzstan and eastern Afghanistan are such pretty places. The war takes away from what could be great scenery and adventure. We manifested for an afternoon flight into Afghanistan. Upon our arrival we still had over 200 people in Manas (from the battalion on previous flights) because the flood of people coming is overwhelming capacity (of the Air Force to move the people into Afghanistan). A surge in AFG, I am sure, is pushing the logistic system to its limits. AFG always had issues with its rickety infrastructure, and I am sure adding more people is really straining the system.

I got into Bagram at 1800 with my S1, S2, S3, OPs SGT, and FDO. We will do our mandatory classes and then push out to Kalagush. My XO told me that the unit we are replacing knows little about the AO and really doesn't do anything. That is a shame. The way I see it, we have to get involved and make a contribution toward making AFG a better place, and that is what 2-77th FA is going to do during its year.

All units going to Afghanistan transfer from a commercial plane to military aircraft in Manas, Kyrgyzstan. The tiny country of Kyrgyzstan is a former Soviet republic about 250 miles north of the Afghanistan border. The airbase is an old Russian airfield near the capital of the country, Bishkek. The construction of the airfield buildings is the typical drab Soviet concrete design with little character. It is an old outpost of the Cold War now used by the United States to support the fight in Afghanistan. Kyrgyzstan is a combination of flat, open plains that remind me of Oklahoma and beautiful mountains. The Pamir Mountains border the Hindu Kush region in Afghanistan. During the competition between the British Empire and Russian Empire in the nineteenth century the Pamirs represented the extreme southern limit of Russian expansion to the south in Central Asia while also signifying the extreme northern limit of British incursions out of India. The mountains are gorgeous and a mountaineer's dream.

Units marshal at the airfield in Kyrgyzstan for onward movement into Afghanistan. Some units have to wait several days to catch a flight because of bottlenecks in the logistic system. When we arrived there was a flood of troops moving into Afghanistan as the troop numbers began expanding. This created a backlog when we arrived, which kept some of my troops there for seven days. I managed to get the battalion staff moving forward that evening so that we could get to our location as quick as possible to start the process of assuming responsibility for our area. The process of waiting to move forward echoes the old adage in the Army that a soldier is always playing "hurry up and wait."

5 June 2009

Spent the day receiving briefs from the CJTF-82 (Combined Joint Task Force 82) staff. It is amazing to me how much Afghanistan has changed over time. In my first two tours we didn't have enough of anything. Now, while there still might not be enough assets, there is at least 3 to 4 times what there was before. I wish we had had all these assets 6 years ago on my first tour in AFG. We might be much further along than we are now.

I ran into several old buddies here today on the 82nd staff and from 3/10th MTN (Mountain), my old unit. It was good seeing friendly faces. The chief of fires for the 82nd is a good man I served with in the 101st (101st Airborne Division). He is a smart guy and will be a good leverage point for us. He finally divorced his first wife; she was quite a pain to him, and it is best for him. Also saw the S3 and engineer officer from 3/10. They caught me up on everything that has happened since I left.

Tomorrow I will move out with the staff to Kalagush. Finally, about to get the ball rolling.

The Army is a small place. Inevitably, in every assignment career soldiers will run across folks they have served with in other units. When I got to Afghanistan my old unit, the 3rd Brigade, 10th Mountain Division, was there. I had served in several positions in that brigade, including the brigade executive officer, which was my last job before I moved to Fort Carson to take command. The friendships you build over a career help to sustain you over time. When I got to Afghanistan it was good to know that many of my friends were there and serving in important positions. These highly competent officers buoyed my confidence coming into theater for my third tour.

Upon arrival I was amazed at the size of our forces' footprint. In my first tour in 2003 our troop strength hovered around 10,000 total troops. In 2006, during my second, we had expanded to over 20,000. However, by 2009 we were well past 50,000 when I arrived with the battalion and continuing to expand. We now had an increased ability to conduct counter-insurgency operations—which are personnel heavy—with greater expectations of success. As stated in the entry, I lamented the fact that it took so long to reach reasonable troop levels in Afghanistan.

6 June 2009—D-Day + 65 Years

Took my last set of briefings this morning. Got an intelligence brief about my AO that is pretty much in line with what I already thought. It leaves me with two COAs (courses of action) for the year. 1. Aggressively push north, but I don't have the forces to do it right. 2. Recommend to boss that Nuristan is fine without our efforts and we would be better utilized somewhere closer to the population centers. There are few people in independent-minded Nuristan. In COIN (counter-insurgency) it is all about population security. Therefore, if we are not where the people are, then what purpose do we serve? I will recommend COA 2 for implementation as we move into the election period.

The Bn will close into AFG tonight with the CSM. Shortly after that I will push out to Kalagush with the S3 by helo (helicopter). Then, on Monday, we will hit all the firebases. Should be interesting seeing all our sites and finally getting down to business.

D-Day today. The World War II vets made tremendous sacrifices. I think our young guys are doing pretty well in their own time.

The reader should recall that during my pre-deployment site survey (PDSS) to Afghanistan in December 2008 I believed that we needed to push north into Dow Ab District to establish our footprint further into Nuristan.

This would have fit nicely with the old paradigm of operations in Afghanistan in 2006 of pushing the enemy into the hinterland and allowing the Afghan government to build capacity while we held the enemy at bay. However, this is not a good counter-insurgency strategy. My thinking had evolved over the six months since that visit. I now saw that our efforts would have a much greater impact if we focused on the population centers in our area of operation. Since the populace is extremely sparse in Nuristan, with the number of people diminishing further north into the province, it made sense to look to the south. The majority of the population in our area was in Alingar District of northern Laghman. Securing the population would isolate the insurgents far better than chasing them into the hinterland. Therefore, I made the decision to focus our effort in the Alingar River Valley. My brigade commander did not see the utility of moving north either and had in mind that we should concentrate our main effort in the southern region of our area. So, our thoughts were on the same page, and it turned out that this was the best decision.

7 June 2009—Arrived at Kalagush

Spent the day getting familiar with the firebase and surroundings. I am troubled by the state of security. The OP (observation post) on the hill overlooking the base and outlying areas is very vulnerable to attack and needs serious position improvement. Further, there is a counter-intel team here because they suspect that we have some infiltrators among the local national workers. Finally, discipline is lax on the base.

So, I pulled the staff together and HHB and gave them priorities for improving defense. I will have the CSM take on the discipline issue and establish the standard. Finally, once the CI team identifies the infiltrators, we will detain them.

Outside the wire we will focus on pushing the road construction northward. To the north is the enemy sanctuary in W. Nuristan. But if we can put in the road and develop the economy, we might be able to reduce "the accidental guerrillas" because they will have employment. Much hard work to be done, but first we have to fix the security situation. Tomorrow I will fly to Alpha's firebases.

When I first arrived at Kalagush I was appalled by what I saw. In my mind the security of the base was weak and the outgoing unit was not enforcing uniform and discipline standards. The observation post, known as OP Loyalty, was located about half a mile away on the Kalagush Ghar (or mountain) 1,000 feet above the firebase. The OP had excellent visibility of the surrounding area and valleys, which branch off the Alingar River Valley. There were ten soldiers manning the OP with six Afghan contract security guards, *but the perimeter and defensive dispositions made it vulnerable to attack. The state of discipline combined with the lax security measures would add up to disaster if we did not make this our first priority when we assumed responsibility. My CSM proved instrumental in fixing this issue. I am glad that we attacked it aggressively because the enemy launched an assault on the observation post and firebase in November. By then we had made great improvements on the defenses and were able to repel the attack fairly easily.*

Another priority was reconstruction. Economic development is an integral part of counter-insurgency operations. Many of the local men are unemployed, and the enemy exploits this situation by giving them "work," such as moving weapons, digging holes for IEDs, or reporting our movements. By emphasizing economic development, we could produce legitimate employment for these individuals. Further, by working on the road, it would become a source of pride for the local population that they would not want the enemy to destroy with IEDs. Therefore, economic development would peel away a source of fighters for the enemy. David Kilcullen, noted author and civilian aide to General David Petraeus, coined the term "accidental guerrilla." His premise is that the reason many military-age males end up fighting in an insurgency is that they do not have good employment. In other words, their decision to fight comes down to pure economic issues. By offering an alternative to fighting, they will not end up in the insurgent camp by "accident." Having read Kilcullen's treatise, I sought to implement some of his ideas in our area of operation.

8 June 2009

Made it out to Goshta and Khogyani (districts in Nangarhar Province where A Btry had guns supporting maneuver) firebases today. I have to say that I was very pleased with our platoons' progress in preparing to take over responsibility. Both firebases were very orderly and the sections rehearsed their missions. Great work. I spoke to the soldiers about maintaining discipline, standards, and fighting complacency over a year. I also talked about not using drugs. A soldier from the outgoing unit overdosed yesterday at Kalagush from some hash a local Afghan gave him. The kid might die—all because he was bored. Complacency kills, and I am determined to prevent that. Keeping people focused and busy, while maintaining standards, is the way to do it. I am spending the night at Khogyani tonight, and they fly to Mehtar Lam tomorrow and back to Kalagush.

As previously stated, the platoons in the battalion were spread out all over N2KL. Goshta is in the northeast corner of Nangarhar Province and well within range of the Pakistan border. The firebase is about 100 miles from

Kalagush. Similarly, Khogyani is in a remote location in the southwestern corner of Nangarhar. The separation from the battalion headquarters meant that the lieutenants and sergeants were on their own in terms of operations. They had a great deal of responsibility, but all of our platoons in these remote locations did an outstanding job over the course of a year in maintaining discipline and providing close supporting fires to the maneuver units. The two-gun platoons supported single infantry companies with artillery fires, demonstrating a high degree of proficiency in their jobs and maturity in doing the right thing without the senior leadership providing constant supervision. While my primary responsibility was our maneuver area in western Nuristan and northern Laghman, I made it a point to visit all the firebases frequently. As the senior artilleryman in the brigade, I had to ensure that our firebases adhered to all standards, delivered their fires correctly, and maintained a high degree of discipline. To the credit of all our junior leaders, they did this with distinction.

9 June 2009

Just got back from Mehtar Lam firebase today. It is not bad, but not in as good shape as Goshta and Khogyani. They currently don't do hot gun/cold gun rotations and only man the FDC with *one* person. When I went in there today a specialist was on duty and couldn't tell me what targets they were laid on or anything else of use. Therefore, in the whole firebase one person was on duty. I told my battery commander to fix all of this when the outgoing unit handed over responsibility and man one gun and the FDC 24 hours a day.

Everyone is now arriving at their final locations, and we start doing our relief in place tasks tomorrow with the outgoing unit. I am glad because we are all ready to take over and get moving on our year here. Our priorities:

- Fix security
- Establish firing capability
- Make initial contacts with local leaders
- Assess our AO in order to determine the way forward in asking the locals what they want

At this point the outgoing unit still retained responsibility for operations. Our units were continuing to arrive and settle into the firebases. The visit on this date references what I found the outgoing unit doing, and I was extremely displeased with the lack of discipline. In an artillery unit in combat the guns must have the capability to provide fires 24 hours a day on a moment's notice.

When I was checking on the operations of the unit at Mehtar Lam in Laghman Province, I noted that neither the guns nor the FDC were ready to do anything on a moment's notice, much less provide fires. To carry out the mission correctly, half the unit had to man their guns and the FDC at all times. This would ensure that if the infantry called for fires in an emergency, the unit could provide this support on short notice—that is, in less than five minutes. My directive to my battery commander was that he would do this when he assumed responsibility for the base. An artillery unit that cannot provide fires quickly and reliably for an infantry unit in contact is worthless, and I would accept nothing less than 24-hour-a-day readiness to provide that support.

10 June 2009

Spent today meeting with various tenants at the base (Kalagush). I met the Marine trainers for the Afghan artillery battery, the KBR (Kellogg, Brown, and Root contractor) manager, and the law enforcement liaison. One thing I learned in my career is that establishing good working relationships is critical for achieving success on the battlefield. Where frictions occur, soldiers suffer and mission success is jeopardized. Therefore, it is critical to build a team and foster the relationships. As I discussed in my books about Red River and Camden, personalities are everything in war. Where they clash, there will be issues.

Tomorrow I begin a three-day fly-around to the rest of the firebases and meeting with 1–32 IN and C/1–321 FA. It is amazing that both of these units are here since I was the brigade XO for 1–32 in the 10th Mtn Div and was in C Btry as a LT. It is a small army.

Our unit had several other entities attached to it when we assumed responsibility for our area. We would partner with an Afghan field artillery battery to train them on sound artillery gunnery. They had a four-man Marine training team called an ETT (embedded training team) that mentored the battery leadership. These Marines were not artillerymen, so our expertise was needed to help the Afghans learn good gunnery techniques. Kellogg, Brown, and Root Contracting Company performed some of the basic life support tasks, and these civilian contractors were also my responsibility. Additionally, we had two civilian police officers attached to the battalion. Their job was to mentor the Afghan National Police, and they worked directly with us in carrying out this mission. These gentlemen were indispensable in assisting us, and we provided them with security as they moved around the area. It was critical for our battalion that I establish a good relationship with these individuals. I did not want friction to reduce the effectiveness of our battalion, so I invested personal time and initiative to firm up the relationship early on. This would prove invaluable as we conducted our mission over the course of the year.

11 June 2009

Flew to Torkham Gate this morning. It is the eastern entrance to the ancient Khyber Pass through which invading armies passed for centuries, including Alexander the Great. I have a PLT there doing border security with the Afghan Border Police. I went down to the gate to visit my soldiers. It was absolute chaos. 50,000 pedestrians and thousands of vehicles pass through the gate daily. It is very tight because of the restrictive terrain.

As I walked around, I took note of the people. Some of the children interacted with the soldiers. I saw one little girl sneer at me. Obviously, her family has taught her to fear us. What a shame. We are actually here to help, but misinformation and prejudice poison the well. It stank down there as well (it smelled of urine, crap, and unwashed humanity). The jingle trucks always get my attention. They are so ridiculous looking with their murals and pictures painted all over them and the ubiquitous jingling chains. Afghanistan is an amazing place.

I feel sorry for the people. The folks I feel most sorry for are the young girls. They are condemned to a hard life because of the attitudes toward women in Islam. What a shame that they can't live and be free as American women are.

Finally, we arrived at firebase Fortress. I have a Bravo platoon here. Shortly after arriving one of the guns fired the first rounds of 2–77 in Afghanistan in a fire mission. I got the first canister for the regimental room. Overall, I am pleased with how we are doing so far. The firing batteries look real good. Just need to get the outgoing unit out of the way so we can fix the Bn AO at Kalagush. Tomorrow visiting 1–32 and Asadabad.

In addition to our mission to secure our assigned area of operation and the fire support from our guns, the battalion had to provide a platoon to provide border security at Torkham Gate, the eastern end of the famous Khyber Pass. It is the passage point for all commerce moving into Afghanistan and back into Pakistan. It is a critical point that the Afghan government had to secure and very dangerous as a place that the enemy would want to target with spectacular attacks. I would continuously worry about this platoon in this critical location. There was more than one attempt by the enemy to conduct attention-grabbing attacks at the gate, but the platoon performed its mission in a professional and competent manner. Spending time at Torkham will give you a good vantage point from which to observe the people. Walking

A 105mm howitzer from B Battery firing a high-angle fire mission over the mountains in Konar Province (courtesy Captain Geoffrey Terman).

among them, one can see every ethnic group and social status. As I stated, it always hurt to see the young girls. They are so happy and carefree when they are young. But as soon as they reach twelve years of age, the cultural norms force them into a burqa and a life of submission for the remainder of their days. They then have to walk behind the men and can only move in public with a male relative. It is shocking to an American to observe such treatment of women.

Firebase Fortress was the most dangerous location that any of my platoons occupied in Afghanistan. There was a firefight in and around this area daily, and our guns there engaged in fighting continuously throughout the year. Knowing the challenges of this location, we put our best platoon here—one with the best leadership from top to bottom and outstanding young soldiers. It was good that we did this because these kids would earn their combat pay every day they spent at Fortress.

12 June 2009

Arrived at 1–32's HQ today and got to meet some old friends from 3rd Brigade, 10th Mtn Div. Of course, I remember them from having been the brigade XO. It is good to have some familiar faces in our area. As I was getting ready to fly out, the base took incoming mortar fire and the birds (helicopters) were waved off. By the time it was all clear, they could not return, so I guess I am stuck here for the night. Oh, well, could be worse. They have a nice base here. I just wanted to get to Asadabad to meet the C/1–321 BC. Guess it waits until tomorrow.

13 June 2009

Made it back to Kalagush today after hitting Asadabad and meeting the C/1–321 Cdr. After that we had an amazing flight over the mountains to Kalagush. It was unbelievable with the Nuristan mountains in view. We flew at about the snow-line level. It reminded me of the movie *The Man Who Would Be King*, based on the Rudyard Kipling story about the two British soldiers who make their way to Kafiristan to become kings. Afghanistan is so beautiful. If it were not at war, this would be a travel destination for adventurers. It is a fascinating place. I just hope that one day the war will end and people can come see its beauty.

I think we are off to a fast start with our preparations to take responsibility and getting the right relationships established to be successful. It is all about the relationships in war.

Tomorrow I meet the Nuristan governor and accompany the outgoing commander to the radio station for his address.

14 June 2009

I met the governor today, and I think it was very productive. He wants more security and road work. He is very concerned that because Nuristan has a small population we might focus on the populated areas to the detriment of his province. He thinks this would lead to Nuristan becoming an enemy sanctuary, and I agree. However, I also understand that counterinsurgency is population-focused and Nuristan is the smallest province in Afghanistan population-wise. Therefore, I am going to be asked to do a lot with very little and in areas that are not critical to mission accomplishment. I have set some very simple goals for security and development. I feel that if we can achieve them, we will at least be making it better than what we found and pushing AFG forward.

Since we did not have the translation for the radio address, I will go down to the station tomorrow with the outgoing commander. The TOA (transition of authority) will be on the 22nd of June, and I will be glad when we finally take charge.

The governor of Nuristan was very polite and expressed great "concern" for his people in our first meeting. As I learned more about him over the course of the year, however, I found him to be one of the most disgusting and corrupt individuals I have ever met. He was working me for resources to line his pockets and attempted to deceive me at every turn to get what he wanted out of our partnership. While our relationship began on the right footing, I came to despise him by the end of my tour in Afghanistan. He is representative of the central issue preventing success in Afghanistan. Corruption is the enemy of good government, and competent political leadership is the key to winning in counter-insurgency. When the people only see their government officials lining their pockets with the resources that are supposed to make the lives of the people better, they lose faith in their government and look for alternatives. This gives the enemy—the Taliban—an opportunity. Therefore, when the government officials engage in these practices, they are undermining all of our efforts to assist them in building a better life.

15 June 2009

Spent the day getting myself organized to take charge. I took all briefs (from the staff) today and prepared myself for the security shura with local leaders on 17 June. They will probably want to address the detention of our 5 infiltrators a few nights ago. The unit here didn't really have a plan for consequence management following the arrests. Now the locals are clamoring for info, and none is coming. If these guys would use their TGTing (targeting) process properly, this could have been foreseen and nipped. Now I will have to deal with the consequences (once the outgoing unit has left).

The COL is coming tomorrow, so we will brief him on our picture of the AO. Also, we are doing an overflight of the area up to the Russian bridge, which should give us a good idea of our AO layout and major terrain features and villages.

The infiltrators whom I spoke of in earlier entries were arrested on Kalagush while I was out making my initial visits to all the firebases. Whenever local nationals are arrested as a part of operations, the relatives of those incarcerated will naturally want information regarding what happened. The responsible unit should have a consequence management plan ready as part of the targeting process. This will provide information to the local officials and relatives to allay concerns. However, the outgoing unit had no plan, and within hours the locals were bombarding the base with requests for information, all of which went unanswered. With the outgoing unit leaving, it was left to our unit to absorb the mess. It was a lesson that we applied for the rest of the year in our operations to ensure that the right information got to the locals in order to build trust and cooperation.

16 June 2009

I did my overflight of AO Steel today, and most of the staff came along. We have a pretty extensive area to patrol and secure with such a small number of personnel. But we will do OK by leveraging all assets (IO, projects from the PRT, HTT, etc.—that is, information operations, provincial reconstruction team, human terrain team). I will also have to talk to the local leaders and attempt to bring in some insurgents willing to talk.

Aside from that, the view from the helicopter was unbelievable. The mountains seemed to go on forever and were amazing. It is just so sad that there is a war here because the beauty is so amazing and I wish I could see more of it. I wish I could bring Mare here to see it. Oh, well.

The COL came to the FB (firebase) today. He received briefs from the outgoing staff and I didn't get much of a chance to talk to him about my way ahead for the AO. I sent him my update by email later, and that was that.

Tomorrow I have the elders here for the security shura. It will be my first opportunity to meet with them and introduce myself. I need to meet with the local police chiefs and NDS (national directorate of security—this is the Afghan intelligence agency) folks as well. Unfortunately, my predecessor did not work much with these folks, so I need to build the relationships myself.

Our area of operation, dubbed AO Steel (for our battalion nickname), encompassed 1,200 square miles, and we had about 60 personnel available for patrolling between our platoon, the attached military police, and Marines with the Afghan Army. To compensate for our lack of assets, we had to make use of other forms of combat power, which included communicating with the people and contrasting the differences between what the government offered and what the enemy could provide. We also had to rely on good intelligence gathering to allow us to maintain the initiative against the enemy. Finally, building projects would help to develop infrastructure while providing employment to young males, drawing them away from the ranks of enemy fighters. In other words, the scarcity of assets forced us to get creative and "fight" using nonlethal means instead of relying on our combat forces.

17 June 2009

Today I attended the security shura. It was good for me to meet the people whom I need to establish a relationship with in order to gain momentum in the area. The big concern is election security, and I assigned a project officer to start working the plans immediately. I met with our counterintelligence guys to discuss ops and to tell them that one of my main focus items is turning insurgents who no longer want to fight. If we can get a few of these local agitators to come around, we can increase development through better security. We are going to start working it now.

The security shuras were an important part of security coordination between our forces and the local government and police. The first one I attended was orchestrated by the outgoing commander, but I did get the opportunity to begin building the critical cooperative relationships. One of the major tasks ahead of us was securing the presidential election held on 20 August 2009. Little planning had taken place up to this point, so we had to start immediately bringing together all the assets required and coordinating the actions of the Afghans with our forces. The election absorbed all of our efforts for two months leading up to the balloting.

18 June 2009

We had a bonehead act today. One of our SSGs had a negligent discharge of a M203 (grenade launcher), of all things. Unbelievable. I will have to bust him to set an example for our guys to be more vigilant about their weapon status. I had a long talk about the elections with the Department of State rep at our PRT. Nuristan is such a challenge because of the remoteness of the province. It is all supposed to have an Afghan lead, but they are still so incapable that we will have to do a lot of hand holding to help them accomplish the balloting. Just to get the materials in we are going to have to rent donkeys to carry the stuff (ballot boxes, ballots, recording sheets, etc.). Then the corruption issue could arise, so we can only pay these people (the election workers) part of the money for salary up front and then the rest when they demonstrate that they actually delivered to the districts. We will do the best we can.

Tomorrow I will attend the first targeting meeting to drive the planning for our way forward. I want to expand our security by using concentric circles expanding out from the center valley by valley. Then, when we have expanded to our limit of capability, we will aggressively work road development to connect Nuristan to the south and grow the infant economy. In a year we won't accomplish a great deal, but if we can push forward the progress, that is success.

Nuristan's remoteness meant that conducting an election was quite difficult. Our planning included the use of pack animals to push balloting materials into the isolated districts. I was already beginning to recognize the limited capability of the Afghan government officials. After eight years they still seemed incapable of carrying out any administrative tasks without heavy coaching from our forces. I would have expected that after this many years the government officials could have at least achieved a minimum level of competence in conducting government business. After my discussions with the representative from the U.S. State Department, I realized that our unit would have to become intimately involved in the planning, preparation, and supervision of the election. The targeting meeting was our vehicle to push for the development of plans for all types of operations, not just lethal targets. As noted in the entry, the initial targeting meeting gave me the opportunity to explain my vision for the year to my staff. They would take this guidance and turn it into plans and orders to expand security and development throughout our area. Our plan was a multifaceted effort to build Afghan capacity while maintaining security for the people to live normal lives.

19 June 2009

Day started off slow and then picked up after 1800 tonight. We did our first targeting meeting today, and although it took a while and was a little rough, we did achieve the end state, a usable FRAGO (an operation order) to drive operations for the coming weeks. Then we got into our first contact with the maneuver platoon. Last night we saw a fire near one of the cell (phone) towers south of here (the firebase). So, today we sent out the platoon to investigate. When they got there a few enemies were in the area and fired on them. After returning fire they pulled back to the vehicles. The ANP was called, and they said the guy holed up there was wanted for murder and he thought we had come to arrest him. The ANP came to the site, but they failed to make the arrest. Our lesson is to take them with us on every patrol.

While they were out there we got A-10s (ground attack aircraft) on station, and they reported two guys digging by the road 1.5 Km from the TIC (troops in contact). So, we sent the platoon there. It turned out to be a graveyard. Unbelievable. They just returned a few minutes ago. Finally, our OP saw lights moving around a historical rocket launch site. We fired illumination at it, but nothing else was seen; at minimum we disrupted whatever was going on there. B Btry got their first BDA (battle damage assessment) today. They fired at a mortar setting up and got them. We are doing OK—just need to refine some of our maneuver tactics. Other than that, we are on track. Final update on relief in place tomorrow then the TOA ceremony on Monday. We will finally be in charge.

While we had not yet assumed full responsibility for the area of operation, our forces were conducting all of the patrols, as most of the outgoing unit had already flown out. Only the leaders of the outgoing unit remained, and they

II. Execution: 2 June 2009 to 23 August 2009

First Lieutenant Tony Great served as the platoon leader of Headquarters Battery's maneuver platoon. He routinely met with local villagers along with his ANA partner to facilitate security throughout our operational area. A former sergeant first class, he attended officer candidate school at 39 years old and is now a fine officer. He has since been promoted to captain (photograph by the 2-77th Field Artillery Public Affairs Officer, Captain Matthew Frye).

were in charge until the transition of authority ceremony. On one of our patrols the maneuver platoon made our first contact with the enemy. It did not go as I would have liked. At the time I wished they had maintained the pressure on the enemy instead of moving back to the vehicles, but in time they would improve, and this was their first firefight as a team. The Afghan National Police who arrived on the scene played on our lack of knowledge of the area and enemy. The individual holed up at the cell phone tower was in fact a criminal, whom I will call Khan Mohammed, and worked in concert with the enemy. Mohammed was notorious for terrorizing the local population, and his criminal activity funneled money to the enemy. What we didn't know at the time was that the police who failed to capture him that evening were in fact protecting him. In return for this protection, Mohammed cut the police in on part of his proceeds. When our patrol arrived on the scene with no police, Mohammed thought that we were there to apprehend him. The police came on the scene and the patrol leader allowed the chief to move in to make the

Sergeant First Class Kyle Riley at the Nurgaram District Tree Farm outside of Forward Operating Base Kalagush. Riley served as the platoon sergeant of our maneuver platoon. He performed his duties in an outstanding manner, enabling the battalion to implement an effective counter-insurgency campaign in AO Steel (photograph by the 2-77th Field Artillery Public Affairs Officer, Captain Matthew Frye).

arrest, as he was trained to do. However, the chief conveniently allowed Mohammed to escape. It was only later that we learned through our intelligence gathering the full details of the corruption that existed with the police chief and this criminal/enemy fighter.

Our firing batteries had already assumed responsibility for fires in their area, and B Battery drew first blood. A mortar team was attempting to fire on firebase Fortress in Konar when the observers located it and called our howitzers for fire. The guns of the platoon were right on target and destroyed the team. While we had only been in Afghanistan for 18 days, we were already heavily involved with the action, and we would continue to remain heavily engaged until we flew out of Afghanistan the following year.

20 June 2009

Slow day. Did AARs (after-action reviews) from yesterday's events and prepped to take charge. Did my final brief on our transition and we are ready.

Got a note from Gen Vessey today saying he is thinking about us. There is an old Corp of Engineers guy here with us who said that the Holy Spirit led him to come here. I think that with people like Gen V. and the Engineer we will be all right.

21 June 2009

We rehearsed for the TOA ceremony tomorrow and calibrated the guns. The maneuver PLT went out on a patrol to the south and got some info on a bad guy, but it was a dry hole. I met with the Nuristan chief of police. Seems like a man very committed to the success of Afghanistan. When he met me he said he was at my service, and I reversed it and told him that I was at his service since it is his country. I think one of the big mistakes we make as Americans is that we condition people to be dependent on us because we somehow believe we can fix the world's problems. But if Afghanistan is going to be a success, they have to do it themselves with us backing them, not leading them. In this area it is clear that the people are dependent on us, and until they take the lead they will never be independent.

The Nuristan chief of police was another official who initially presented himself as a dedicated servant of the people, but the reality of the situation was that he was another in a long line of corrupt officials. In our initial meeting the chief was very self-deprecating and deferred to me a great deal. As with all the other officials, I learned later that he was deeply involved in smuggling. Further, he routinely skimmed the payroll of his police force. It would take us some time to figure this out, since he and all the other officials would maintain a façade of dedication in all our dealings. In the entry I also noted that the Afghan officials would have to take the lead in their own affairs and administration. I knew this implicitly; yet I still did not internalize it and execute accordingly. I was guilty of taking the lead and not pressing the Afghans to do their own jobs. They were only too happy to allow us to do things for them while they stood on the sidelines and enriched themselves with the funds provided to operate their government. Within a few months I would change my approach to and assessment of these officials.

22 June 2009—TOA

We did the TOA today and started implementing our standards to improve FOB readiness. And it was none too soon. We have reports tonight of a planned attack on the FOB. I immediately assembled the primary staff and HHB security folks. We are going to take some immediate actions to improve security and also start battle drills tomorrow. Everyone has to know exactly what they are supposed to do if attacked, and that is what we are going to practice. The CSM walked the NCOs around the FOB tonight, pointing out important aspects of defense. The big worry I have is our 10-man OP on the hill to the north. We can't immediately reinforce it, so our only alternative is indirect (fires) and air (support). I don't like that thing, but we fell in on it, so I have to deal with it for now. I just pray that we can finish position improvement in time to make it and the FOB invulnerable. I am really pissed at the professional laziness of the previous unit in looking to their combat mission and defense.

The outgoing unit leadership left that day, and we immediately began working to fix many of the issues they left behind. Improving the defensive posture of the observation post and the base was the first priority. There were many holes that we had to plug to make any enemy attempt to attack a suicidal endeavor. We were able to accomplish this task after several weeks, and it proved prudent, since the enemy tested both the observation post and the forward operating base on multiple occasions over the next several months.

B Battery at Firebase Fortress firing in direct fire mode as the enemy attacks from the surrounding hills. Note that only one crew member is visible, as the rest of the crew is taking cover until it is time to load the next round due to enemy fire impacting around the howitzer (courtesy Captain Geoffrey Terman).

23 June 2009

We did a series of battle drills today, and thank God we did, because we got rocketed tonight at about 1900 (7 PM). Everyone reacted well and we had no casualties. We counter-fired, but I doubt we got anything because they like to set their rockets up on timers. Then they are gone when it fires. I want to become more efficient at running these people down to prevent attacks. We have got to clear the Titin Valley and Mashpah to secure the area, and that is our next priority once we get position improvement fixed here.

The rocket did destroy one of our buildings used for meetings. I am glad it didn't hit a living area. Tomorrow I have a meeting with the sub-governor for the area (governor of Nurgaram District), and I will discuss security with him and what we can do to fix it.

This was the first attack on Kalagush since we arrived. The other contacts had occurred while outside the base on patrols. The enemy began testing our unit to assess our mettle and reaction to the attack. This is fairly common across Afghanistan when one unit replaces another. Our rehearsals and drills had paid off, since nobody was hurt. However, the rocket impacted inside the perimeter and destroyed one building. It landed within 25 meters of an ammunition bunker and our mortar pit. The reaction of the troops was swift, with everyone taking cover and our howitzers returning fire. The fact that the enemy could place a rocket within view of the base gave me some concern for the security of the location. As previously stated, our first priority was to improve the physical position at Kalagush and then move outward, starting with the valleys closest to the base and expanding further from there. This would provide us with a security "bubble" from which to conduct our operations and give us freedom of movement. The security thus established would also allow the local residents to carry on a normal life, which was an important objective for our operations.

24 June 2009

It was Ashley's birthday today, so I called and told her happy birthday. It is so hard to believe that she is already 17. Too bad I have to be gone for another one. I did order some flowers for her, and I will pick up some items at the bazaar to send home.

We sent out an early patrol this morning to the area of the rocket launch and came up empty. The patrol talked to some of the people and distributed our IO (information operation) message demonstrating that all the Taliban does is destroy while we try to help build and secure the area.

We are planning an operation into the Titin Valley that should help us alleviate some of the security issues with freedom of movement and force protection. If we can restore the police presence there, clear out the weapon caches, and drive the TB factions out, we should disrupt them until winter. This will secure the election and push the road paving in the main valley. Then we can work some of the other hot spots.

I met with the district governor (of Nurgaram, whom I will call him Sikander Laghmani) today, and he was upset at the destroyed building. He did a radio message for me condemning the attack, and we worked through some election issues. Also, he agreed after our op to reestablish the police checkpoint in Titin Valley. I think we will work well together. Tomorrow I am going to visit 3-61 with the State rep to discuss election plans for Nuristan. I will also have a chance to visit one of the platoons from C Btry while I am up there. Then to J-bad (Jalalabad) to talk to the COL about our plans.

We made it a habit after every enemy attack to point out what little they have to offer the people and then contrast that with the positive things that our operations were bringing to the area, such as road building. It is critical in counter-insurgency to communicate with the people. Our mode was to illustrate positive (our efforts) versus negative (destructive acts of the enemy) aspects. The information operations we used enabled us to build trust with the people, which angered the Taliban. Months later our enemies would attempt to break this trust as their frustration boiled over.

The Titin Valley was an area that the Taliban liked to use to stage rocket attacks; therefore we devised an operation to clear it and reestablish police presence, which for some reason was pulled from the area before our arrival. District Governor Sikander Laghmani *was one of the most likable characters whom I ran across in Afghanistan. He was very polite, spoke some English, and presented himself as a dedicated public servant. Laghmani did have some commendable qualities and administrative ability, and I had a very good relationship with him throughout our time working together. However, he, too, had a streak of corruption that, while not as pronounced as that of other leaders I had to work with, was still detrimental to forward progress in Afghanistan. Nevertheless, Laghmani was capable enough that we were able to accomplish some positive things for the area, particularly regarding the upcoming election.*

25–26 June 2009

The past two days were very interesting. I flew out to 3-61 with the State Dept. rep to talk about the Nuristan elections. I had been there about 45 minutes when a runner came and got me to tell me that an IED hit one of the PRT vehicles. Miraculously, only 5 people were wounded, with no deaths and no loss of limbs. But, again, it points to the fact that this is not an easy area, as we were led to believe. I think that the complacency of the last unit has led the enemy to believe that there is an opportunity to turn back any previous progress and appear to inflict defeats on us. I only wish I had more force to knock them back, but I really only have enough to do local security. An infantry company would allow me to set out a nightly ambush. Since I don't have it, instead I just pray that we can gain a tactical victory in the short term in order to gain some momentum.

I went to the brigade TOA today (26 June). I am glad we are finally in charge. Hopefully, we can turn things around and help Afghanistan to victory. They deserve a chance at freedom and peace.

The IED that hit the provincial reconstruction team patrol was another in a series of challenges to our unit after we took over in the area. The bomb that hit this patrol destroyed a Humvee, turning the vehicle over on its roof. It is a miracle that no one was killed in this attack. Further, no one lost any limbs, although the vehicle gunner suffered some severely broken bones. This attack occurred only five kilometers from the base in the Mashpah Valley. This indicates how close the enemy was to Kalagush and their boldness in staging their operations so nearby. We had to secure the local area if we were to be effective in doing anything else, like road construction. Without security, nothing else of any consequence could happen.

The last paragraph of the entry is an indicator of my mindset at this point. While I had already seen some things—and even stated in this journal—that demonstrated that victory was up to the Afghans, I still believed that the United States would make the difference. While we can do much, ultimately the determination for and impetus to victory has to come from the Afghans. We have set the conditions for their ability to win for themselves. Will they take the opportunity?

27 June 2009

Little happened today. I did some refining to plans and the O&I (operations and intelligence) brief. There was an IED in the village of Ja'laam south of here. But it was a family feud between a couple of rivals in the village. It's crazy in this country. A guy has a beef with his neighbor or family, and he decides to blow the other one up. I know that Americans do dumb things, but this is just stupid. The society is so primitive that it is difficult for us as westerners to understand, and how do we help a people who are so far behind us in development culturally, economically, etc.? I guess the answer is to let them do it their way and assist them in achieving Afghan normalcy, whatever that is.

Personal vendettas and revenge killings are routine in Afghanistan. I knew this going into Afghanistan for the third time; yet I still found it shocking. This incident would not be the last case of family and tribal feuding that we would encounter in our year in Afghanistan. No matter how many times I witnessed such incidents, I was no less shocked with each occurrence.

28 June 2009

Went out on the patrol today and came up empty, but it was eventful. Before leaving we got word from a local that there were two IEDs in separate locations. We sent the PRT patrol to one at Parwai village, and the other patrol, which I was with, went up the Mashpah Valley. The PRT found the one at Parwai and EOD (explosive ordnance disposal team) blew it up. But it took so long for us to get past the first one that it would have been close to dark before we could even arrive at the site. EOD told us that they would not go and work at that location in the dark. This would have isolated 22 guys in the vicinity of a known enemy area (this is where the PRT hit the IED two days ago). So, I made the call to abort because of that and the fact that we had no air (support) and EOD wasn't staying on-station. It is so frustrating to be so weak with combat power. If I only had an infantry company, we could take on this threat. Instead, I have to use indirect approaches like the HTT, IO, and cooperation with police. Oh, well. I think they (the enemy) are challenging us and trying to disrupt the elections, but we won't let them.

The enemy was indeed challenging our unit as the new guys on the block. The idea was to inflict numerous casualties on us to produce defeats, demoralize our forces, and make it appear in the eyes of the people that we could not provide security. Further, the elections were less than two months away, and weakening the security situation would enable the enemy to disrupt this critical event. To counter their efforts, we continued to aggressively patrol our area to prevent them from having success with roadside bombs. We also placed great emphasis on the nonlethal efforts such as communicating with the people. It would take time to see results, but the lack of assets actually worked to our advantage because it forced us to focus on the nonlethal aspect of operations. Ultimately, this effort paid great dividends, as we were able to make a connection with the people that the enemy was not able to form.

29 June 2009

A slow day today, which is OK. Did have a meeting with the brigade commander regarding Nuristan way ahead. I think the COL supports my thought that the best outcome from our year would be to conduct the next

TOA with the Afghans here. It would represent a serious victory for the Afghans if they took over the area as the first piece of ground they have full responsibility for. It is semi-permissive, so the ANSF (Afghan National Security Forces) could start working independently without worrying about getting smacked by the enemy. It would force the GoA (government of Afghanistan) to take charge, and Afghan forces would be less of an irritant to the people here. It is a winning hand. We would then shift to the south and partner with an ANA unit with a small AO. I time-lined it out today, and if the higher levels will approve it, we can start moving forward. For now we have got to work on Titin and Mashpah valleys. Right now my main effort is nonlethal, but soon I am going to have to get some forces to physically clear the area.

At this point we had the opportunity to refine our plan of action for the coming year. The plan that we developed involved preparing the Afghans to assume control of the area of western Nuristan and northern Laghman instead of turning it over to another American unit the following year. The area was, and is still, not as violent as other places in Afghanistan. Therefore, we believed at the time that, with the right mentorship, the Afghans could take control of the area, serving as a model of how to conduct transitions of authority with Afghans throughout the country. The factor that I had not considered was the competence (or lack thereof) of the Afghan leaders in the government and security forces. The key to the execution of such a plan was the ability and willingness of these officials to accept this responsibility. I did not know enough about them at this point to realize that they were neither competent nor willing to step forward. The officials were happy to stand aside and allow us to expend resources, including human ones, in order to keep their hands in the till. I still believe that assuming control of their own security is the way ahead for Afghanistan, but until the Afghan leaders are willing to take charge, winning is problematic.

30 June 2009

Fairly light day today, but I let the CSM have it. I need him to start being a CSM and not a section chief. He is a good leader, but he can't seem to make the transition to higher-level leadership. He has a bad habit of pulling people from tasks without asking why they are doing what they are doing. This tends to upset missions and cause things to get dropped, which makes him mad; yet he caused it. He has to use his chain of command and develop leaders. If he doesn't learn to do this, I can't see him going any further than a Bn. He has to stop looking at the 10-meter target and look longer range, plus think cause and effect. The negativity is killing some of the soldiers. They work all day, and then he grumbles about things being screwed up, so the soldiers think he doesn't appreciate them. I told him to concentrate on working through the chain of command and confine criticism to the leaders and not show this to the troops. The problem is that I had to blow up before he would listen. Well, no one said command was easy, so I guess I earned my pay today.

1 July 2009

Today I attend 3 shuras, and it was interesting across the board. The first one was the security shura with the district governors, their police, and NDS. Since I don't have the strength to go after people, I have to use the local security and reach the population to compensate. The governors and CoPs (chiefs of police) are an interesting bunch when together. When they start arguing it reminds me of a Baptist church argument.

From the security shura we learned of some names that might be involved in the recent IED attacks, plus a couple of people wanting to reconcile with the government. If we can work our leads, we might be able to pull a couple of these people off the battlefield, thereby increasing security for the election.

The election shura went well and informed the Afghans of their responsibilities and what we would provide. Only the most remote locations in Nuristan may have issues with the plan. Their ballots will be moved in by donkey. I will establish a coordination center at the District Center in two weeks to begin coordination with the local leaders to work with them on security and distribution of materials.

Shuras, or meetings, with Afghan leaders were a routine part of my duties. I used them as a means of steering the Afghan officials toward solving problems in the districts. They were always cordial, and it seemed at first that the leaders took the meetings seriously. However, much of the engagement was for my benefit, with few tangible outcomes on the part of the security forces. There was always a great deal of squabbling among the officials as they argued over petty issues among themselves. In the run-up to the election we laid out a coherent plan for the conduct of the election and prodded the Afghans toward accepting responsibility for their own process. This would be a constant struggle over the next several weeks.

2 July 2009

We had a shura with the Mashpah village/valley elders today. It went pretty well, but there was no real information coming today (with reference to the IED incidents). It is obvious that they don't want to come forward publicly with information. So, I reassured them that they could report anonymously and we would take it from there. They are concerned that the ASG (Afghan security guard) posts are not vigilant, and they want more police presence in the valley. We will have to work on that. We should have our award program on line to start getting some of the munitions out of the hands of the enemy. Also, we will be executing our operation in the Titin and Mashpah soon, and hopefully that will help clear some of the issues in the side valleys. If only I had more combat troops. The firing batteries are shooting well, and it shows that our training program worked. We have confirmed BDA in several instances, and our guns are providing great support to the infantry.

I met with the elders of the Mashpah Valley in an attempt to win their trust and see if we could gain some information about the IED cell in their valley. In this first meeting it was obvious that they feared the enemy. They would not divulge information that I believed they had because the threat of retaliation was too great. To get around this fear, we set up two programs to enable them to get involved in preventing future attacks without revealing their identities. We set up a telephone hotline (everyone in Afghanistan has a cell phone) for anonymous reporting of suspicious activity. Second, we implemented a reward program for turning in weapons and explosives that could be used against us. This program had worked in areas around Afghanistan, and if it worked in western Nuristan, it would take a bite out of the enemy's ability to support themselves logistically. I then used the radio station to publicize the programs in addition to putting out the word with every one of our patrols and whenever I met with the people. Over time the programs worked and became a great irritant to the enemy.

3 July 2009

Another rocket attack today. We had intel that it was going to happen. The frustrating thing to me is that we can't prevent it. We can react, but I just don't have enough forces to set up ambushes and catch them before it happens. One of the two rockets fired hit a living quarters and fragments hit the mess hall. Thank God no one was injured. We were able to counter-fire the launch site, as we noted in our surveillance camera an individual attempting to egress the area following the second round. Our observers saw the counter-fire impact on the enemy and assessed one enemy casualty. This was gratifying considering the damage the rockets caused on the base.

As soon as we can launch our op to search for cache sites, we should be OK, provided we can find rockets there. We also will have some money on hand to start buying them from people who want to turn them in through our weapon buyback program. We are sending out a patrol to search the area to see what we can find.

Tomorrow we are doing our ceremony to award combat patches to our new guys. All the old guys will put the 4 ID (4th Infantry Division) patch on. I can't believe after 20 years that I now have three. When I came in the Army some of the old Vietnam vets had two, and everyone was amazed by that. Things have changed so much since the days of the Cold War Army that I joined. The current war was certainly something that I never expected, but we have adapted and, God willing, we will win to ensure the free world stays free.

Within ten days of assuming responsibility for the area, we had already had five attacks at the firebase or out on patrol. The enemy was still testing us, and our counter-measures had not yet taken effect. The second rocket from the attack blew the roof off of one of our living quarters and sprayed the dining facility with fragments that would have killed several of our soldiers had they been in line waiting for a meal. Luckily, since it was the second round, everyone was under cover. The individual firing the rockets did not find the range until the second round. Therefore, we had time to react appropriately. The drills that we had instituted paid off, and our counter-fire caught the enemy fighter before he could escape from the area.

4 July 2009

Conducted the patch ceremony this morning, so now everyone here is considered a combat veteran. Simultaneously, we had a patrol out looking for the rocket launch site. The S3 went with them, and they found it at around 6,000 feet (on the side of a mountain in the Wadawu Valley). Primitive but effective. They had one rock stood up as an aiming pole and two other stacks that they likely propped the rockets up against to launch. They will certainly improvise.

We also had intel today that fighters are moving into our area from Pakistan. If true, this is an issue. It was going to be tough enough for us to deal with what we had. If true, the enemy may be trying to make a statement by attacking what they believe to be a soft target. If attacked, we have to make them pay so they think otherwise.

Finally, there are some fighters and leaders who want to reconcile. If this is true, this development is the true path to winning the fight in our area. I will work it.

The receipt of a combat patch on the right sleeve of one's uniform is an important event for a soldier. It represents initiation into an exclusive club, as the soldier joins a long line of veterans who have served in harm's way, and the unit patch on the right shoulder is a source of great pride. A soldier receives it after 30 days of serving in a hostile fire area. I wanted to mark the occasion by having a short ceremony to recognize those soldiers who did not already have a combat patch. It was very appropriate that the 30-day mark for most of the battalion fell on the Fourth of July.

My operations officer accompanied a patrol to find the rocket launch site so that we could disrupt future attacks and learn more about the enemy's methods. In our area the enemy would prop a rocket or series of rockets up and site them in using an aiming reference like a stick or rock to provide a rough estimate of the range and path to the target. Without a tube to stabilize the rocket, firing was a haphazard endeavor. I was very impressed with the way the enemy could "jerry rig" a rocket, prop it up on a rock, site it with a stick, and then fire it with any chance of accuracy. In the first two rocket attacks on our base, they destroyed one building and heavily damaged two others. Despite the crudeness of these methods, they were effective. Our patrol sanitized the site by knocking down the rough aiming references and discussing with the locals ways they could report such things anonymously.

5 July 2009

The day started out uneventful, but then we got a report of an IED south in Parwai. We sent the QRF (quick reaction force) and EOD met them there. There were actually two IEDs: one to stop vehicles moving in and the other to get the first responders. The enemy must have watched how the response to the PRT IED incident went and were trying to replicate that event and then kill the medical response. Disgusting. At least the local people reported it. As long as we have their support, we can defeat the enemy.

Tomorrow I will cover this during the radio address. Also, I am going to push the reconciliation program so that we can make some headway there and put a stop to the recent rise in violence. As I have said before, without combat forces, I have to use indirect means to defeat the enemy, so IO, reconciliation, and development is the way ahead.

Parwai was the site of a Mujahideen raid during the Soviet-Afghan war and is described in the book *The Other Side of the Mountain*. Parwai was a dangerous location for our forces. The IED setup here was designed to disable or destroy a vehicle, and then, when the first responders came in to treat the casualties, the enemy would blow the second one to maximize injuries and spread terror. However, residents of Parwai reported the presence of these IEDs to us using the hotline. This was the first evidence that our hotline was beginning to work. Over the course of time the hotline would reveal the location of many IEDs, saving the lives of multiple soldiers. We were beginning to make a connection with the population.

6 July 2009

Very busy today meeting with officials. First, I did the radio message with Sikander Laghmani, the Nurgaram sub-governor; then I met with the Nuristan governor. Finally, I met with the Alingar sub-governor down at his district center. I like Nurgaram and Alingar district governors because I think they are truly concerned for their districts, but I don't have that impression about the Nuristan provincial governor. I think that Mullah Kabir (the Nuristan governor) is more concerned with his own self-interest. He seems to be working on cronyism and would make a good Chicago politician. But I have to figure out how to work with him.

C/1–321 had some issues today firing artillery, and we have to investigate and get to the bottom of it. One of the rocket-assisted projectiles fell 5 km short tonight, so we will have to check to find out why. Human error is always the most likely cause, but if we eliminate that, we will look for mechanical error. More to follow.

Every day I met with a myriad of Afghan officials. In only one month I realized that the governor of Nuristan was nothing but a corrupt, self-interested politician. Everything that he did was motivated by personal monetary gain. He routinely found ways to skim funding for his province and continually bombarded me with requests for development projects from which he would receive a portion of the outlay from the contractors. He always attempted to abscond anything of value he could obtain for himself. His continuous demands wore me and my staff down until we could barely stand to meet with him. The district governors from Nurgaram and Alingar gave the impression of being concerned leaders. In the case of the Nurgaram district governor, he did have some ability and a degree of care for his duties and district. The Alingar district governor gave this impression as well; however, he was quite incapable of rudimentary administration. In both cases these men were involved in graft on a low-level scale. It took me some time to figure out that these officials were not what they seemed because of the façade they put forward.

7 July 2009

Big event today was the Bde Cdr visit. We gave him our view of the situation here in Nuristan and our proposed way ahead. We proposed a TOA (transition of authority) with ANSF (Afghan National Security Forces) in the spring of next year while preparing them to take over before the changeover. Simultaneously, we would prepare a new FOB to partner with the Afghan Brigade headquarters that was supposed to move into Laghman. The new FA unit (American unit that would replace our battalion) coming in would TOA with us there next May. The COL approved it for future planning with the key condition that the Afghans had to demonstrate the capability to assume responsibility for the area. We will pitch the plan to the division when they come here and at the commander's conference next week. This will give us some nice long-term goals to shoot for next year and give us a good mission. In the short term we are going to get Alingar District as a boundary change because our adjacent unit rarely gets there and it is directly connected with what is going on here. The unit south didn't like it, but it makes perfect sense. The Dow Ab district governor (I will call him Hamid Osmani) met with some insurgents to begin working on reconciliation and has future meetings scheduled. If we can turn a few of these guys, we will be in good shape for security.

As I had stated in earlier entries, we developed a plan to prepare the area for transition to the control of Afghan government and security officials and then assume a partnership mission with an Afghan brigade headquarters. This was our first opportunity to propose the idea to the brigade commander. He approved it in concept, but he was rightly concerned that the Afghan officials might not have the ability to assume control. As we got to know the Afghan leaders from continuous interaction, this proved true.

8 July 2009

Met with the Dow Ab sub-governor and Nuristan Parliament rep. The Dow Ab sub-governor is still not formally seated because the old guy won't leave. I have a feeling that there is going to be some violence up there. The governor (of Nuristan) did not do the replacement correctly, so the old guy thinks that he is still the legitimate sub-governor. The governor and chief of police are going to have to get personally involved to fix this, or there will be trouble. The Parliamentary rep was concerned that the road contractors working on the road to the north were not hiring local labor, which is a legitimate concern. The PRT commander is working on it.

We have a patrol out tonight reconning activity around the IED hotspot, and it is supposed to meet with a source to confirm where the Taliban cache is at. If we can find that, we will be in business because we can take their weapons and disrupt their operations, enabling us to secure the elections. Ultimately, it will guarantee our freedom of maneuver.

When I talked to the Dow Ab sub-governor, I asked him who is responsible for the violence around here; he didn't hesitate to reply that UH[3] was, and he outlined his area of operation and activities—exactly what our intel was tracking. I think he will be valuable.

The Dow Ab district governor was one of the few Afghan leaders whom I respected. Of all the officials I encountered, Hamid Osmani was the only one who had the leadership skills and genuine concern for the people of his district to get the job done. Unfortunately, his poor relationship with the provincial governor, Mullah Kabir, deprived him of the necessary support to achieve full effectiveness. He proved an energetic leader who took the initiative on several occasions to solve problems without the usual prodding required for every other leader we dealt with.

9 July 2009

Traveled out to FOB Joyce and Fortress today. We worked through D30 (Afghan howitzer) clearance of fires and training plans. It is unbelievable that the last FA unit did not want to partner with and train the ANA FA unit. Because of this, we lost a year of getting them better. The Marine ETT (embedded training team) stated to us that it was breath of fresh air to have us here and willing to work to make them better. It is one of the things I think is enormously important if Afghanistan is going to stand on its own. Its forces ultimately have to be capable of taking charge. Right now they can't. But we will help get them there. I visited B Btry at Fortress, and they are doing fine and shooting every day.

A source came back tonight with 3 107mm rockets from the cache. Tomorrow we will know the location. Once we know that, we are going to launch an op to take it. This will get most of their munitions in the area, disrupt their ops, and allow us to secure the election.

I was astounded that the Afghan artillery unit was so poorly trained. This was a result of our predecessors' lack of emphasis on partnership. In order for Afghanistan to stand on its own as a country, it has to have capable security forces, particularly in the army. Therefore, one of the areas that we dedicated time and resources to was training the Afghan army artillery unit in our area. Over time they made amazing progress in their ability to employ indirect fire with precision.

10 July 2009

I received word that Nana died on the 8th. I am shocked. She was always so resilient and strong willed. She made such a rapid recovery from her broken hip last year. She apparently died in her sleep. Last year when she broke her hip she was upset because she had to depend on others to help her. All she wanted was to be home and independent. Well, that is how she died, with her dignity, not in a home, but on her terms. She was always there for me. It hurts that I can't go home. I have a mission and 500 people to take care of in this war. So, I will do my duty. Nana was very proud of me, and I am glad I was able to give her that. She loved Maryellen, Andy, and Ashley. We gave her family, and she was happy. Just wish I could go home. Since I can't, I pray that God will deliver us a victory so we can secure the valley for the election and make for safer ops for the soldiers.

The unexpected death of my grandmother stunned me. While she was in her late 80s, I never expected this to happen because of her strength and willpower. The fact that I could not go home for her funeral compounded the shock. But, as a battalion commander, I could not leave the theater. In addition, Army regulation does not authorize leave from a combat zone for the death of one's grandparents. The regulation clearly states that it only applies for immediate family members in time of war or en loco parentis[4] situations. I could certainly not go home if I knew that I would have to tell some soldiers that they could not do the same in similar situations. I had to uphold the regulation, and that included doing the right thing myself.

11 July 2009

Had the mega-shura today with all the W. Nuristan elders. 200 showed up. The Nurgaram sub-governor said that nothing like it had ever happened before. One of the participants suggested that the shura should be a recurring event to solve problems. I thought that was a great idea because it could function like a regional council. I spoke to the sub-governor, and he agreed. In concluding the shura he suggested to all that we do this monthly with 15-20 reps from each district with a set agenda each month. They agreed. I hope that the things we are doing indirectly with the people will undermine the enemy, making our mission easier to accomplish.

Our source for the cache did not show up. He is in Barge Matal fighting the TB (Taliban) there. So, our op to take it down is on hold pending the source coming back with the pictures and grid (location to the site).

Talked to Maryellen today. She is flying to Chicago on Sunday to start taking care of Nana's estate. I appointed her as the executor in my absence. Mare is a good lady, and I am thankful she is my wife and doing all this for me while I am here. I would give anything if I could go home, but I can't.

We planned to conduct a "mega" shura—a slang term for a large Afghan meeting of elders—since assuming responsibility of the area a couple of weeks before. The purpose was to introduce ourselves to the elders of the villages in the area and discuss the way ahead for the region, assessing the desires and concerns of the people. This was one of the ways in which we sought to establish a rapport with the people that would build trust and simultaneously deny the enemy space to operate. The overarching concept was to use such indirect methods to separate the enemy from the population.

The failure of the source to report the information on the weapon cache was only the start of a series of frustrations with our sources. While we did have some success with our turn-in program and phone hotline, our effort to determine where the enemy stored their weapons produced little in the way of results.

12 July 2009

I was finally able to not run around like a chicken with my head cut off today and get some things done in preparation for my next meetings this week. I have my joint radio address tomorrow with the sub-governors and then the road shura. Paving the roads is going to cut down on the IEDs, increase our mobility, and foster economic growth. It is a key to success here in Nuristan and part of our overarching indirect approach to winning here. Had a guy request to turn-in 3 suicide vests today (as part of the weapon turn-in program). The MPs are checking them to ensure they are legitimate and not a hoax to bilk money from us. If they are real, then it is big, because they could be used for attacks at polling sites during the election. No word from our source on the cache. I want that thing bad, but without the location we won't be able to do much.

Maryellen flies out tonight to start getting Nana's estate in order. I pray she won't have any hitches in putting everything in order.

The shura on road building was both a ground-breaking ceremony and a meeting to inform the people of the plan for expanding the road network. This plan was in the works before our arrival and finalized after we assumed responsibility. The improvement of the roads in western Nuristan proved one of the great successes over the course of our year there. It greatly improved mobility to some of the remote valleys in the region and generated a flurry of economic activity in the district capital of Nurgaram. An added benefit was the fact that the enemy generally avoided placing IEDs in paved roads because of the difficulty in digging them in (and the population also became indignant when they damaged the road).

13 July 2009

I had a busy day today. I had a joint radio message with the Alingar and Nurgaram sub-governors. Sikander Laghmani is very good. The Alingar sub-governor, Mangal Abdullah, had never done an address, which amazes me. The radio is one of the best mediums we have to get in front of the enemy. The radio should be used to help get our message out and every opportunity to get the local leaders on (the radio) should be made. I just can't believe it hasn't been done earlier. Further, the PRT needs to get on the radio and talk development, and the new cdr is on board to do this.

Next, I went to the road shura. This was a very good shura because it gave us the opportunity to talk with the people about the benefits of the road, which will provide jobs, enhance the economy, and provide greater access for the people. Further, guys working won't pick up guns to fight us and will take pride in construction so that they will protect it for what it means. I asked the contractors to hire all the local men they could, and the elders to support them. Overall, a good day.

Mare made it to Chicago and is going to the apartment today to start packing Nana's things.

I made it a point to get the local leaders on the radio weekly to speak directly to their constituents. In Afghanistan the radio is the top means of communicating with the people. Literacy rates are so low that print media is not viable, especially in the remote mountains of Nuristan and Laghman. Additionally, there is no access to the Internet or television in these areas. The enemy does not have a mass media capability. Therefore, we had a major advantage with the local radio station for communication with the people. The use of the radio station in western Nuristan—which was funded by U.S. forces—represented a way to separate the enemy from the people by illustrating the positive things that we were doing with the government and contrasting the negative acts of the enemy. Prior to our arrival in Afghanistan, the radio was not exploited on a routine basis for targeted messages. After we took charge we made radio programming and government communication a top priority.

14 July 2009

The FECC (brigade fires and effects coordination cell) came down to visit today and we worked through a few things. I am concerned about the overuse of WP (white phosphorous) munitions. Some units use it like HE (high explosive). The problem is if it hurts innocent civilians, it is going to get played up in the press that we are using it as a terror weapon. I recommended to the Bde Cdr that he talk with the Bn Cdrs to rein in the use of it. If that doesn't work, he is going to have to restrict its approval for use to his level.

Our source is now in Jalalabad. If we could just get him to move back up here, we could get the info on the cache site. We will have our coordination center for the elections set up tomorrow at the district center (in Nurgaram). I am flying out tomorrow to do an Art. 15 (Article 15 disciplinary action) with C Btry. I will make it a visit too. Finally, I am working the security shura on Thursday and a "friendship" shura on Saturday. IO is the main effort for us without enough combat forces.

White phosphorous is an artillery smoke shell used to mark targets and produce smoke screens to protect movement of friendly troops. It is also very incendiary, burning at temperatures of 2,000 degrees when detonated. My concern as the senior field artillery officer in the brigade was that this shell was overused in the brigade for purposes other than those for which it is intended. Therefore, after a few weeks of observing our fires in the brigade area of operations, I determined that we had to limit its use to prevent the possibility of needless civilian casualties and damage. Since we were in Afghanistan to secure the population, we could not use ammunition that was counter to our intended purpose. It would take time and persistence, but eventually we cut back the use of white phosphorous by over 50%.

Even in combat you have to maintain discipline and enforce it in formal proceedings. Article 15 is a form of non-judicial punishment for minor offenses. It is used as a tool by a commander to get the attention of the offender so that he/she does not go on to commit larger offenses, and also to deter other soldiers from committing minor offenses. Unfortunately, I had to take formal action to discipline soldiers during our time in Afghanistan to maintain the unit's fighting edge.

As a part of our ongoing effort to connect with the people in our area, I scheduled a series of "friendship" shuras in which I met with the elders of each district within our area of responsibility. The purpose of these meetings was to build trust and rapport with the leaders at the village level by working with those individuals whom the people looked to for direction.

15 July 2009

This day started off very good and ended very bad. I flew to Asadabad with the CSM to visit C/1–321, and it was good to talk to those guys. I wore my old 18th FA Bde combat patch, which was kind of funny. Then everything went downhill from there. I fell in a pallet of pickets in the dark last night and needed 8 stitches in my right hand. Then the rear detachment called me at midnight, saying it was urgent. When I called back (to Fort Carson) they said to call Maryellen. She was very upset when I reached her. She told me that this character, whom Nana trusted, had gained access to her bank accounts and cleaned them out about a week before her death. What kind of low life steals from a dying woman? Had he been here in

Afghanistan, I would have shot him on the spot. She saved all her life for the purpose of leaving us something, and this guy stole it in her last days. I really don't care about the money. He stole her dignity, and it disgusts me. The Lord will have His way with him in the end.

16 July 2009

I did not sleep much last night due to the situation with Nana. The only compensation for my feelings is that Mare misses me and needs me. She told me that I am the only one that she talks to, and she needed me to be there for her. She doesn't often tell me that, so I know that when she does, she means it. I need her too, and it sucks that I am here right now.

I had the security shura today, and it went very well. I think if we can get these caches, we will have a safe election in our area. I met the Mandol (District) sub-governor and his wife today—smart folks who seem to really want to help the people of their remote region. Meeting an Afghan woman was strange. She was fluent in English and outgoing, something I have never seen here in Afghanistan. We will work to help Mandol, but its remoteness will make any help limited.

The USO was here today, and I had them autograph the journal. Amazing when folks from Hollywood actually care about soldiers. I thanked them for what they did, and then we let them fire the howitzers. They had a great time with the Joes (slang for soldiers).

This was the first time I had met the leaders from Mandol District. This district is in the northeastern corner of Nuristan and is the most remote of any in the province. There are very few people in the district, and the terrain is characterized by mountains rising close to 20,000 feet. Further, there is no road connecting the district to the rest of the province. Therefore, none of our patrols ever made it to this district. With a population density of only a few individuals per square mile, it made no sense to contribute precious assets to this region when the largest concentration of people was in the southern part of our area of responsibility. Given the focus on population security, Nurgaram and Alingar districts became our top priority for presence.

17 July 2009

Fairly slow day today until our patrol started coming back in tonight. We still don't know exactly what hit them, but we believe an RPG (rocket-propelled grenade) was shot at them on the way back (to the firebase). They were able to make it back with no further incidents. We pushed the patrol out in the morning to exploit the site for info. They did a pretty thorough investigation, but there is still some evidence an IED might be involved. The enemy obviously is challenging us not to patrol at night, but we will continue to do it. We have to prove that we own the area and the initiative. The enemy will not have freedom of movement at night because our presence disrupts them, so we will keep doing what we are doing.

Maryellen made it home this morning to help Ash get ready for her swim meet in Oregon. She got the funeral arrangements done; she just has to go back to attend the service and finish closing out Nana's apartment.

The attack noted above took place near the village of Sundawar on the main road in Alingar District. This little village was the site of much fighting during the Soviet-Afghan war and is situated right across the river from Parwai. The enemy was still challenging our presence in the area. Sundawar was a transit point between the dangerous Nuralam Valley and points south and west in Laghman. The patrols we were sending out at night in the area disrupted the enemy's ability to move fighters and weapons between Konar, Laghman, and the capital region. The enemy used safehouses in Sundawar to rest and refit fighters on their movement. Therefore, they did not want us out on patrol. Over the course of the next month we would have further problems with this village until a natural disaster occurred that gave us the opportunity to help the village in ways the enemy could never match. We won the population over as a result. This will come out in subsequent journal entries.

18 July 2009

Today was a very busy day. I had PBS network reporters from *Frontline* here today, my friendship shura with the Alingar elders, visited the OCC-P (election operation coordination center for the province), and we did training with the D-30s (Afghan howitzers). I did an interview with the PBS director, and I guess the show will air in October. They wanted to know about the new COIN (counter-insurgency) strategy in Afghanistan, and my opinion is that what we are doing here is not new—it is what we wanted to implement several years ago. The difference is that we have more forces to better implement it than 6 years ago or even 3 years ago, the last time I was here. COIN is personnel intensive, and the mistake made previously by the politicians was to force a technological substitute on a problem requiring human interaction. War is a social phenomenon and not scientific. Therefore, technology cannot account for human behavior because it does not act in a logical way in many cases. Only human interaction can solve human problems. Humans must leverage technology in war but never forget that people fight wars, and focus must remain on convincing people to do your will in war.

The synopsis above is essentially what I told the PBS reporters. Early in Afghanistan our resources—particularly in personnel—were too meager to implement a solid counter-insurgency strategy, even though we wanted to. As a result, we tried to push the enemy into the hinterland of Afghanistan with that meager force to give the government and people breathing space. This did not work. Only the influx of thousands more troops to focus on securing the population would facilitate what we had sought in previous years.

To work the counter-insurgency strategy that I described to the reporters, I implemented the first of my friendship shuras. We invited area elders from each district to meet with us to just talk without referring to anything relating to business. The intent of the shuras was to build trust directly with the people and show them our human side. The shuras did result in starting to establish that rapport, and we soon received word that the enemy leaders in the area were quite upset at the progress we were making with the people.

19 July 2009

We had a turn-in of munitions through the small reward program today. Combined with our earlier success, we have pulled in quite a bit of small arms. The guy turning it in supposedly has 3 suicide vests too, but he is haggling for money. We have made him an offer, and hopefully we will get them soon. Our source for the cache is supposedly back. If we can get him to come in tomorrow, we should be able to move on it this week. That would be huge for us to get the vests and the cache.

A bomb went off at Torkham Gate today. Nobody was hurt from our platoon. That gate area is so disorganized and my PL down there doesn't really have a clear chain of command, so he gets pulled in 20 different directions. I will try to help him out tomorrow by speaking to the commander in charge of the gate. He might not be very helpful, though, because from the sound of it he is part of the problem. More on that later.

Our weapon turn-in program was building momentum. When this program was combined with our outreach efforts, development, and security patrols, I believed that we were really beginning to make a difference in our first month. Unfortunately, the source with the information on the cache never provided the details that would allow us to find it. This was extremely frustrating because we expended a lot of time and intelligence effort in trying to develop this information. It turned out that the source wanted a large profit from the information and the price was too high. So, rather than acting in the best interest of other Afghans, this individual was only interested in himself. It was an attitude we would encounter all too often in spite of the efforts we were making at building our relationship with the people.

As noted earlier in the discussion of where our platoons were located, we had one at Torkham Gate on the western end of the Khyber Pass. This was the port of entry for all goods moving east and west between Pakistan and Afghanistan. Our cannon platoon was posted there to provide security for the gate and mentorship to the Afghan border police who were supposed to control the entry point. The gate area is a frequent target of terrorists because a spectacular attack here will likely garner much press coverage and demonstrate the ease with which they can operate. In this incident a suicide bomber disguised as a woman wore a vest under a burqa. The vest was packed with explosives and steel ball bearings to cause maximum casualties. When it detonated, there were a great number of civilian pedestrians in the area, and the explosion caused numerous injuries to the bystanders, including women and children. The platoon from Bravo Battery reacted quickly, and they were collectively able to secure the scene and treat many of the wounded. Several of the soldiers and leaders involved were recognized for their actions that day.

20 July 2009

I had a semi-busy day today. The PRT changed out today; the naval change of command ceremony was interesting to see. The COL came and we spoke briefly, but he spent most of his time with the PRT. I then did my radio message, and the new PRT Cdr is on board with doing a message with me on a weekly basis to talk about development. I think this has been needed for a long time. He did his first one with me today. Then I spoke to the UN military liaison about getting the Afghan election officials here to start working with us. It is taking them too long to get down here to do the planning needed to accomplish the mission. Finally, met with the Marine team on D-30 training. We gave them our proposal for a certification program for the Afghans. If we can get buy-in, I think it represents the best way to get the ANA Artillery moving forward.

Talked to the commander responsible for Torkham Gate today, and my PL attached down there is in a tough spot. At Torkham there are many people interested in what he is doing and sticking their hands into what is going on. Therefore, this lieutenant gets pulled in multiple directions, and as a LT, he can't stop it. What he needs is top cover.

The PRT in our province was commanded and manned by a team from the navy. Their primary mission was development of government capacity and infrastructure to establish a functioning administration and economy. PRTs change out every nine months in Afghanistan, and this team was one of three that we would work with over the course of our year. In the meantime, *the election was one month away, and the provincial election officials and United Nations advisors had yet to visit the province to discuss the mechanics of the polling. I was becoming concerned about the level of interest and planning for this important event when I met with the military liaison and pressed him to assist us with getting the interested officials to the province to discuss the plan and requirements. The Marine training team attached to our battalion was an outstanding set of individuals. The partnership that we established for training the Afghan artillery unit in the region proved very successful in building the competence of the battery. The dedication these Marines showed in doing their job and in cooperating with us was one of the most satisfying aspects of our year in Afghanistan.*

21 July 2009

We had a couple of contacts come on line today to offer us more weapons, and of course we will take it. One is bringing in the vests and the other is a new contact. He is bringing in mortar rounds, rockets, fuses, etc. We are really trying to work that one. Also, today some mediators for TB cdrs want to have a meeting to reconcile to the government. I have been inviting people to do that, and word is getting out. I have pledged to cooperate with any who will work with the government instead of against it. Our patrol last night shook things up in the Mashpah Valley where the PRT hit the IED. The bomb guy and his buddies apparently left the area because we went in so heavy. They had never seen anything like that, and it spooked them. We fired multiple illum rounds over his house too, so that he knows we will go where we want, when we want, and no tinhorn TB is going to stop us.

Finally, I talked to Maryellen, and yet again we have to pay for something dumb. Nana's lease runs out in September, so we have to pay the August rent for a dead woman. Even in death greed reigns supreme in this world.

As I had mentioned in earlier entries, we planned to move into the valleys in the immediate vicinity of the firebase to establish presence and demonstrate our ability to move freely. Further, we went into the Mashpah Valley to establish contacts with the local elders, build trust with them, and send a signal to the local IED maker that we would not be intimidated by his activity. He got the message. In subsequent reports we learned that he left the area and remained gone for quite a long time. He would not reemerge for many months, and our operation into the valley achieved the intended purpose of expanding the security bubble to ensure our freedom of movement and physical security at the base.

22 July 2009

We conducted a reconnaissance of the ford site today and found that the river in that spot is *not* fordable. The river is too swift and deep, so if we are going to achieve surprise in the Mashpah (Valley), we will have to do a short AASLT (air assault by helicopter) on the west side of the ridge, and then walk over the mountain to Ma'in (a small village in the valley).

On another front, my announcement encouraging people to reconcile seems to be working. We had mediators arrive today to inquire about two TB commanders in Dow Ab reconciling. We have another meeting scheduled for the government officials to meet next week with the actual TB cdrs. If that works out, then they can make a formal arrangement to renounce their association with the TB.

Our source with the vests did not show up, and now we know why. Apparently, providing the stuff to us has caused the Alingar cell (enemy cell) and Alishang cell to accuse each other of stealing munitions. So, they are removing it from the area to protect it, and the source is scared that if they found out who is selling it, he could end up dead. So, he is laying low. It is all good for us because we have created a rift and made it tougher for them to supply munitions.

Following our Mashpah operation, we wanted to find another way to get into the valley undetected should the bomb maker come back to the area. The narrow mountain road that we had to travel to get into the valley always forfeited any hope of surprise. We knew of a potential ford across the river that might support a dismounted (foot) movement that could provide us with the element of surprise. The Alingar River, however, would not allow for a dismounted movement. When we conducted the reconnaissance of the ford site we found the river raging from snow melt and runoff from the mountains. We attempted to ford the river, but the danger was too great, and we aborted the attempt upon finding the depth of the river well over six feet.

Our information blitz was beginning to pay dividends for the security of the area. The small rewards program to buy back weapons was encouraging people to bring them in. Certain contacts were raiding the caches of the enemy, and the various cells began to accuse each other of taking their munitions. This created a temporary split that worked in our favor, since it temporarily neutralized some threats. Given that the election was less than a month away, it proved very advantageous to our efforts to secure the area for polling.

23 July 2009

I am in J-bad tonight for the Bde Cdrs' conference. It is so hot in Jalalabad, I am so glad we are at Kalagush. It is hot where we live, but not degrees. Everything went well tonight, and we are going to go over the way ahead in Afghanistan for the rest of the year here. Some of the things that have happened in Barge Matal are going to slow down some of the proposed moves, like our own proposal to TOA with the ANA at Kalagush and move to a new FOB. Oh, well, the enemy has a vote, and that will dictate much of what we do.

Back at Kalagush we have a patrol out all night. It got into position safely. The enemy supposedly has an ambush set out tonight, but they will be waiting a long time because they (the patrol) are not moving until morning. We are trying to draw in one of our targets, a local bomb maker known as Mohammed al-Rahman, but I don't know if it will work. If we could get him, we would disrupt the IED cell. But we will see what happens.

The purpose of the commander's conference was for the brigade commander to provide his vision for the way ahead to all the battalion commanders for the rest of the year based on an assessment of the situation from our first month in the area. This would unify the efforts of all the subordinate units moving forward. However, the enemy in eastern Nuristan was upsetting the plan. The Taliban began a major push in this region to wrest control of the remote district from the government. To stabilize the situation, our brigade was forced to send in part of an infantry battalion and several Afghan units. The fight in the district dragged on for months, culminating in a desperate struggle at Kamdesh and combat outpost Keating. The drag on our resources seriously upset plans for future operations by our brigade.

24 July 2009

I got back from J-bad this evening, and thank God. It is so hot down there. The temperature is in the 110s every day. It gets in the upper 90s here, but that feels like fall compared to Jalalabad. The Cdrs' conference continued today, and it was good to get everyone together and ensure that we were all on the same sheet of music. I got to voice some of my concerns and discuss the way ahead for our region (in western Nuristan and northern Laghman). Bottom line is I am cleared to discuss our plan for an ANSF TOA with the CJTF (commanders and staff from the combined joint task force, the brigade's higher headquarters) when they visit and can plan for it, though it may not happen now that Barge Matal happened.

Maryellen wrote me a note and asked me to write a eulogy for Nana. I will work on it tomorrow after my shura.

As a part of the brigade commander's conference, the battalion commanders explained the situation in their individual areas and the way ahead in consonance with the vision for the brigade. I had already discussed my assess-

ment and plans individually with the brigade commander, but this was the first time I had pitched them to the assembled battalion commanders. In doing so I was also seeking permission to pitch the plan to the division headquarters, which was the combined joint task force headquarters. In accordance with protocols of command, I could not pitch it to the division until the brigade commander granted that permission. With his approval, I could then explain it to the command team and staff when they visited Kalagush.

25 July 2009

I conducted another friendship shura today, this time with the elders of Nurgaram, and again it went over very well. One elder spoke for the group and said how much he appreciated what we had been doing since we arrived. He is happy that our troops are so respectful and that because of their efforts we are winning friends while the TB is losing support. This was later confirmed when our patrol in the Titin Valley today was informed that local villagers told the Taliban to leave because the coalition was making a difference for them. The first time we went in there we got shot at. Now the locals are helping us. We are gaining momentum with our indirect approach, and we are going to keep it going. Also, pulled in more munitions on the small rewards program. This is having an effect in that the enemy can't resupply themselves right now, so we have the initiative.

I started Nana's eulogy today. It is hard for me to do, but I will do it as a tribute to her. I need to send it to Mare tomorrow so that she has it for the service on the 30th. I tried to call her today to see where she was at, but I couldn't get her. I worry about her on a long trip alone.

The elder who spoke that day, I later learned, was the Wakil Sakhi. (A wakil is a member of Parliament.) This gentleman was in his 80s, and he had participated in the Constitutional Jirga in 2003–2004. As a signer of the document that established the government of Afghanistan, he was a well-respected leader and would be the rough equivalent of a founding father in our own country. He was a great supporter of our efforts to bring security and stability to the area, and over the course of the year I would visit with him to discuss matters of political importance and cultural significance.

The patrol into the Titin Valley represented the execution of the operation we had planned to clear this valley when we first arrived. The intent was to expand the security bubble that we started working on a few days earlier in the Mashpah Valley. The information received from the elders of Titin Valley was quite welcome and confirmed that our effort in using the indirect approach with information, personal relationships, development, and security patrols was working. We were on the right track; however, what was the Afghan government doing to build capacity in order to capitalize on the work we were doing? Not enough, as I would learn.

26 July 2009

Today I used to knock out a lot of admin things I needed to do. I did a couple of OERs (officer evaluation reports), wrote a couple of letters of recommendation, and letters of concern over a firing incident at Fortress.

A Naval War College IO (information operations) guy came through today with the Bde PAO (public affairs officer). He came to provide us with some help and to check out our operations. The Dr. said that we are the model for IO in the region and with our use of the radio station.

We have gained momentum lately in staving off enemy initiative, and I now believe that we have it. I just wish we could find a couple of caches and roll up the IED maker. That would definitely ensure our momentum going into the fall. Regardless, we will continue our IO offensive because I believe it is helping us with security and allowing us to not operate with a heavy hand.

I completed Nana's eulogy and sent it to Maryellen. It was tough because of the memories.

While we made great progress with our efforts in so many areas, we never did capture the IED maker and only made minor progress with finding caches. The best way to have done this would have been in cooperation with the district police. However, they never seemed capable or sufficiently motivated to prevent crime or investigate incidents when they occurred. All efforts to enlist their assistance and push them to take ownership for their areas failed. As noted in these entries, I still believed that what we were doing represented the path to victory. However, our efforts really only set the conditions for the Afghans to take eventual control. It was incumbent upon the Afghans to take the opportunity we offered them to make a better region and nation.

27 July 2009

Did my radio address today with sub-governor Sikander Laghmani. Also, the first article from the Brazilian embedded reporter came out. (A couple weeks ago we had a reporter from one of the biggest Brazilian daily newspapers in that country.) We made the front page of the São Paulo daily there. Too bad I can't read Portuguese.

The rest of the day was taken up by planning for an op that the brigade is directing we do. It has us doing an AALST to kill/capture our IED guy. I don't think we have the intel, so I am going to work on reshaping it into a disruption operation in the Mashpah Valley. I think if I go in and talk to the elders, I can get more traction than coming in heavy handed with an AASLT. Besides, I think if we did that, I would lose some of the momentum and trust I have gained through the IO campaign we have been running. More to follow if I am successful in convincing the brigade to try my plan.

This operation was the brainchild of the brigade operations officer. I did not agree with executing an air assault to snatch the IED maker from the village. First, I did not believe we had adequate information and intelligence to carry out the operation. Had we executed it, I worried that we would not capture the target and only anger the villagers. Second, I had been trying to enlist the support of the people, and executing such an operation would have come across to the population in the Mashpah Valley as hypocritical. Therefore, we started the planning stage, but while this was progressing I worked to convince the operations officer to modify the proposal in such a way as to enable us to get the IED maker through cooperation with the people, which is what eventually happened. We executed the operation a few days later, but it served as more of a security patrol and meeting with the local elders. Further, as we later learned, the IED maker was not in the village, as he had left after our earlier operation. Thus, conducting the operation as originally planned would have resulted in breaking the relationship with the people before we got it fully established.

28 July 2009

We held the road ground-breaking ceremony today down at the district center with sub-governor Sikander Laghmani, and it went very well. This was a huge step forward for the area, and with this project now moving ahead, the province's economic development should really start moving. After the ceremony I did an interview with Al Jazeera. It went OK, but the reporter was completely focused on trying to trip me up by admitting that we indiscriminately bomb civilians. I told him that this was not the case and rattled off all the positive things we do. Frustrated, the reporter finally gave up and thanked me for the interview.

We finally got the suicide vests today. I think this will have a great effect on disrupting enemy plans for the election. Plus we got a bunch of other items, and the guy will be back tomorrow with more. His car broke down here today, so we installed a tracker on it to see if we can find where this cache is and get the stuff ourselves and then save the money.

With road construction in full swing, economic development now had a chance to spread north into Nuristan. This road was the first paved road in the whole province, and we were very proud to be a part of the ground-breaking ceremony. The interview with the Al Jazeera reporter was very unusual. I knew going in that Al Jazeera is a hostile network in the Muslim world, but some of the questions were truly ridiculous. The reporter asked me outright if it was American policy to attack civilians. I simply explained to him that our policy was never to attack civilians but instead to provide security for them to live their lives in a normal manner. After pressing me with this line of questioning and not achieving his objective of tripping me up, the reporter finally gave in. As important as the ground-breaking was, securing the suicide vests proved a major coup. Reports we had received stated that the enemy intended to use suicide attacks to disrupt the election in our area. For a relatively small price, we managed to get these things off the streets, and there were no suicide attacks on the day of the election.

29 July 2009

I conducted the security shura today and focused on the elections. The governors are starting to get frustrated with the process because the central government made the plan without consideration for local issues. Plus the people hired (to administer the election) are not actually from the area and therefore have no credibility. I share their frustrations, and after the meeting I got with the state rep from the PRT to find out when the election officials will be coming down. She said by 1 August, so I had my interpreter, Daud Mohammed, call them (the election administrators) and let them know the plan. We also scheduled an election shura for 5 August. This should help get the ball rolling. We had another turn-in of munitions today and confirmation that the suicide vests were real. The SRP (small rewards program) appears to be really helping us.

I talked with the COL about conducting our op a little less heavy-handed, and he agreed to let me go forward with our softer approach so that we can maintain the momentum we have achieved with our IO campaign and the goodwill of the people.

With about three weeks to go, we had still not met with any Afghan election officials; in addition, the central government in Kabul had predetermined many procedures best decided at the local level. As a result, the sub-governors were very frustrated and anxious to meet with the appointed election workers. I shared their concerns. The State Department representative assisted us in obtaining the contact information for the election officials, and I immediately had my interpreter contact them to determine when they could make their way to the district to begin the process of planning with the local leaders. Our cajoling got the ball moving, and within days the officials were in the district to begin the hard work of establishing a plan to execute the election process in cooperation with the district governors.

30 July 2009

Today was a slower day, but that is OK because I caught up on several things. Planning is almost complete for our disruption op to keep the IED cell off balance. Six years ago today I arrived in Afghanistan for my first tour here. I can't believe this is my third time back here. I didn't think the war would last so long, but it has. The problem is that Afghanistan has so far to go and the government has not made progress as quickly as I expected. Also, this place was not much further advanced than the first century A.D. when the war started in 2001, and developing basic infrastructure will take a great deal of time. Patience is not an American virtue. Americans somehow think that bringing a country from that point into the modern world is relatively simple. But it isn't because it takes time, money, and dedication. Plus, Afghan attitudes are rooted in the past (so progress is difficult because change does not come easy to Afghanistan). This is difficult stuff. Hopefully, if we can defeat the insurgency, progress will quicken the pace, and that is what we are trying to do now.

Nana's funeral was today. I hope it all went well.

In 2009 the U.S. forces had been in Afghanistan almost eight years, and in this entry I reflected on the time our military had spent there. At that point I had seen many polls stating that the American people had lost patience with our presence there and thought that it was time for our nation to end its mission in Afghanistan. To make a difference in a place such as Afghanistan, with its many complex issues, requires patience on the part of our nation. It also requires that the Afghans do their part to pull their nation out of the quagmire of war and focus on good governance. Therefore, I would say that our commitment must be proportional to the efforts of the Afghan government officials as long as they are making genuine efforts to develop a stable country for the sake of their people.

31 July 2009

The ANA LNO (liaison officer) team arrived to work with us on the election today. This was a very good development. I went down to the district center to meet them today. They seem fairly competent and I finally think we are starting to make some headway on getting the planning done. The only thing still missing is getting the civilian Afghan election officials here. Once we get them here, we will finally have all the pieces in place to get the election process moving. The Afghans have to take the lead in this. For over a month we have been waiting for these folks to get here. During that time the local leaders kept asking me questions that put us in the lead.

I can't do that. This is their election. If we appear to take the lead, it reduces the effectiveness (of the election) and gives the enemy a victory. With them (the election officials) here, they will get out front and I can step back.

Tomorrow I have a shura with the Dow Ab elders to establish friendship as I have with all the other districts.

I was very concerned at this juncture about the still absent civilian election officials. The longer they remained away from the districts, the more it forced us to push the planning process. I did not want to take the lead here because it would weaken the credibility of the Afghan government. They simply had to take the lead in planning and execution of the election. If we as Americans took the lead, or even appeared to take over the election process, it would make the Afghan government look like a puppet of the United States and give the enemy a leverage point for weakening the government. Therefore, we had to get the officials down to the district as soon as possible so that they could take the reins and direct the election process.

1 August 2009

I had my friendship shura with Dow Ab today. It went very well, and we surprised them in that we disproved all the propaganda that the TB had put out concerning us. I know there are probably certain individuals who are "playing" us. But if we keep on message and demonstrate that we mean what we say, I believe we will continue to win the vast majority of the people over, and hopefully it will continue to pay dividends with security. If only I could build some militia forces, I think I could run the TB completely out of the area.

We had our op order brief today for our disruption operation to set the conditions for the election. I hope that we can knock the enemy off balance so that we can secure the election. The DFCs (district field coordinators, for the election) did not show up as expected today. They had better show quickly, for the election shura is on Wednesday.

Maryellen is now home and I am glad about that. She has done so much lately dealing with Nana, and I hope that it is now put to rest. The police are supposedly investigating the individual who stole Nana's savings in her last days, but who knows? I just want it done so she can finally rest in peace.

Our friendship shuras seemed to go very well for us. The Dow Ab District was the most dangerous place in our area of responsibility, and because of this I really wanted to establish a good rapport with these people. It appeared that we had accomplished this during our meetings with them, including this occasion. Based on what we had done up to this point, it appeared that we had made great progress, and my confidence was growing daily.

2 August 2009

I met with the ANA artillery officers to discuss our certification training plan and seek their buy-in. There was no issue. They agreed that as soon as the elections are over they would like to work with us in implementing the plan. Unfortunately, the elections are the main focus for now. Another 18 days and that will be behind us. We still need the Afghan election officials to show up to make the detailed plans. We believe they may finally show tomorrow.

Other than that, we briefed our plan for disrupting enemy attempts to challenge the election (to the brigade). I think our plan is good, and if we can capture our main target, it would be even better.

Tomorrow I do my radio message with the governors.

The Afghan National Army artillery needed training to refine their skills, which were rough. They could conduct crew drills relatively well, but their ability to compute gunnery data was poor at best. Part of the reason for this problem was the education level of the enlisted soldiers in the battery. Our training plan would improve their crew drill and provide basic gunnery skills to the soldiers who had the highest education. The objective was to enable the unit to function independently with adequate competence to support Afghan maneuver forces. Getting buy-in from the battery leadership was key because we did not want to force our training regimen on the unit without the leaders being fully on board.

3 August 2009

An interesting thing happened yesterday that we got more details on today. There was a dispute between the Pashai and Gajour tribes over grazing of the Gajour tribe's animals. The leader of the Pashai tribe took some men and went to confront a member of the Gajour tribe. In the confrontation they murdered the guy, so the Gajour tribe in turn went and burned down Mashpah village. The governor of Alingar told me this at the radio station today. Sikander Laghmani from Nurgaram did not come for the address, so I called him about the situation. He said he knew and would mediate the issue. This is a golden opportunity for the government. If they can assert justice and mediation in this case, they can gain credibility. If not, the TB will fill the vacuum. I pushed Laghmani to do this, and he stepped right up without me having to get involved. Plus, I don't want to get involved; if I did, then I would weaken the government. The TB can then say that we are in charge (rather than the government), and that is unacceptable. We will see what comes of it over the next few days. If it turns out well, the people and government win and the TB is further marginalized.

The Afghan election officials finally showed up today. I am meeting with them tomorrow to go over the plan and the election shura agenda with them and Laghmani so that we are all clear going into the meeting.

The entry above is actually not correct. The initial information I received was erroneous. In Afghanistan it is traditional for the nomadic tribes like the Gajour to pay "rent" for the right to graze their animals on the land of the sedentary tribes like the Pashai. The Gajour had arrived from the mountains and squatted on Pashai land. According to the cultural norms, the Gajour should have paid for the use of the land. However, the Gajour refused. The Pashai tribal chief did go down to the village where the Gajour were camped, called Demagal. However, rather than the Pashai chief murdering a Gajour, the Gajour actually murdered one of the members of the chief's party and wounded the tribal leader. Upon their return to Mashpah, the Pashai formed a mob that went down to Demagal and burned the Gajour encampment and much of the village. The Gajour lost most of their possessions, and they went to the Alingar District Center for assistance.

At this point I realized that the government had a great opportunity to adjudicate and mediate the situation. The Taliban uses perceived injustice among the people of Afghanistan to fill the vacuum created when the government is incapable of solving basic problems that civil and criminal courts should hear. Therefore, I believed that if the district governors, in concert with the provincial officials, could adjudicate a fair civil settlement and punish the perpetrators of the criminal incidents, then they would gain great credibility with the people. Simultaneously, the Taliban would be pushed to the margins. As a result of this assessment, I pressed the officials at district and provincial levels to begin the process of mediation and investigation. The district officials took the bull by the horns and began to plan a jirga to bring about a settlement. However, the Nuristan governor refused to be bothered by the proceedings. This would have a chilling effect on the attempts to mediate because, in the minds of the Afghans, the blessing of the provincial governor was necessary to implement the agreement. Over the course of the next few months this situation frustrated me and diminished my confidence in the care and competence of the provincial leadership.

4 August 2009

Today went well in a number of ways. First, I met with the DFCs, the sub-governor, and security chiefs to work on the agenda for the election shura. We got everything ironed out, and I believe we will have a good shura *led* by the *Afghans* to get the election ready. Also, we made a big buy on our small rewards program today—many RPGs (rocket-propelled grenades), rocket fuses, and an anti-aircraft gun. Intel reports are telling us that the combined effect of our IO and small rewards program is making it tough for the cell leaders here to recruit; plus they can't resupply themselves locally. Therefore, with our op starting Thursday, we should be able to completely knock the enemy off balance and secure the election.

The sub-governor also made headway on the goat grazing–murder–village burning issue today. He submitted the grievances to the provincial judge for adjudication. If this thing is successfully handled, the government gets a big win and the TB loses its foothold. Now we have a displaced persons issue, but we will get on that tomorrow and get the UN (United Nations) and NGOs (nongovernmental organizations) in here to work on it. The governor (of Nuristan) will do a radio message here tomorrow.

The arrival of the Afghan election district field coordinators was a huge step in the right direction. Once we met with them I felt much better about the status of the election. This would enable us to hold the election shura with the elders from the districts with the actual election officials leading the meeting. Afghan ownership of the process would give the election credibility, and I was very relieved that we could finally move things forward.

The indirect approach to our operations in the area was paying big dividends. The reports we received at this time pointed to the enemy becoming frustrated with supply issues and their inability to recruit, and they could not carry out operations that would disrupt the election. It appeared that we were reaching the people and making a solid connection with them. If the government could competently do its part, as with the Pashai-Gajour dispute, then the enemy would lose any influence in the area. Unfortunately, the government leaders were not up to the task. The Nuristan governor failed to show up for the address the next day to address the issue. In his place the district sub-governor, Sikander Laghmani, filled in. However, his lower position in the government would not provide the power and credibility required to settle the issue.

5 August 2009

Did two major things today: First, worked with Laghmani on the displaced persons (the Gajour tribe) issue from the tribal conflict. Second, we did the rehearsal for our election disruption operation.

Laghmani went on the radio at my suggestion to discuss the tribal dispute and what he is doing about it. Then we met the displaced elders for an impromptu meeting to work through some issues of providing assistance. Half the village still thinks they are in Alingar. But Nurgaram is prepared to help, so after wrangling for 1½ hour the elders finally agreed to accept Laghmani's help. Tomorrow the UN should arrive to start working on long-term help.

We then did our rehearsal for the op. Only the ANP was not present. The ANA was excited to help, and I am glad we are working with them.

Tomorrow is the election shura, and if it goes well and the op works as planned, the election will be a good event for W. Nuristan.

Sikander Laghmani was making an honest effort to mediate the dispute between the Pashai and Gajour while we contacted other agencies to assist the displaced persons. However, the provincial governor refused to get involved in the settling the dispute, stating that "it was not his problem." This lack of interest made solving the issue impossible and demonstrated to the people that the government at the provincial level did not care. This emasculated the district leaders who needed this top cover to remain effective.

6 August 2009

We had the election shura today and all went very well with that. The outstanding issue is the voter registration cards. The government has got to come up with a solution to people voting who did not receive their cards. I hope we get the word soon because the election is now two weeks out.

We kicked off our disruption operation today to knock the enemy off balance before the election, and that is going well so far. In fact, the target may potentially be in our hands in the morning. If we get him, it is proof that our soft approach was much better than a raid.

Maryellen and Ashley are going to Seattle this weekend for the junior national swim meet that Ash qualified for. I hope she does well. Andy started school today and is excited because he is now past the halfway point. He had his commitment dinner where the juniors actually make their formal commitment to serve in the AF for 7 years. No turning back now.

We will see if we got our TGT on the patrol.

During the election shura many of the elders pointed out that they and their villagers had not received their voter registration cards after going through the registration process. Without these cards, the villagers would not be allowed to vote because they had to present them at the polling site. The Afghan government had to develop a solution to fix this problem, or the perceived disenfranchisement would destroy the credibility of the voting process. This issue would dog us until the last days before the election.

While our disruption operation proved very successful, we did not get the IED facilitator. As stated, previously, he was out of the area and would remain so for several months. So, his absence due to our activities was in itself a positive result.

7 August 2009

Our patrols made it back in today with no issues, but we did not get our target. He never came back last night (as we anticipated). However, that is OK. He knows that we know where he lives; therefore he has to lay low, making anything he wants to do more difficult. So, in the long run we have achieved the objective of disrupting the enemy's efforts to affect the election. The op continued today and will go on for the next 5 days. I will go out with them tomorrow night as we do some more disruption operations.

We have another embedded reporter from CBS, and we have been showing her how we operate. She is coming out with us tomorrow to do some reporting on women.

One piece of good news is that I got selected for the War College alternate list. I couldn't believe it. It was the best personal piece of news I had heard in a long time. I called Maryellen to tell her, and of course I sure thank God for this news too.

The embedded reporter was Mandy Clark of CBS, who has done extensive reporting in Afghanistan and spent several days with our unit.

8 August 2009

I worked with sub-governors Sikander Laghmani and Hamid Osmani (of Nurgaram and Dow Ab) yesterday (I am writing this on the 9th, having spent the evening out with our patrol) on petitioning the government for funds from MoI (Ministry of the Interior, which was responsible for the election) to hire local security for the election. We found out there is a process and there is a fund for this, so I worked with them to make the system work. We will see what happens.

I went out on a patrol last night as a part of our election disruption operation with the maneuver platoon. Our op is working well and the PLT has done a great job. We walked up (and I do mean up) the Wadawu Valley to Zirat village. Walking in the mountains with a flak jacket on is ridiculous. It is heavy and hot. I can't see how the protection offered makes up for the mobility you lose and increased water intake. To me it is ridiculous. We had a good visit with the villagers and talked about the election and the radio station, which they love. We handed out a lot of radios.

Later in the evening we went down to Alingar, where we talked to the police chief and governor about some intel we had on guys who wanted to attack the district center. They appreciated the visit, and we had tea and watched an Afghan news broadcast on TV. That was funny, because they had some commercial with the Afghan version of Bono advertising Roshan phones. It made me laugh.

Then we went back out and set up a checkpoint N (north) and S (south) of the village to do biometrics on people moving at night. From 2200 to 0200 we had a grand total of two people come through. This tells me that the locals just don't move around at night. So, those who do are likely enemies. And if they aren't moving, then we have freedom of movement and the TB doesn't. We have the initiative, something we did not have two months ago.

The Afghan government actually had a fund set aside for the election to hire local villagers to protect polling sites. Our state department representative on the provincial reconstruction team provided me with this information, and I met with the district governors to go over the request process, which was routed through the provincial government. At my suggestion, they prepared written requests to obtain funds to hire local security.

Our disruption operation was going very well and the enemy was off balance. Our visit to the Alingar district governor and police chief that night was interesting. We provided them with the intelligence that an attack was planned on the district center, to take place sometime before the election—which actually occurred. However, they were prepared, as the district governor had police positioned all around the compound and he slept with a loaded Makarov pistol by his bed. The district governor was one of the few Afghans in our area with a television. He was able to receive the Jalalabad TV station and watching the programming was very comical to the Western mind.

As we continued on with the patrol and established our checkpoints, I was struck by the lack of activity after 10 PM at night. The people in rural Afghanistan, and western Nuristan specifically, simply did not move at night. Once the sun went down the people retired to their homes. Much like rural areas in the United States, the people did not go out at night. This information allowed us to understand what represented enemy or criminal activities and what was not so that we could counter it effectively.

9 August 2009

I caught up on some counselings, wrote my radio message, and arranged some meetings with locals for next week.

9–10 August 2009

After I had written last night, a couple of incidents occurred that ruined the night. First, our patrol returning last night was ambushed. In the process of sweeping the area, an ANA soldier was killed. None of our troops were harmed. We did our own mini ramp ceremony for the soldier with the ANA Cdr and our troops at the helipad at 0230. The body went back to J-bad for burial. Then, 30 minutes after that, PFC Birr at FOB Fortress was wounded while sitting at an MWR (morale, welfare, and recreation) computer. An RPG was fired into the compound and he caught a piece of frag (fragment) in the back of the head that exited above his right eye. The initial report did not contain any information on an entry wound, only the exit, which was originally considered superficial. Only after he lost consciousness was it realized that the frag had passed through his brain. He is in a coma now, and we are praying for a miracle in this case. As usual, the first report was wrong.

Today we took to the airwaves to report what happened last night. Mangal Abdullah and Sikander Laghmani joined me at the radio station. We have evidence that the enemy was upset that they killed the ANA soldier. They wanted to kill an American. So, we used the radio message against them to show that they killed one of their own people.

The JTF (joint task force) deputy commander came today, and I briefed him on our proposed way ahead. He was enthusiastic about our plan, and I

Before and after pictures of Private First Class Mathew Birr, who was shot through the right side of his head in August 2009. He is pictured with General John Vessey, U.S. Army Retired. General Vessey commanded the 2-77th Field Artillery in Vietnam and later served as the chairman of the Joint Chiefs of Staff for President Ronald Reagan. He was our guest speaker for the annual artillery ball in December 2008. I asked him to award Private Birr his Purple Heart and Commendation Medal at the Minnesota veterans hospital where Birr was convalescing. He graciously accepted, which was an important act of service for our battalion and this young man. Birr fulfilled his enlistment and was promoted to sergeant before he was medically retired from the Army in late 2011 (photograph by the 2-77th Field Artillery Public Affairs Officer, Captain Matthew Frye).

think if it makes it up to the CG (commanding general), we will get to execute our proposal for a TOA with an Afghan unit and move down toward Hwy (highway) 1A (in Nangarhar) and partner with the ANA Bde. I hope we will get to do it. It would be a victory for Afghanistan if we do.

As our patrol returned from another night of operations, they bumped into the enemy near the village of Sundawar. The enemy initiated an ambush from a steep embankment overlooking the narrow road that snakes along the Alingar River. The enemy was trying to disrupt our pre-election operations, which were having an appreciable effect in preparing for a successful day at the polls. They used RPGs, machine guns, and AK-47 rifles to attack the patrol, which incorporated a platoon from the Afghan artillery battery at Kalagush. The patrol dismounted from the vehicles as they were trained to do and attempted to flank the enemy moving uphill. As they were moving forward, an AK-47 round hit the young Afghan soldier in the chest. The patrol immediately evacuated him to the base, where he died while our medical team was trying to stabilize him. To honor him, we hastily organized a "ramp" ceremony whereby soldiers from the Afghan battery and our battalion lined the helipad in formation as his body was moved to the helicopter. The Afghan unit was our partner and we were all part of a team. Therefore, we wanted to show our respect for their loss by doing the same thing we would do for one of our own soldiers. We would go back to Sundawar in a concerted effort to remove the Taliban from the village over the next several months.

Forward Operating Base Fortress was the most dangerous firebase manned by one of our platoons. As Private First Class Mathew Birr sat at a computer in the recreation hut on the firebase following a long day of duty, the enemy attacked the base with small arms fire. The initial report stated that a fragment from a rocket-propelled grenade had hit the young man above the right eye, causing a superficial wound. However, he passed out in the aid station. It was at this point that the medics at Fortress discovered the entrance wound in the back of his head; the wound over the right eye was in fact an exit wound. The fragment, which we later learned was a bullet, had passed through the right side of PFC Birr's head. Over the next several months we would remain on pins and needles as we followed the medical status of this young man. Against all odds, Mathew survived. For me, Mathew's survival is a miracle of God. By all accounts from medical personnel whom I talked to, he should have died shortly after being struck.

11 August 2009

Today was a fairly good day, as we took in another small rewards turn-in. We got some good weapons and munitions and put a "package" on the source's car to track where he goes so we can just take the cache ourselves and save the taxpayers' money. We will see where he takes us.

Then I got the Dow Ab sub-governor on the radio for the first time today. I think Hamid Osmani will command great respect in Dow Ab once he really gets his feet under him. He is a charismatic guy who fought the Soviets and later the TB in the civil war. This is the way an Afghan leader earns respect.

PFC Birr was evacuated to Germany today and is still in a coma.... The parents were notified and we are praying for a miracle here when he comes out of the coma. After a bullet passes through your head, it will be a miracle if you recover without serious loss of function. I know God can provide the miracle, so I am hoping it will turn out that way.

We also attended the memorial service for the fallen Afghan soldier from the other night's firefight. It was good for us to be there in support of them. Their ceremony had the soldier's clothes, boots, and an Afghan flag. They were the clothes and boots he was wearing when he died, and they were all blood-stained. We would not do this at one of our ceremonies, but they don't look at things like that the same way we would. Where we attempt to sanitize death in our society, the Afghans accept it more readily. We have built a good relationship with the ANA, and our attendance solidified it.

The bad item for today is the encounter I had with the provincial leader. He went into a tirade that I had informed the sub-governors about the fund for election security hires. He cursed at the sub-governors and then accused them of running to me instead of relying on him. I corrected him and told him that they did not come to me; I provided them with the information to make the government work—information that he withheld from his district governors in order to use it as a source of power. I am on to him and working through my channels to get this corrupt turd fired. Got pictures from Andy today at his commitment dinner. He is now committed to 7 years' service in the AF. Good-looking cadet.

PFC Birr was still in critical condition, and we did not know what would happen to him. As already stated, he did recover from the injury in what was surely a miracle. Although he has issues with seizures and fine motor skills, the fact that he survived and recovered so much of his normal functions is absolutely amazing.

My encounter with the governor of Nuristan was the first contentious meeting that I had with an Afghan official. I was infuriated by his embarrassing behavior and effort to enrich himself. He had dressed down the district governors publicly for supposedly running to me for help, which was not true. There would be many more incidents like this in the future, and the provincial governor's behavior typifies why Afghanistan is still struggling to establish a stable government and defeat the only moderately competent Taliban. This corruption, combined with lack of competence and concern for the people, is the biggest obstacle to victory in Afghanistan. Ultimately, it is up to the Afghan leaders to achieve that victory with our assistance in setting the conditions to make it possible.

12 August 2009

Today was mine and Maryellen's 21st anniversary—sorry I missed another one. Today was a pretty good day until the PRT got hit with an IED. Luckily, they had two wounded who returned to duty and one with a broken arm. The vehicle was destroyed, but the MRAP (mine-resistant ambush protected vehicle) did its job and protected the crew. Thank God for that. We thought we had the trigger man on the IED, but he got away. I wish we could come to grips with these people just once and kick them in the backside. They are very elusive, but someday they are going to slip up. Until then we will continue our indirect approach; it has worked, and

The G Company Recovery Section in the process of recovering a mine resistant ambush (MRAP) vehicle that was disabled by an improvised explosive device. Note the rear wheel of the vehicle, which has been blown off, and the burn marks on the side of the vehicle (courtesy Major Carrie Brunner).

we intend to keep doing it. Incidentally, the PRT was doing a MEDCAP for the people of the valley, part of our indirect approach. And, in their disgusting way the TB attacked them on the way out. I sent our maneuver platoon to secure them and G Co recovered the vehicle.

On a good note, PFC Birr woke up today, spoke, moved his extremities on command. If he comes out of this after taking a bullet through his skull and brain, it will be a miracle from the Lord. I just pray that this is the case. I spoke to his parents tonight; they seemed to be hanging in there, and I gave them the latest.

Well, I am thankful to have been married for 21 years; it has been a wonderful marriage and I am happy and blessed to have been married to Maryellen for this long. I hope we have at least 21 more.

The poor leadership of the governor (of Nuristan) was on display in an article that the reporters from Zuma (a German news service) wrote while they were here with us. During our election shura on 6 August it seems the governor of Nuristan was actually here (unbeknownst to any of us) at the Nurgaram DC (district center). Yet, rather than asserting his leadership and joining the shura, he sat downstairs eating grapes. The reporters noted this, interviewed him (asking him why he wasn't there), and published an article about his poor leadership. Instead of informing the elders of the plan for the elections, he sat on his lazy rear end and ate grapes. He has no credibility, he is weak, and as corrupt as a Chicago politician, if not worse. I sent a copy of the article to the BCT Cdr, who in turn sent it to the Division Cdr. If I could get this guy fired, it would be a great achievement. Nuristan deserves better than this.

The IED strike greatly surprised us, particularly because the PRT was on a humanitarian mission providing medical care to people who rarely had access to any health care. The road into the Nuralam Valley where the PRT was working is very narrow and the only access to this beautiful valley. Once a convoy moves up the road, it can only come out of the valley by the same route. The enemy monitored the entry of the PRT into the valley and set the IED while the team was in the village. Then, as they were coming out, the triggerman initiated the IED, which resulted in 2 slightly wounded and one wounded with a broken arm. However, the villagers were very upset by the incident and the Taliban actually hurt their effort to wrest the people from our influence.

The governor of Nuristan continued to demonstrate his lack of sensitivity to the need to lead his people and his supreme incompetence. His nonexistent leadership only created chaos within his jurisdiction. This chaos in turn created an opportunity for the enemy. Regardless of the positive momentum we—the American military—were generating or the things we did, the governor's continual corruption allowed the enemy to fill the vacuum that he left in his wake. Had the governor done anything positive, the enemy would have had no foothold in the area and the Afghans would certainly have been able to assume responsibility for the area from our forces. But this could never happen with Mullah Kabir as the governor of Nuristan.

13 August 2009

We did the first ever security shura at the DC today rather than at the FOB. The governors had always been so reluctant to conduct the meeting anywhere but here. Today I changed that. And I told them that after today they will lead it. I am not an Afghan, they are, so they need to take charge and lead. The focus was of course the election, which is now a week away. It is so hard to get Afghans to develop solutions to problems. They always want me to provide the answers. They are like a bunch of welfare cases that can't break away from their dependence. But I forced the issue and made them come up with their own solutions to security rather than me. Only sub-governor Hamid Osmani of Dow Ab seems able to do this confidently, and that is because he is an old Mujahideen Cdr. The others argue. Eventually, they came to agreement on the plan (for the election), so I guess the lively talk is actually good. Maybe that is how we started out as Americans. Tomorrow we will rehearse the plan with them and then execute. I pray that God blesses the effort for a safe election.

Up to this time all the security shuras had occurred on the firebase. This was one of the most basic things that I wanted to change after taking charge. As long as the security shuras continued to take place on the firebase, it would appear that the American forces were in charge of the area. Additionally, the Afghan district governors and police chiefs would look to us to set the agenda for security issues. This had to change if the Afghans were to take charge of their own affairs. Therefore, I pushed them to start hosting and leading their own meetings. In this first meeting at the Nurgaram District Center the Afghan chiefs of police and district governors finally agreed to a detailed plan on how they would use their resources to secure the polling sites.

14 August 2009

Today we held the election rehearsal with all the players involved. These included the police chiefs from Nurgaram, Dow Ab, and Alingar. Plus their governors came too. The only ones missing were Mandol (district officials). We went over the whole plan, and I have to say that based on their resources they are ready for the election. The guy that impressed me most was sub-governor Hamid Osmani of Dow Ab. His tactical ability is clear, and his charisma is inspiring to Afghans. If the plan to hire local militias comes through, Osmani will quickly bring Dow Ab under control. And we will have a great ally.

I had them come to dinner with me afterward and they thanked me for my hospitality, saying that my hospitality was better than theirs. I had my rear d. brief today, and I will be so glad when I get my replacement CPT back there to replace the current guy. He is the guy I need to organize things and take care of families. Tomorrow I will host the Bde commander and take him down to the OCC (province operations coordination center).

The rehearsal for the election gave me confidence that the Afghans would be able to carry out the election as the lead agents. They all knew their roles and had a good plan for how to secure the sites and what to do if the enemy attacked in specific situations. Most impressive was the district governor of Dow Ab. He was clearly the best leader among the Afghans and had the best interests of the people as his top priority. Among all the leaders I worked with, Hamid Osmani was the one whom I believed was capable of doing his job.

After a little over two months into the deployment I began to realize that my rear detachment commander was not measuring up. The families needed a solid, compassionate leader to assist them and prepare for our redeployment. I already had a replacement designated for the mid-point of the deployment, but what I was hearing about what was happening in the rear forced me to accelerate my plan. Taking care of families was too critical to not have the right leader at home to ensure success.

15 August 2009

Our Bn XO left a couple of days ago. While I am kind of sad to see him go, I also know that he was part of the problem with the Bn being labeled as a non-team player. He always resisted things from higher up, and within the Bn he was such a poor communicator that it caused friction. My new XO (old S3) will fix a lot of this, and the new S3 seems to have a good handle on things, so I feel we have improved a great deal.

Also, the Bde staff has changed out, so the old XO and S3 are going. They were real Neanderthals and the S3 was so lazy and non-communicating that he caused friction, contributing to ineffectiveness in the Bde. Good riddance.

We had the COL down today and we took him to the OCC, the radio station, and he gave the signal officer his ARCOM (Army Commendation Medal). I think he is pleased with our efforts.

I also spoke with the Afghan #2 election official about the lack of registration cards, and the decision is they can't vote. Because of the incompetence of the government they would disenfranchise the Nuristanis, and if they do that (because they don't care), then in the long term they provide the TB with a recruiting pool. Instead of thinking like that, they (the Afghan government) only consider their narrow process and won't deviate outside it. So, I took it upon myself to issue instructions to the DFCs, saying that for those who didn't receive registration cards an elder (from the village of the prospective voter) could vouch for identity. I know I am not supposed to do this, but the long-term negative effect would be worse than letting 10,000 poor Nuristanis vote in a race they can't change anyway.

It is routine, even during combat operations, to change personnel for a number of reasons. My old XO was actually nursing a severe back injury at this time. In addition, several new officers were inbound to our brigade from the United States after having graduated from the Command and General Staff College at Fort Leavenworth. The rotation of officers keeps the unit fresh and allows for professional development of the officers by providing them with a wide variety of positions within units. Further, it makes the Army better because the more well rounded the officers, the more able they are to see the "big picture."

The election official whom I met with at the Nurgaram District Center was the number two man within the Afghan National Election Commission. I specifically brought up the issue with the registration cards in order to force the national government to deal with a problem that it had created. There were several thousand Nuristan citizens who had registered to vote, but they had never received their voter registration cards. While the issue had been reported by the district governors several weeks before, nothing had happened to remedy the situation. Therefore, I pushed the issue to this senior official who came down from Kabul. However, he told me in a matter-of-fact way that there was nothing he could do. He seemed completely undisturbed by the fact that these poor mountain people would not be able to vote. When I brought up the fact that disenfranchisement could only benefit the enemy by creating a perception that the government didn't care, the official just waved me off. I could not believe this lack of competence or care for the people. So, I took matters into my own hands. I called in the district field coordinators and the sub-governors and told them that if the village elders vouched for individuals at the polling sites, they should accept their votes. This would allow all residents to vote, take away a potential wedge issue for the Taliban, and encourage the democratic process in the region. I was not authorized to do this, but I did it because it was the right thing to do for the people. If we had not done this, our unit would have had to deal with the consequences in terms of deteriorating security.

16 August 2009

Woke up to a rocket attack this morning. I was lying in bed at around 0530 thinking that I would need to get up before long when 30 seconds later I heard the whir and boom. I jumped up and ran into the TOC (tactical operations center), but we were unable to counterfire because we couldn't determine quickly enough where it came from or that there was more than one round. I was not happy with the battle drill in there and ordered the staff to practice all day and night to make sure we are better next time. I think we may have got hit because a new source from Ma'in (in the Mashpah Valley) who brought us weapons began demanding more money than we can give him. So, I think that this incident may have been his signal to us that we should give him what he wants. Not happening. Crater analysis showed that it was fired from just north of Ma'in.

I flew down to J-bad today to see my old brigade commander from the 10th Mountain Division. It was good to see him again after a couple of years. He was the best brigade commander I ever had, and he has a brilliant mind. He talked to us today about the background on how N2KL got the set that it has now, which he was able to articulate so well. It was an effort in 2006 to get into the enemy sanctuaries and allow the GoA to transform things in the populated areas (while our forces took on the enemy in the hinterland). This didn't work because the GoA did not step up. So, now we are going to pull back from the remote areas like Nuristan and Korengal to help the GoA transform the environment in the populated areas. Therefore, my plan to pull our base and give it to the Afghans is right in line with the strategy we are going for.

The rocket attack was unexpected, and yet we should have known something might happen. The source who was turning in the weapons had pestered my intelligence section for more money the previous day. Afghans who cooperate with Americans will sometimes execute "attacks" on our forces to make a point with us if we do not give them exactly what they want. I had heard of many such incidents in the past. However, we were not going to let him extort more money from us. If he wanted to cooperate, then that was fine. If not, we absolutely could not bow to pressure because it would weaken us in the future.

Listening to my old brigade commander—whom my current commander had asked to come speak to us—was very good for all of us to understand how our unit got to where it was in 2009. The plans we had executed in 2006 seemed sound, and if the Afghan government had held up its end of the bargain, the strategy might have worked. But it did not, and we had to change tack. Therefore, our unit and all others in Afghanistan began to pull back from the remote locations we held and came down into the valleys where most of the people lived. Securing the people and facilitating growth of government capacity and the economy would do more to keep the enemy separated from the people than what we had done previously. However, the wild card remained: Would the Afghan government take the ball and begin to run with it? At this point, a little over two months into the deployment, I was having my doubts.

17 August 2009

Today was a very busy day as we move into election week in Afghanistan. We did a ribbon cutting at the Nangaresh Agriculture Center. It was a good opportunity to get the radio guys there to talk to the local leaders about the election and publicize another developmental project. After that I did my radio address with the sub-governors and paid out the election security fund to them. Mandol's sub-governor sent a rep to draw the fund. Mandol is so isolated that I don't think there is much we will ever be able to do to help them. Plus the sub-governor (of Mandol) seems more interested in his wife than doing his job. Regardless, we will have a successful election with the three districts we can affect.

I did have lunch with the locals today. It consisted of bread, rice, potatoes, and beef. You have to be careful with the beef, since you could get sick.

I also began building a file to document the corrupt behavior of the governor. I will do my part to bring him down.

As previously noted, the governor of Nuristan had refused to assist the district governors with funding for local security for the election. In response, we acquired a small fund through our channels to provide to the district governors so that they could hire villagers to secure the polling sites. I distributed these funds to officials to enable them to augment their police forces in the last couple of days prior to the election. This system actually paid great dividends on election day, with the exception of the Mandol District. Here the district governor did little to ensure a safe election. The isolation of Mandol made it difficult for us to support him; however, he did little to help himself with regard to leading his district. He spent most of his time in Kabul, rather than in his district, and his priority seemed to be paying attention to his Westernized wife.

One of the things that units must do in counter-insurgency is identify corrupt and incompetent officials for removal. The presence of such leaders only gives the enemy an issue they can exploit. Therefore, it is incumbent upon the government to replace inefficient leaders to deny the enemy this opportunity. The poor local leadership was very disturbing, and allowing it to remain in place would destroy any possibility that the people would learn to trust their government. As a result, I had my intelligence team start putting together a file of the governor's actions and behaviors so that we could forward this through channels to the national government to have him removed.

18 August 2009

Went on patrol today with maneuver PLT. Saw a lot of evidence that the things we worked through in the security shura were put into action, such as the community security initiative. I saw it in a village south of Alingar and in Sundawar of all places. It was gratifying to see, and hopefully it will translate into a secure election in Alingar and Nurgaram. I also talked many people on the street today, and all except for one are voting for Karzai.

Also, yesterday our first incidents directly connected to the election occurred. In Dow Ab a DFC and his assistant were attacked, with both shot, neither life-threatening. ANP did respond. In Mandol the election materials were burned by the Taliban as they were coming over the mountain by pack animal from Panjshir. In the Nuralam Valley of Alingar a polling site (in Kowlak village) was attacked while writing (this entry). The good news here is that the ANP, with local hires, successfully defended the site. We fired illum in support and the TB broke contact. The bottom line on the election is this: Those places we can reach and where the sub-governors and CoPs developed a plan will have a successful election. But Mandol, which we cannot reach and where the sub-governor has done nothing, will not have an election.

Two days before the election the enemy was beginning to become active in the area. Where the government officials had actually put forth an effort to plan and execute a safe election, things were going well. However, where the officials had done nothing, as in Mandol, I expected failure. This entry proved prophetic. The election went very well in Alingar, Nurgaram, and Dow Ab, but it was a disaster in Mandol. The community security initiative proved a positive development because the local villagers took ownership of the election. Their involvement made the event personal, and thus they were invested in its success. As I moved among the villages I saw great enthusiasm for the election. With this excitement for the opportunity to vote, I did not believe that the enemy would prevent a successful election.

19 August 2009

It was an amazingly quiet day before the election tomorrow. That can only mean two things: either the enemy is gone or they are waiting to hit us hard tomorrow while people are out at the polling sites. We have been shooting illum tonight in support of the police chiefs in both Dow Ab and Nurgaram. Both chiefs said our fires were right where they needed it to deter the TB. Our fires last night were certainly effective in breaking up the attack at Kowlak.

Our patrols start pushing out after midnight to pre-designated locations to respond quickly to calls for help from the ANP, and the ANA is deploying out tonight too. Overall, we have a good plan and everyone understands it, so I think we will be fine. Then we will have to worry about getting the balloting material back to Kabul.

Mandol won't have an election. Their DFCs showed up in J-bad today claiming they were too disheartened to carry out their duties and left their posts. Plus they claim the ballots were not burned, but they just abandoned them at the DC (district center). They are suspect, so the NDS (National Directorate of Security intelligence service) is questioning them. We don't know what to believe. They might have taken a bribe to leave their posts. We will see.

The eve of the election was eerily quiet. I suspected that we would hear from the enemy on the following morning. To preempt potential attacks, our plan called for deploying patrols forward into the districts at pre-designated locations where they could respond quickly to any threats to the polling sites. The police were already in position and the ANA moved out that evening to reinforce the police. We were ready.

Word that the Mandol district field coordinators had abandoned their posts and made their way to Jalalabad did not surprise us. We knew that Mandol would be the weak link in the election process. However, we now had conflicting information as to what had happened. The initial report was that the Taliban had captured and burned the election materials. Then the field coordinators claimed that this did not happen, but they were too scared to carry out their duties. What actually occurred was what we suspected: they had accepted bribes to leave their posts. This was yet another instance of Afghan incompetence and ineffectiveness.

20 August 2009—Afghan Election Day

The elections finally took place today. After all the planning and preparation they finally came off, and with the exception of Mandol it all went well. There were three weak attempts (by the enemy) to disrupt the polling, including a rocket attack here, but none had any effect at all. Turnout was high and we had our security forces out everywhere to help, but they weren't needed.

Now all we need to do is ensure the balloting material gets consolidated at the OCC-P safely and then ensure they are secured for shipment on to Kabul. Then we will see the outcome. If Karzai does not win 50%, we have to do it all over again on 1 October.

We will do an election AAR (after action review) with the security forces next week and an elder shura on 1 September for W. Nuristan. Plus, we are going to start shifting to Ramadan ops on Saturday. I think the local hires for security had a great effect on the success of the election, and I hope this program can be a permanent arrangement so that the people can be involved in their own security, much like how the Sons of Iraq worked.

Election Day went very well in our area. The three attacks by the enemy were very weak, and in Pashagar village in Nurgaram the local hires were able to drive away a Taliban attack from their polling site. With the polling complete, we now had to monitor the consolidation of the ballots at central counting locations. We believed that this process would come off without complications. Our only concern was that Karzai would not win the 50% of the votes needed to avoid a runoff, which would mean doing the election over again. I had hoped that the security arrangements we made with hiring local villagers could become a permanent arrangement. However, Karzai would never allow this because he feared that doing so would lead to the rise of local militias. The local armed bands were detrimental to the country in the 1990s, fueling the civil war. The Taliban emerged from this turbulent period with its brand of hardline fundamentalist Islam government. Based on this history, it is understandable that Karzai would have reservations about the provision of local militias for security. But the situation had changed since the 1990s, and I believed that the time had come to have the people become a part of their own security to drive out the Taliban.

21 August 2009

Today was another successful day, as the balloting materials have almost completed consolidation, with the exception of a single polling site from the Pasagar Valley. I am happy to have witnessed the positive outcome here in AO Steel. The best part is how the sub-governors pulled this off with their police and leveraging the citizens. It proves what they are capable of if they just set their minds to it. Hopefully, this will give them confidence that they can run their own affairs, and we can turn this area over to the government as I have been pitching for a while.

I did get a piece of disturbing news today, as Birr is back in surgery. Apparently, he has an infection that he developed in the past 24 hours. He had been doing so well and the progress reports had been so good. I can't believe this happened today. I just pray that all will be OK with him. I will check in the morning.

The election had strengthened my belief that the Afghans could run their own affairs; unfortunately, that confidence would steadily erode over the next few months. They certainly could manage their own affairs, as the planning and execution of the election had proven. But they quickly reverted to an attitude of dependence and a constant stream of demands for more development projects.

Birr's turn for the worse worried me greatly. He had seemingly done so well in his recovery, and this infection threw it back several steps. This relapse made me realize that his road to recovery would be much tougher than I had anticipated.

22 August 2009

Another slow day, but we did get a good weapon turn-in today. The election materials in Nurgaram are now consolidated, and we just need to move Dow Ab down. Once the PEO (Provincial Election Officer) certifies everything, then it can ship to J-bad and the election is complete, barring a runoff.

Birr is in ICU again and is sedated. He came out of the surgery, but is critical again due to the infection in his brain. The Bde Surgeon told me he could fully recover in 4–5 days, or recover with some neurologic function loss, or he could die, which is least likely. I just pray that he comes out of this all right. I have the chaplain and his study group praying as well.

I talked to Maryellen today, and everything is fine at home. She said that Nana's lawyer called and the investigator has subpoenaed the bank records of the individual who made off with Nana's savings. Apparently, he has found irregularities, and there is a chance a civil suit could recover Nana's lost assets. I don't want to grovel over money, but I don't want this con artist enjoying himself on my grandmother's life savings either.

23 August 2009

I made a trip down to the Nurgaram DC today to talk to Sikander Laghmani and Hamid Osmani about some Ramadan activities. I took along our DoS (Department of State) rep so that she could talk to the PEO. We have a plan to do several mullah shuras during Ramadan to now work the religious leader component of our IO campaign. I think it will pay us big dividends to establish good relations with these critical leaders.

Osmani described how he pulled off the safe election in Dow Ab by co-opting two TB Cdrs. He is going to try to reconcile them in the next few weeks, and this will seriously weaken the TB in Dow Ab. Once they come in I will begin working with them to demonstrate good faith, but not until the government has completed the reconciliation process.

Finally, we talked about alleged instances of fraud during the elections designed to prevent balloting in two districts, all to produce a desired outcome. I suspect the governor is behind this. He is such a dirtbag. I reported it right up, and the DoS rep is working it too. We have to get this guy fired to have any chance of pulling off a semblance of good governance in Nuristan.

Ramadan was coming within a few days of this entry. This meant that there would be almost no government activities, including security operations, due to the religious observances. Everything comes to a screeching halt during this month. So, I needed to discuss how we would coordinate security activities to prevent the enemy from gaining any ground.

While the election went well in our districts, the governor of Nuristan attempted to prevent balloting in two districts in the province where the vote might have gone against Karzai. Since the governor owed his position to the president, he fully intended to deliver the vote to his patron. We found out about these activities, and it was incumbent upon us to report it. Nuristan would never reach its potential as long as officials like Mullah Kabir continued to hold such high-level positions.

Phase One—Execution Through the Afghan National Election—Ends

The successful Afghan national election was a significant milestone for the government and proved that, given the appropriate motivation, the Afghans were capable of managing their own affairs. Yet I witnessed many distressing indicators that demonstrated that while the Afghans might have the ability to take care of themselves, they did not have the desire to do so. The incompetence and corruption exhibited by almost every official I encountered confounded our hard work and is analogous to the old adage that for every step forward that we took, the Afghans took two steps back.

In my previous two tours in Afghanistan there had been demonstrable progress in many areas, including infrastructure development. The nascent government was in its infancy, and after 30 years of war it would take time to build a viable government. Therefore, all the Afghans needed was time and coaching to develop the required competence. This would lead to an eagerness among their leaders to take charge for themselves, or so I believed. Yet, nine years on, I did not see this eagerness.

The election was the highlight of our first three months in Afghanistan. This event absorbed all of our attention as we cajoled and mentored the local security and government officials through the process of securing and carrying out an election. These Afghans were able to protect the polling sites and conduct a relatively sound administration of the election. This convinced me that the Afghans could govern their own affairs, if they would rise to the challenge. Unfortunately, the election was the exception to the rule.

Normal operations within the government in Nuristan and Laghman consisted of activities designed to line the pockets of those in charge. The officials were involved in smuggling, skimming of development projects, and avoiding the hard work required to advance the business of the people. The police in Alingar were actually reporting our movements to the enemy while those in Nurgaram protected timber smugglers in exchange for a portion of the profits. Finally, when difficult problems arose, as with the Pashai-Gajour tribal conflict, the provincial officials washed their hands of the issue. It was this deluge of corruption and incompetence that eroded my confidence in progress.

As I continued to observe such despicable activities, I would ultimately conclude that, regardless of our best efforts, the Afghans would have to win the war for themselves. The problem was that in late 2009 the Afghans were more than willing for us to bear the weight of responsibility. This realization hit home as we took losses in our effort to assist the Afghan people, leading to my change of heart. I still believe that we can and will make a difference in Afghanistan, but I changed my opinion as to what our contribution would need to be. Instead of primary responsibility for victory in Afghanistan resting upon us, the prospects for success lie with the Afghans. Within weeks of the election I came to this conclusion. We would not quit and would remain fully committed to victory, but we would push the Afghans to do it for themselves.

III

Execution: Mounting Frustrations and a Change in Outlook, 24 August 2009 to 6 December 2009

Following the Afghan national election, we entered a new phase of our deployment. We began to focus on building the capacity of the Afghan government and their associated security forces. We entered this phase with a nagging skepticism as to the level of dedication the Afghan officials were prepared to exhibit in bettering their country. Based on our initial observations of the leaders at district and provincial levels, there was little to recommend their collective competence. By December I was convinced that the Afghans were simply not prepared to take the lead. A shocking event solidified this assessment.

In spite of the growing skepticism, we still had a mission to accomplish. Our task was to provide security for our area while simultaneously partnering with Afghan army and police forces to develop their skills. Further, we had to coach the government leaders in the administration of their districts. They required mentorship in budgeting, security planning, and prioritization of infrastructure development. Regardless of our efforts, most of the Afghan officials refused to step forward and lead. Instead, they shirked responsibility in favor of allowing us to run their affairs. This we would not do.

The lack of dedication to our partnership on the part of the Afghans exhibited itself in many ways. First, almost every meeting we held started with the Afghan leaders presenting me with a list of unreasonable wishes designed to enrich them. Second, there was an irritating tendency among the Afghan leaders to blame coalition forces for any failure that occurred within their jurisdiction. They were all too eager to pass the buck to us to avoid appearing as incompetent as they truly were. Finally, the police demonstrated no initiative in carrying out real police work. They would not patrol and were not proactive in preventing crime. In fact, the police actively engaged in illegal activities themselves. This provided monetary benefits to supplement their meager pay, which was absconded from their leaders at district and provincial levels. This series of frustrating tendencies created a cynicism in my mind that wore on me mentally.

When an IED blast in December killed one of my best soldiers along with seriously wounding another, my anger reached a boiling point. At this point I came to believe that we that we cared more for Afghanistan than the very officials charged with leading the people. We were sacrificing our blood to make Afghanistan a better place, and there was seemingly no appreciation of that fact among the Afghan leaders. This represented the turning point of our tour. No longer would this be our fight. It had to be the Afghans who led from the front. Only when they began to make their own sacrifices for something bigger than themselves would their struggle result in victory.

This chapter begins at a point when we had enjoyed success with the Afghan election and ends following the tragedy of 5 December 2009. From that point forward we would focus on pushing the Afghans out front. Further, we would tenaciously identify corruption and use whatever means we could to cleanse the corruption within the establishment. This was the essential requirement for success in Afghanistan. The Afghans had to introduce transparency in their government and work diligently to win for their own fight. They would take the lead for their own good with our unwavering support.

24 August 2009

I made it down to Torkham Gate today to visit the platoon out there. They are doing pretty well, and all seems to be working smoothly out there as they continue to work as border guards with the Afghan Border Police at Khyber Pass. They had no incidents during the election.

We got a warning order today to prepare for the move next spring. I guess my IO campaign to turn Kalagush over to the ANA and move us south to partner with the new brigade worked. I really thought that we would not get to do it, but when I pitched it to the DCG (deputy commanding general) and got the staff on board the momentum started building. The good thing is our current AO will be the first one turned over to ANSF and the government in all Afghanistan. To me it is a victory for them and us, and we are going to call the plan Steel Victory. Also, found out today that my request to stay a third year in Colorado got approved, so I can stay for Ashley's senior year of HS.

I had not been able to make many trips to visit the platoons scattered around the brigade area. The election forced me to focus on our own battalion area of operation. Now that it was concluded, I was able to start moving about the battlefield to see my troops. I did not like the fact that I could not visit everyone, but the mission dictated that my first priority was to ensure a safe and well-executed election.

I was pleased to receive the warning order to prepare for a transition with the Afghans at Kalagush. By the spring we would move the battalion headquarters to another location yet to be determined to establish a partnership with an Afghan infantry brigade. We actually executed this mission later during our year, but with one hitch: we did not turn the area over to the Afghans. Based on my assessment after working with the officials in our area for several months, I judged that they were not ready to accept responsibility. My first couple of months in western Nuristan and northern Laghman had raised my hopes that the Afghans would be able to take charge for themselves. Following Ramadan that confidence began to wane. Rather than gaining in capability and competence, the Afghans continued to wrangle for assistance as if it was 2004 instead of 2009. I became frustrated with this mentality since the officials should have begun demonstrating their own capability and, more important, the desire to take charge of their own affairs.

25 August 2009

I did my radio address today with Sikander Laghmani and Hamid Osmani. They did a good job discussing the election and security. I congratulated the people on how well the election went and their cooperation with security forces. Later this evening the preliminary results came out and Karzai and Abdullah are neck and neck. Therefore, there will probably be a second round in October, so I guess we will start preparing for that. The enemy has been quiet around here for a few days, so we will take that. But I know that they are just re-cocking for something else after Ramadan. Hopefully, what we do with the mullahs during Ramadan will build us some support and deny the enemy any sanctuary among the people. We have our first mullah shura for Nurgaram tomorrow, where we will provide gifts for the poor for Zakat (gift offering in Islam) and express our respect in order to build those good relationships we need for security cooperation.

Our next initiative was to engage the mullahs of each district during Ramadan. In addition to the local government leaders, the most influential individuals in Afghanistan are the mullahs, or Islamic preachers. These men form a key link between the government and the people. Therefore, if we could gain the trust of the mullahs as we worked with the government, then perhaps we could make a connection that would keep the Taliban out of local politics.

This would isolate the enemy, allowing the government to solidify its own relationship with the people. Then peace in our area might actually take hold. This was my thought process as we prepared to enter the month of Ramadan.

26 August 2009

We conducted our first of three mullah friendship shuras here today. Since it is Ramadan, we decided to begin establishing these relationships to augment the good relations we already have with the local government leaders. If we can solidify both, then we will have made inroads with the leaders that the people respect, government and religious.

It went very well, and I gave each mullah a personal gift; the PRT also put together some food and clothing packages to give the mullahs the ability to give to the poor in the villages as well. Showing respect for their culture is a way to calm their fears of us and hopefully win them over to create a more secure environment while encouraging them to deny the enemy a safe haven.

Tomorrow is the security shura.

Our attempt to connect with the mullahs and allay their fears was a well-intended effort that seemed to fall short of the mark. While some of the mullahs responded positively to our effort, others were clearly keeping us at arm's length. So, the mullah shuras only met with mixed results, and I was let down by our inability to reach some of the participants. Regardless, we would continue in an all-encompassing effort to reach the people in order to prevent the enemy from maintaining any foothold among them.

27 August 2009

Today was the security shura and once again Sikander Laghmani did a great job because he led the shura. I helped develop the agenda but told all the participants that I could no longer lead it. They have to because it is their country, and they take charge and I support. If we are ever to get out of here, then they have to step up. That is what I am pushing them to do. Overall, successful.

One patrol went to Titin Valley today and no contact. Three days in a row moving into our high-threat areas and no contact. I think the enemy used what they had for the elections and are refitting themselves to hit us again after Ramadan. No word on a runoff on the election yet, but Karzai does not have 50% right now. I think there will be a runoff. If not, there could be unrest because they will think he stole the election. We will see.

Birr got better again. If the infection has drained, it looks like he will be out of the woods again. I keep praying and believing everything will be all right.

Enemy activity had dropped off for two reasons. First, the enemy had expended a lot of effort in their ineffectual attempts to disrupt the election. Second, it was Ramadan, and even though we expected that the enemy might take advantage of the opportunity to hit us during their holy month, this did not come to pass. Therefore, we made continued efforts to build our relationships through the shuras and patrols to keep the enemy isolated from the people.

28 August 2009

We finally got our generator up to the top of the mountain to run our radio repeater for the radio station. It will allow us to push the signal north into Dow Ab. I flew to the OP (observation post) with the squad today. It dropped us below the OP, so we had to hump to the top. The view was unbelievable from up there. It is just too bad that there is a war here in Afghanistan; it is so beautiful. It would be great to go for hikes in the mountains. Unfortunately, right now you would get shot at.

We also had another SRP turn-in of 7 rockets today from a new source who wanted to turn in last week (but was wary to do so). I guess he finally got around to it. At least the program is working and we have evidence that our message is convincing people to work with us instead of the enemy. Our nonlethal approach appears to really be working and gaining momentum, and if it keeps up, we will turn the base over to the ANA. Tomorrow is our second mullah shura with Alingar.

Since we arrived in Afghanistan the radio repeater at the top of the mountain on the east side of river had not worked. The generator was not operational, and without a power source our signal could not reach the northern part of our area. This meant that Dow Ab District did not get access to our radio messaging. To remedy this issue, we sought to get a new generator to the top. The observation post would maintain the generator and the power would project the signal to previously untouched areas. Since Dow Ab was our most troublesome district, the opportunity to get our message to the people there would facilitate making a connection with them.

29 August 2009

We conducted another mullah shura today. Although it went well, we did not have the turnout that we expected. The reason for this is that some who wanted to attend did not for fear of retaliation for meeting with the coalition. While most of the valleys in Alingar were represented, one was not: the Nuralam Valley. This is the valley where we know the enemy is most active, and it connects to the Chapa Dara (in Konar Province adjacent to the notorious Korengal Valley). That is where some of the worst TB are and they transit through our area. Clearly their failure to attend shows where the TB is really operating in our area. Well, hopefully word will get out as to what we are doing, and we can then work with the populace to find the bad guys and deny them a sanctuary anywhere in our area.

We did the mission analysis for moving to a new location and turning over this base to the ANA. It will be a huge undertaking, but the payoff of having this be the first place in Afghanistan to transition to them will be huge.

Again our mullah shura fell short of the mark. This time some mullahs did not even show due to intimidation. The Nuralam Valley was connected to the most volatile areas of eastern Afghanistan in Konar Province. Nuralam proved a contested valley during our entire time in Afghanistan. The Taliban would avoid contact unless they had a distinct advantage over our forces, but they did use the valley as a "highway" to move fighters from east to west into the capital region. Once we identified this problem, we focused our patrolling to disrupt their freedom of movement.

While we began to plan for our move and new mission, we would not make the transition with the Afghan forces and government. Their lack of capability prevented this, and instead we transferred responsibility to another American unit later in the year.

30 August 2009

Today was a slow day—which is OK—but we did have one significant development. A new source came in to turn in a mortar round to us under our small rewards program. The PRT did a patrol to Tupak today, and the man who turned the round in found it next to the Tupak Bridge. He said 2–3 TB put it in a hole next to the bridge. So, he went and got it, called the police and they sent him here. A great development and may have prevented someone from getting hurt. Other than that, nothing all day. I will have the commander from our replacement unit here tomorrow and will bring him up to speed on what we do here over the next few days. They have only been to Iraq, but they need to break that mentality and get prepared for the environment here in Afghanistan.

The report through the hotline and turn-in of the mortar round was evidence of the success of our information campaign. We were making inroads with the populace and preventing the enemy from dominating the area. We believed that if we could keep this momentum and facilitate the building of government competence, then the area would be a model of stability in Afghanistan. The key was government capability.

31 August 2009

We did our radio address today with the SGs (sub-governors) and then a mission analysis for our operation into the Nuralam Valley. We had a patrol go into the Nuralam today and we were able to gather some intel and info on tribal divisions. Since the operation we are planning is focused here, it should help us do what we need to do. Still no word if there is going to be a runoff election, but Karzai still doesn't have 50% of vote, so I would say chances are good. If that is the case, then our operation will focus on setting the security conditions for the election. If not, then we are going to try to knock the enemy out before winter. Tomorrow is the post-election shura. It will be a good chance to bring all of the people together to discuss what went well and what went wrong, plus how we can fix it. We may need the input for another round.

Finally, today would have been Nana's 86th birthday. Still can't believe she is gone.

Based on our previous assessment of the Nuralam Valley, I decided to conduct a short operation in the valley for the purpose of gathering intelligence and disrupting the enemy's ability to use the valley for their own purposes. We began some preliminary reconnaissance into the valley to help direct our effort later in the month.

1 September 2009

We had a very busy day today with several more to come. We conducted the post-election shura at the district center with all the elders from W. Nuristan. In any Afghan meeting, even with an agenda, it takes hours to get to the heart of the matter because of all the flowery talk, but they eventually do. Today the issues they presented to the government election officials were the lack of registration cards, DFCs who did not get to know the people in the district, and the failure to have an election in Mandol. Very pertinent. I hope the election officials will actually take the info back to the government and develop solutions to the problems. A good AAR (after action review) by Afghan standards.

Then we did the final mullah shura and it went well. The one thing that came out of it was the Dow Ab mullahs said that previous projects (development projects conducted in the district) there were done in a shoddy manner or not at all, with corruption being the cause. I put the sub-governor in the lead and said that any new projects would go through him and they would not be complete until he was satisfied. He readily accepted the responsibility.

I also received the Cdr for the next unit today on his PDSS (pre-deployment site survey). I will take the next several days to get him oriented so he understands the mission.

Finally, Maryellen called and the detective is close to indicting the individual for stealing Nana's assets. They want his bank accounts frozen, but that can only be done civilly. So, I am thinking about suing him for justice.

The complaints of the mullahs from Dow Ab became a typical refrain in my discussions with the population. As I was beginning to discover, many development projects carried out before our arrival in Nuristan were of low quality in terms of construction. The reason for this was that the previous district governor forced the contractors working in the area to "cut him in" on all projects. In other words, the district governor would allow the projects to go forward as long as the contractors paid him protection money. However, his demands cut into the profits of the contractors. Therefore, they used shoddy materials in the construction of the schools and clinics they were contracted to build. This corruption on the part of the government led to much discontent among the people, driving them into the orbit of the Taliban, which claimed to offer justice instead of corrupt government practices. This made our job more difficult. While the district governor was dismissed shortly after our arrival, the memory of his actions hurt our efforts. Further, such corrupt practices were still pervasive among the government officials, as I was starting to learn. So, while I, with my battalion staff, might plan to turn over responsibility for the area to the Afghan government, reality would dictate that this was not possible due to the continuing corruption and incompetence, which would not allow me to recommend that the Afghans were actually ready. This would be a great disappointment to my battalion and myself after the painstaking effort we put into our mission to prepare the Afghans for taking responsibility.

2 September 2009

Another very busy day. I spent it showing the incoming commander around the FOB and in an aerial recon. We also had the start of our D30 certification plan (with the ANA artillery battery). If we can get the ANA artillery moving in the right direction, it will be a positive step forward for developing their Army. This is a goal that I have while we are here. Our aerial recon took us throughout our AO and down to where our new FOB would go if we do transition with an Afghan unit. After the overflight I gave him a full brief on our way ahead and our ops and intel.

We got info today that our recent disruption ops before the election convinced a couple of our targets to leave the area. Apparently, they were spooked by our continuous presence in their villages and building relationships we have with the people. They thought, rightly, that we are targeting them, so they left. The purpose of the ops before the election was disruption, and based on the evidence it worked.

Massive thunder and hail storm tonight.

The storm that hit the area brought several inches of rain. The precipitation was so heavy that it caused mudslides throughout all the valleys of western Nuristan and northern Alingar. In the village of Sundawar a mudslide destroyed a home and killed many of the villagers. The road—the only access we had to the south—washed away, and there were more than four feet of mud and large boulders covering the road bed. This tragedy gave us an opportunity to help the villagers and turn them away from the influence of the Taliban. It should be remembered that Sundawar was where our troops were ambushed before the election, resulting in the death of the Afghan soldier. The unfortunate circumstances offered us the chance to help where the Taliban could not, thus demonstrating that it was in the best interests of the people to work with the government instead of the enemy.

3 September 2009

I took the incoming commander around to see A & G (battery and company) at Mehtar Lam to see maintenance ops and our firebase down there. Good visit, and I gave the 2nd gun section there an award for being the best 155mm gun section during our section certification. We then moved on to Torkham Gate to see my B (battery) PLT at the western end of the Khyber Pass. We visited the border entrance and it was utter chaos; the Afghans weren't doing anything. When the platoon arrived they immediately got everything moving smoothly and started vehicle searches. After we left I am sure the Afghans went back to doing nothing. They are so lazy and are willing to just let us do everything for them. We have to make them begin doing things for themselves. They make a great case for why welfare doesn't work.

Back in our AO the rain last night caused huge mudslides that blocked the main road to Kalagush at, of all places, Sundawar. The slide was 4 feet deep and 350 meters long. 8 people apparently died when their house was covered. Although bad, we have an opportunity to win their goodwill by helping, and that is exactly what we did all day back there.

As part of the incoming commander's visit, I took him to a couple of the

A massive mudslide over three feet deep engulfed the main road in the Alingar Valley following the torrential rains of 3 September 2009. The village of Sundawar, where we had several engagements with the Taliban, suffered immensely from the storm. Within days we visited the village with the district governor and his officials, assisting the town in recovering from the effects of the storm. This effort turned the village from an enemy sanctuary into a town that supported the government and ejected the Taliban (photograph by the 2-77th Field Artillery Public Affairs Officer, Captain Matthew Frye).

locations where we had platoons so he could get a feel for the brigade area and what we were doing to support it. At Torkham Gate I was appalled by the incompetence of the Afghans. Our troops manned the gate several hours a day to help train the Afghans and mentor them in their operations. However, whenever the Bravo platoon left the gate the Afghans would simply melt away, resulting in a snarl of traffic trying to enter Afghanistan and, in the other direction, Pakistan. As soon as the platoon arrived, the platoon leader and his sergeant and squad leaders took charge to get traffic moving again. The leaders then found the Afghan border guards and got them back to work managing the flow. It was hard for me to believe that the Afghans could exercise so little initiative when not under our direct supervision. It was very frustrating.

4 September 2009

Completed the PDSS today with the commander of the unit that would replace us. Got up to Fortress today and the platoon up there is doing very well. No issues with their training and hard work to stay proficient. Following the PDSS I made it back to Kalagush and saw the road washout. It was unbelievable. The Afghan governor of Laghman hasn't done anything, and the contractor who was supposed to start clearing the road lied and said he was already on site. He was not because our patrol was there and he wasn't. These people are so corrupt and lazy. Even when their own people need help they won't lift a finger until they know what's in it for them. There are no George Washingtons, Adams, or Madisons in this country. Everyone has a hand out. Great case for ending welfare.

After the storm hit on 2 September we immediately gave out an emergency contract to have the main road up the central valley cleared. It was critical to clear the road not only to assist the local people but also to open our main supply route, as the mud and rock slide prevented any supplies from reaching Kalagush. I was angered by the fact that the contractor failed to do the work. I flew over the area and noted that nothing had been done, and our ground patrol observed the same thing. Based on this information we cut payment to the contractor and found another one who would actually do the work. Further, within the next few days we would put our own plan to assist the people into action while placing the district governor in the lead. The Laghman provincial government did nothing to meet the emergency, so we took the initiative to back up the Alingar district government with assistance.

The reader will probably note that the tone of my entries is beginning to change. Previously, there was a note of optimism in the way that I discussed our progress and the potential of the government. However, I was now becoming frustrated by the corruption that I continued to witness. What was worse is the fact that even in the face of obvious disaster and hardship the government did nothing to help the people and the contractors were only interested in profit. Afghanistan needs leaders with an attitude of selflessness and dedication. Yet these were few and far between, and altruism was a rare trait indeed. Because of this lack, it would be hard for our unit to turn over responsibility for the area to a government that was neither ready nor willing to take charge.

5 September 2009

Today was fairly interesting, as we conducted our Iftar (a celebration of breaking the Ramadan fast with a large meal) with the leaders of W. Nuristan. I actually wore traditional garb, which was a hit with the local leaders. The more we build the relationship, the greater our cooperation and hopefully a resulting drop in insurgent activity. I believe that this approach has worked effectively since implemented upon our TOA. I will continue to do it.

We contracted our own road crews to begin cleanup efforts around Sundawar. The crew got about 25% of it done, but work slowed due to some large boulders. The government has been fairly disengaged in spite of the disaster. None of the SGs or Laghman governor have visited the area. The result is they have done nothing, so we are taking on the relief effort. Nevertheless, we did get out a message on the radio that the government was working on it even though this was not true. I just don't want them to lose face with the people, so we put a message out on the airwaves stating that the government was working to fix things. I will work to get the district governor motivated.

In spite of my frustrations, I was determined to continue forging our relationships with the local leaders. One of the things we did was to hold an Iftar dinner in honor of the government officials as they broke their Ramadan fast. My belief was that a consistent effort to build trust and demonstrate our concern for the people would serve as a motivating factor for the local leaders.

I went on the radio that day to inform the people of the area that the government was actually working to assist them. I stated that the Ramadan religious observances had slowed the cleanup efforts. This, as noted above, was not true. The government had done nothing, but rather than allow the officials to lose face with the people, I covered for them while organizing our own relief effort. We developed a plan and then brought the Alingar district governor in and placed him in front of the effort to give the government credibility. This effort turned out very well after we got the ball rolling.

6 September 2009

Not too much happened today, although the PRT did have some shots fired in Wadawu while they were there. It is either tribal or someone there was trying to let us know that we are unwanted.

The main road is now almost reopened in Alingar. We put out a radio message today stating that the government was on top of the situation with our help. Tomorrow there will be a shura in Sundawar to discuss the way ahead for the relief effort. Once we get the district governor Mangal Abdullah involved and out front, the messages on the radio station will be more genuine. Up to now we have done all the work, but the government needs to pony up now.

We will do a fires conference this week at JAF (Jalalabad Airfield) to work out the way ahead for artillery in our fight. Key is to fit it into the overall COIN (counter-insurgency) strategy. So, less fires and more precise is better and our goal.

We planned a shura in Sundawar for the following day, with the district governor leading the effort. Once we met with the village elders and learned their needs for relief, we would press forward with assistance to get the people back on their feet. The key was to get the government out in front of the effort, and with a good deal of prodding we were finally able to get the district governor involved.

I was also working on the other part of my responsibility as the artillery battalion commander for the brigade area. Based on a couple of months of observations, it was my assessment that our fires were at times heavy handed and not in line with a solid counter-insurgency strategy. If our primary task was to secure the population, then we had to employ artillery fires judiciously. The fires conference's purpose was to bring all the artillerymen from across the brigade area together to discuss how to better employ fires within the spirit of our mission. Overuse of fires could only work against our counter-insurgency strategy. Over time the use of fires should recede.

7 September 2009

We attended the shura in Sundawar today and checked on the road progress and other damage caused by the storm. Aside from the mudslide, there was some major damage to their canal; the retaining wall gave way, which caused most of the damage to the village, 150 acres of crops were destroyed, and 9 people died in one family. I knew the storms were bad, but it must have been a wall of water coming down to have caused this damage. It is amazing how poor the people are here. It is also unbelievable how women are treated here. They are kept hidden and treated as property rather than humans. Literally an animal is of more value than a woman in this society. It is ridiculous. Any woman in the West who complains of lack of rights or the like is nuts. Further, she doesn't know what she is saying. The women of Afghanistan are the ones who have issues.

I allowed the soldiers to have half the day to relax for Labor Day. I thought it was good to allow them a little time to unwind because I have been pushing them hard since we got here.

The elders of the village of Sundawar welcomed us with the district governor. The storm had destroyed their livelihood, and they would need immediate assistance as well as a long-term approach to restore the village's viability. The district governor Mangal Abdullah led the meeting and the elders laid out their immediate and longer-term needs. We all agreed to assist and asked for one favor in return: to deny the Taliban access to the village. The elders were reluctant to make this promise out of fear of the enemy. However, they did commit to do their best to prevent the enemy from entering and to inform us when the Taliban was in the vicinity. With this assurance, we set about imple-

menting a plan that would help the villagers get back on their feet. The recovery plan would take the rest of our time in Afghanistan to complete, but it did restore the village to its previous level of productivity. Further, the elders held up their end of the bargain and the enemy was never able to reenter and use the village for anti-government activity after September.

8 September 2009

Today I visited with A Btry at Goshta (Firebase Garcia) and they are doing well, just a little bored. They are at the firebase that shoots the least. Part of the problem is that the unit they support won't clear the fires that are requested. They are so afraid of collateral damage (even with illum) that they won't pull the trigger. I understand you don't want to overuse fires, but someday, when someone really needs it, they won't get it or it will be too late.

The PRT was in an uproar when I got back because the ML (Mehtar Lam) PRT wants to survey the storm damage, but it is across my boundary. The state rep says that we should just give Laghman the governance and development mission and I would just concentrate on security in Alingar. This is ludicrous. COIN (counter-insurgency) at its heart is a political problem. Therefore, how can you separate security and governance? You can't. One goes hand in hand with the other, and I will maintain that I am in charge of all in my battlespace to maintain unity of command and effort.

Alingar District is in Laghman Province, and the PRT at Mehtar Lam is the team in charge of reconstruction and governance for Laghman. Yet my unit boundary extended into northern Laghman. If I had given up responsibility for everything but security, it would have been difficult to synchronize activities—which included political and reconstruction considerations—in our area to ensure that all focused on the same outcome. Only unity of command under a single individual can do this. Therefore, I would not relinquish responsibility for anything within my area. Besides, we had already begun to implement a plan that we could supervise and ensure proper execution for, which would enhance our security. In addition, we already had a relationship with the people of the village, and changing horses in midstream just didn't make sense. Further, we were only 15 kilometers from the village while the Mehtar Lam PRT was about 45 kilometers. It just made sense for us to retain responsibility.

9 September 2009

Today the CA (civil affairs) guys met with the contractor in Sundawar to assess the canal. The work will start tomorrow. Sikander Laghmani returned from Kabul (following a visit to his family to celebrate Ramadan) and began doing his own assessment of Nurgaram (following the storm). He will meet me tomorrow to discuss priorities for relief and I will help him with resources. Mangal Abdullah and Laghmani will give radio messages tomorrow to discuss storm relief.

The district governors had spent a great deal of time away from their districts recently due to Ramadan, which would continue for several more days. This made it difficult to get the government involved in storm relief. However, the Nurgaram District governor did return from his home in Kabul to make an assessment of what was needed in Nurgaram. With this information, we were able to provide him with resources to alleviate the issues in his district, which was not hit quite as hard as Alingar.

10 September 2009

The two SGs met me today and they did radio addresses discussing what is being done to help with relief from the storm last week. After that I met with Sikander Laghmani to get his priorities so we can start planning our resource assistance. In the course of the conversation, a pay issue with the ANP came up. It seems that the ANP has not been paid for 3 months. This is because the money goes to Parun, the provincial capital, making it difficult to move here because of the geographic isolation (of the capital in the mountains of central Nuristan). But the centralized bureaucracy in Kabul insists that it must go there. We floated the alternative of having the pay go to Mehtar Lam so that it is accessible to the district in order to pay them (the police) on time. We will see how far this goes.

Our patrol tonight thought they encountered an IED, but it turned out to be a boy with wires. Maybe the enemy wanted to observe it and see how we react to make it tougher for us. Just glad our platoon was vigilant.

I am heading to J-bad tomorrow for the fires conference with the BCs and FSOs. We are working on improving our FS (fire support) system to enhance COIN ops.

The Nurgaram district governor introduced me to the issue of paying the police for the first time in the meeting of 10 September. In accordance with Afghan law, the payrolls for all provincial police must be deposited in the bank of the provincial capital. Once on deposit, each district police chief is to send his pay officer to the capital to draw the pay for the appropriate number of officers in the district. Upon arrival in the district each officer then receives his pay. Nuristan's geography prevented this process from unfolding in a simple manner. The capital at Parun is in the central part of the province, completely isolated by mountains east and west rising over 15,000 feet. It took six days of travel for each district pay officer to make the round trip for the payroll.

However, this was only part of the issue. Of greater import was the fact that money passing through several hands has a habit of disappearing. After a little investigation we were able to determine why the police salaries were so far behind. It seems that the payroll was making it to Parun for deposit at the provincial bank. However, once there, the provincial bureaucrats who worked for the governor levied a "tax" for depositing the funds, transporting it, and paying it to the individual officers. Therefore, most of the funds were simply not making it back to the district after all the government officials siphoned away their shares. The individual officer in the district on average made between $80 and $120 a month. Yet, if he did see any pay at all, one third to one half was gone, leaving only $40–$60 a month for the policeman to support his family. The whole process infuriated me. In order to help solve the problem, we suggested that the pay go to an alternate location to enable the officers to receive their full earnings in a timely fashion. Once again the government officials were purposely obstructing normal operations in a corrupt manner. As long as this continued, the government would never gain any credibility and the Taliban would be able to use its incompetence as a wedge.

11 September 2009

Today I switched gears and focused in on my artillery commander role. We held a fires conference in J-bad with all the BCs, FSOs, and targeting officers. I wanted to map out the way ahead and determine lessons learned plus how we can make fires more efficient for a COIN environment.

We outbriefed the brigade commander afterward, and he approved all of our proposals. We will begin working on them immediately to upgrade our efficiency and capability across the region.

Tomorrow I have the security shura in Alingar.

Our assessment of artillery operations concluded that we needed to increase our accuracy to enhance counter-insurgency operations. Therefore, the battalion's leaders committed to focus on improving accuracy through use of precision munitions when we could and tightening up our gunnery procedures. We also pressed usage of less lethal munitions to reduce risk of causing collateral damage or civilian injury. It took some time to fully implement these changes, but once we did it greatly enhanced our overall efficiency as an artillery unit in support of infantry maneuver forces and counter-insurgency operations.

12 September 2009

The security shura went very well today in Alingar. Mangal Abdullah followed the agenda very well. He led the proceeding, and it was the most productive non-election shura so far. We agreed to work some combined patrols during Eid (the post–Ramadan holiday celebration) and shared information on the turds in the area.

I spoke to Sikander Laghmani about storm relief, and he gave me a prioritized list of which villages (in Nurgaram) lost what. We have now developed a plan to help. Again, if we can help the people, they might reject the TB, and that makes things more secure.

The security shura was an excellent forum for sharing information and working through the planning for storm relief. The combination of security and provision of recovery assistance to the people would have a number of benefits. First, it would facilitate confidence in the government's ability to organize recovery. Second, it would help the economy return to normal. Finally, the combination would demonstrate that the Taliban was an obstructing force, which would draw the people closer to their government, thus improving the overall security situation.

13 September 2009

Today was quiet. Just did some planning for our movement to new FOB and turnover to ANA. I don't know if we will execute it, but we are going to be ready. I did go to an Iftar with the ANA BC (battery commander) tonight. He invited me to it since I had invited him to the Iftar we held last week. We are working hard with his battery to raise their artillery skills, and he appreciates that we have brought him on the team rather than ignoring him like the old unit did. Tomorrow we are going to Nangaresh to do a dismounted patrol, visiting the high school, bazaar, and the Wakil's (parliament member roughly equivalent to a senator in the United States) house.

14 September 2009

I went to Nangaresh to walk in the village and met with the school headmaster, doctor at the clinic, and the Wakil Sakhi. It was a good opportunity for me to get a feel for the village and their issues. The biggest issue is the teachers have not been paid for 6 months. I swear this government in Afghanistan can't seem to get anything right. It is corrupt, doesn't live up to its responsibilities, and then complains about everything. Then, because the government is no help, the people ask me for everything. It is so irritating, but I took their concerns and reported them up my chain.

Meanwhile, I launched an investigation into the U.S. Army Corps of ENG (engineers) rep's activities, and the investigators found that he has been accepting substantial gifts from the locals. Since he is in a position to steer contracts, this is a serious issue. In cooperation with the PRT, I sent him packing. If we can't avoid corruption, then how can we expect the Afghans to do it? Plus corruption leads to shoddy projects, which leads to frustrated Afghans, and eventually breaks down our progress in security. The best thing is to weed these people out, and that is what I did. The PRT S3 tipped me off, and I took it from there.

Tomorrow I visit FOB Monti.

The teacher pay issue was similar to the problem with police pay. When the money reached the provincial capital, at least one third of it was "taxed," and the teachers would receive the remainder once it finally arrived in the districts. Of course, the "tax" found its way into the pockets of the provincial officials. Since the teachers could not get satisfaction in complaining to the district or provincial government, they came to me.

I was upset to hear that the civilian U.S. Army Corps of Engineers representative was receiving "gifts" from the Afghan contractors. After initiating the investigation we found that he had routinely received gifts in the form of jewels and other expensive items. In turn, these contractors received lucrative work from the PRT for reconstruction projects. I was very displeased with the fact that the Afghan officials were so corrupt, but learning that an American engineer was caught up in anything that appeared corrupt was even worse. How could we encourage Afghans to do the right thing if an American was involved in corruption too? Therefore, I had to take action to ensure that our practices were completely transparent in order to facilitate honest business among the Afghans.

15 September 2009

Today was a crazy day, and all indicators are that the enemy is going to come after us hard. First, we learned that an IED cell in the area is attempting to recruit and accelerate production of devices to target our soldiers. Second, the TB in Dow Ab attacked a police station and were threatening to attack the district center. Third, the Gajour and Pashai tribes clashed again, and this time over a dowry. One guy was shot. Plus, there is a rumor that there is about to be a dispute over pine nuts. If you add the meetings the IED cell has been having lately, then there is likely to be something starting after Ramadan and before winter. But we are planning to hit them hard in our operation in the Nuralam to prevent that and maintain our momentum.

Several things were beginning come together that threatened an interesting period for the unit once Ramadan ended. To prevent the enemy from gaining the initiative, we were planning on launching our own operation to counter enemy plans. It is interesting to note that within a couple of months of the release from Bagram of the three individuals from the IED cell, our level of IED contacts tripled. We had had our share of these incidents to date, but they were sporadic in nature. However, by December we were making routine contacts or having locations reported to us on an almost daily basis. Regardless, we had to maintain our patrol routine to ensure our own freedom of movement while disrupting the enemy's capability to do what they wanted.

The problem with the tribes was becoming acute because of inaction from the provincial government. The district governors were trying to bring the two tribes together for a jirga to solve the dispute, and this was an honest and valiant effort on their part. However, without the support of the provincial government, any agreement would not have the stamp of official sanction. The tribes needed this authority to enforce the decision of a jirga. Now, with fall closing in, it was almost time to begin gathering pine nuts, which provided a lucrative means for the tribes to sustain their people over the winter. They had a traditional arrangement much like the land use "tax" for grazing animals that applied to gathering nuts in the fall. But since the dispute from August was still unresolved the gathering season could prove just as violent as the situation arising from the failure of the Gajour to pay the land "tax" to the Pashai. The provincial government had to become involved in the resolution process or a full tribal war would result.

16 September 2009

Another interesting day. We found out today that I can purchase livestock, so I am going to buy some goats and cows to replace some of those lost in the storm. Also, I am encouraging the sub-governors to form a "pine nut" shura to come up with a solution over the nuts before fighting starts over the gathering. I never thought in my career that I would be buying goats and negotiating over pine nuts, but I guess there is a first time for everything.

We also got word tonight that Sikander Laghmani of Nurgaram has been named the new sub-governor of Barge Matal (in eastern Nuristan). It has been utter chaos in that district since July when the TB attacked the town. Laghmani is from there and has always had an interest in becoming the SG there. However, there are huge problems there now, and without our forces to back him and no budget, he might struggle. The one good thing is, he is fairly honest, but I don't know if that is enough.

To alleviate the effects of the storm, I obtained funds to buy some livestock to help the people of some of the hard-hit villages. Nothing in my military training had ever prepared me for such endeavors, but we did what we had to do to assist the people.

Sikander Laghmani was fairly effective as the district governor of Nur-

garam, and we had a very good working relationship. Yet when he took the job in Barge Matal and was no longer under the direct observation of a U.S. commander, he engaged in corrupt activities in his home district. This was a huge disappointment for me since I had placed a lot of confidence in him up to that point. Another letdown for me with regard to government competence and capability, and my faith in the officials was steadily eroding.

17 September 2009

Today we finalized our goat purchase and will deliver tomorrow. I can't repopulate the whole herd, but hopefully they will mate and repopulate for us. Ha. Police backpay will be here in the next day or two, and this should get the police back on track for their pay. The system is so dumb. All pay has to go through the provincial capital in Parun, which is isolated from the rest of the province. To deliver the pay you risk getting killed, and the person picking up the pay is charged a delivery "fee." So, the police get screwed. No wonder they (the police) aren't that good.

Tonight we have an IED situation. A local reported one in the Wadawu Valley and the ANP cordoned it. Our platoon arrived and EOD has to come on station to blow it. There has been small arms fire, but we have plenty of force there and have been shooting illum all night to cover them. The good news is a local reported, the police responded, and we helped.

The arrangement that we made was to have the pay come to the Nurgaram District Center before it went to Parun. In this manner, the police in the local area could receive their full pay before it was "taxed" at the provincial capital. Although we put the plan into operation, events in the next few days would work against a clean execution.

The fact that a local reported the IED to the police was a positive development. Unfortunately, IED incidents were beginning to pick up. Some of this was attributable to the IED cell becoming active again with the release of the three detainees from Bagram.

18 September 2009

We bought 20 goats, two cows, and 30 chickens today and gave them to the sub-governor for distribution to the Shemgal and Titin Valleys. We took a bunch of pictures of them so that we could laugh about it later. The guy we bought them from brought the chickens in the back seat of his car. Unbelievable.

The IED was a small one that we think would have been used to initiate an ambush. We had enough firepower on the scene to ensure that not much could be done to the patrol. We are going to cut off the valley for a while from development projects. Then, when they ask why, I will tell them because they harbor insurgents. When they turn them in, we will restart it. We will see if that works.

The police pay will be here tomorrow. This will get them back up to date on pay and with no middleman. Now we just have to get the right officials here to receive it. Most are leaving tomorrow for Eid (the post-Ramadan holiday). I wish they would stick around for a few more days to take care of their people, but I don't think they will.

19 September 2009

Police pay did not arrive as it was supposed to, but we expect it any time. Now all of the leaders have gone home for Eid and there is no one to actually pay the police. It is so frustrating. The government finally gets the money headed this direction, and then there is nobody here to receive it and pay it out.

On another note, the police chief of Alingar asked us to guard their district center until Tuesday for Eid. I told him to pound sand. What a dirtbag. If we would do it, these officials would never lift a finger and do anything for themselves. Afghans, while claiming to have so much pride and honor, are so lazy when it comes to taking charge of their own future. This is just another example of it. We are welfare for them. They could do it themselves but won't because we are here. They are the perfect case study as to why welfare can't work.

We got rocketed tonight and had no casualties with the thing landing outside the wire. We have been anticipating that after Ramadan things would pick up with the enemy, and that has happened, starting with the IED the other night. I just wish we could get at these people.

Actually, we could have tonight, but missed the chance because the TOC failed to get the available info to me so I could make the call. The tower saw the launch, but because my Btl CPT (battle captain) and NCO were dead on their rears, I didn't get the TGTing info until over 10 minutes after the launch, so they (the enemy) were gone by then. I was so mad I chewed the whole TOC out. The purpose of the TOC is:

- To gather info quickly
- Provide it to the decision-maker (me) so he can make the decision
- Pass orders

The first two did not happen in a timely manner, so we missed an opportunity to kill the guys who did it.

This was a bad day for me, starting with the encounter with the police chief in Alingar and culminating with the failure of my command post to get the information I needed to fire back at the enemy. I could not believe that a chief of police would have the audacity to ask me to have our troops guard his headquarters while he and his police took a holiday. This inability of Afghan officials to take responsibility for their own operations was astounding, and it was occurring all too often. There was no way I was going to relieve any Afghan of their responsibility to do their own jobs.

Enemy fighters fired rockets by physically igniting the explosive train at the firing point. With this knowledge we had a chance to engage them with counter-fire before they could vacate the area. But we needed to get this targeting information within two minutes to engage the enemy effectively. The inability of the command post to do this angered me beyond description because this is something that a field artillery operation center is supposed to do as a matter of routine. Following this incident I made them rehearse counter-fire drills for hours the next day so that this failure would not occur again.

20 September 2009

Today was a very quiet day after the events of yesterday. All of the government officials are gone and the enemy seems to be celebrating Eid somewhere else. The PRT Cdr finally came back from Barge Matal. We had a sitdown with them tonight to work through developing a joint vision for our AO. For too long there really hasn't been one, and I couldn't get them to adhere to our standards. With him back we should be able to fix both.

I had the TOC doing drills today to get our CF (counter-fire) procedures down. Plus I had a UAV (unmanned aerial vehicle) flown over the launch site during the historical attack hours, and we are going to continue doing so from now on for proactive counter-fire. Also, we are going to do "registrations" (live fire of artillery) at those locations during the historical times to deter future launches or kill the enemy in the act.

The PRT commander had spent over a month at Barge Matal during the fight there to work on addressing damage caused by the fighting. In his absence the PRT was in chaos without a firm leader. His return would provide order that had been missing for some time.

21 September 2009

No enemy activity today and no local government officials either. They are all gone for Eid. That made my weekly radio address tough. My interpreter, Daud Mohammed, is gone to Kabul, and I had to use one of the other guys. Well, none of them is even close to being as good as mine. It was pretty painful getting through the address without him.

The ANA BC invited me to lunch with him today for Eid, which was nice. Especially since I am actively trying to get rid of him. As I have had a chance to observe him over the past several weeks, I have noted that he is a horrible leader who does not set an example and doesn't know what he is doing. As we have tried to implement the training program for certifying his guns (as we would do with ours), he has been the single biggest factor that is holding the unit back. The soldiers want to learn, but the BC disrupts everything. He just doesn't want his battery to know anything so that he can retain all knowledge and thus power. What a poor way to lead. Well, he won't be there much longer if I can help it.

COL is coming tomorrow, and we will brief him on our Nuralam operation. Then on Wednesday I am headed out to Abad to see C Btry.

The Afghan Army battery commander was becoming a thorn in our sides in our effort to train the unit to better execute its mission. As the leader of the unit, he should have been at the forefront of training, but instead he sought to prevent his officers and noncommissioned officers from learning anything. In the Afghan culture many leaders seek to retain all knowledge of something in order to use it as power over those whom they lead. Any sharing of knowledge is seen as a threat to that power. Therefore, many leaders guard their prerogatives rather than building a better team. If the Afghan Army is going to become a capable and independent force, they have to be well trained. The obstructionism of the battery commander would never lead to a competent unit. So, I made it a priority to get him replaced with a better leader.

22 September 2009

Today was a crazy day. First, the COL visited today, and I had him meet the ANA BC. The BC demonstrated for me exactly why he should be relieved through his own antics. Then we briefed the COL on the Nuralam operation and he gave us some guidance on it.

The maneuver PLT almost tipped a vehicle today on the ASR (a dirt road designated as our alternate supply route) east of the river, but luckily the recovery team was able to right it with no injuries or damage.

Then the real excitement came with the PRT. First, they lost a pair of NVGs (night vision goggles), and then one of the Navy senior NCOs hurt himself going down a cliff to the river to check an intake pipe—while carrying a fishing pole. These guys act like we are in one big game here. They are killing me. If it were my soldiers, I would hammer someone, but they cover it up under the mantle of checking a pipe. The NCO (who works in the intel shop) should not have even been there in the first place. He wasn't there to check a pipe. He was there for fun. I don't want my soldiers seeing this stuff because they will then do the same thing. I just can't believe the stuff that goes on in that organization. I am getting sick of it and want it to stop. As the landowner (commander of the area) here, they need to get on board (with our standards).

I go to Abad tomorrow to visit C Btry.

I was becoming frustrated with the PRT. Their commander had been gone for over a month, and many standards were loose during this time. The incident in which the noncommissioned officer was hurt attempting to go down to the river to fish is an example of the lowered standards. A medevac helicopter had to come in to pull the NCO up from the river, which was walled by a steep cliff on both banks. This wasted a precious medical asset in a combat zone. Further, there was little security with the group of people that made their way down to the river. If the enemy had noted their presence and decided to attack this gaggle, there might have been several unnecessary casualties. Finally, I was concerned that my own soldiers might see this behavior and start to mimic it. Fortunately, the leadership of headquarters battery remained tight and the discipline of the soldiers stayed intact, and we never had such an incident in our unit.

23 September 2009

Police pay finally arrived today, and then we found out that it was promptly withheld (rather than paid out to the district police paymasters) because it has to go to Parun. Then why the heck was it sent here in the first place? It is so frustrating in this country. You try to do the right thing, and then you can't because of some dumb law, or corruption, or something that prevents you from assisting effectively.

Also, I had a soldier from HHB shoot a machine gun round through the floor of a hut today. Luckily, no one was killed, but it was just ridiculous. So, yet another stupid situation that I have to deal with.

Tomorrow is the security shura. Hopefully, we can make some headway on police pay.

While I was up at Asadabad visiting C Battery, the pay for the police finally arrived. My executive officer began making the arrangements to have the pay distributed to the district police. However, the provincial bank found out that the money had come to Kalagush and alerted the governor, who stopped the paymasters from drawing the pay. He sent instructions to have the money moved to Parun first and then distributed. The governor was correct in doing this, since it is the law that the money must first go to the provincial bank. However, this provides the opportunity to skim. Also, it would add at least two more weeks to the timeline before the police would actually receive anything. By having the pay transported to Kalagush we could ensure more timely payment and guarantee that the police would get their entire earnings. The governor's order would prevent this and frustrate the police in the districts. My concern was that this delay would cause the police to walk off the job, creating an acute security situation to the detriment of the people of the province. Again, our effort to streamline administration was obstructed for the corrupt purposes of a government official.

24 September 2009

We did the security shura today down in the Nurgaram district center. Sikander Laghmani ran the meeting, which went pretty well. Both SGs (that were in attendance) are upset about the police pay issue and worried about corruption if the police don't get paid before the money goes to Parun. Hamid Osmani also is mad about the lack of action by elders in the area. He thinks if they would take a more active role in their own security and turn in weapons, then things would be a lot better. He is right. He spoke about his frustration with others who won't take action to make things better.

We have intel that there may be a bomb maker present in our AO teaching the cell here how to construct bombs. This is not good. We have been hearing for some time that the cell in our area wanted to bring in a trainer to help build bombs for IEDs. Now it looks like it is happening.

We launch our Nuralam operation on Saturday, and hopefully that op will help us take out this cell, or at least the munitions they have stockpiled. I am really hopeful that this op can help us tip the scale in our favor for the local area. We rehearsed with the ANA today.

Tomorrow we will have our commander's conference. All the BCs and 1SGs are here tonight, and it will be a good day tomorrow.

The sub-governors had a legitimate concern over the status of the pay. They understood as well as I did that if the pay was not distributed at Kalagush, it would be weeks before the police received their wages. Further, they knew that the police would not get their full pay if the payroll went to Parun. This was a source of irritation for them as well as myself. We were attempting to convince the governor to distribute the pay locally for many logical reasons that we hoped would appeal to him. However, our efforts were not working out as we desired. I found the intelligence about the bomb maker in the area disturbing. If the enemy gained the capability to make IEDs locally, it would seriously affect our freedom of movement. We believed that our operation in the Nuralam could have a disruptive effect on the enemy, forcing the bomb maker to leave the area. We would launch the operation within 48 hours.

25 September 2009

Today I conducted the Cdr's conference. We covered a lot of ground, including personnel moves, realigning our firebases, taking care of and training new soldiers, and making our fires more effective through lessons learned. The main thing we needed to do was ensure everyone was on the same sheet of music. I think we are now set for the next phase of our tour.

I had Sikander Laghmani come in today to talk with the COL about Barge Matal and what was happening there. The COL came in for the Cdr's conference, and it was a golden opportunity to have Laghmani talk with him. Laghmani has been tapped to be the Barge Matal sub-governor if he is willing to accept the job. The heavy fighting there recently makes the job very difficult. Laghmani is from Barge Matal and is ready to take the job with some conditions.

1. Support for defense (of the district)
2. Budget to get the job done and form shura
3. Provincial governor out (Laghmani did not like the governor and no longer wanted to work with him)

The last item on this list will be the toughest to pull off, but that guy has got to go because he is the most corrupt and ineffective leader imaginable. While Laghmani would be great for Barge Matal, that would leave Nurgaram hurting. This district has done very well under his leadership, and what worries me is that a dirtbag could get appointed in Laghmani's place. I asked him for recommendations as to who would be a good replacement, and he said the current SG of Mandol. He might be OK, but he has been fairly ineffective in Mandol. However, he gets little support, so he might be OK here (in Nurgaram). If Laghmani recommends him, then he is probably OK.

Tomorrow we will launch our op in the Nuralam.

My conference with the battery commanders enabled me to implement much of the changes agreed to at the fire support conference. Pushing changes and the new agenda for fires from the direction of the commanders combined with the fire support officers would ensure that we could actually see them through to fruition. With our commanders' help, we would make our fires align with sound counter-insurgency strategy.

The Nurgaram district governor's impending move to Barge Matal con-

cerned me because any replacement might be far less effective than Sikander Laghmani. He was a known quantity, and I was already aware of his strengths and weaknesses. There was a real possibility that his replacement would have little ability and engage in corruption. However, the situation in Barge Matal was critical and Laghmani's presence there could potentially stabilize the situation. Therefore, he had to go to attempt to bring the area under control.

26–27 September 2009

I went out into the Nuralam for the past two days with our maneuver platoon, the MPs, and the ANA battery. We planned this op to gather intel over an extended period of time to try to fill gaps in our information about the Nuralam Valley. And we got a lot of good info. We figured out shortly after we got there that, rather than Dow Ab being our biggest problem, instead it is the Nuralam in Alingar. It is a major transit area for bad guys, arms, and money. Our enemy cell operates there as well, and our whole intent was to fill in some blanks while disrupting enemy operations in the area. We did just that and confused the heck out of the enemy. Some of the info we got:

- We learned who killed the ANA soldier during the election disruption operation
- Figured out that the ANP CoP (chief of police) in Alingar is protecting the cell
- Took pictures of the house where the cell leader lives and operates
- Did some biometric survey

Now hopefully we can turn some of the info into action against the enemy.

Today I sponsored an Eid shura for Alingar with the PRT. It was good to finally have the PRT Cdr involved with me in a shura. Our combined effort could make some real headway in AO Steel. Lack of cooperation will only cause friction.

I spent a couple of days in the field with our platoons, patrolling the area around the mouth of the Nuralam Valley. The operation, as noted above, gave us a treasure trove of information that our intelligence team would use to analyze and piece together what was happening with regard to the enemy in the Nuralam Valley. This valley represented a key piece of terrain that the enemy had to control to maintain their operations and a link to the Konar's notorious Waigul, Pech, and Rechalam valleys. Our operations in the Nuralam disrupted the enemy to such an extent that it became a strongly contested area. Therefore, we determined that this valley would become our priority for operations for much of the remainder of our year.

28 September 2009

Today was the second Eid shura, this time for Nurgaram. It went very well and focused on security. Sikander Laghmani could not attend because he went to Barge Matal to assess the situation there to see if it is feasible to become the SG there. His deputy (hereafter noted as Sakhi al-Nuralam) took charge and did fine. SG Hamid Osmani, who is the district governor of Dow Ab and lives in Nurgaram, also participated. He is the best pure leader I have met in Afghanistan. He asks for little and expects his people to do the right thing for Afghanistan. I think he should be the provincial governor instead of Mullah Kabir. The only issue is that he is not well connected politically in Kabul and it would be hard for him to get the appointment. I will offer up the name and see if we can get some momentum.

I also talked to Osmani about some of the intel we gained. He is all about taking out bad guys. The problem here is that our rules are so restrictive that it makes it difficult for us to do it. He would be willing to get some people together to do the job. This is something that could work. An Afghan solution to an Afghan problem.

Tomorrow is the Dow Ab Eid shura.

As with all other major holidays and events, I made it a point to honor the Afghans by hosting shuras with them. This enabled us to maintain our strong relationships, but it was also a chance to discuss issues like security. Much of the intelligence we gained in the Nuralam was confirmed by several of the local leaders, including Hamid Osmani. He was an aggressive leader and, as I stated previously, is one of the few Afghans whom I maintained respect for throughout my tour in Afghanistan. His assistance to us was certainly appreciated and a rarity among the leaders I encountered.

29 September 2009

Today was the final Eid shura for Dow Ab, and it went very well. Hamid Osmani again impressed me with the way he handled the meeting. He focused on what the elders should do to ensure security in the area and that they have to take responsibility. Also, he said the elders should convince the enemy to reconcile. He is actively working this himself, with one already brought in and two more in the queue ready to come in. I had worried before we got here that Dow Ab would be my biggest concern, but with Osmani in charge it is not. Our Nuralam op uncovered some great intel and really helped us piece the puzzle together in Alingar. This area around the Nuralam is our biggest concern, and if we could defeat the cell there, we win in AO Steel. We just need to find an indirect way of doing it.

I am going to start actively working to get the Alingar chief of police relieved and a new guy in place. This is part of that indirect approach combined with our IO and engagement plan.

Good news from the FA (field artillery) evaluation team. They told me today in the outbrief that we are the best FA Bn in RC (Regional Command) East, hands down. My biggest worry in taking command was delivery of fires, but now it is our greatest strength and I am proud of all of our artillerymen.

While it was absolutely correct that our biggest challenge in the area of operation was the Nuralam, it was premature of me to think that Dow Ab would not become a thorn in our side. The district governor had done an excellent job with attempting to reconcile low-level fighters and welding the village elders into a security network. Yet he lacked resources to solidify his gains. He needed the provincial government to provide him with support in the form of political capital and other resources, but the governor would not provide this aid. As a result, Osmani struggled to expand the authority of the district, provincial, and national governments in his area. The enemy used this vacuum in governance to regenerate power in Dow Ab and then conduct operations in the district and into neighboring Nurgaram. However, for the time being all was calm in Dow Ab District.

30 September 2009

I had a good chance to catch up on some things today, including counseling my former rear d. cdr who arrived a couple of days ago (from Colorado). He was so bad back there that as soon as his dwell time was up I had him come over immediately and sent my top staff officer back to take over in the rear. I had wanted to keep his replacement in Afghanistan longer and switch out in November but could not afford to do it any longer. When I counseled him I laid it out that if he did not work on the things that I told him were deficient, he would never command and his career would be over. I hate to have to tell someone something like that, but it is the truth. I can't place a guy in command who can't hack it or take care of soldiers. It would be wrong. So, either he improves or he is done. The most painful part of command has been having to tell guys along the way that they were not cutting it. On a personal level I like all of the guys whom I had to be honest with, but on a professional level I have to tell it like it is. If an officer either through laziness or pure inability cannot properly command tactically or care for our nation's most precious resource, soldiers, then they have to go. Therefore, I have to tell them the truth as part of my duty as a commander. I just hate having to do it.

1 October 2009

I visited our A (battery) PLT at Khogyani today, and they are doing fine while making many improvements to their firebase. All the firing elements are doing very well, and we have had only a couple of issues since we have been here and I am happy with the performance of the LTs and PSGs.

We did 3 patrols in our AO today, and the only thing of significance is that the chief of police in Alingar is his usual corrupt self. He would not patrol with the MPs today without us providing him fuel, and when we said we couldn't, he would not do it because he said he did not have any gas for his vehicles. Then, while the MPs were out, they saw multiple ANP vehicles transporting civilians like it was a taxi service. He also refuses to patrol at night because "there are no issues at night." This is just a way to protect the movement of people (enemy) and munitions through the area. Since he gets a cut, it is in his interest to not patrol and keep us away too. One of my missions is to get rid of this guy. We will never be able to beat the enemy east of the Alingar River until he is gone and a competent guy is in place.

The chief of police in Alingar routinely asked us to provide him with fuel so that he could patrol with us. He would then take the gas and sell it on the black market. About a month into our deployment we stopped providing any fuel to the Afghan government officials or police, which was common practice previously. I quickly realized that all this did was create a dependence on our forces, and worse, a source of income for corrupt officials. So, I put a stop to it. Many of the officials did not like the fact that we had cut them off and became belligerent with us, as in the case of the chief in Alingar. Nevertheless, if Afghanistan is ever to stand on its own, the government must look to its own resources rather than depend on the United States.

2 October 2009

Today in the TGTing meeting I went in with the PRT Cdr to brief our joint vision to both staffs. For too long we were not moving in the same direction, and while he was in Barge Matal there was not enough cooperation. With their Cdr back and us both having made a joint statement of the way ahead, everybody should get on board. Success here depends on us both moving ahead in the same direction.

3 October 2009

Disaster today at Kamdesh in the east. COP (Combat Outpost) Keating was overrun. The enemy breached the wire by the ANA camp and rolled up the rest of the base until the 3–61 soldiers were holed up in one building. The ANA ran away, leaving only a few defenders and the U.S. unit. It was disgusting. We sent multiple artillery resupplies to them today and prepared our guns from two firebases to move forward to provide more support. 7 KIAs and 11 WIA from the fight so far, with several of the remaining ANA dead or wounded. There are 50 dead enemies in the compound. I am disgusted by the lack of leadership by the Afghans from the governor to the ANA. They are a big joke. If they won't make their own country better, then why should we? 8 years into this thing and they are content to let us do everything for them. They need to step up, weed out the turds, and take charge, or we should leave them to their own devices. I believe in what we are doing here and that we must win, but the Afghans don't seem to care about their own cause. It is very frustrating.

Above and opposite: The first photograph depicts G Company soldiers preparing to hook up a generator for slingload by a CH-47 cargo helicopter. In the second the soldiers have hooked the load to the aircraft and are running out of the way so that the helicopter can take off with the load for delivery to the outlying location. Our logistic company kept the battalion running by conducting ground and aerial resupply every day during our year in Afghanistan. Without this hard-working company, our unit could not have sustained operations in the manner we did for twelve long months (courtesy Major Carrie Brunner).

III. Execution: 24 August 2009 to 6 December 2009

Our artillery firebase at Naray supported this battle, firing more than 1,000 rounds of 155mm ammunition in the effort to defend the base over a 48-hour period. They were firing so fast that we had to scramble to push ammunition by slingload to the platoon in Naray. At several points during the fight the guns were short on high explosive rounds. To keep the guns firing, we stripped several of our other firebases of ammunition.

This is the first entry in which I directly state the opinion that the Afghans are doing little for themselves and allowing our forces to carry the majority of the burden in the fight. The Afghan Army at COP Keating performed very poorly in this battle, allowing the enemy to penetrate their portion of the perimeter, thus endangering the whole base. Further, the politicians did little to build credibility or govern altruistically, which provided an opening for the enemy to make inroads with the people. The result is that Americans shouldered the majority of the responsibility in Afghanistan, with the local leaders all too happy to sit back and let us do most of the hard work. At this point, with several Americans dead and many more wounded, my patience was nearing its breaking point, although it would not break until I lost some of my own soldiers a short time later. I was beginning to come to the conclusion that our tactic in Afghanistan had to change. Our policy had to force the Afghans to take the reins for their own good. Until this was the case, victory was not possible.

4 October 2009

All the wounded and KIAs were flown out of Keating today, and tonight it looks like the whole post will be evacuated. We were planning on leaving the post in a week anyway, so I am sure the enemy got wind of it and made the attack as an opportunity to say that they forced us out. Of course, a lie, but something this enemy does well in spite of their platitudes about their religion.

I had my staff working on a couple of plans to send reinforcing artillery in the future if we need to. I wish I had my platoon back from Torkham (where they performed the border security mission) because if I did I would have the capability to do it without taking down a firebase. But I don't, so we are making plans for it anyway.

Also, have the staff working on a plan to clear the Titin Valley. There is a legal gem mine there now, and a secure valley could stimulate economic growth associated with the mine. I have been wanting to do some work up there for a while and now I have an excuse.

Evidence of the success of our Nuralam Valley op came in today. Reports came in that the IED cell dispersed because of worries that we were getting too close to them. We will keep up the pressure.

The enemy in Afghanistan has a very good network for gathering information about coalition operations. Our brigade had planned to close COP Keating in Kamdesh District of eastern Nuristan for some time. The actual closing date was within one week of the attack on the outpost. Armed with the knowledge that the base was closing, the enemy decided to attack before that date. The idea behind this assault was to make it appear that the base's closure was the result of the attack, thus providing the enemy with a victory. I had seen this before in previous tours in Afghanistan, specifically at Bari Kowt in late 2003. The enemy spun this incident as a victory in their effort to "liberate" Nuristan from the coalition forces.

When we assumed responsibility for our area in late June, we had planned to conduct a short operation in the Titin Valley because we had thought that this area was a hotbed of enemy activity. As we learned more about the area, we found that it was of lesser importance, and we focused our operations on other places such as the Nuralam Valley. The impetus behind planning a new operation in the valley was the arrival of a consortium of gem miners at the base. A group of men presented me with the deed for a gem mine that they legally owned in the Titin Valley. After confirming the validity of the claim, we decided to plan a new operation in the valley to confirm that it was safe for them to begin working the mine. The mine apparently produced high-quality emeralds, which are found frequently in the mountains of Nuris-

tan and Panjshir. I viewed this as an opportunity to stimulate some real economic growth in an isolated and depressed area and therefore sought to foster this growth by ensuring that the security situation was stable.

5 October 2009

I went to Sundawar to check on the storm relief effort with SG Mangal Abdullah, and I was very pleased that the canal was repaired and the washout near the retaining wall was nearly fixed as well. The locals were ecstatic and even offered to kill a goat for us for lunch. We had tremendous difficulties here previously with the two ambushes, but now the locals are on our side. We took advantage of the opportunity the storm offered to make headway in the village, and it worked.

In my radio message today I changed the tone a little and spoke about the locals' responsibility for security and corruption. If we are going to win here, two things have to happen:

1. Locals have to take charge of their own security.
2. They have to get rid of corrupt officials.

If these two things don't happen, we can't win, and that will be my focus from now on.

The success in Sundawar represents one of the things our unit did in Afghanistan that I am most proud of. This village was clearly anti-government and anti-coalition when we first arrived. There were two ambushes there—one costing the life of an Afghan soldier—and numerous other reports of the enemy using the village for planning and executing attacks. The village sat astride our main supply route and was a pivotal point in the area that the government and we had to control to maintain stability. The storm, while tragic, gave us an opening, and our focused effort there turned the situation around. From this time forward Sundawar was among the most cooperative villages that we dealt with, and it served as an example to other villages of what they could accomplish if they would seek a peaceful alternative to the Taliban.

The last paragraph of the entry shows that my approach to what we were doing in Afghanistan had changed. Previously, I focused on what we as Americans could do to win. At this point I was starting to shift my attention to what the Afghans needed to do for themselves to achieve victory. In short, they had to take responsibility for their own security and the officials had to govern as servants of the nation rather than serving themselves. Convincing Afghans of the need to get on board with this philosophy would prove extremely frustrating, but it was now our main line of effort.

6 October 2009

Everyone is out of Keating now and the old base is being leveled by B-52s. Apparently, 150 fighters died in the attack, a 15:1 ratio. They did this just to make it look like the pullout was forced by them even though it was something we were planning for some time.

The ANA LNO (liaison officer) in Nurgaram told me that the TB is not done in E. Nuristan. He said the TB plans to attack three other locations, including Monti, where I have a firebase, to isolate. He would not reveal his source to me, but I think it is credible because I would do the same thing if I was the enemy.

I immediately called the BCT S3 and Cdr of 1-32 to let them know what was going on. The 1-32 Cdr, whom I knew from being the former XO of 3/10th Mtn, said that he had been getting the same info to that effect and said it corroborated some of the info he was getting.

We staged more ammo to push to our guns at Naray if they need it tonight from 3 other FBs in the AO.

Tomorrow I will travel to ML (Mehtar Lam) to visit A & G.

Immediately after the election the Afghan National Army posted a colonel at the provincial operation coordination center in Nurgaram. The colonel became a great friend of our unit. He was competent and worked hard for Afghanistan. As illustrated in this entry, he never hesitated to seek me out to share important information that could facilitate our success. Attacks did pick up in the east, but the enemy was defeated in their effort. Within another few weeks we would become the target of a serious assault at Kalagush.

7 October 2009

I went down to Mehtar Lam today to visit A & G, and all is going pretty well there. I am concerned about where the ANA compound (at Mehtar Lam) is situated. It is right behind both of the unit CPs (command posts) and is not very defensible. The last three attacks on our locations in Afghanistan have focused on breaching the ANA side (of the respective firebases). If they (the enemy) did that at ML, they would quickly be right in the middle of the perimeter. So, I told both A & G to reinforce the wall to the rear with wire, fighting positions, and fixing a couple of gaps.

Other than that, it was a quiet day in our AO. Tomorrow I have the security shura in Alingar. It is time to start turning up the pressure on some of those guys (chiefs of police) to start contributing.

8 October 2009

I had a notable success today. The CoP of Alingar was fired today. This was an objective of mine so that we could get a competent guy in place. I don't know if the new man will be any better, but I am hopeful. With the right officials I think we can make a difference.

The police may finally get paid in a few days. We have had to put pressure on the governor to do it, but it looks like that might finally happen. If the DoS rep had not obstructed our plan to pay it out here when it arrived (at Kalagush), we would have been fine a month ago. But we are still screwing around with this because she said the governor was correct in having the money deposited in Parun because of Afghan law. Funny how Afghan officials never follow the law, but when it comes to their financial interests they are all for it.

The information on the firing of the Alingar chief of police proved premature. He was recalled to provincial headquarters, but he was not fired. We would have to build more evidence and enlist assistance from the people to actually get him removed.

The pay issue was finally coming to a close. At the time the cash had arrived at Kalagush it was our intent to have the three local districts of Nuristan paid before the money went to Parun so that the officers could receive their full salaries. However, the Department of State representative at the PRT did not support our effort to distribute the pay from Kalagush before reaching Parun. She was absolutely correct in asserting the irregularity of this procedure. However, I knew what would happen if the money made it to Parun before our districts were paid: the police would only get one half to two thirds of their earnings. I sought to prevent this, but failed. So, I clashed with the state rep in my anger. Nevertheless, we continued to try finding a viable solution to the pay issue so that our police would not lose any of their earnings. By the time of our departure from Afghanistan, we finally developed a fix for the problem.

9 October 2009

We continue to move ammo around to support C Btry, which is firing a lot to defend the positions in E. Nuristan. In our own AO we continue to learn more about the characters that are moving through the Nuralam and the IED cell. The cell has been disrupted and we learned that Parwai village is not very supportive of us, primarily because they are being coerced. We will try to have some nonlethal effects in there to sway opinion, similar to what we have done in Sundawar directly across the river.

We got pictures today from PFC Birr's award ceremony. GEN Vessey pinned on Birr's PH (Purple Heart) and ARCOM (Army Commendation Medal). I was very happy to see that and his family was very appreciative. Birr was missing a good chunk of his head on the right side. That was a little disconcerting, but considering what he has been through he is doing great, and it is a miracle he is alive.

10 October 2009

I went up to Gandalabuk today to gauge the threat to the north. There have been reports that, with the loss of projects in Dow Ab and the attack in Kamdesh, the enemy up there wants to attack down here. In talking to the road construction site manager and the ANP up there, I don't believe that anything will be coming down this way, especially with winter coming on. I think our focus on the Nuralam in Alingar is the right place to get results and stop the enemy in our AO.

Worked through some of the police issues today and I think the pay might actually start moving this way, plus we should be able to keep their current manning levels. We will need them because without any other presence from ANSF we need as many police as we can get.

I was wrong in my assessment that we would not have issues with the enemy from Dow Ab. Within a month of writing this entry we would have a series of incidents and a major attack on our firebase perpetrated by the Dow Ab cell. The reports that I had been receiving were correct, and I should have given them more credence.

While we were close to solving the pay issue, there arose an effort to cut the number of police in the local districts. The police were critical to security because they represented tangible evidence of the government's control of the area. Any effort to reduce the number of police would prove detrimental to security operations. Therefore, we fought these efforts to slash the force and were ultimately successful.

11 October 2009

Met with the Nurgaram chief of police about retaining his police force intact, and I think we will be able to do it. We had a guy call wanting to turn in a mortar with some rounds, but he never showed up. The NDS chief in Alingar vouched for him and said he would help bring him in tomorrow. I sure hope so. The last thing we need is an effective mortar attack here with the lack of hardened roofs on the FOB. Not too much else happening today. Did get some pictures from home, where they had an ice storm.

Nothing like that here, but I wish it would happen so the enemy would freeze out there at night.

12 October 2009

Many developments today. First, I went down into the Nuralam to a village that lost its retaining wall in the storm last month, meeting with the district village affairs rep. This village is a good place to build relationships and deny the AAF (anti–Afghan forces, a euphemism for the enemy) operational space, so if we can do a couple of small projects, we can potentially place an obstacle in the way in the Nuralam.

Last night the Mangow ANA CP (a checkpoint that the Afghan Army had in the village of Mangow east of the Alingar River) was attacked by the enemy, and we fired illum in support as they successfully defended their post. We will visit there tomorrow and also begin work on projects there to deny the enemy that place as well.

Finally, there was some timber smuggling going on in Nurgaram that has implicated certain provincial officials, which, if true, could be the break we need to get rid of them. We might have a date for the Pashai-Gajour jirga finally. I find out tomorrow.

My visit to the village of Paranieh in the Nuralam was part of an effort to target specific villages with development projects around our area in key locations. These locations were critical for the enemy in carrying out their operations. Denying the enemy access to these villages would enable the government to expand its authority and facilitate our own freedom of movement. Therefore, we focused on villages in the Nuralam, on the east side of the Alingar River, and along our main supply route on the west side of the river. Using Sundawar as our model, we believed that we could replicate the same success and win the people over to the government.

The attack in Mangow was significant because this was one of our targeted villages. We had several small-scale development projects starting in that village. The enemy was attempting to prevent us from carrying these through by intimidating the people there. The Afghan Army had established a checkpoint at this critical location with about 15 soldiers. Their sustained presence protected the people and the projects, frustrating the enemy in their attempts to wrest control of the village from the government.

Timber and gem smuggling were recurring problems in eastern Afghanistan, including in Nuristan Province. Smuggling activities were run by thugs with the approval of government officials. Engaging in these illegal activities avoided taxation and brought enormous profit to the smugglers, who paid the government officials to look the other way rather than enforcing the law. The enemy noted this blatant corruption and used it to demonstrate the weakness and graft of the government. This presented us with a challenge because if the government did not act honorably, then the people would turn on them, creating a difficult security situation. Again the governor of the province, along with his chief of police and some of the district police, was engaged in corruption. I had to find a way to get these men removed for the good of the people of Nuristan and ultimately Afghanistan.

13 October 2009

I went to visit FB Garcia (on the Pakistan border in Nangarhar Province) today, and within 10 minutes of my arrival there I found out that an airplane crashed in AO Steel up in Dow Ab—we think. I couldn't believe it. We spun up our maneuver platoon to be the force to secure the site for the search and rescue people. The problem is that the crash site has still not been located as of tonight. So, we are on standby. The place where they thought it went down was in the Showk Valley of Dow Ab, which is known HiG (Hezb-Islami-Gulbuddin, a political group in competition with the Taliban for control of the insurgency) country. If it is in there, we would have to fight just to get to the site and to get the bodies out. The bad guys have been heard on the radio saying that they think we are getting ready to attack up there. There have been other conflicting reports about the enemy having found the bodies. We don't know what is happening but are standing by should we be needed.

The information we were getting on the plane crash was sketchy. All we really knew was that a fixed-wing military aircraft had crashed somewhere north of Kalagush. The aircraft actually went down on the side of a 14,000-foot mountain in the Dow Ab District. The remoteness of the crash site prevented the enemy from discovering its location. It took a few days to figure out where it went down to enable the recovery team to clear the site. The enemy, seeing all the overflights searching for the wreckage, thought that we were conducting reconnaissance in preparation for an attack to the north. Many reports came in through our intelligence channels telling us of the rumors swirling through the enemy network. The enemy was in the dark, which worked to our advantage.

14 October 2009

Another unexpectedly busy day. First, I met with the Dow Ab SG Hamid Osmani to discuss the plane crash and we ended up talking about politics and other items. He again laid out how the governor was corrupt and that there is now a movement among Nuristanis to have him removed. There are a few candidates to replace him, but none are really viable.

There were many overflights today by the recon aircraft looking for the crash site, which still has not been located. Then this afternoon 2 Apaches were shot at from the Wadawu by tracer fire. They (the aircraft) engaged with rockets and machine guns, and we watched the whole thing. It was unbelievable.

Tonight Osmani brought a shifty character named Mawlawi Mohammed who said he knows people who know where the plane went down. But he wants money to tell us. I couldn't believe it. The greed of these people is beyond disgusting. Everything has a price, and every Afghan just seems to want to know what is in it for them before they do anything, if they are even willing to do anything to begin with.

We are making arrangements to have this guy mark the location so we can find it, with the understanding that he gets nothing if we can't get the bodies and wreckage safely. This guy knows where the plane is and he just wants a payoff. It is unbelievable. Are these people who always tout the superiority of their religion to us a true representation of the faith? How can they possibly want to profit from the deaths of a couple of pilots if they are true to their religion? Every person here is a conniver seeking their own benefit and wouldn't do anything to help themselves, much less anyone else. It just makes me sick.

Once again I was thoroughly disgusted by the greedy nature of the Afghans. I had arrived in Afghanistan with the idea that the people would act in a more honorable manner. This expectation was based on previous tours in the country and the wealth of literature I read in preparation for the mission, all of which pointed to the noble and independent nature of the Afghan people. Yet most of what I had seen so far convinced me that finding anyone with altruistic motivations in Afghanistan was truly a rarity. This latest incident further eroded my expectations. When the source arrived I thought that we might have a break in the mystery of where the aircraft went down. Shortly into our conversation the source immediately turned the discussion toward payment for the information. He would not even begin to speak of the location of the aircraft until a price was negotiated for finding it. I became very irritated, but I knew that we might have to "get dirty" in order to recover the bodies of the pilots. The whole process was extremely distasteful, and I despaired of achieving success in Afghanistan if we could not find an honest man.

15 October 2009

Our source got a couple of items to mark the site of the crash today and then departed. I think he knew all along where the plane went down but would not tell because he wants reward money. We should find out something tomorrow. I have the maneuver platoon ready to provide support if they are needed. However, we have them out doing their patrols because I did not want to cede AO Steel to the enemy while we were waiting for word about the A/C (aircraft) location.

The platoon went down to the Mangow CP to see the ANA that fought off the enemy the other night, and there was evidence of quite a fight. The platoon also found evidence that they (the ANA) did at least wound one enemy, finding a blood trail. We gave them some more ammo. Those guys and their SGT have done a great job on that side of the river. I just wish there were some more troops to help them have more of an effect. I am working it, though. The MPs were informed that there might be an IED on the Mashpah Valley road. The ANP will head there tomorrow, and if one is found, we will get EOD up here. Finally have date for the jirga between the Gajour and Pashai. If the government can finally settle this, it will go a long way toward demonstrating their effectiveness and preventing enemy inroads.

The source did not actually know the location of the downed aircraft. He went up into Dow Ab for several days in search of the crash site without success. One of the reconnaissance overflights finally found the site, and we did not have to deal with this slimy individual again. I was very happy that I did not have to pay for information to such a disgusting person. Subsequent entries describe the actual outcome.

The district governors finally came together to plan a jirga to bring peace between the Gajour and Pashai tribes. They did this with no help from the provincial government. I had prodded the government officials since August to bring about a solution to the problem so that it would not recur and, more important, to prevent the enemy from filling the vacuum. This was a gratifying development among all the frustrations of the week. Yet the conflict between the tribes was still not resolved.

16 October 2009

Source is in the Showk Valley, which we did not expect. If the downed aircraft is in this valley, it could be a very bad situation because there is a lot of known enemy in there. It would require a lot of force to go in, extract the bodies, destroy any components remaining and then get out, but we will see where this thing ends up.

We sent out two patrols tonight, one north and one south. Signal flares went up when they left. We have seen that to the south before, but never to the north. This is in line with our recent reports that say the enemy believes we are preparing an attack to the north. Also, we saw lights flashing in the ANA CP outside the base. These are MoI (ministry of the interior) soldiers and not MoD (ministry of defense personnel), therefore of questionable quality. It seems these guys were signaling their buddies in the hills. So, we sent the ANA and marines out to question them, which scared them to death. Tomorrow I will have them questioned by our intel team. Then I am calling their commander to have them placed under arrest and replaced by more reliable people.

The enemy was watching the base due to the fact that they expected an attack to the north. The flurry of activity in Dow Ab made the enemy edgy, and they were closely monitoring our activities to prevent a surprise assault. Of course, we did not have any intention of attacking the enemy in Dow Ab. The enemy signaling revealed the extent of their network, including the fact that they had infiltrated the security guards of the Ministry of Interior. Understanding how the enemy network gathered intelligence was important to our own security, and the crash was providing us with usable information.

17 October 2009

Still nothing in the effort to find the crashed aircraft except that another freaking aircraft went down looking for it. Unbelievable. This one had a hard landing on a 14,000-foot mountain. Luckily, the whole crew was extracted safely, but the aircraft is still up there and will probably have to be destroyed because it can't be lifted out and probably can't take off at that altitude. We will see tomorrow.

Today the Wadawu Valley elders came to see me. They are concerned after hearing our radio message discussing the attack on the helicopters and stopping development in the valley. I told them that if they didn't start rejecting the Taliban, then we would not invest anymore in their valley. They were profuse in their promises that this would not happen again, but said that they do not know who the "thieves" are. I told them that they know, and if they want development, they have to report enemy activity. Finally, they went down to the radio station with me and did their own message denouncing the enemy and pledging their cooperation with us.

Following the attack on the Apache helicopters from a few days before, I went on the radio to denounce the attack. At that time I intimated that all development projects in the Wadawu Valley would be cancelled unless the elders began to cooperate in stopping the enemy. The elders came to see me in order to convince me of their loyalty to the government and their commitment to peace. I played hardball with them, telling them that they were not committed to peace if they were not willing to identify insurgents in the valley. I told the elders that unless they began to cooperate for the security of the area, development projects would not continue. Further, I told them they had to make an announcement on the radio indicating their stance. The elders did so, but insurgent activity unfortunately continued and we were no longer inclined to assist with development.

18 October 2009

After a month of pushing, the Gajour-Pashai shura/jirga started today. This should finally solve the problem of the village burning and hopefully will result in a land use deal between the two tribes. The semi-nomadic Gajour use lands where they move, which "infringes" on the owners, who demand a "tax" for use. This is what ignited the problem in the first place. It was important to solve this problem because failure to do so will result in the Gajour becoming a recruiting pool for the TB. They are already discriminated against by the other tribes, and so they make a readily exploitable manpower pool for the enemy. When the government does not solve their problems, then the TB takes advantage and co-opts those who feel there is no justice.

I was very pleased to witness the start of the jirga. The government had to solve the land use issue in order to prevent the two sides from becoming susceptible to enemy propaganda. The Gajour, because of their semi-nomadic culture, are looked down on in Afghan society. As an already downtrodden tribe, the Taliban targeted the Gajour as recruits for their movement. Solving the dispute was paramount in maintaining security in our area—thus my intense interest in a peaceful solution.

19 October 2009

May have a break on the timber smuggling activity. If we can get rid of some of the corruption in the province, we may have a chance to build a semi-competent government focused on the people rather than self-interest. However, I have to admit that I am losing confidence in finding any honest officials. A functioning government starts with trust, but I despair that there might not be anyone who places the interest of the people above their own. All I can do is try to find a few good people, but there is a serious deficit of that here.

Looks like the crashed airplane was finally found. Tomorrow we are going to provide assistance to the Division Aviation with recovery. The plane is at 14,000 feet and north of the Showk Valley, where the enemy is at. So, they should recover it without issues from the enemy. The real enemy will be terrain and altitude.

As one can see in the entry above, I was losing confidence in the local officials and my frustration was increasing steadily. Nevertheless, I had to keep pressing to build better governance in the area. That meant I had to have patience to facilitate bringing in leaders with a greater level of competence and ethical behavior. I was becoming jaded by the constant stream of corruption I witnessed. A few honest government and police officials could have made a world of difference for the people. Our battalion, along with all the other Americans in Afghanistan, did amazing work in providing security and facilitating development in the country. Yet the Afghan leaders seemed intent on enriching themselves rather than working for the betterment of their people. This lesson was sinking into my mind, and I came to the realization that it was not up to us to win in Afghanistan. The battle in the country was political. Competent politicians were required to win. Our forces could only create the conditions for Afghan success; they had to take advantage of the opportunity we were providing them. The more I observed, the less I believed that the Afghan officials would actually take charge of their own affairs.

20 October 2009

The COL brought the ANA Bde commander up today to gauge the leadership ability of the ANA BC. I have sent many updates to the COL about the incompetence of this guy. Today the (ANA) Bde Cdr saw it firsthand. So, that guy will be out of here and another one will replace him shortly. I just hope he is competent and cares about what he is doing.

I have come to the conclusion that I can have the greatest intent in the world to help in Afghanistan, but until leaders here begin to take charge competently and with care, it doesn't matter what I do. Winning in Afghanistan depends on competent government leaders. Since most are corrupt, all we can do is maintain a stalemate. The balance between winning and losing will only tilt positive when there are more competent leaders here than incompetent. The government holds the key. If they are not willing to step up, then we are wasting our time here in Afghanistan.

Word today of a runoff election after Karzai conceded under pressure that he didn't win 50% (of the vote) outright. So, we will get ready to do it all over again.

The battery commander for the Afghan artillery unit was an incompetent leader who provided a textbook case for how not to lead a military unit. I had for some time suggested that a change in command was in order for the good of the battery. Our brigade commander suggested that the Afghan brigade commander visit so he could see for himself the gross incompetence of the battery commander. On this day our commander brought his counterpart along for an inspection visit, and the Afghan brigade commander was not pleased with what he saw. Within days the battery commander was replaced in favor of another man. The new captain was a godsend for the unit and made our training efforts successful. The relief of the old battery commander and his replacement with a competent successor was a source of satisfaction for me as we continued to try to weed out those who could not do their jobs.

The entry above notes my change of heart with regard to what was possible for U.S. forces to achieve in Afghanistan. This was my first overt statement that it was up to Afghans to make the ultimate difference. The nonstop bombardment of demands from Afghan officials combined with their unethical behavior had worn me down. Even after this point I continued to harbor hope that we could turn the corner ourselves. But this attitude would finally and permanently change on 5 December.

21 October 2009

I met with the Nurgaram chief of police today to discuss crime, training, and patrolling. If any progress is to be made here, then we have to have leaders who will step forward and do their job. The chief was not comfortable with me pointing out that there was in fact crime in Nurgaram. Every official will tell you everything is fine in their area while the town is burning down behind them. I told him that the only way to fix a problem is to identify it first. I told him about two corrupt officers he has on his force. We ended with agreement on all after he realized I wasn't going to let go of the subject of patrolling and firing his corrupt officers. We will see if he follows through.

This afternoon the village of Paranieh, where I visited 10 days ago, reported an IED to the police. We got the call and pushed to the site with the maneuver platoon, RCP (route clearance package, made up of military engineers) and EOD. They removed it and brought it here for fingerprinting.

This is good news. I told this village when I was there that development depends on security and, if they saw anything, to report it. Well, they did, and now we will help with their retaining wall.

We were beginning to receive some good information from our sources on the activities of local officials and their organizations. The Nurgaram police had several individuals who were associated with corrupt, illegal, or insurgent activities. Continued behavior such as this would eventually destroy the credibility of the police in the district and hurt the overall security situation. The key to effective policing is honest officers and leaders who are willing to investigate and fire those involved in unethical activity. Transparency is the hallmark of competent institutions. I tried to impress this truth upon the chief of police in Nurgaram. We argued for well over an hour about the fact that his force was not as good as he claimed and that there was crime occurring in the district, sometimes facilitated by his own officers. In Afghanistan government and security officials are reluctant to take on poor performers within their departments because they believe it reflects on their abilities. Honor is critically important to the worth of an Afghan. Admitting that there are problems within the organization is an admission that they cannot do their jobs. Therefore, an Afghan government official will rarely concede that there is anything wrong with their area of responsibility. I had to wear down the chief to get him to agree that there was a problem and to commit to doing something about it. Then I had assure him that I would not embarrass him publicly by calling him out on his corrupt officers to the elders. Such negotiations with Afghans are very tedious and take up a lot of mental energy.

22–23 October 2009

I spent two days in Jalalabad at the Bde Cdr's conference. While I was there we had an earthquake. It was centered in Badakshan north of here and apparently registered 6.2 on the Richter scale. I slept through the whole thing. I was very tired last night and just conked out.

It is much cooler in Jalalabad now than just a couple of weeks ago. I am glad of that. We went over a number of things in the conference with regard to our way ahead. It focused on partnership with the government and security forces. I am in complete agreement that this is what we have to do. But until the right leaders are in place it seems like pissing up a rope. You can only do so much with people who don't care and don't try. Like I have already said, if we don't have the right people in place, I can only take things to a stalemate. They (the Afghans) have to tip the balance to victory.

24 October 2009

Very quiet day today. While we had patrols out, there was no contact or hint of enemy activity. So, the staff focused on preparing for the election runoff. We will publish our order tomorrow providing the direction for the next few weeks as we focus on bringing off another safe election. We did well in planning and executing the last round, and I want to do that again. Some of the Afghan leaders we have talked to are frustrated because they think Karzai already won and it is a waste of time doing it again. Others believe it is right under their constitution. All are resigned to the fact that they will be doing the whole thing over again.

My own staff officers asked me why this is happening again, especially knowing how corrupt Afghans are. I asked them if they had ever heard about the paradoxical trinity, as Clausewitz noted. This is pure politics, and not for the benefit of Afghans, but for the U.S. and Western audiences. For the president to maintain our presence over here, the U.S. public must perceive that we have a legitimate partner. With Karzai tainted by fraud in the first round, this will clear up that stain so that the U.S. population and the NATO allies can stomach sending more people. Therefore, we do it all over again. Then the decision will come out announcing a "surge" of troops to support GEN McChrystal's COIN strategy.

The Afghan constitution states that if the leading candidate does not garner over 50% of the vote, then a runoff is required between the top two candidates. Karzai attempted to gain the required plurality through corrupt means. When this did not work, he conceded to outside pressure to conduct a runoff. This required our unit to once again plan for the safe conduct of elections within our area. As alluded to in the entry, the administration was undertaking a review of the situation in Afghanistan in preparation for a "surge" loosely modeled on the change of strategy in Iraq. For this policy to gain traction with our people, the Afghan government had to adhere to their constitution, which Karzai was reluctant to do. The decision to hold a runoff would make sending additional troops to Afghanistan more palatable since it appeared that the government was abiding by its law.

25 October 2009

Overall a slow day. The patrols started their polling site assessments today to prepare for the election on 7 November. We did engage SG Hamid Osmani today on a number of issues, starting with the governor's complete lack of interest in anything going on in Nuristan. He is not supporting his sub-governors and, as childish as he is, he will end up causing the situation to deteriorate like it did in Barge Matal and Kamdesh. Osmani wants to quit because he is sick of dealing with him (the governor). I don't blame him.

We did talk about reconciling an enemy fighter from Nurgaram today. Osmani knows this guy and that he is a target of ours. I believe that he is related to him (the target), and that is why he is reluctant to talk about him. But with the offer of reconciliation Osmani is more enthusiastic and said he will begin to work it. He apparently has two nephews in Pakistan with the TB who are dangerous men. But Osmani said that he (the target) is not. He is more of an opportunist who could probably be brought in through reconciliation. This would reduce the threat in the Titin Valley to near nothing, leaving the Nuralam as our main concern.

I often had long conversations with Hamid Osmani, the district governor from Dow Ab. He was beginning to tire of working with the Nuristan governor, and I could not blame him for feeling this way. The governor caused a great deal of friction and was completely uninterested in actually serving his people. His disinterest was at least part of the reason for the deteriorating security situation in eastern Nuristan, and I was concerned that this attitude would affect western Nuristan. The sub-governor shared this concern.

Sub-governor Hamid Osmani was the only district governor who actively attempted to reconcile enemy fighters with the government in order to reduce the threat in the area. In this case, the enemy fighter we were interested in was a relative of his. When I made it clear that we would respect the reconciliation of this individual, Osmani felt relieved and promised to work on bringing him in.

26 October 2009

Today I met with the elders of Paranieh with the Alingar district governor. We discussed security and I thanked them for reporting the IED last week. Then we provided half the fund to the governor so they could start repairing the retaining wall that was damaged by the storm in September. If we can cooperate with them in things like this, we can prevent the enemy from having freedom of movement in the Nuralam. That could stop the flow of arms and fighters into the Chapa Dara in Konar. We will keep working this avenue.

I also got word that the Nurgaram chief of police is hiring more police for the district, which sounds good. But I learned today that many of the new hires are thugs, some of whom are directly connected to the IED cell. Apparently, they are trying to infiltrate the police to get weapons and uniforms and then launch attacks on us, leveraging their inside position. I called the provincial police chief tonight to inform him and asked for a hiring freeze. I swear that none of these people are trustworthy. I thought that the Nurgaram CoP would be a good chief, but he is proving to be like all the rest. Again, without good Afghan leaders, I don't think it is possible to win. All we can achieve is a stalemate. Only good leadership will tip the balance.

I found the news of the police chief hiring infiltrators disturbing. Armed with this information, I had to move quickly to prevent the district chief from bringing in enemy infiltrators who could then turn their weapons against us, report our movements, and so forth. The provincial chief honored my request and froze all hiring until a proper vetting process was in place to screen the candidates to determine their loyalty.

27 October 2009

We held the election shura today down at the Nurgaram District Center and had over 100 elders attend. The meeting went very well, but Afghans often talk a good game while execution is another matter. The only one that I really trust to get the job done is Hamid Osmani. But he is frustrated because the governor does not support him in his efforts and treats him badly. I provided the sub-governors with their fund for security publicly so that they would not be able to hide it from the people and thus pocket it. If used correctly, they can pay for local security for each polling site to help the police. There is a question as to whether Mangal Abdullah paid his elders last time or pocketed it, so I sought to prevent that today.

Other than the shura, it was a quiet day. I think the enemy will prepare for the election to disrupt the polling, so we won't hear from them for a few days, then, just prior to election day, they will come out with a vengeance. We will see.

28 October 2009

Today was mostly uneventful. We issued our order for the election. Then tonight something unusual happened. A local came in to have several wounds dressed that had been inflicted by a bear. I couldn't believe it. Apparently, this guy was a shepherd tending to his flock when a bear attacked. In the melee the thing tried to take his face off. I thought I had seen it all over here, but I guess I was wrong.

29 October 2009

I have been sick all day with something that hit me last night. I had to lay down for several hours and got absolutely nothing accomplished. There was a munition turn-in today.

30 October 2009

I feel much better today. We had another earthquake last night that rattled the place, and I was awake for this one. It broke the sewage pipe in the john. It is always something here.

We had reports today that our number one target attended the wedding of his sister in Tupak today and that there were 30 fighters in the area. We called the police to check it out, and they said that the wedding had occurred yesterday. I wish we could get some real-time intel to act on. Unfortunately, since we are an economy of force effort, it is not likely that we will get something we can act on. Even if we did, the Karzai 12 and incompetence of the police make it difficult to do anything.

The Karzai 12 is a set of rules established by the Afghan president that restricted our ability to act unilaterally on targets of opportunity. While they are absolutely appropriate for counter-insurgency, the rules also inhibit taking reasonable action against targets that present themselves. This enables the enemy to hide and take advantage of the restrictions. These rules were not in place during my first two tours in Afghanistan, and thus our forces were able to act with greater agility. The enforcement of these rules forced us to rely on the police to arrest insurgents. The lack of professional competence on the part of the police made this dependence very frustrating, since they were never able to arrest anyone of value.

31 October 2009

I visited Joyce today and took Chief (my radar technician) with me so he could stay a few days to check the radar and see if we could make the

In this picture G Company is conducting a combat logistic patrol, moving supplies for the battalion from Jalalabad to Laghman and Nuristan provinces. The body of water is the Kabul River in Nangahar Province. A dam at this location provides hydroelectric power for the surrounding villages (courtesy Major Carrie Brunner).

system more efficient. It is difficult in Afghanistan to acquire enemy mortars and rockets because of the terrain here. It masks the trajectory so that the radar can't "see" the bullet coming. Chief will see if he can adjust the settings to make the system more efficient.

G Co got hit with an IED today, but it missed. Thank God for that. Those stupid things make me angry because it is nearly impossible to fight back. I am just glad we have successfully avoided them so far.

Hard to believe it is Halloween.

The mountains of Afghanistan make the employment of radar systems designed to track incoming mortars, artillery, and rockets extremely difficult. The enemy was very astute in using the terrain to prevent us from taking advantage of our technology. They would fire their rounds from behind a mountain so that our systems could not pick up the trajectory. In order to give us a better chance of acquiring the enemy targets, I shuttled my radar technician around to refine our procedures and system settings.

1 November 2009

Just worked on election preparations today. There will be a new ANA BC here tomorrow. I just hope he is competent and cares about what he is doing. If we can get that, we might have a good battery here soon. We will see. I promoted a good young man to SGT today. A little over a year ago he returned to us after deserting from Iraq. I had charged him with desertion in a court-martial. He pleaded with me to give him another chance to clear his name and serve out his time. Needing guys in the S1 (personnel) shop, I decided to take the chance at rehabilitating him. Now, a year later, he did it. I was happy to promote him because he did everything we asked and cleared his name.

Abdullah withdrew from the runoff today. Now what?

The new Afghan battery commander was not only competent but also one of the best officers I have ever seen in the Afghan Army. It was a pleasure working with him, and his unit became a very good artillery battery. Facilitating the removal of his predecessor was a success for us in our counterinsurgency efforts, and the Afghan Army was better for the decision to bring in the new man.

Rehabilitation of soldiers facing disciplinary action is a tool that a commander can use to help an individual and the unit. I was wary of giving a deserter a second chance because I have strong feelings about abandoning one's post and leaving tasks to those who stay behind. However, extenuating circumstances led me to take a chance with this young man, whose wife divorced him while he was in Iraq. He not only took the punishment of the court-martial but also became the best soldier in our personnel shop. I was able to promote him to sergeant, and he has advanced even further today. Seeing a young man turn his life around was very satisfying amid all the frustrations I was experiencing in Afghanistan.

Finally, the challenger in the runoff election, Abdullah, suddenly withdrew from the race with less than a week to go. We were stunned by this development. We had made many preparations for the event and felt that a great deal of time was wasted in readying ourselves for the election. We quickly changed our focus within our area with the election no longer hanging over our heads.

2 November 2009

Last night the battle CPT woke me up to tell me that one of our soldiers from B Btry at Torkham Gate had died in his sleep while at home on leave. I was stunned. This guy apparently died of a heroin overdose. Unbelievable. In all my time as a Bn Cdr I had never known this kid to get in trouble. He had always seemed steady and was recently in the promotion board to SGT. In going through his personal effects for inventory and shipment home, the officer found drug paraphernalia. So, he was using and probably getting it from locals (Afghans). It was a favorite tactic of the Mujahideen to sell the Russians laced heroin to take advantage of their high to attack. Now the same thing has affected us. Why young people use drugs I will never know. There is no benefit and a high cost ... today is a great example, as a family is mourning over his dumb decision.

Today the runoff was cancelled and Karzai declared the winner following Abdullah's withdrawal from the race. All the planning we did is out the window. Oh, well, we will still do the disruption op to stay on the enemy.

3 November 2009

Today we had the ANA Bde commander back with the COL to see his new BC. CPT Hafizullah has made a good impression and is much better than the old guy. I think we took a step in the right direction by pushing this change; now if I could only get rid of some other incompetent Afghan leaders. I am working on that and provided a list to the brigade commander while he was here.

Even though there is no election, we are still launching our disruption operation, which we are calling Dejavu. I think that we need to be out there on the enemy before he can formulate plans to hit us now that the election is cancelled. We kick it off at midnight.

4 November 2009

Our patrol last night ID'd about a dozen guys way up the side of a mountain on the southern rim of the Nuralam. Nobody moves at 0300 in the morning in this area, so we knew that these are obviously fighters moving along through the valley. We sent 3 rounds of illum their way and they scattered. Before doing so, we noted signaling between the fighters and the radio tower at the head of the valley where one of our targets likes to hang out. I know that the Nuralam is a major link between Konar and Laghman for arms and fighters. I think our future ops must focus on securing that link to prevent the enemy from moving freely.

I am at Torkham Gate tonight for tomorrow's remembrance ceremony for our soldier who OD'd. 3 guys took it very hard. Chaplain is here and has been working with them, and we have combat stress coming in a few days.

Even though the election runoff was cancelled, we executed our operation anyway, simply modifying it for the changed situation. Putting out night patrols in areas our enemies liked to use gave us a better understanding of how they operated while also serving to change their patterns. With our paucity of forces, a disruption operation was a good way to deny the enemy the initiative, and it helped us to maintain our own freedom of movement to sustain development and other activities.

5 November 2009

We did the ceremony at Torkham Gate today for our deceased soldier. So sad to lose someone to drugs. I just hope that at least his life might be an example for someone else to not go down that road. What a waste.

I called back to the TOC (tactical operations center) today, and the S3 said they saw absolutely nothing in last night's patrol. We will conclude the op this evening. Hopefully, we have disrupted the enemy and made them wonder what is going on.

I went to the border tonight on a patrol with the platoon here. All went well. Just like the last time I visited, the Afghans were doing nothing and the platoon had to get everything straight so that traffic could flow correctly. It was disheartening to see that the Afghans were not taking charge and the chaos at the border before the platoon arrived. They have to take the lead, and we will continue to impress this upon their leaders.

It is traditional to conduct a ceremony to remember a deceased soldier and to assist those left behind cope with their loss. We did this at Torkham Gate to enable a healing process for the soldiers of the platoon. I also took the opportunity while I was there to discuss with the unit the issue of drug abuse and how the enemy will use something like that to weaken us. The unit there never had any other issues. It is tragic that such things happen.

6 November 2009

I got back today and learned that the NDS finally did something positive. They conducted a raid last night in Ja'laam that netted an insurgent with 10 IEDs. The area to the south of us has been hit hard lately, and I believe it has been flowing through the Nuralam. We have known for a while that this village harbored insurgent activity like this, but we never knew exactly where. The NDS helped answer that question.

I called the NDS chief in Alingar to congratulate him and asked if we could work more closely. He agreed to conduct a meeting with me next week to start the process.

The NDS "sting" was the signal success for Afghan security agencies during our deployment. The police never achieved anything of substance, and the Afghan Army only had moderate success. However, the NDS seemed to have the most dedicated officials of any I encountered in Afghanistan, and yet it was the most under-resourced agency. In this case, the NDS operation temporarily disrupted the IED cell and gave us a reprieve from the threat of IEDs for a short period of time.

7 November 2009

What started off as a slow day quickly turned exciting, as our patrol returning from the Shemgal Valley got hit with an unblocked ambush when returning to the FOB after handing out HA (humanitarian assistance materials). A couple of days ago we got information from SG Hamid Osmani that a guy named Jamaluddin Gajour and 10 fighters came down from Dow Ab a few nights ago for an unknown purpose. Osmani told us that the 173rd (Airborne Brigade) had killed Jamaluddin Gajour's brother about 2 years ago. Therefore, he has a vendetta against the coalition. If he was involved today, it looks like he was just taking advantage of an opportunity.

I still can't believe the platoon appears to have run from another fight. They never seem to be able to get around to taking advantage of terrain to defeat the enemy. I just wish for once they would destroy the enemy instead of appearing to run. When they returned to base we turned them around and I jumped in with the MPs, and we all went back to the site. Upon examining the location I determined that the platoon did the right thing. The ambush was set up in such a way as to suck the platoon into a fight that would inflict a serious defeat. The enemy used the terrain to their advantage, dominating the high ground and channelizing the platoon into a crossfire if they moved into the draw where they arrayed their fighters. So, moving quickly out of the kill zone was the right call. But the enemy believes that they won and we ran, and that is frustrating.

The ambush was designed to trap the platoon in an impossible situation so as to inflict a serious defeat on our forces. There had been several reports in the preceding days pointing to an attempt to wrest control of the area north of the FOB from the government. Further, there was chatter that the enemy intended to assault the FOB proper in order to "liberate" Nuristan following their perceived success in the eastern part of the province. I had disregarded these reports before this incident, but afterward I took the threat very seriously. The ambush was also designed to monitor our patterns in preparation for a major attack that would come within a week.

8 November 2009

Very quiet today because of heavy rains that started last night and continued throughout the day. It was also very cool today, not even making it out of the 50s. Amazing change in the weather that will hopefully cause the enemy to finally go to ground. We may have some mudslides like we did in early September. That could represent another opportunity for us in the area to help the locals. That is something the enemy can't do.

Hamid Osmani visited today and told us that it was Jamaluddin Gajour and his group that attacked us yesterday. He said that Jamaluddin does this from time to time to try to kill coalition soldiers, and then he goes back to Dow Ab. Most of the folks opposed to us here are vendetta-based people. They are so primitive, like the old Kafirs.

Regrettably, the change in the weather did not cause the enemy to go to ground. Instead, they were planning their attack for the coming days, and the buildup of intelligence would begin to come in a torrent.

9 November 2009

A very cool day today. After the radio message we did a budget meeting with the DSG (deputy sub-governor) of Nurgaram to coach him through laying out his priorities against available money. Next week we will do a shura with the people/elders of Nurgaram so they can see how the money is spent. Also, I will emphasize that where there is questionable security, there will be no projects.

My sources provided some surprising info today. They told us that the guy arrested last week with the IEDs was ratted out by another IED maker.

This guy apparently plays both sides because he is a survivalist. Afghans are famous for doing whatever it takes to survive, including playing both sides. Loyalty is not a revered trait here and is another reason why it will be difficult to win in Afghanistan.

10 November 2009

Today we had several reports of enemies in the Titin Valley. They were intimidating locals for money and are apparently planning a rocket attack tomorrow on the FOB. We will do a counter-rocket fire plan tomorrow at the historical times to prevent it. Hopefully, we catch them in the act and teach them not to screw with us. We have focused a lot of effort around the Nuralam, and with our small resources it was about all we could do. But I think the enemy may think they have a safe haven to the north (in Titin Valley) and use that area to hit us. So, we are planning an op to disrupt this.

I met with SG Mangal Abdullah and the Sundawar elders today about helping clear their damaged fields from the flood. This village is a success story. They were harboring the enemy for a while, but when we go there now, with our focused effort there and around the Nuralam, this village supports the government If only I had more resources to affect more.

Several reports were coming in of enemy plans for attacks on the FOB, though they lacked specificity at this point. Regardless, I was beginning to see that an attack of some type was imminent in the next several days.

11 November 2009

Busy day today, and I am still in the office. I did a shura with reps from national security services today in an effort to gain better information in a more timely manner. Previously, neither of these guys would really talk to us because they do not trust the police who attend our security meetings. Getting them one-on-one without police attendance has proven better for our ability to get info. So, if we can build on this relationship, I think we can actually get better at keeping the enemy off balance and maybe even inflict some serious defeats.

We have had several reports today of enemy fighters intending to move down from Dow Ab to attack the FOB. Tonight we have had drones with eyes on dozens moving south. There could actually be some validity to this report, unlike most that we get of the enemy intending to attack us. We have never seen this much movement south before. This combined with the ambush last week leads me to believe that we could have something. We are ready. More to follow.

The meeting that I held with the national security officials turned out very productive and would lead to a more cooperative working relationship. They always attended the security shuras along with the police, but we had rarely received any useful information from them. As we learned in this meeting, the reason was that they did not trust the police. Thus, they would not share any information of substance because they believed that the police would relay that information to the enemy. From this point forward we held separate meetings with the officials so that they would feel free to speak without fear of police duplicity.

Among the things we learned at this meeting was that a significant force of enemy fighters was coming down from the north to attack the FOB. The purpose of this assault was to "liberate" Nuristan and replicate the perceived success in Kamdesh a few weeks earlier. Based on the reports, we were able to obtain drone overflights to confirm or deny movement to the south into Nurgaram. That evening we saw several formations of fighters moving south along trails around Gandalabuk. Due to the quality of the video we could not determine if they were armed and thus could not attack. Yet the reports, combined with the video, led me to believe that a large assault was coming. I just had to determine when and from what direction I would need to defeat it.

12 November 2009

We lost contact with the group moving south last night. When the ISR (intelligence, surveillance, and reconnaissance, used as an all-encompassing acronym for unmanned aerial vehicles) came back up, we couldn't find them. However, today a number of unusual things happened. First, we were observed from several different locations today simultaneously. We have not seen that before. There was an explosion audible at the FOB south of here IVO (in the vicinity of) where we had a report of an IED. But we got no confirmation of what it was or reports of injuries. Reports continue to come in of attacks here. It is probably the enemy's last shot at us before winter really sets in. We did some contingency planning and have continued to step up our base defense procedures. We fired at the enemy rocket launch locations to deny the area to the enemy as well.

The reports of an impending attack on the base were now reaching a crescendo. Our own observation posts and cameras confirmed that there were several points at which military-age males were scouting our locations. Based on these reports and observations, we believed that an attack was coming from the north and most likely aimed at our manned observation post, after which it would proceed onto the FOB proper at the ANA compound. There-

fore, we began a series of rehearsals to ensure that our defensive procedures were sufficient to meet the threat.

13 November 2009

More indicators of an attack today, with reports and threats against local people. Tonight our surveillance cameras picked up movement of several individuals at one of our historic rocket launch sites. We could see they were carrying heavy loads on their backs and what appeared to be rockets. Then the group was milling around at the site, appearing to set up something. I had the S3 request CAS (close air support), and we dropped two 500-pound bombs and followed with artillery on the target. The bombs and rounds were off by 20 meters. Don't know if we got any of them, but they know we are watching too. Still a threat to the base, but we will see what tomorrow brings.

On the night of the 13th I was actually in a video teleconference with our rear detachment when the S3 came in to inform me of the sighting of the individuals at the rocket launch site. When I walked into the TOC we could see about 12 men at the location. They were carrying loads, which we suspected were rockets, but we could not confirm our suspicions. Nevertheless, based on what we knew of the local area, we were aware that this was not normal activity. Combined with the reports of an impending attack on the FOB, I determined to attack the position. Rockets launched on the FOB the next morning in conjunction with a ground attack would have suppressed our position, enabling the enemy to get in close and penetrate the FOB. Attacking their rocket launch site on this night would make their attempted assault more difficult. So, we attacked. We did not immediately know the results, but we later learned that six of the dozen enemy fighters were killed and others wounded. We had neutralized the position. This was the right decision, for the next morning the reports of an attack were confirmed.

It is important to note that my entry of 13 November lacked detail, since I had spent most of the previous night up checking defenses. The following entry filled in some of the missing details after I had more time to record the event.

14 November 2009

This morning at dawn we were attacked on our OP and the FOB by about 60 fighters. Last night at around 2200 we detected 10 (it was actually 12) enemies with our cameras moving into the old ANA OP to set up what appeared to be either rockets or a mortar. Since this was out of the ordinary,

I had the S3 request CAS to bomb the location. I told our Bn FDO to work up a fire mission at that location AMC (at my command). We got the bombs in at about 2300. Then, 30 seconds after impact, we fired the 155s HE/VT (meaning high explosive with variable time fuses to burst above the ground) on the target. Result: 6 killed, including the leader (whom we learned was the old Dow Ab sub-governor's brother). This probably prevented an effective indirect fire attack in the morning. At 0600 we were in stand-to (meaning everyone at their fighting positions before daylight ready to fight) when the OP came under fire and the FOB took some RPGs. The whole base was ready, and the mortar quickly had rounds on TGT (target) supporting the OP. It broke up the attack. As the enemy attempted to regroup, the Predator (unmanned aerial vehicle) picked them up and we dropped two 500-pound bombs on them. Result: mortar 3 X KIA (enemy), bombs 7 X KIA, including their commander, who was from Dow Ab. The attack was defeated and two leaders killed. The unit did a great job, and we had no casualties.

I am anticipating another attack in the morning, as we have had intel all day that the enemy wants to do more. However, when word spread that their commander was killed, it seems to have sapped their morale. We have

The explosion of a 500-pound bomb on the western ridge overlooking Forward Operating Base Kalagush. This was the culmination of the defense of the base on 14 November 2009, when the Taliban attempted to overrun our observation post on the ridge and assault the base proper in an effort to "liberate" Nuristan. The attack failed, resulting in 16 enemy dead and 6 more wounded (photograph by the 2-77th Field Artillery Public Affairs Officer, Captain Matthew Frye).

III. Execution: 24 August 2009 to 6 December 2009

A 155mm howitzer from A Battery direct firing into the mountain at Forward Operating Base Kalagush (photograph by the 2-77th Field Artillery Public Affairs Officer, Captain Matthew Frye).

now gained the upper hand. If they attack again tomorrow, I believe we will defeat them again and put an end to this business.

We successfully repelled the attack, and I was very proud of our unit. They were well trained and ready for what the enemy could bring and beat them without loss while inflicting a heavy price on them. The ANA unit did an outstanding job under their new commander; however, the police did nothing but hide at their station. This event was my proudest moment in command because all of the training and preparation we had conducted at Fort Carson and in Afghanistan paid off. The enemy was gone, and we would have a short period of quiet.

15 November 2009

A very quiet day. We sent out a couple of patrols, including one to exploit the site we bombed by the OP, and got a mountain of evidence and several bodies. I spoke to the provincial police chief today, and he gave me a good rundown on the local attitudes and the enemy's reaction to the defeat. Bottom line: we crushed them. We killed three of their leaders, including the brother of the TB shadow governor of Dow Ab, along with 15 other fighters and several wounded. That is close to 40% of the estimated force that attacked us. The local officials are ecstatic, and most of the people are happy as well. Some, of course, are indifferent, and that is OK as long as they don't support the enemy. I have several officials set to come to the radio station with me to make addresses. I really want to solidify this victory from all points, especially on the IO front.

Also, gave the ANA BC a (unit) coin to congratulate him on the job they did.

I spent 15 November gauging the attitudes of the local people and the officials. By and large the defeat was welcomed by the people in Nurgaram District. The enemy had intimidated many of the villagers north of the FOB, and their retreat enabled the locals to return to their normal pursuits. While the defeat was significant, it also produced a desire for revenge among the remaining fighters. We would hear from the survivors again.

16 November 2009

Today I focused heavily on IO messaging with my own address and having five local leaders give addresses on what happened over the weekend. All of them drove home the point that the enemy suffered a heavy defeat and their leaders were killed in the attack. The new ANA BC did very well, not only providing a review of what happened but also covering the purpose of the ANA and why young men should serve. Very well done, and nice to have a good leader commanding the battery.

I met with the NDS, and they said the enemy from up north was thoroughly defeated and would not come back for months. But they asked the cell to the south to place IEDs to take revenge. Funny. They attack us after all the development work we do, and when we kick them in the butt they want to take revenge on us. What a bunch of fools.

Following our victory I felt it was imperative that the local leaders weigh in what had happened with public addresses from the radio station. Putting them out front would serve to build their connection with the people and concern for their security. Of key importance to this message was the ANA, which was heavily involved in defeating the enemy. Therefore, we wanted to get the battery commander on the radio to discuss his role and the importance of the Afghan Army.

The report from the NDS was chillingly accurate. The cell to the north was rendered ineffective by the defeat on 13–14 November. Yet they wanted to strike back in any way they could. Thus, they asked the enemy cell operating in Alingar to ramp up the placement of IEDs in order to exact revenge. Our patrols were alerted to this development, and we elevated our own vigilance. Unfortunately, within a few weeks the enemy would have their revenge.

17 November 2009

I traveled to Jalalabad today to do an Article 15 (disciplinary proceeding) on a soldier in C Btry. He fell asleep on guard and missed inputting a no fire area in the computer (fire direction computer), and the unit later fired IVO the NFA (no fire area). I busted him. Unacceptable in combat. More reports today of the enemy wanting to take revenge on us for spanking them the other day. We will see what happens. Tomorrow I travel to Fortress to promote the fire direction officer out there.

Falling asleep on guard duty cannot be tolerated in combat. Further, failing to manage the fire direction computer database can cause unnecessary losses. A "no fire area" is used to designate areas on the battlefield where friendly forces are located or that are places of civilian interest or population. When this soldier failed to input this data into the computer, he endangered the lives of numerous civilians. It is our policy to always protect the lives of civilians in Afghanistan, and when a soldier fails to do his job, placing civilians in danger, you have to take disciplinary action. In this case I did, and the soldier lost his rank and pay. As I stated before, I hated to do this in combat, but it is necessary to maintain discipline and instill the importance of following proper procedures in combat. There is no margin for error in what we do.

18 November 2009

We got four patrols out into the AO today, including one north (the IED clearance team) and three to the south with the PRT at Sundawar, maneuver platoon at Parwai, and MPs in Alingar. No issues anywhere and no IEDs to north—as we may have expected. So, overall a quiet day. A Btry smoked 8 insurgents last night attempting to attack a construction crew. They have finally won over the confidence of their maneuver unit and now appear ready to take a bigger role in supporting that unit.

I visited B Btry at Fortress today and promoted the FDO, presented 14 combat action badges, and gave coins to the guys from D/1–32 who have taken care of that platoon so well for the past 6 months. They will be leaving soon. Their 1SG even visited Birr in the hospital in Minnesota. It will be sad to see them leave. I hope the next unit is as good.

A Battery had some issues winning the confidence of the unit it supported at Mehtar Lam, but this fire mission ended all doubts. It is common practice for the Taliban to threaten contractors to get them to stop working on projects.

B Battery at Firebase Fortress firing over the mountain to support an infantry company in contact with the enemy (courtesy Captain Geoffrey Terman).

In this case the contractor was working on the main road up the Alishang Valley in Laghman. The Taliban wanted to prevent coalition force access to the valley and facilitate placement of IEDs into a dirt road rather than pavement. Intelligence reports stated that the enemy planned an attack between 16 and 20 November. The maneuver unit established surveillance of the area and aimed the artillery on the target. When the Taliban launched its attack, the intelligence assets identified the assault and gave the command to fire on the target. The artillery impacted on target and stopped the enemy cold, leaving eight dead. The contractor was able to continue work on the road free of enemy interference.

19 November 2009—Afghan Inauguration Day

Another quiet day, which is a very good sign. Our patrols today again did not see anything or receive reports of the enemy. Also, in a very positive development, SG Hamid Osmani went back up to Dow Ab. Apparently, the enemy commander who led the attack on the FOB had threatened to kill him, but with his death in the fight on Saturday, Osmani sees his opportunity to reassert leadership. The TB have been threatening for some time to attack and take the DC (district center) up there, and so far the CoP has managed to resist. Osmani's presence should stiffen that resolve. I did meet with the governor today, and he finally agreed to announce the decision of the jirga to the Pashai-Gajour tribes. This should finally solve the problem between the two over the burned village and murder. But in another development we learned today that the governor might be arrested for corruption in the coming days. This would be very good. In Karzai's inauguration speech today he spoke of cracking down on corruption and incompetence. He can start with the Nuristan governor. If Karzai follows through, we can actually win after all these years.

The jirga had negotiated a settlement between the Pashai and Gajour tribes after almost a month of deliberation. The agreement allowed both tribes to save face while implementing a practical solution to land use by the Gajour tribe. The jirga requested that the provincial governor announce the settlement publicly to give the decision credibility. I argued with the governor for what seemed like hours, trying to convince him of the importance of this simple step. All that was required of him was making an address at the radio station providing his stamp of approval on the process. He finally agreed after all the wrangling and then dragged his feet afterward without ever making the announcement. I could not believe how lazy and disengaged this man was. He simply could not be bothered with carrying out his most basic responsibilities. This is because he was more concerned with enriching himself at the expense of his province.

20 November 2009

Another quiet day. We did run a patrol into the Nuralam today to establish our presence. They were able to gain some intel about places the TB uses to laager when moving through the valley. Daud Mohammed, my interpreter, was named in a report as someone the enemy wants to kidnap or kill. I can't stand this enemy. Daud is a better young man than 99% of this entire population. He is working as an interpreter to make enough money to go to college in the United States. When he gets there I have told him not to come back to Afghanistan unless it finally stabilizes.

Tomorrow I have the security shura and a budget meeting with SG Mangal Abdullah.

The enemy wanted to kill my interpreter because he was very effective in communicating my messages, and they viewed him as a traitor. As more of these reports came in, I gave him some guidance on what to do to avoid becoming a victim of enemy retaliation. Eventually, I would get him out of the area in order to remove him from the threat.

21 November 2009

We held the shura today and found more evidence of the extent of the enemy defeat from SG Hamid Osmani, who had just returned from Dow

Ab. He told us that the TB up there needed a victory to receive any pay from the provincial TB commander. Since they failed in attacking the FOB, they cooked up a plan to collude with the police in Dow Ab to make it appear that they had overrun the DC. They would take some pictures of their "victory" as proof of their success, enabling them to receive their pay. The police chief in Dow Ab refused to go along with this, leaving the TB no option but to physically attack the district center. As they were preparing to carry out the attack, the village elders in Dow Ab intervened to stop it, saying that the TB could not do this because their sons were part of the police. So, if the TB did attack, they would have to fight both the police and the elders. With this ultimatum the TB gave up and went back into the mountains. Further, they can't agree on who their new leader should be with the death of their commander—a clear sign of discord and more proof of our decisive victory. SG Osmani is going to try to capitalize on it by reconciling some of the willing TB to further divide their ranks. This should put a nail in the coffin.

I talked to Maryellen tonight, and it is always good to talk to her. I sure miss her.

The Taliban fighters in Afghanistan only get paid when they can demonstrate success. If they are defeated, then they lose their earnings. In light of the defeat on 14 November, the Dow Ab cell needed a victory. To claim one, they tried to bribe the chief of police in Dow Ab, but he would not cooperate. Further, the local elders would not allow an attack because their own sons constituted most of the police force. As a result, no attack on the Dow Ab District Center ever occurred. In addition to all of this, the cell was struggling to identify a new leader. The division in their ranks worked to our advantage, giving us the opportunity to drive a permanent wedge between the various members. The district governor took the lead in this effort, although he was only partially successful. Nevertheless, the cell to the north was effectively neutralized for the next several months.

22 November 2009

We conducted the budget shura today in Nurgaram, and it went pretty well. The best part about it was the lack of bickering over who got what project and nobody came to me begging. The DSG covered the projects approved and talked about security and why continued development depended on it. Not too bad, and they were in the lead.

One note was that the governor was at the district center today and the deputy sub-governor asked him to attend the shura. He said he was too busy. Doing what? No one knows, but he did come to lunch. What a turd. He shows no leadership and is always on the take. I can't stand him.

The ANP called us today, saying there was an IED in Wadawu Valley. We launched the QRF and secured the site, calling EOD. There was no main charge placed. So, either the enemy did not finish the job or it was a hoax to watch us react and note our tactics.

23 November 2009

A quiet day as we prepared for our operation in the Titin Valley. We did our rehearsal today with the ANA; they did very well and have a good plan. We will be going into the Titin Valley to the north to clear some caves that could hold caches. Also, I will meet with the local elders and we will ID the gem mine that the mining company has gained a permit from the government to operate. This valley was used by the insurgents two weeks ago to attempt their attacks on the FOB (unsuccessfully).

We had planned to carry out this operation sooner, but due to the recent enemy activity we had postponed it. Opening the gem mine was part of our overall economic development plan, and if operations got under way, it could have a positive economic effect on the entire area. We just needed to confirm that the mine was not being used by the insurgents and to gauge the level of influence the enemy had in the area.

24 November 2009

We conducted the op today, which went very well. We cleared over 20 caves, none of which had any weapons. I met with the people and contrasted our visit and the road project with what the TB did two weeks ago, which was shake them (the people) down for money. I think what we did today reinforced their support for the government and further separated the enemy from the people. The deputy sub-governor came out and led the shura, and he brought the deputy provincial CoP. He did very well. Our target in the valley actually showed up at the shura. We have had him on our list for a long time. He says he wants to reconcile, which we support, but we believe he is trying to play us because we still get reports that he attended insurgent meetings as recently as two weeks ago. We will keep tabs on him.

When we were headed back we got a report that the police found multiple IEDs in Wadawu Valley. I decided to wait until we have the RCP (route clearance package) tomorrow to clear the route with the engineers. We will see what happens tomorrow.

Our operation into the Titin Valley was a success, and in addition to finding no weapons, we were able to meet with the elders of the village. The oppor-

tunity to speak directly with the local leaders was important to facilitating the government's reach into the area. Further, confirming that there were no weapons and a relatively supportive population would facilitate opening the mine. Security combined with economic development, and backed by a relatively competent government, would encourage stability in the region. While the government leaders played a good game on this day, the question was whether they sustain it after we assisted them in establishing the environment. Good government requires more than just talk at a shura; it requires follow-through on what they promised to do.

25 November 2009

The RCP found nothing in the Wadawu today. A report came back to us that the enemy dug them up last night. I don't know if I believe that, but regardless nothing was found. I got down to Connelly (in Nangarhar) today and promoted Mazella. He is my teenage-looking LT. I wonder if I looked that young to my Bn Cdr as a LT. I am sure that I did.

In November 2009 I flew down to Forward Operating Base Connolly in Nangarhar Province to promote Jason Mazzella to first lieutenant. He was later severely wounded in Konar Province after I had moved him to an infantry company to serve as a fire support officer. Mazzella is now a captain and again serving in Afghanistan. Pictured from left to right are Captain Anthony Brunner, Lieutenant Mazzella and myself (photograph by the 2-77th Field Artillery Public Affairs Officer, Captain Matthew Frye).

Hard to believe that tomorrow is Thanksgiving. I am glad time is moving quickly, because I am tired mentally from worry about our people. Hopefully, the next few months will go quickly too.

Lieutenant Mazella was an outstanding fire direction officer and lieutenant in our battalion. Within a couple of months I changed his duty position so that he could gain experience as a fire support officer with an infantry battalion. Field artillery officers need to perform jobs with the infantry to understand how the entire fire support system works. This makes them better leaders as they rise in rank and responsibility through the Army. In February, while I was on leave, I received word that this fine lieutenant was severely wounded while on a mission with his infantry unit. I was horrified by this development, since I made the decision to place him in that position. Thankfully, he has recovered from the wound, and he and his wife celebrated the birth of their first child within one week of my penning this paragraph.

26 November 2009—Thanksgiving

I flew up to the OP today to visit the guys up there and take them some good food. They asked for stuff to grill rather than turkey, so that is what we took up. Even though a lot of work was done up there to improve protection, it still needs more. The problem is getting materials up there. It all has to be flown up to the top. But we are going to work it until we leave. That is the most vulnerable point we have, and we need to keep working on it.

The CG flew in today with the Undersecretary of the Army. I asked them to award some combat action badges, and they did down at the mortar pit. It went very well.

This evening I called Birr and his parents, and he sounded very good. God certainly performed a miracle for that kid. Thank God he is even still alive. He said he wanted to come back. If I only had 100 more like him. I have at least 25 slackers on rear d. claiming to have ailments from a sore knee to a hangnail so they can avoid coming to Afghanistan. Meanwhile, Birr got shot in the head and is ready to come back. What a big heart. The slackers should be ashamed, but they aren't because they are just selfish.

Finally, I talked to Mom and Dad, Maryellen and the kids. That was good. Sure do miss Mare.

27 November 2009

Today I flew down and promoted two LTs at Mehtar Lam. Both of them have done a fairly decent job as PLT Ldrs in G Co. Today in the AO we did two patrols, one to Paranieh and the other to Ja'laam. Both turned up nothing. The maneuver PLT in Paranieh was told that the east-west movement through the Nuralam Valley has stopped. I can believe this because the snows have finally come in, and heavy enough to close the passes. I hope it becomes a lot more snowy and cold so the enemy can freeze.

Winter tends to slow the pace of operations in Afghanistan because the enemy cannot cope with winter. They fade back into Pakistan or in remote mountainous villages to avoid contact and rebuild strength for the warm weather. A difficult winter is harder on the enemy than us, and I welcomed heavy snow and cold.

28 November 2009

Nothing today except for a report that the enemy in Dow Ab is meeting to try to determine another time/way to attack us again. Right now I don't credit it because of the snow up north and the fact that there is no clear leader among the TB. IEDs and rockets are probably the most likely ways we will be attacked.

I was exactly right in my assessment. However, we continued to receive many reports about the enemy's desire to attack the FOB directly. These reports distracted me from concentrating on what I believed was the true threat. The enemy played their hand very well.

29 November 2009

Nothing happened again today, although we were able to connect the dots on one of our targets today. While the MPs were out on patrol they were talking to some kids who said they were those of a member of the Nurgaram police. We know who he is and have seen reports that he has met with the IED cell previously. They asked the kids if they knew who the IED cell leader was, and they said that he was their uncle. So, the police officer is the brother of our number one target. Unbelievable. This guy blows up the PRT a while back, and the whole time his brother works for the local police. This demonstrates the duplicity of many of those who work for the government. It sickens me. Incompetent leadership continues as an issue in the department. That is the entire problem with security here: Poor Leadership.

My interpreter is still getting death threats against him. I told him again not to go anywhere alone or wander away from any patrol when we are out.

The entry above demonstrates the challenges facing our forces in Afghanistan. We were tracking the IED cell for some time and searching for hard evidence that would allow us to detain the cell leader. Little did we know that his brother was part of the local police force. We patrolled with them frequently, and there can be little doubt that this guy would report our movements to his brother to either avoid contact or set IEDs in an attempt to inflict casualties. Discovering information like this made me very skeptical about progress after all the hard work we had done. If the police were undermining us in such a way, it negated everything that we were attempting to accomplish. Further, this was at heart a leadership problem. The local leaders simply would not remove an incompetent or corrupt member so as not to embarrass that individual. Worse, they kept them on in order to maintain their network of corruption. It was disgusting. I began calling this the "crisis of leadership" in Afghanistan. We had done much to facilitate security, development, and good governance in our area. Yet at every step some government or security leader would undermine our best efforts. Until Afghanistan is willing to take a meaningful step toward reducing corruption and incompetence among their leaders—such as firing them to make an example—then all we as Americans can do is maintain a stalemate. The Afghans will either push the issue across the finish line to victory or forfeit the opportunity for a better life that we have offered them.

1 December 2009

I had meetings most of the day with NDS and Hamid Osmani. The threats against my interpreter, Daud Mohammed, persist. The reason, according to NDS, is that he has taught us about Afghan culture, and therefore we know how to act around the people. So, the people actually like us and the enemy has not been able to recruit from the population. This frustrates them, and they believe removing this young man would make us inept. Plus, since he works for the TF Cdr (task force commander, meaning myself), the enemy thinks they could get a lot of information out of him if they captured him. Turds. We have Daud under wraps so that no one can touch him. If we can get our hands on these people (the enemy), I would like to take them out.

We gave Hamid Osmani his budget today, and if he uses it right in Dow Ab, he can reassert himself as the power in the district. That would be huge.

Tomorrow all the Bn Cdrs fly up to Bagram to hear GEN McChrystal speak to us. I am sure that he will summarize the president's announcement of a surge.

I was very concerned for my interpreter's safety. This young man could fluently speak every Afghan language. A good interpreter gives a commander a great deal of credibility, and I had enormous clout with the leaders and people due to his command of the languages. *The NDS report confirmed our success in making a connection with the people and building their trust. The enemy somehow believed that if they killed Daud, that bond would be broken, which of course was nonsense. Nevertheless, we took measures to ensure that he was protected from harm.*

2 December 2009

Went to Bagram today to hear GEN McChrystal speak following the president's announcement this morning. It looks like 30,000 more are coming and the focus is in the south and east, which means we should see some increase in N2KL, but there were no specifics. The unbelievable thing about the president's speech is the fact that he set an end date. In my opinion, this is stupid. A smart enemy would just lay low until we start pulling back, but our enemy may not be that adept.

When I got back I noted several indicators that another attack is coming in the next few days. For some time we have been getting reports that the enemy wanted revenge for the butt kicking they got on the 14th. Until today I discounted it as talk. However, we now have indicators that confirm the reporting. First, movement through Tag Valley. Second, the MPs got shot at near Gandalabuk this morning, and third signaling around Titin. Finally, more reports through our sources. Apparently, the enemy will get cut off from financial support in the local area if they don't have a successful attack on us to exact revenge. So, the local groups are pressing to achieve that success. I think something could happen in the next 72 hours.

There was indeed an attack within 72 hours but not on the FOB. Instead, it came in the form of an IED, as I had suspected a few days earlier. We found out later that the flurry of activity to the north of Kalagush was related to the movement of timber as part of the smuggling operations. What were the police doing about the smuggling? Or IEDs in the area? Nothing, and this complacency and corruption pushed my frustration with Afghan leaders beyond the breaking point.

3 December 2009

I visited Monti today and counseled my new PLT Ldr there. He is a very good kid and was the FSO at Keating when that place came under attack. He is going to be a good PL. Today there were not a lot of indicators of an attack, like we saw yesterday, but there were a couple. Tomorrow is Friday, so it isn't likely the enemy will attack tomorrow, but Saturday would be a good day. We will see.

Friday is the Islamic day of prayer, and enemy activity normally dropped off significantly on this day. Therefore, we anticipated that if an attack were to occur, it would happen on Saturday. It did.

4 December 2009

More enemy contact today, and there is signaling going on tonight. Plus there are individuals at the rocket launch site as I write. It is a replay of 3 weeks ago, with a couple of exceptions. It looks like the attack will come from the east, and it is led by one of the commanders that was at Keating. We will be prepared, though, and I intend to attack the rocket launch site before it starts in the morning. We have reinforced the OPs and have rehearsed our defensive plans. I pray God will bless us with success again. This is all part of the enemy plan to "liberate" Nuristan and avenge 14 November. I don't intend for that to be the outcome.

In spite of my intentions, the enemy did carry out a successful attack, and I was unable to counter it. It was the worst day of my command.

5–6 December 2009

The day turned out much different from what I expected. We did not have an attack on the FOB in the morning. I thought the day would turn out OK. It didn't. While I was meeting with the officials at the security shura I got word of an IED blast, followed shortly thereafter by word that SPC Rao had died in the blast. I was pissed. I cut the meeting and moved to the site with the MPs.

They (the maneuver platoon patrol) were doing all the right things, clearing culverts and moving deliberately. The enemy had the perfect position, though. Using an irrigation tunnel, the triggerman waited until the dismounts got to the culvert and then blew the IED. The dirty coward ran through the tunnel out the other side of the hill and out without anyone ever seeing him. Meanwhile, Rao was gone and SSG McClintock was severely injured. We called in EOD, which did the investigation while we searched the area for Rao's remains. We found pieces of him scattered all over the place. He was such a good young man. He was quiet and just did a good job every day, one of the good ones. Now he is gone. I am stunned. I had seen him this morning getting ready for his patrol as I was leaving with the MPs. Little did I know it would be the last time I would see him. He has a young wife and 18-month-old daughter.

This enemy, for all their talk of religion and piety, are simply evil hypocrites. They say what suits their purposes and do what they want without

Sergeant Elijah Rao, who was sadly killed in action by an improvised explosive device on 5 December 2009. In this picture he is meeting with young boys at a local school. A much-loved soldier in the battalion, he had a positive effect on everyone he came into contact with, as this photograph demonstrates (photograph by the 2-77th Field Artillery Public Affairs Officer, Captain Matthew Frye).

thought for anyone else. They claim they do it all for God. Well, in the Bible God is described as love. So, how could God condone killing "in his name"? Everything I see here confirms me in my beliefs that God's sacrifice of his own Son is true love and thus the only true religion.

We staged our own ramp ceremony tonight to properly send off Rao's remains from the FOB.

* * *

This morning (0500 on the 6th) I flew out with the CSM and BC with Bde Cdr to Bagram. There we did the ramp ceremony to send Rao home. I am so sad. Command is tough because of the responsibilities borne by the leader. And when one of the soldiers dies due to enemy action, it hurts because the weight of responsibility becomes heavier. You second guess your decisions and wonder, if you had changed the mission or a procedure, would that person still be alive?

The C17 (aircraft) had only the single casket on board. An enormous plane for such a small package. But the small package is the most precious of cargo. He is going home.

Finally, I saw McClintock today, and he will make a full recovery. The doctor said none of his injuries would disable him. Thank God. I called his wife tonight and gave her the news. McClintock is now headed home too.

Second Phase of Execution Ends: The Reality

The death of Specialist (posthumously promoted to Sergeant) Rao was a sobering event in our unit. It rendered the effort we were making in Afghanistan nobler, and yet at the same time it produced a deepening cynicism. The previous behavior of the Afghan leaders and their endemic corruption, incompetence, and lack of dedication to their people made the loss hurt in an indescribable way. We had traveled more than 10,000 miles to assist the Afghans in building a better life. Yet I felt that our effort was not appreciated by the Afghan leaders. This tragic event convinced me that we had to change tactics and press the Afghans harder to take on the mantle of leadership.

The death of this young man brought out feelings of inadequacy in my own ability to command. I questioned my decision-making ability and wondered if there was something that I could have done to prevent the tragedy. I was becoming very angry at the Afghans because I believed they were feckless. The leaders expressed their condolences for our loss, and yet they did nothing to improve their own performance with regard to governance. I would no longer accept words of assurance from the Afghans—I wanted action.

From this point forward we changed our approach to working with the Afghan leaders. I had believed that we were pushing the Afghans to the forefront in taking on the mantle of leadership. But I realized that the American effort from my first tour of duty in 2003 until 2009 had focused on how we could help Afghans rather than on how we could empower them. This is a subtle difference in the strategy of assistance, but an important distinction. From now on we had to force the Afghans to perform their duties rather than do it for them because it was easier. Doing the job of the district and provincial leaders had not fostered growth on their part. While frustrating, we had to put the Afghans in the driver's seat. This was the true path to progress and facilitating victory (and our eventual exit from Afghanistan).

Our time in Nuristan would last about four more months, at which time we would receive orders for a change of mission. As part of this new mission, we would move the battalion headquarters to establish a partnership with an Afghan National Army brigade headquarters, much as we had planned shortly after our arrival in theater. We had hoped that our departure from Kalagush to assume the new mission would mean transferring responsibility for the area to the Afghan government. However, the lack of capacity on the part of the government meant that this was not an option. In the meantime, we focused on readying the local leaders to assume that responsibility at the earliest possible time. The next phase of the deployment represented a continuing commitment to our mission, but with a sobered attitude and a change in direction to empower our partners.

IV

Sustaining the Fight and Making a Difference, 7 December 2009 to 3 April 2010

After the death of Sergeant Rao, we resolved to continue our mission with renewed commitment and a changed attitude. While we would still focus on building up our area of operations in terms of security, governance, and development, the onus for leading was now squarely on the shoulders of the Afghan officials. Simultaneously, we would begin preparations for the new mission we would receive during this period.

The new year would hold in store a mix of successes and new woes. Our relationship with the people, particularly in the villages of Sundawar and Paranieh, solidified into one of mutual trust and respect, which we found gratifying. The Afghan officials began to manage a simple budget for their districts by setting their own priorities and incorporating the people in the decision-making process. Finally, we were able to assist the elders in Alingar District in ousting their corrupt and incompetent chief of police.

At the other end of the spectrum, we witnessed a threefold spike in the number of IEDs in the area, as well as the tragedy of several Afghan schoolgirls getting caught in a blast meant for us. In addition, the Afghan officials continued to search for ways to line their pockets through corruption in spite of efforts to curb these activities. This pointed to the fact that they still lacked altruism and failed to understand the need for transparent, honest government. Further, we received a lead on who was responsible for the IED that killed Sergeant Rao. The identification of this individual illustrated better than anything else we observed during our time in Afghanistan that poor leadership was the central issue that made achieving victory difficult. As we prepared for our next mission, I made the assessment that, based on their practices, the Afghan officials were not ready to assume responsibility for the area when we moved out. Instead, we would turn the area over to another American unit.

The new mission involved establishing a partnership between our unit headquarters and that of an Afghan Army brigade; our staff would provide mentorship to our Afghan counterparts so as to build competence and capability within the brigade. This mission would provide us with an exciting change from what we had experienced at Kalagush while keeping us engaged as we moved toward the culmination of the deployment. Yet even this mission brought significant frustrations.

However, until we moved to our new location, we had to maintain the pressure in Nuristan and Laghman. It is common for units to get into a "rut" at the halfway point of a deployment. This is a dangerous period because the tendency to let one's guard down can lead to needless losses. As a result of previous experience, I pressed my leaders to prevent the soldiers from becoming complacent. To my great satisfaction, we made it through this period without further tragedy. This phase is about sustaining the effort as we changed our focus and starts as we begin to recover from the losses of 5 December 2009.

7 December 2009

HHB changed command today, and now another captain is in charge. I will put Carpenter in as the cdr of A Btry next month for a second command. The COL spent the day here. He was at the CoC and pinned on SPC Davidson's ARCOM (Army Commendation Medal) for valor, and we talked about the way ahead for Nuristan.

We got the maneuver platoon back out today. It was good for them to keep active and not sulk after what happened on Saturday. I wrote letters today to Rao's parents and wife. Very painful.

We are still searching for the person responsible for the attack. We believe he is well connected to some corrupt leaders, which will make apprehending him difficult, if not impossible. If the Karzai government can't get rid of people like this, then winning is an issue. Regardless, we intend to ensure justice is done, whether the government is capable or not, by pressing the local officials to start taking corruption seriously.

Captain Chris Carpenter was my best battery commander and among the finest young leaders I have ever seen in the Army. Giving him a second command was meant to provide greater leadership opportunity and development. Additionally, it represented a considerable honor for officers selected to command two batteries as a captain.

Our maneuver platoon had to stay active to prevent the brooding that inevitably occurs when a close personal loss occurs. So, while we worked to provide the soldiers with needed counseling to assist the healing process, we also pushed them to maintain their focus and keep their minds occupied.

Finally, the discovery of who was responsible for the IED on 5 December 2009 was extremely disheartening. Success in Afghanistan depends on good Afghan leadership, but poor leaders worked against success, which motivated us to push our Afghan counterparts to make transparent, responsible government their top priority.

8 December 2009

I met with Hamid Osmani today at the radio station with the Nurgaram chief of police as well as the ANA BC. We all did our messages, and afterward I spoke with Osmani about his progress in Dow Ab. He told me that he had formed a shura and with them drafted a letter to the enemy telling them to stop attacking and work with the government. He, with his shura, is going to use the projects we can assist with to target some specific villages to solidify his hold in Dow Ab while reintegrating some of the fighters. If it works, we might be able to neutralize the threat to the north.

More reports today of Haminullah Khan's part in the IED attack. There is now momentum at higher HQ to take the (IED) cell out. If we can do it, that eliminates the threat in Alingar. Then we can deal with the traffic through Dow Ab. Regardless, the members of that cell need a bullet in their heads.

The Headquarters Battery maneuver platoon out on a patrol at dusk along a ridge overlooking the Alingar Valley (photograph by the 2-77th Field Artillery Public Affairs Officer, Captain Matthew Frye).

9 December 2009

Flew down to Mehtar Lam today and met with the Agriculture folks to see if we could work some assistance on long-term Ag development in our AO. Good meeting, and with their help we should be able to get some worthwhile projects off the ground with the buy-in from the local elders and officials.

Our intel deck is really building. Today we were able to get a great deal of info on our targets, including pictures, 10-digit grids (locations), and biological data. If we can roll this all up, we should get the green light to make a hit on them and take the scourge out of the area.

Tomorrow is Rao's memorial.

10 December 2009

We did the memorial today. It was very well done. I managed to get through my remarks without choking up too bad. The weather held up. It was raining this morning but cleared up by mid-afternoon, so we did it outside. Rao had a positive effect on the whole unit. He was just the kind of guy everyone liked to be around and who did his job in a professional, respectful manner. It was tough on the soldiers. I called his wife tonight, and she is holding up well in spite of it all. I feel so bad for her because she is young and will raise their little girl alone. This war has a cost that most Americans don't understand. They think the cost is too high. It is high, but the alternative is unbridled terrorism exported everywhere and an oppressive Taliban here in Afghanistan. To continue enjoying our freedom and security, someone has to pay the price. For America less than 1% of the population is doing it. Rao was among that small number so that everyone else can live under a blanket of security. Some appreciate it. Polls are showing that most Americans now believe it is not worth the effort and that winning in AFG is not important. But to us losing is not an option. That cost would be too great.

Sergeant Rao had influence within the unit far beyond his rank and responsibility, and that came through in the memorial service we conducted at the firebase. I had a difficult time making it through my remarks, as I became choked up at a couple of points. In the entry I mused about the cost of his sacrifice. At that time and since there have been a number of national polls asking Americans whether the war in Afghanistan was worth the cost. All of them have shown that support for the war has waned and well over half of Americans believe that it is no longer worth the effort. To me, this is hard to understand. The events of 9/11 were launched from Afghan soil and without our commitment to the Afghan people the Taliban could retake the government, making future terrorist acts possible. Would this not cost more than the current effort in terms of human loss and treasure?

11 December 2009

I went with the platoon on a long patrol today down to our southern boundary. We stopped in the Salaw Valley to talk to a village and discuss enemy movements and concerns of the people in their valley. We gave some gifts of clothes that our family readiness group sent over. We also checked out communications the entire way using our new 100-foot antenna tower on the base. Since it appears to work as good as having one up on the OP, we will bring all our soldiers off the OP and use Afghan guards instead. It will get us back 10 soldiers for patrolling.

We got some good information on the IED cell leader—specifically, we got clean fingerprints from an associate of the cell leader. They were found on the notebook of a guy detained in another area recently. This should allow us to detain him if we can match them (the fingerprints) with the IED that hit the PRT on 25 June, but his connections to certain officials mean he will be difficult to capture. Nevertheless, we are working this very hard. Finally, we had a tip come in telling us about the location of a cache in Lowkar, the village where Rao was killed. We are going to get it tomorrow.

The reader should surmise from the entry above how difficult it is to actually apprehend an enemy combatant. In order to take action against a target, we must gather evidence much as police would in a criminal investigation. The evidence must provide at least probable cause to apprehend the suspect. Contrary to popular stories of haphazard raids of civilian homes, all operations to kill or capture an important target require this standard. Once the standard is met, detailed planning occurs to conduct an operation against the target. The plan must ensure that the target can be captured or killed with accuracy and a minimum of collateral damage. This is a necessarily high standard to meet, and at the same time it is extremely frustrating to a unit that has suffered losses at the hands of the enemy.

12 December 2009

It was a quiet day today. We were unable to get the cache because it is in a house and the ANP have to be present. As usual, the Alingar CoP is unresponsive and ineffective, refusing to help. I can't believe we can't get rid of him. The governor (of Nuristan) is still in place, and things like timber smuggling and illegal "taxes" are rampant. Meanwhile, local officials don't get paid, and when they do some of the pay is missing. Karzai said he was going to crack down on corruption in his inauguration speech. Yet almost a month later we have seen absolutely nothing. The governor should be the first to go, but he remains in place. He is so incompetent, corrupt, and cares about no one. Once again the leadership deficit is killing Afghanistan. Ridiculous. If they don't do something soon and in radical fashion, we will lose any opportunity to tip this thing to victory. It is doable, but the Afghan government must act.

I am calling Rao's parents tonight.

My frustration at failing to get the weapon cache comes through clearly in this entry. As with apprehending a target, we could not just go to an Afghan house and search it. We had to have evidence, which in this case we did. Also, we had to have the Afghan police with us to do the searching and make the arrests. However, the incompetent and corrupt Alingar chief of police refused to participate in the action. Thus, we were unable to secure the cache. We would actually secure it at a later date, but for now we were left to brood over a lost opportunity. The point here is that our rules of engagement forced us to act much as a police force. While this is sound counter-insurgency practice, it is hard for those who have to abide by the rules. Yet we did in order to ensure that our actions were in accord with our national values and would protect the Afghan people from arbitrary acts.

13 December 2009

A very quiet day without any incidents or even reporting. We conducted a mission to blow up the Wadawu cave complex, and that went very well. These caves were used to attack the Apaches (helicopters) back in October during the downed aircraft search. Two guys popped out of these caves and shot at the aircraft. Well, now there are no more caves. Our maneuver PLT and EOD did a nice job sealing them with explosives.

I spoke with Rao's mom tonight. Very tough.

14 December 2009

I hosted a lunch today for the Wakil of Nuristan to commemorate the sixth anniversary of the constitutional loya jirga. I continue to try and solidify the relationship we have with the local leaders. The Wakil is always very supportive of our efforts, and gaining his trust and confidence is an important part of our overall goal to develop a connection to the people through the local officials. The difficult part of it is getting the local officials to do their jobs properly to live up to the promise embodied in the constitution. But I will still keep pushing.

The Alingar CoP called saying there was an IED in the Nuralam. We told him when he found it to cordon it off and we would then come take care of it. He never called back. Typical.

Patrols had no issues today and no enemy reporting.

Tomorrow we are doing an education shura to assist with developing the education system.

In my continuing effort to maintain the trust of the people and the local officials, I hosted a lunch to honor the wakil of Nuristan, who, as mentioned in an earlier chapter, participated in the drafting of the Afghan constitution. I took the opportunity to point out that the this document represented an opportunity for all Afghans to build a better life and a nation. Would they take it? This was still the unanswered question, and as I noted in the entry, in order to realize the promise of the constitutional convention, the leaders of Afghanistan have to work hard in a more altruistic manner than they previously have done.

15 December 2009

The election (I meant to say education) shura went well today, and we learned the following:

- Teacher pay is an issue in that, like the police, it goes to Parun (the capital), where it is "taxed" before it is disbursed to the teachers
- Teachers are not professional because they don't know their subjects and are madrassa trained
- Many kids come to school primarily for WFP (World Food Program) handouts instead of education

While we intend to work on this, it was not the event of the day.

The event of the day was the RPG attack on the FOB. What made it interesting was that it matched a tip we got 3 hours earlier. We believe it was a planted tip to test our reaction to an attack and encourage us to trust the tipster, who would later lead us into a trap. We have to be very careful about who we trust so that we don't walk into an ambush.

In my discussions with locals during visits to the villages, I had learned that there were many issues with the schools in the area. To dig deeper into the problem, I decided to host the district and provincial education directors along with some of the school principals. Plus, I invited some representatives from the Department of State to come down to hear the discussion in the hope that we could highlight it at higher levels and assist with the problems.

There are many nice schools in the local area, built through development funding over the past few years. However, there is a critical shortfall in the number of qualified teachers, and those who are in the system are "educated" in religious madrassas. As a result, there is no standard curriculum, and critical subjects are taught inexpertly by these individuals. This problem is compounded by the pay issue in which the teachers are paid haphazardly and "taxed" by the provincial government, reducing their overall compensation. By gaining an understanding of the issues, we could attempt to assist with needed changes. Regrettably, we were not able to make a lot of progress in this area.

The second event was very perplexing. My intelligence officer briefed me about the impending attack, including the time it would occur. As if by clockwork, the attack happened at precisely the time predicted in the report. My young intelligence officer offered the hypothesis that the report was a plant, and its purpose was to encourage us to trust the tipster, who would later lead us into a trap. This hypothesis turned out to be correct because the district sub-governor informed me later that the source had known ties to the enemy in the area and intended to do exactly what my S2 postulated.

16 December 2009

From the looks of it, the S2 was right about the tipster because Hamid Osmani called to inform me that the source was untrustworthy. How he knew this information is open to question, but Osmani has never steered me wrong. Absolutely nothing happened in the area today. I visited Torkham Gate, and the PLT is doing fine. The shock of the death of the young soldier by overdose has actually had a deterrent effect on the rest of them. That is good.

Osmani called from Dow Ab to let me know that the enemy up there responded to the shura's letter, stating that they were ready to cooperate and potentially reintegrate. Great news. If we can neutralize the Dow Ab TB and destroy the IED cell, we have won in AO Steel. We will keep on it.

This was great news from the Dow Ab District sub-governor. He was the only official who was actually working with his local elders to make a difference. The enemy, however, was talking out of both sides of their mouths, using the negotiations as an opportunity to get some breathing space to regenerate their lost capability from the battle in November. We would hear from them again.

17 December 2009

Our patrols again had no problems, and the trail of the IED cell has gone cold because last night the special forces folks again had success in knocking out another target. The cell here is scared. That is good for us.

At the security shura today Alingar finally admitted that there are security issues. It was like the "no kidding" statement of the entire deployment. But, as usual, nothing in the way of names or specifics came out. It might make them look bad. The Provincial Deputy CoP for Nuristan briefed the plan for a QRF (quick reaction force) Bn in Nurgaram. The only problem is they have not done any logistic planning for this organization. Therefore, they have no housing or food for them, not to mention transportation. He brushed my questioning off as an MoI (Afghan Ministry of Interior) problem. So, yet another huge problem I will have to deal with. No thought is put into anything by these officials. Tomorrow I am putting on my hat as the fire support coordinator and conducting a brigade fires conference in J-bad.

Following the IED incident in Alingar, the chief of police finally admitted that there might be some issues with security. However, other than this admission, nothing of real use came out of the meeting. In Afghan culture any admission of a problem in one's area of responsibility is an issue of honor. Unlike in America, where criticism is common, in Afghanistan criticism is seen as an insult. As a result, it is difficult to make any course corrections even when it is clear that things are not working. This held true in west Nuristan and northern Laghman. Despite a mountain of evidence pointing to the ineffectiveness of the police force, changing anything was like attempting to move that mountain.

The presentation by the provincial deputy was a good idea to facilitate security. However, absolutely no thought was put into supporting the quick reaction force. I could see that once the Afghans established this organization they would immediately look to us for the necessary logistical support. My questioning of this shortfall only resulted in a denial of the problem. More work would have to take place to solve this issue.

18 December 2009

We did the fires conference today and set some pretty reasonable goals for ourselves as the fires system. First, we will reduce the lethal fires in COIN and make it more effective. Second, we are going to get our AASLT capability stood up to provide the Bde Cdr with flexibility. Finally, we are realigning some COLT (combat observation laser teams) teams to provide fire supporters to the BSB (brigade support battalion) for CLPs (combat logistic patrols) going north. Overall, a good conference, and division reps told me we are doing the best with fires across the board in the JTF.

When I got back the state department rep was all up in arms about a kidnapping and our lack of effort to help. First, we can't do police work.

That is what the police is for. Second, the Karzai 12 prevents us from doing police work. I guess she didn't catch that. Then, when I needed some documentation on the skimming of the police pay (financed by U.S. tax dollars) so we can get rid of the governor, out came an emotional tirade on how I can't replace officials anyway. There isn't anyone better, etc. Further, she pointed out how little I understand of Afghans. She then proceeded to tell me how arrogant we are. Funny, I have been here 3 times as long, she wants me to do police work, and yet won't help me police something up that we can actually do: get rid of the corrupt governor. And I am arrogant. She should listen to herself.

The entry above does not contain the full story. What I failed to mention in this entry is that the kidnapped individual was a young woman of 18 years. She had been promised in an arranged engagement to a young man in Alingar. She refused the arrangement, and in anger the young man "took" her into a forced marriage. This is commonplace in Afghanistan and considered acceptable under the tribal system. Of course, I found the situation with the kidnapping both tragic and disgusting. Yet, in accordance with our rules of engagement and the sovereign laws of Afghanistan, there was absolutely nothing I could do. When I conveyed this to the PRT state department representative she flew into a tirade, accusing me of lacking compassion and of knowing little about Afghanistan. This outburst did not change the fact that the Afghan police would have to act in any case of civil or criminal law, and if I took it upon myself to take action, our unit would have been in violation of numerous established directives.

The source of my extreme irritation in this case is that the representative knew this and yet still had a tantrum in which she essentially called me a stupid and uncaring incompetent. When I had asked her some days earlier to assist me in gathering evidence about the skimming of police pay—something that we were capable of doing—all I received was stonewalling. In my mind, if corrupt behavior is not sufficient reason to fire an irresponsible leader, then I don't know what the appropriate situation is.

19 December 2009

I went to Nangaresh today and met with the acting sub-governor and the village elder to identify the location where they want to build a municipal sporting field. They want to do it right by the school, so we agreed to get started on it. After that I went back to the FOB and met the 4th Kandak (Afghan term for battalion) Cdr, who came to observe his battery going through certification. The Btry did very well today. They have made enormous improvement and the change is attributed to the new BC. If I have had one success in changing leaders, it was in getting rid of the old BC. Now this unit is really improving thanks to that simple change.

20 December 2009

A very quiet day. Our patrol went down the entire length of the east side of the river with no issues and to the end of the road in the Nuralam Valley. They took the agricultural team with them to assess the possibility of ag development in the valley. A lot of potential, but we need the commitment of the good locals to move forward. We are going to start with a demonstration farm first outside the FOB and bring in the locals to teach modern farming methods. Then the effort will move out to the villages after they receive the instruction.

The suspected perpetrator of the IED attack that killed Rao was detained and interviewed today. He accused everyone in the world of setting him up while denying any wrong-doing. But they got his biological data and other info. They will polygraph him tomorrow. Hopefully, we can connect him to some bad activity so that we can take him off the street permanently.

Andy's economics professor from the Air Force Academy is here to work through the timber and gem smuggling issue. Small world.

The leader of the local IED cell was drawing interest beyond our area of operation. However, his connections made it difficult to permanently remove him from our area. Though he was detained and interviewed, his story that he was framed by his enemies was accepted, leading to his release. It is still hard for me to stomach that we had him within our grasp but could not hold him.

Incidentally, the professor mentioned above played a key role in assisting me to land a position teaching at the Air Force Academy following my command.

21 December 2009—21 Years in the Army

It was a quiet day. We sent out three patrols, and with the exception of a couple of pot shots from a rifle, there was nothing. We are moving forward with our plan for ag projects with buy-in from the local elders. My AS3 (assistant operations officer) put a lot of work into a plan to develop the ag economy, and it will give us direction for the rest of our time here. We will begin an education program, demo greenhouses, farms, and a fishery in the watershed. All is feasible, according to the agriculture experts, and we are targeting it to villages where we can separate the enemy from the people.

Andy's economics teacher from the AF Academy is here working the timber and gem issue. The bottom line is that Afghan ineptitude is causing the problem. Gems are legal but overtaxed, so it is easier to pay a bribe and move them through the lax law enforcement than pay the 30% tax. Timber is just flat illegal for forest preservation, but this has only made it more valuable. So, smuggling is big business that, with proper legal structure, could provide jobs and tax revenue. But without a good legal initiative and leadership this will be difficult. Again, leadership is the issue.

As seen from the entry above, we made great efforts to develop the agricultural economy in our area, and we achieved a good deal of success. Other issues, like smuggling, did not turn out so well. Timber and gem smuggling were huge industries in western Nuristan. Government policy has pushed these industries into the illegal arena, causing a loss in economic growth and tax revenue. Yet, rather than exhibiting leadership in fixing the problem for the good of all Afghans, the government's incompetence produced a situation in which criminals benefited, funneling some of the proceeds to corrupt officials and the insurgency. This was yet another example of the leadership deficit at work in Afghanistan.

22 December 2009

Nothing today, but did get some interesting reports. First, Hamid Osmani came in from Dow Ab and told us about his success in turning some enemy Cdrs away from fighting and instead working with the government. Also, he is working on some community-based projects to help the people up there. We provided some funds for him to continue what he is doing and use it as a separation mechanism to keep the enemy away from the people.

Also, more reporting of caches in Lowkar near the IED site and in Parisaw near where the PRT hit the IED on 25 June. Problem is precisely locating them. If we can, we are going after them.

We heard in the U.S. news today that President Obama announced a time line for the end of the surge, our phased withdrawal, and end of combat operations over the next four years. I suspect that the announcement of a time line for withdrawal of any kind plays into the enemy's hands, because they will simply wait us out.

The time frame above was shortly after the announcement by the president of a time line for withdrawing American troops from Afghanistan. The Taliban is very astute in the use of propaganda, and this announcement was used immediately by the enemy in an attempt to wear on our morale. The news reports provided the enemy with several options. During my previous deployments I saw the enemy leverage open-source news to make it appear that they had influenced American actions by waiting us out, stepping up attacks, and attempting to cut deals with the government. What we actually saw in our area was an increase in IED activity that would begin within days of this writing.

23 December 2009

Our patrols encountered nothing today. However, our reporting seems to indicate that all of our current issues enemy-wise are coming from Tupak, Dareng, and Lowkar, where the IED took place. So, we are going to work these heavily over the next couple of weeks.

I took the ANA BC with me to (FOB) Joyce (in Konar) today to see his guns out there and to talk partnership with the ETT (embedded training team) on site. The BC noticed that the crew drill was not as good as at Kalagush. So, he started providing some mentorship. Then his LT started acting stupid. At that point, he called the Bn and relieved the LT on the spot, appointing another LT as the new PL. I was happy. This LT was like the old BC, not receptive to new ideas or change. If we had more leaders like the current BC, the ANA and other Afghan agencies would be a lot better off.

24 December 2009

I visited the OP with the CSM today, and they had done a lot of work on improving the force protection since we were up there last time. We will be pulling it down soon and turning it over to the Afghans within a few weeks, and one of my concerns will then be gone.

We received reports that the enemies under the local leaders have been ordered to take revenge for all their losses in S. Alingar over the past couple of weeks. They have taken a beating down there, and so we will have to remain vigilant, as it is very likely they will attempt to lash out to demonstrate that their losses were insignificant.

Hard to believe tomorrow is Christmas. Doesn't feel like it. This is now the fifth one in my career spent away from home in foreign lands.

Our plan to pull the observation post down was continuing to progress, and in less than a month we would turn it over to the Afghans. The observation post, which was about half a mile from the FOB, always worried me. The post was one of the targets of the attack in November, and the enemy would have exploited any victory in the press. Replacing our soldiers with Afghans was a cost-effective solution, as we could still maintain surveillance of the surrounding area and gain ten more soldiers to reinforce our patrols in the area. It was a win-win decision.

As noted in the previous week's entries, the enemy cells to the south of our area were hit hard by special forces, seriously weakening their capability. The cell in our area was linked to those in the south, and the overall Taliban commanders ordered our cell to step up activity to avenge the losses. This increase in activity occurred within a week of this writing.

25 December 2009

A quiet day for Christmas. No patrols and no issues. The troops got a chance to relax and not have to worry about going out. I caught up on all of my counselings and other administrative crap. Sure would have rather been home, but that is the way it is.

26 December 2009

We had a patrol go all the way up the Mashpah Valley today. No issues in or out. The platoon was checking on a completed project in Malel, which is done. Also, maintaining presence in the area where one of our IED facilitators, Mohammed al-Rahman, lives. We don't want him to get too comfortable.

Dow Ab is still stable, and it looks like there will be few issues from that direction. Hamid Osmani has things well in hand with his reconciliation effort there. So, we are going to concentrate in the south on both sides of the river between Tupak, Parwai, Sundawar, and Lowkar. For now this is where we can have the best effect on the enemy.

Things were quiet in the period immediately following Christmas, but the enemy was planning future attacks. Within days we would see IED activity spike to a level we had not observed before at a rate three times that of our previous experience.

27 December 2009

I went into Titin Valley with an engineer team to QC (check quality control) of the road project. The road is coming along very well, and we encountered no enemy activity. In a breakthrough today, we managed to locate one of the enemy commander's safe houses from a source. If we can track this guy's activities, we will be able to hit him at the safe house in the near future, which is what I would like.

Our MPs did a night patrol this evening with the ANP, and more timber smugglers came through. The ANP confiscated it. What they will do with it is probably an easy guess: take a bribe, and it will move out to Pakistan. I just wish we could have some credible police to work with. That would make all the difference. Probably not happening any time soon.

The enemy commander referred to above fled to Pakistan within days.

28 December 2009

After the radio message today I met with the Nurgaram and Alingar sub-governors to discuss the long-term economic program. The staff has done some good work pushing this forward and developing the plan, and the SGs seemed to like the proposal, so we will move forward on it in the next few days.

We learned from a source that a target from Chapa Dara named Mohammed al-Nuristani may have moved into our area. Apparently, he is a dangerous criminal and is so bad that even the TB kicked him out. He is supposedly in the Nuralam, and incidentally we are kicking off an op focused in there for the next two days. It also turns out that he is connected to many targets throughout the region. Hopefully, we will be able to track him and take him down soon.

Our actions were in accordance with sound counter-insurgency strategy. We were continuing to provide security throughout the area. All of our patrols were partnered with the Afghan police and Afghan Army to provide mentorship and guidance. Plus, we continued to partner with the government leaders to facilitate competence and attempt to identify corruption for elimination. Finally, we strove to develop an economic plan that would provide long-term growth and employment. All of this activity required buy-in from the local government leaders and village elders, which our frequent shuras were designed to achieve. Combined, these pillars had the potential to lead to real change and make the enemy irrelevant because they were incapable of providing any of the above. The major element that could upset our progress was the government and the security apparatus. Unfortunately, it proved the major obstacle in spite of our best efforts.

29 December 2009

We currently have the PLT, MPs, and ANA out in an op we are calling [redacted] in the Nuralam. The new battery commander is in command on site in his first operation. We are trying to pinpoint the cache location in the Nuralam, plus see if we can find out more about the area cell leader Khan Mohammed. Further, we are trying to confirm/deny Mohammed al-

Nuristani's presence in the valley. They went out six hours ago and so far nothing, but we will see in the debrief.

I received one piece of disturbing news today. Hamid Osmani came back from Dow Ab today and told me that he had been replaced by the former sub-governor of the district. This guy is completely corrupt, and he collaborates with the enemy. If this is true, it is yet another example of the idiocy of the Afghan government. They will replace a relatively effective SG with a criminal. It goes against everything that we are working toward here. If true, I just have a hard time believing that expending any more blood or treasure is worth it for such a clearly bad government.

The information that Osmani brought back was erroneous. The rumor was planted by the former district governor in an attempt to erode the support that Osmani had built in the district. It was a matter of jealousy and rivalry between the two men. Many times in Afghanistan such competition causes disruptions in the public discourse, and this was a case in point.

30 December 2009

I flew down to ML (Mehtar Lam) today to meet with Mangal Abdullah and the Laghman provincial officials in order to ensure that we are providing him with unity of effort in accordance with his province's priorities. Because he is connected down there, it makes it difficult to avoid friction that can occur because we are in Nuristan with an artificial military boundary that splits his district. We ironed out all issues, and the PRT down there (in Laghman) is very user friendly in solving problems. I was amazed at how the Laghman PRT is working so hard to make things better compared to our PRT, which has already quit, has no vision, and is the most undisciplined military organization I have ever seen. If you really want unity of effort in an area, then you have to apply the old principle of war of unity of command. As the AO owner, they should work for me. But, since they don't, I continually have to deal with their half-baked responses and lack of leadership in development and governance. They are pathetic.

Much friction developed between our battalion and the PRT we were partnered with. This arose from the fact that there were two officers of the same rank in command of both organizations. I had a vision for what I wanted to accomplish in our area, and initially both units generally worked to achieve that vision. However, about halfway through their rotation—which was nine months compared to our year—the PRT diverged and essentially became a nonfactor in the area. Therefore, we took it upon ourselves to take the lead in matters of development.

IV. Sustaining and Making a Difference, 7 Dec. '09 to 3 Apr. '10

31 December 2009

The NDS called me today as we were about to roll out the gate for the security shura. The chief told me there was an IED in Nangaresh. I diverted the convoy, and we met him in the village. From there we moved with the patrol to the site and found it hidden in some tall weeds. We called in EOD, which took care of it from there. It was a propane tank filled with explosive and had wires in a plastic bag. It had been staged for placement. Also, it was meant to target dismounts, probably searching culverts for IEDs. I think the enemy has seen the PRT checking those things so many times that they are purposely trying to target this TTP (tactic, technique, procedure). Bottom line: the enemy is watching and you can't do the same thing over and over. They will catch you.

Then, tonight, as I am preparing for the brigade update, G Co Cdr calls me stating that a soldier attached to her unit was stabbed by a local national in his B-hut. She was almost hysterical. She apparently happened upon him immediately after he was stabbed, falling down in front of her bleeding profusely. A few minutes ago I got word that he had died. It just proves that you can't trust anyone.

I am again frustrated by the incompetence of the local leaders. I came here wanting to believe in them and help them. What I discovered is they (Afghan leaders) lack the altruism, selflessness, and dedication to duty required to make a difference for their people. They are only concerned about themselves, which plays right into the hands of the enemy, and they take advantage of it. If Afghanistan goes back to the TB, it will not be our fault. Afghans will lose it. This stabbing is one of a couple of other incidents in the past 24 hours where Afghans have killed Americans on bases. It is hard to trust them when we see these things. We must remain vigilant.

In spite of the enemy attempting to bribe the Nurgaram NDS chief, he was one of the few officials who maintained a positive level of integrity. After he passed the tip about the IED, I led a foot patrol to the site where the enemy had staged the bomb, and EOD came in to diffuse it. The trust and cooperation we developed with the Nurgaram chief was one of the few bright spots in dealing with the Afghan officials.

Contrasting with our positive relationship with the NDS was a series of incidents across Afghanistan in which Afghans with access to American bases had killed our soldiers. On 31 December there were three murders of American soldiers on their bases. My young company commander was profoundly affected by witnessing the death of the young man attached to her unit. The criminal investigation division of the Army initiated an inquiry to determine the culprit. The investigation cast a wide net to determine who might have committed the crime, questioning local nationals, contractors and our soldiers. We never learned who did it. All we found out was that all soldiers were eliminated as suspects. This left us with a lack of closure in the wake of the incident.

1 January 2010

The young man from last night's incident died, as I noted last night. ML has been locked down all day. They have not yet found who did it. When they do, he needs to be dealt with swiftly. If a soldier, a court-martial resulting in the death penalty is in order. If an Afghan, then through their justice system. It was a disgusting act.

Quiet today, as all patrols were in. I flew to Firebase Connolly to visit down there and meet our new FDO. He is a good young man and will do a fine job. Once all the new LTs arrive on the 5th, I can complete all the job changes for the rest of the deployment. It is good to rotate the LTs so they get experience in fire support and gunline. They will be better, and so will the Army.

2 January 2010

We had a lot going on today. First, I had the security shura. Second, the ag reps did the assessment for the greenhouses in the area, and finally we began the process of building the school wall in Nangaresh. A very busy and productive day. The interim district governor did a very good job with the school wall, as he made the Malik and elders sign a contract stating that they would do it right. He has grown into his job. The security shura was silly, as the Alingar CoP of all people accused the Nurgaram police of corruption. He said they are part of the timber smuggling problem. Then an argument ensued. I think AM is just pissed that he hasn't been cut in. He is such a jerk and never does anything that could be remotely considered policing.

The kicker of the day is the PRT. They are actually trying to send one of the provincial leaders to Yale. That, to me, is criminal. It seems to me that there are a lot of young Americans who are more deserving of a Yale education rather than considering this program for such a dirtbag. It makes me sick. I have lodged my protests, but the state rep arrogantly said that I am not nuanced enough to really understand Afghan society. Well, here is what I do understand:

1. The provincial leader is not worthy of a free education based on some of his actions.
2. Stealing is wrong in any culture.

3. The Afghan president and ours have stated that stopping corruption is a top priority.
4. Supporting him going to Yale rewards his corruption.
5. The U.S. taxpayer would be pissed to know that the PRT has not got the balls to take a proper stand and is taking the easy way out.
6. I guess my Murray State, LSU, and SAMS education just isn't good enough to understand how things work in Afghanistan.

I don't care. It is wrong and I will fight them on it. Most Americans can't go to Yale, and neither should he on our dime.

The U.S. State Department has a program through which it will fund some education in government at Yale University for officials from developing countries. It is a good program, but it should only be used for those officials who demonstrate some capacity for actually governing. Further, there should be some litmus test of credibility before nominating an individual to attend a premier university in the United States. The PRT was working to remove the governor from his position, as I had wanted for some time, but I took issue with their methods. Most Americans cannot attend such a prestigious and expensive university, and yet the PRT was prepared to give this man an opportunity in spite of his incompetence. In my mind this was just wrong, and I could not allow it to go forward as planned. If the governor was to be removed from office, it should be a means of holding him responsible for his corruption rather than a reward.

3 January 2010

Another quiet day with no contacts. In spite of the fact that we have had multiple patrols out, there has been no activity. We sent one into Mashpah to ID a potential cache site and the other one was the MPs on the east side of the river. Little happened. I am going to meet with the provincial police chief tomorrow to discuss issues with the ANP after the radio message. Hopefully, we can get through some issues with smuggling, stealing fuel, and corruption. He is corrupt too, but not quite as bad as many others.

4 January 2010

We did a very large patrol into the Shemgal with the PLT, MPs, and even the PRT. Their commander actually let them do something today. We wanted to assess the valley sentiments and gauge whether they knew anything about our planned retrograde of the OP on 17 January. They knew nothing, which is good. I don't want the thing attacked as we are pulling out like the enemy did at Keating in eastern Nuristan and then claim a victory. I think everything will be OK.

The radio address included the provincial CoP today as well as the provincial prosecutor. These were important firsts, and the prosecutor in particular did very well. Afterward, I met with the CoP to talk about some things. I think he would be far more effective as a chief if there was a different governor. But the Afghan government is too cowardly to remove him and the PRT's solution to the problem is to send him to Yale. It still pisses me off, the very thought.

5 January 2010

A quiet day again, and I am happy about it. Only one night patrol that made no contact. Tomorrow I will meet Mangal Abdullah in the Nuralam to visit Paranieh and provide them with the rest of the funds for their retaining wall assessed in October. They (the villagers) have done a good job, and now they will get rewarded for their effort. The village has also proved anti-TB and supports the government, so we are trying to keep the faith with them.

Paranieh, like Sundawar, was a village on which we, in conjunction with the government, expended a lot of effort in order to build a solid partnership. With our help, the government identified several things that could be done to improve the villagers' lot. Once village affairs chief assessed what needed to get done, we provided the resources and the villagers provided the labor; as a result, they were able to complete a flood retaining wall that would protect their fields from threats like the storm that hit in September. In return, they kept the Taliban out and worked with us for the security of the whole area. This was another gratifying success that we had during our time there. However, the very next day a tragic event would test all of us.

6 January 2010

The patrol into the Nuralam went very well today and Mangal Abdullah (Alingar sub-governor) made the final payment to the village for their retaining wall. Then everything went downhill. We visited the school, providing school supplies, etc., and then left to come back to the FOB. When school let out, 4 girls ages 10–11 were injured in an IED blast. This cowardly enemy will do anything as low as it can possibly go. Then, as we were returning, we had another report of an IED at the site where Rao was killed. Sure enough, we found not one but two in the escape tunnel the triggerman used on 5 December.

The TB would do nothing but ruin this country if they were in charge again. We are trying to assist, and the enemy is just tearing everything down. I couldn't be more angry about today.

As we were sitting in the cordon (around the IED site) waiting for EOD to arrive, I saw through my binoculars several little girls playing a game that looked like Frisbee, and they were having great fun. As I watched I could not help but feel sorry for these young girls, who will be condemned after age 12 to a hard life of work, multiple pregnancies, and mistreatment at the hands of an older husband. Yet they will bear it in dignity while their mostly lazy menfolk do nothing to make the country a better place. Today was a prime example of our challenges. I am sure the police will do nothing in the way of investigating or making arrests following the incident in the Nuralam.

The IEDs on this day occurred in two different locations in Alingar. The first was in the Nuralam. As we learned later, the IED was actually targeting us, but the triggerman missed horribly. The IED killed one of the girls and mangled the three others. It was a horrible event that thoroughly disgusted all of us. The enemy demonstrated once again what they were all about. Rather than doing anything positive for the people, as we did, the Taliban destroyed and left nothing of value in their wake. The only thing that kept the Taliban in the game regarding the people's loyalty was the incompetence of the government leaders.

The second incident occurred in Lowkar, where we finally found the previously identified cache. It was actually a staging location for IEDs in preparation for placement at a later time. We received a tip from an anonymous caller to our hotline. Our patrol moved to the location, where we met a patrol from the PRT. We cordoned off the site and brought EOD forward to diffuse the bombs and remove them for evidence collection. This brought the total of IEDs in the past week to four, and the trend would continue. Regardless of the uptick in IED activity, a number of tips and reports from local citizens enabled us to avoid casualties. This was the payoff for our hard work in developing a relationship with the residents of our area. It was the common citizens who provided us with the information to find the explosives without experiencing losses. Most of the people understood that we were in Afghanistan to help them build something better than what they had in the past. I am still grateful for the assistance the people gave us, and I hope that what we did make a difference in their lives.

7 January 2010

Today we found out more about the IED in Wat-e-Jabbarkheyl; 1 girl was killed and 3 others wounded as a result of an IED in the road that was meant for us. Apparently, it was a remote control device that didn't go off since we were jamming (the signal). After we exited the valley it went off, killing and wounding the girls. We did an IO blitz today. First, the ANA with MPs went out to express condolences to the families. The ANA provided some humanitarian assistance. Then we did an info message on the radio, and later Mangal Abdullah came to the station to denounce what the enemy did.

Tonight I got a tip from a source in Alingar telling me that the TB had posted night letters in the village threatening people who work with us and claiming we were responsible for yesterday's IED. He said the villagers don't believe it, but they are scared.

We used the events of 6 January to illustrate the enemy's nasty nature. The enemy realized that they had erred in killing and maiming these girls. There was a backlash in the Nuralam against their activities. In response, the enemy attempted their own information campaign, accusing us of causing the IED blast. Of course, this was erroneous, and the people did not believe this story. We set the enemy on their heels as a result of their enormous misstep, and we solidified our relationship with the villages in the Nuralam.

8 January 2010

A very quiet day following the past two. We had the platoon go out and gather some intel around Lowkar, and some of the village elders are embarrassed by what is going on around their village. Further, they know it will affect future development in their village. So, I think our continuous presence is helping, plus they understand the math: support the enemy = no help from government or coalition and the enemy offers nothing. Support the government = development and a peaceful environment. Our continuing effort will reinforce this to separate the enemy from the people. If I only had some good police to make the effect permanent.

9 January 2010

We had several patrols out today. Of note was one we sent into the Nuralam. We were there to assess the people's attitude following the IED. The bottom line is they do not believe the TB propaganda that came out in the night letters saying that we did the IED. The multiple patrols made it difficult for the enemy to carry out anything, so it was a good day.

I met with three sub-governors today regarding the development shuras and Hamid Osmani's idea for a W. Nuristan reintegration shura. We are ready for the development shuras over the next couple of days as we prepared the SGs for their meetings. But the interesting thing is the initiative that Osmani is undertaking to get reintegration moving in W. Nuristan. He now has 3 commanders identified who want to stop fighting and come in with their fighters. I am going to help with the shura to get it moving. The catch is they want the governor (of Nuristan) to participate. However, true to his lazy self, he has expressed no interest. So, I will see if I can put some pressure on there. Regardless, it is looking like we will do the reintegration shura around the end of the month.

Our patrols confirmed what the source had already told us: nobody believed the Taliban's misinformation campaign. The people placed the blame for the loss of the girls squarely on the shoulders of the Taliban. This development allowed us to further reinforce our relationship with the people.

The district governor of Dow Ab worked very hard to reintegrate Taliban fighters back into society. He planned to hold a reintegration shura to discuss the terms of having these men come over to support the government and lay down their arms. Sealing the agreement would require the provincial governor's support. However, he was not willing to lend the authority of his office to this effort to make Nuristan a safer place. So, as will be seen, while the district governor made a valiant attempt, his hard work would eventually come to nothing as a result of this lack of support. Nevertheless, we did everything we could to support Osmani in his endeavor.

10 January 2010

Today Alingar held their development shura. Before it started I met with the families of the girls who were hurt in the IED incident in the Nuralam. I hope that our condolences may have at least let them know that we were disgusted by what happened and are there to help, as opposed to the enemy.

The shura went well, but it focused more on how bad the police are than on development. They are right; the CoP is so bad that he is destroying the credibility of the government and Mangal Abdullah. I am struggling to get him fired, but I can't because his boss is just as bad. Again the issues in Afghanistan come back to poor or corrupt leadership. If Alingar only had some decent police, the district would have no issues. But he is such a disruptive force that the enemy runs wild and the people rant about poor policing at a development shura. When you come down to it, I am the CoP in Alingar.

The elders in the shura agreed to sign a petition pointing out the incompetence of the police chief and a demand to have him removed. The SG and I will take it to the provincial governor for action. Maybe this will work, as nothing else seems to have had an effect in getting him fired.

I was taken aback by the fervor the elders demonstrated in their anger toward the Alingar chief of police. The shura on this day was intended to discuss the development and budget plans for the district. Instead, it turned into a referendum on the incompetence of the police chief. Elder after elder took his turn at lambasting the performance of the police. After listening to their tirades for some time, I hit upon the idea of having them sign a petition and running it up to the provincial government to see if the governor would have the fortitude to do something about the issue. I had tried other forms of pressure before and nothing had worked, so maybe this idea would change the dynamics. The elders enthusiastically stated that they would draft and sign a petition and put it in the hands of the district governor. Within days the district governor and I would meet with the Laghman provincial governor to force his hand on the issue.

11 January 2010

A quiet day. Our patrol went down the entire length of the road on the east side of the river with no issues. After the radio message the Nurgaram CoP provided me with a couple of documents showing that certain provincial officials are involved in trying to move confiscated timber, demonstrating widespread corruption at several levels. The governor (of Nuristan) is in Kabul right now, apparently under Karzai's orders, with his resume. Could he finally be getting fired? I sure hope so. That only leaves the Alingar police chief and then the most corrupt of the Afghan leaders will be gone. Hopefully, they will be replaced by some competent leaders. Tomorrow is the Nurgaram development shura. I hope they don't beg too much.

The NDS came in for our regular meeting. He thinks the enemy is currently down due to the night letters and IEDs. They are moving munitions in position for future operations.

The Nurgaram chief of police, in presenting the documents implicating corrupt Laghman officials, was simply trying to deflect attention from his own police department. Just a few days earlier the Alingar chief had accused the Nurgaram chief of corruption involving timber smuggling. The sniping back and forth between the two districts would have been almost comical if the situation were not so serious. But this kind of childishness and incompetence was reflective of the problems in Afghanistan. Until someone was willing to do things right for the sake of the people, progress was all but impossible. Yet we continued to plug away.

The governor was not fired and somehow managed to keep his job, much to my dismay.

12 January 2010

Today I attended the Nurgaram development shura. The shura was well run by Sakhi al-Nuralam, the interim SG, and the best thing about it was I did not speak. Exactly where I need to be, allowing the government leaders to take charge. al-Nuralam has got a decent handle on things. He sets priorities, and we will help him with the resources.

Hamid Osmani called today and told me that the former district governor of Dow Ab is trying to reassert himself as the SG in the district. This would be a very bad development. He had a forged letter claiming his authority to take charge as SG. My concern is that what he is doing will disrupt Osmani's efforts in reintegration and stabilizing Dow Ab. Also, this guy's brother is in the TB, and he is personally corrupt and helped the enemy attack the unit we replaced. Bottom line is he has to be stopped before he mucks up everything we have going.

I am heading to Garcia (in Goshta) tomorrow to meet the new LT in the platoon.

The acting district governor for Nurgaram had been performing his duties since October and had done an admirable job. I made a bid to have him permanently appointed to the job but was unsuccessful in this attempt. This man was a relatively competent official, but he was not well connected politically, and thus he was destined to remain a minor administrative assistant.

The former district governor was attempting to disrupt the efforts of the current sub-governor. Although he would not be successful in this effort, he did cause major issues in the district as Osmani attempted to implement his plans for development and reintegration.

13 January 2010

Everything went well today, especially with the large patrol sent into the Tag Valley (which is the western extension of the Nuralam Valley). We put in ANA, ANP, MPs, the maneuver PLT and the SECFOR (security force) from the PRT. We got a couple of sources, and that was about it.

The news of the day came in this evening. The enemy apparently knows we are bringing down OP Loyalty because they are planning an attack on it in the coming days. This is the same MO (modus operandi) they used at Keating and Lowell (in eastern Nuristan), and what they are doing is making an attack before we pull it down in order to show that they "forced" us out. Well, it won't work.

We are going to prepare for them by reinforcing it tomorrow, patrolling in the Shemgal Valley and with air assets we have lined up. If they come down again, I pray the Lord will give us another decisive victory as on 14 November.

Observation Post Loyalty would come down within days of this entry. This post always caused me loss of sleep because I felt it was too isolated to defend against a determined assault. On 14 November 2009 the enemy had attempted to overrun the post, but our intelligence enabled us to know their plans in advance and implement measures to defeat the attempt. I could not count on this luxury in every case. The post was manned by ten American soldiers and six Afghan security guards at all times. The post did provide us with good observation of certain places in our area, but it was limited in many ways. Therefore, after doing some cost-benefit analysis with the staff, I determined that we would accrue greater benefit from manning it exclusively with Afghans and pulling our ten exposed soldiers back to the FOB. These soldiers would then reinforce our patrols and give us a little more flexibility.

The enemy was very adept at learning our intent in Afghanistan. For example, the attack on Camps Keating and Lowell in the eastern part of the province in October 2009 was designed to make it appear that the Taliban had forced us to withdraw from those locations. This was not true, as we had always planned to move the soldiers to new locations. However, the Taliban is very skilled at using information to sway opinion in the press. To prevent this from happening when we left OP Loyalty, we planned some disruptive operations to deny the enemy the ability to mass and carry out an attack. The plans worked, and our operation pulling out the soldiers resulted in no loss of personnel or equipment. Further, it gave the Afghans responsibility for an important post to build their confidence in their ability to defend themselves and take charge of security.

14 January 2010

Today we reinforced the OP and made preparations to meet the enemy if they do decide to attack. I went to the security shura today and gained some commitments for assistance to defeat the enemy should they attack. Here is what we are ready to do with the Afghans:

1. ANP will conduct patrols into the Wadawu and Shemgal (valleys).
2. Combined patrol into Shemgal on Saturday before dawn.
3. Ambushes night of the 16th–17th to catch them moving.
4. Plus we have Predator and other assets coming.

I think we are ready, but the enemy could always pull something unexpected. We will also be doing several drills tomorrow.

We also started a new IO program. I am having my interpreter do some readings on the radio from the book *Taliban* to inform the public of the nature of the TB. Many rural people did not have contact with the TB and don't understand their true nature. This will help them know why they should resist and why we are here.

The disc jockeys at the radio station put together a nice production of the readings. This may seem like a mundane sort of programming to an American, but in Afghanistan such programs are listened to with great interest. Since television, the Internet, and other means of mass media are very limited in Afghanistan, most Afghans keep informed by means of radio broadcasts. The programming is much like that of the United States in the 1920s and 1930s, with music, readings, public announcements, and entertainment programs. Afghans gather around their radios to glean information or be entertained. Thus, the bulk of our information operations revolved around the radio station. We distributed free wind-up generator radios to people so that they could listen to the station. As a result, we had a monopoly on the use of this medium that the Taliban could not rival. The reading of the book Taliban *by my interpreter was well received and reminded many Afghans of the reasons why the Taliban should not come back to power.*

15 January 2010

We spent the day prepping for the retrograde of the OP today. We got some very good intel from Hamid Osmani. He called this evening and told me that the commander who had intended to attack called it off. He returned to Dow Ab with his 15 fighters. Osmani told me that the reason was that after conducting a recon, they believed that they would be defeated and it wasn't worth the risk. So, it looks like we won. We are still going to kick out our patrol tomorrow and ambushes the next night, but for now it looks like the retrograde will be uneventful. We will follow it up with an IO message immediately following the success.

16 January 2010

Today's patrol into the Shemgal confirmed that there was no enemy in there, so the report that the enemy went back to Dow Ab appears correct. However, our cameras picked up a lot of activity in Mangow last night that appeared suspicious. So, we vectored the patrol down there but turned up nothing. Whatever was going on, at least we disrupted it.

I held the (battery) commander's conference here with all the BCs. We had a good discussion with lessons learned, how we are training the ANA, and we worked on redeployment. It is good to know that the light at the end of the tunnel is in sight. Tomorrow we bring down the OP. With no enemy activity and an ANSF (Afghan National Security Forces) takeover of the site, it is a clear victory for us.

17 January 2010

We were able to bring down the OP today with no issues. It was very smooth, and in spite of the tough LZ (helicopter landing zone) up there, we had no safety issues. I went out with the MPs to the blocking position as an outer ring of security, and it was a good op. The only thing we saw was Gajours gathering firewood and bringing it down out of the mountains.

The PRT had a patrol planned into the Wadawu today and for the seemingly hundredth time cancelled it. For no apparent reason. It does us no good to synchronize our targeting effort and patrol schedules because the PRT never follows through. The only reason we were able to get the SECFOR (PRT security force) involved this week with the OP Loyalty security operation was the fact that their Cdr was gone. Now he is back and nothing will happen.

The retrograde of Observation Post Loyalty represented a great success for us. First, we were able to remove all of our equipment from the post via helicopter external loads. Second, we no longer had 10 Americans in an exposed position and had more personnel available for patrolling. Finally, the Afghans took over the post and assumed responsibility for security. Since this was our main reason for being in the country, we were pleased with the outcome. The enemy made no attempt to disrupt the retrograde, and as a wrap-up for the operation we announced on the radio station the positive results of the day, including the fact that Afghans were in charge. It was a win-win situation for the Afghans and us.

18 January 2010

Quiet day. Our patrols encountered nothing. Reports say that the enemy leaders are in Pakistan to regroup. Could be true, based on the low level of activity. There were coordinated bombings in Kabul today. The media jumped on it to depict a deteriorating security situation. Of course, what the attack was really about was targeting the media to get out just that message. And they obliged by providing it without ever realizing that they are being duped.

Mangal Abdullah did give me a letter of petition today from the elders of Alingar requesting the removal of the Alingar CoP. I endorsed it and will meet with the Laghman governor on Wednesday to lodge my own effort to get the turd removed. If they won't remove him, it is indicative of the corruption and failure of the government to get good leaders who could make a difference, plus the fact that they don't care.

The elders in Alingar quickly drafted the letter, as promised, and it contained the signatures or marks of every major village leader across the district. I scheduled a meeting with the Laghman provincial governor to present it to him through the Laghman PRT. I had great hopes that this would finally lead to a breakthrough in weeding out corrupt leaders in our area.

19 January 2010

Today became pretty interesting early this morning, as a protest was organized in Nangaresh and the demonstrators marched from the village down to the DC (district center). It was peaceful, although they did burn some tires and throw rocks at a government billboard. The purpose was to protest the governor. Apparently, he refused to seat the elected representative from Nurgaram on the provincial council. He is the first Pashai ever elected, and the people are angry because he (the governor) seated one of his cronies. Again, corruption enters the picture as the great enemy here. This crap plays right into the enemy hands, and the governor is either too dumb or too interested in himself to do the right thing. Hopefully, the local people can get the attention of Kabul, since we can't seem to. Tomorrow I go to ML to meet with the Laghman governor in the attempt to get the Alingar CoP fired.

Nothing seemed to work in our attempt to hold the Nuristan governor responsible for his outlandish corruption. However, this protest, rising spontaneously from the discontent of the people, seemed like an opportunity to finally hold him responsible by elevating the news of unrest to the highest levels of the government. Even this did not work, however, and the governor remained comfortably in his job with a council of cronies who fed his pockets from the bottom up.

20 January 2010

I met with the Laghman governor and CoP today about the Alingar CoP. After three hours of rambling they finally agreed to get rid of him. Hopefully, they will follow through quickly so we can get a new guy on board. Now my only fear is that the new guy will be no better. The current guy is:

- Corrupt
- Talks to the enemy
- Does no police work
- Doesn't speak Pashto (this makes no sense to me)
- Has no support from people

Tomorrow I fly out to Fortress to visit those guys. Only a couple more weeks and I start moving toward home. I can't wait.

Getting the Alingar chief of police fired was an important step forward, but even this task would not be easy. The governor and provincial chief of police attempted to put a crony in the place of the fired chief to maintain their corrupt network. We learned the background of the new district chief and protested the arrangement. After almost two months of wrangling, we finally got an acceptable replacement.

21 January 2010

Today the RCP (engineer route clearance package) hit an IED near Parisaw. This is roughly the same place that the PRT was hit last June near Mohammed al-Rahman's house. Once again this area is hot and this guy is involved. The MPs were going to do a patrol up the valley that evening, but a few days ago I told the AS3 that I wanted the RCP to clear the route first. The RCP had no injuries. The enemy has gone almost exclusively to IEDs in the area, and this is the big threat. Their sole purpose is to cause U.S. casualties.

If I only had the intel to know where the supplies were coming from and when the IED cell was meeting, I could break it up. But we just don't have the resources. Also, if the police would do their job, it would help, but again the crisis of leadership in Afghanistan intervenes to hurt the country.

The IED cell had certainly stepped up the pressure since 31 December, and this was yet another incident. Rather than challenging us in a stand-up fight, the enemy was now taking an indirect approach, allowing them to preserve their own strength following their losses in November and their success in the IED attack on 5 December. The local people had supplied us with very good information in finding IEDs and preventing casualties, but we could never get the "golden nugget" that would enable us to break up the cell. We had to build our intelligence network to facilitate neutralizing the cell in a more proactive manner rather than reactively.

22 January 2010

Uneventful day. Our only patrol encountered nothing and we got no reports. We did have two guys that we had to evacuate for mental health issues. These things are killing us. Of the 10 or so cases that we have had during this deployment, only two to three are legitimate. The rest use the system to malinger while they leave their buddies short-handed to do their job. If I don't send a guy back, then I can be considered hurting his mental health when most of the time guys are faking to leave. I know that there are legitimate cases and guys who need help. Those I support. But the guy who has an affair before he leaves to come over (to Afghanistan) only for his wife to decide to leave is hiding behind a veil of deceit he himself created. Then all the other "joes" have to pull that guy's load after he did it to himself and then claims he can't take it. It's crap. Failure to take responsibility or care for the guy next to you is pure selfishness. But I guess my comments here make me intolerant when I am being honest and shining light on something that we can no longer talk about because of political correctness.

23 January 2010

It was a very uneventful day until this evening. First, the Alingar CoP is now gone, and thank God for that. He was a horrible police chief and he is finally fired. Mangal Abdullah called me tonight to tell me that he left and the new CoP has come on board. I don't know about him yet, but I hope that he will get to know the people and do some actual police work. Also, if he will not cooperate with the enemy and take bribes, we will stand a much better chance of making a difference in Alingar. Then, around 2000 (8PM), I got another call from Abdullah saying that the TB IED cell leader from Mehtar Lam was holding a shura in Lowkar with a group of insurgents. He requested our help in getting him. So, we met the ANP, took some ANA with the maneuver PLT, and went to the site. Before we got there the enemy scooted. We missed them by no more than 5 minutes. I think the ANP blew it because they got to the site before us and spooked them before we could set the cordon. When the insurgents saw the ANP coming, they went to the school in the village, out the back door, into a ditch behind the school, and escaped west toward the mountains. So, we lost an opportunity. The inept actions of the ANP convinced me that we should tuck them into our convoy in the future rather than have them leading because they won't keep the convoy intact. They got too far ahead of us and did not use stealth approaching the target. Next time, if we put them in the center of the convoy, we can control their movement, allowing us to set the cordon. Then we can feed them in to conduct the search. At the least we disrupted the enemy and forced them to change their plans from what they wanted to do.

We finally got the "golden nugget" and the ANP botched the operation. We organized a cordon team, with the understanding that the ANP would conduct the actual search. We held a rehearsal of the operation to ensure that everyone knew their roles. Then, when we prepared to roll, the ANP left without the rest of the convoy. They arrived with a clamor and spooked the enemy, resulting in their escape just before we could set the trap. I was disgusted by the outcome after we had finally received the intelligence we were looking for. Bagging the Mehtar Lam IED cell leader would have disrupted enemy operations in all of Laghman province. Yet we missed the target.

24 January 2010

Very busy today. I went to Najil with the ANA BC so he could see his people. Once again he has done a great job with his people. Their crew drill out there looked much better, and he made several corrections of discipline to ensure they were doing the right thing. While I was there the new CoP from Alingar came in to do a radio message and discuss last night's raid with Mangal Abdullah. He seems to be pretty good and he has experience, although the drawback is that it was with the Russians and then the Northern Alliance. If he is at least somewhat competent and generally uncorrupted, it will be a huge leap forward, but we will see.

Then this evening a source brought in 6 IEDs. That means we have had 11 in our AO since the first of the year. How many more are out there? I just hope God steers us away from them and we get rid of the rest before they can hurt anyone.

Our relationship with the locals once again paid off with the turn-in of six IEDs. This made eleven in 24 days, which was far more than we had seen in any other comparable period, and the pattern would continue for the duration of the time we had left. The enemy had definitely modified their tactics in order to preserve their forces while inflicting maximum casualties on us. However, the trust we built with the people early on was giving us protection from the intentions of the enemy.

25 January 2010

I met the new CoP for Alingar today, and he seems promising. Then this afternoon Mangal Abdullah told me that the Laghman CoP is going to screw it all up by sending the guy just fired from Alishang (District of western Laghman) over as a permanent replacement in Alingar. We expressly told him last week not to do this, and yet he appears to be doing exactly that. Again it comes down to poor leadership.

I met Abdullah in Lowkar today to discuss the security situation with the elders. The recent uptick in insurgent activity there is surprising. This village has had a lot of development, like the clinic, school, canal, road, etc. Yet insurgents are back. The TB could have never done any of these things for the people, which I pointed out. Abdullah hammered the people for not reporting and working security. And he told them that until they do, development is at a halt. I hope this pressure will produce results, but we will see.

The new Alingar police chief had been on the job a grand total of three days when the provincial chief decided to bring in another man who was one of his cronies. In our meeting the previous week I had specifically asked that the chief supply a credible replacement. Initially, it seemed that he would follow through on my request. However, it appeared the provincial chief had just appeased us temporarily in order to insert a chosen ally so that he could continue his corrupt enterprises. I would not let this happen.

The Alingar district governor did a nice job of steering the meeting in Lowkar. Over the past couple of months security had deteriorated to a troublesome point in this once stable village. Before our arrival the village had received a great deal of development and was seen as a model for progress. Yet the enemy had somehow infiltrated the village, and the elders had done nothing about the situation. Mangal Abdullah forcefully told the elders that if they did not get control of the security situation and start cooperating with the government, then all development and assistance would cease. The elders agreed to implement measures to clean up their poor security, and we agreed to observe their efforts with a view toward restarting development. But we would do nothing without cooperation on security.

26 January 2010

Everything was very quiet in the AO. The switch of the Alingar and Alishang CoPs is true. The COL is mad, and so am I. He is going to engage the provincial CoP himself over this idiocy. Hopefully, he can reverse the stupidity. Then the surprise of the evening: we received COAs (courses of action) from brigade that have us moving in one month. I was floored by this. One has us taking over all of Laghman and moving (to Mehtar Lam). The other has us moving to Gamberi and taking over that base and the Qargyhee district in Laghman. Looks like we are going to be real busy for the rest of our time here. Should know what we are doing by the Cdrs' Conference on Friday.

The Laghman police chief had simply switched the two district chiefs from one district to the other. So, Alingar got the former chief from Alishang, while the Alishang got the former chief of Alingar. I reported this up my chain of command, and our commander was steamed. He decided to intervene directly with the provincial chief and launch his own effort to rid the province of this corrupt leader. It would take weeks to fix this issue. In the end, we did get a decent chief and the provincial chief was finally removed.

Our plan for a move and change of mission had been on the shelf for several months. We had put a great deal of effort into planning for transferring authority over to the Afghans and moving our headquarters to another location with a mission of partnership with an Afghan Army brigade. It had been such a long time since we had engaged in this planning that we believed that execution would not happen. However, with this order we once again began preparing for a changed mission. It would certainly keep us busy for our remaining four months in Afghanistan.

27 January 2010

The RCP hit another IED, this time at Parwai. Once again we were sending a patrol out and I told the AS3 to send the RCP in before the patrol to clear the route. Good call. Luckily, the patrol was saved from hitting the charge on a day that we had the clearance package. Divine Providence. This one was a large one, over 100 pounds (of explosive), and it smashed up the MRAP (mine-resistant ambush protected) vehicle. However, no one was killed (in the RCP), no broken bones, and only a couple of bad headaches. They had concussions, I am sure. If only Rao had not been outside the vehicle, he would still be here.

The security shura went well, and I met the new CoP in Alingar. However, the guy was in only one day. Pressure from above finally prevailed, and he is gone too. I guess the COL was angry last night following my brief to him, and he got the ball rolling to prevent the sleight of hand that was going on. The Laghman CoP was finally forced to get rid of our old guy and this new guy. So, now we will see what shakes out.

Tomorrow to Bostick (FOB Bostick in Konar) and then the start of the Bde Cdr Conference. Thank God no one was killed today. Parwai is now cut off by us. More later.

Once again the route clearance package did its job and saved our patrols, with their less protected vehicles, from hitting an IED. The engineers whom we received once or twice a week did great work for us keeping the routes in our area open for traffic. I had made it a policy that whenever we had the engineers, they would clear the route that our patrol would use that day to mitigate risk. This policy had great payoff, as the engineers detected many IEDs for us, preserving the lives of our soldiers. We owe those brave young soldiers a great deal.

The new Alingar police chief lasted only one day. The pressure on the Laghman chief came from all directions, and he finally succumbed. We did not have to take another corrupt individual, but now we would have to play a waiting game until we got a credible replacement.

28 January 2010

I was flying up to Bostick today before the Cdrs' Conference, but the weather was bad up north, so I got stuck in J-bad. It has been raining all day and the XO told me that it was snowing back at Kalagush in the mountains around the FOB. I am glad. I hope the enemy freezes. I met the COL and hit up the FECC, S3, DCO, and (Bde) XO. We are straight and the decision has not been made if we get Laghman Province yet. Everything is contingent on where the new National Guard unit 1–102 Infantry goes when they get here to replace Wildhorse (1–221 Cavalry).

Back at the FOB, the XO said Mangal Abdullah may have a lead on the IED guy. He said he intends to make an arrest on Saturday. If true, it is a huge step forward.

There would be no arrest of the IED leader. It was another false alarm.

29 January 2010

We had the Cdrs' Conference today. We will move within 3 months to either Mehtar Lam or Gamberi. It all depends on where the replacement for Wildhorse goes. We will know in a few days. Regardless, I am kind of happy about it because it gives us something fresh for our last 4 months here. It is so easy to get stagnant even though we try so hard to push things forward. I know we have done some good things since we have been here and made good progress, but there are times when I get so frustrated with the Afghans. I guess we just have to keep pushing them until they begin to take charge of their own affairs. So, you have to work with the ones who can achieve, remove those who can't, and just keep pressing ahead. It will be good to take my leave because I do feel jaded.

In the end, we went to neither Mehtar Lam nor Gamberi. A few days after this entry I made a reconnaissance to Gamberi and then to another forward operating base known as Hughie in Nangarhar. Following that reconnaissance, I recommended a third course of action to better support the intent of the plan, and that was to relocate to Hughie. This is where we would move our headquarters to establish a partnership with the 2nd Brigade, 201st Corps, Afghan National Army.

30 January 2010

I flew down to Mehtar Lam today for A Btry's change of command. It was a perfect day for the ceremony. We did it on the gunline and one of the big snow-capped mountains was in the background. The A Btry commander did a good job for 22 months, and the former HHB commander (who changed command at Kalagush in December) will keep them moving forward.

Patrols had no issues today. There was a piece of intel that the enemy is now targeting me specifically. There is a local here on the FOB who tells the enemy when I leave the base. Then they will try to hit us based on what vehicle I am in. Apparently, the RCP on Wednesday was hit because they (the enemy) thought I was in the convoy and specifically that vehicle—as I do tend to ride in a vehicle of a similar type. Whatever. If they are that desperate to kill me, then it must mean that we are being effective here. That is what I am after, and God will take care of me and all the soldiers.

A Battery at Forward Operating Base Mehtar Lam firing a 155mm rocket assisted projectile in support of another firebase in contact with the enemy (courtesy Major Anthony "Tony" Brunner).

31 January 2010

Today was quiet until 1630 this evening. We got a call on the tip line about a cache in Baba Kala (near Lowkar). The source came to the FOB and volunteered to lead us to the site. ANP arrived and we moved to the site. Jackpot. For the first time we have a significant find. The cache found a couple of weeks ago was only two IEDs, and they were staged for placement. But today we found IED-making material, mortar rounds, 107mm rockets, machine gun ammo, ammonium nitrate, etc. The hotline works, and because of it we may have saved somebody's life. It had been so frustrating for so long getting this kind of info. Now that we have this one, if we can get a couple more, we may finally break the cell's logistic capability and better connect the government to the people. Hamid Osmani starts the reintegration shura tomorrow; let's hope that goes well.

The discovery of this cache was another demonstration of the trust and goodwill we had built with the people. Early on we established a hotline, much like a 911 operator in America, and we publicized it over the radio station daily in public service messages. A translator answered all the calls, and while many of the tips proved unprofitable, there were several others, like the one on this day, that had great payoff. Our continuous efforts to connect with the people, our engagements with the local leaders, and the respect we demonstrated for the Afghan culture enabled us to operate effectively. It was this fact that led to the intelligence reports stating that the enemy desired to kill me and my interpreter. Nevertheless, we would continue with our program.

1 February 2010

A very quiet day. I did the radio address with Mangal Abdullah today. Then I had my meeting with NDS. The IED cell leader has threatened the source who led us to last night's cache, which turned out to be a significant find of IED-making materials. He called the guy's uncle to make the threat. We then reassured the uncle, and we will keep pushing the envelope to clear the area of the IED threat.

More evidence implicating provincial officials of participation in timber smuggling. Today, I learned that they are accepting bribes from smugglers to get their timber past the ANP checkpoints. The guy who bribes them also kicks some money back to the enemy to allow him to continue operating. So, in an indirect sense, the officials are enabling the enemy. Unbelievable.

As the reader can see from the entry above, I had become very frustrated with what I perceived as a situation that had many of the features of mafia rule. Provincial officials were running protection rackets to move illegal timber, which also benefited the enemy. It was very disheartening to attempt implementing a normal sense of government when the very people you had to work with were an inherent part of the problem.

2 February 2010

We spent the day planning for our now impending move. I went to Torkham Gate to brief that maneuver PLT that it will be coming to us while the XO went to a logistic meeting to begin planning for the impending moves. The whole brigade is realigning and the earlier plan that we pitched, moving us to Gamberi, is now in motion. I think this is great because it will partner us with a new ANA brigade to mentor, allow us to focus on the FA mission, and give us a good mission as we prepare to redeploy, which is now less than four months away.

Also, today we had some success in Ja'laam village with a patrol. The purpose was to pay a visit to the IED cell leader's house. And it worked. We found unauthorized munitions and a lot of useful data that could lead us to all the cell members, plus we scared the piss out of him. If we can get the connections made, hopefully his days are numbered.

Finally, the reintegration shura was attacked, wounding three people, including the OCC (Afghan Operation Coordination Center) intel officer. This actually plays into our hands. The government holds a peace shura and the enemy attacks it. This paints the TB as disruptive and destructive. Further, the elders were angered by the act. Several fighters are prepared to reintegrate and the elders are ready to sign a pact. Hamid Osmani has shown some real leadership, and in spite of the provincial governor and CoP's lack of interest, Osmani has demonstrated that he is the power in the area. We need more like him.

Part of the plan for the move would involve bringing our security platoon at Torkham Gate back to the headquarters battery to provide an extra security element. While we would continue to plan for the move to Gamberi, ultimately we would not go to that location, as events will show.

We sent a patrol to the cell leader's house following threats he made to several of the local people who were cooperative with the government and our forces. We aimed to demonstrate that this thug would not be permitted to intimidate the local people and that he was not immune to questioning about his illegal activities. While the patrol was in the village, the ANA followed a lead that brought us to yet another cache of weapons and other materials used for attacks on our forces. We were beginning to make a dent in the enemy's ability to sustain their operations. Unfortunately, we still did not have enough evidence to connect the cell leader directly to the enemy activity. We hoped that the evidence we gathered this day would enable us to make a detention that would stick.

Finally, the reintegration shura, which was focused on making peace up in Dow Ab, turned into a chaotic event. The enemy up there actually attacked the proceeding, injuring three individuals. The district governor was making a valiant effort to bring about peace and normalcy in his district, and yet the enemy (as well as his superiors in the provincial government) was making it difficult to achieve success. Nevertheless, the inept enemy offered an opportunity for success. In attacking the shura, the enemy made the elders of the district extremely angry. If the district governor had been able to leverage that anger against the TB, he could have finally turned the corner for peace in the northern part of our area. Regrettably, time would demonstrate that too many factors were at work against the sub-governor for him to achieve that level of success.

3 February 2010

I flew out to Gamberi today to recon what could be our new FOB. There are several limitations right now that could make moving problematic. There are a lot of ideas and plans swirling around at Brigade, so for now I will just lean forward and wait until the realignment plan comes out before getting too excited.

There was yet another IED today. It was called into our tip line again, and the RCP with the maneuver platoon were able to successfully remove it with no harm. This one was booby trapped, which is something we have not seen previously. It appears to have been laid for us to intentionally find it. Once removal attempts occurred, there was a grenade strapped to the bottom of it to get the team removing it. Fortunately, a numbskull must have placed it because the pin was still in it. Thank God for the tip and the ineptitude of the enemy.

I go on leave tomorrow, and I am very happy about that. I am mentally worn out and ready to go home. I can't wait to see Mare and the kids, plus Trigger (my dog).

Once again our hotline paid off. An anonymous tip from a local citizen told us the location of the IED, and we were able to move the engineers, along with our maneuver platoon, to the site to avoid yet another blast. As stated above, this IED was rigged to wound or kill the first responders. The engineers are trained to search for booby traps around an IED site and were able to discover the grenade attached to the device. However, the enemy did not pull the pin on the grenade to set the fuse, so that when the engineers attempted to remove it from the ground it would detonate. Once again the Lord was with our troops.

4 February–2 March 2010

I had a great leave at home and got some much-needed rest. It took a total of 8 travel days to complete getting back and forth on top of the 18 days of leave and TDY (temporary duty). We did not really do anything other than go to the state swim meet for Ashley and to the hospital in San Antonio. Ashley won the meet, and there were several college scouts there looking at her. She did very well. At the end of my time home Maryellen and I went to BAMC (Brooke Army Medical Center) in San Antonio to visit the soldiers in the hospital. (Staff Sergeant) McClintock is making a great recovery following the severe wounds he had from the IED on 5 December. The only thing that irritated me was finding out that McClintock's wife told him she wanted a divorce when she went down to BAMC to be with him. Apparently she has some other soldier on the side. Unbelievable. I am so happy that I never had to deal with that with Maryellen. She has always been wonderful. The visit was good and the leave with Mare was great. We just spent our time quietly together, and it was the best thing I could have asked for. Andy got to visit a couple of days from the academy, which was good. He is doing very well. So, I had a great break, but now am back and will have to deal once again with the issues at hand in Afghanistan.

During a year-long deployment each soldier gets 15 days of leave. Commanders are permitted three additional days to visit hospitals where wounded soldiers are recovering. This much-deserved leave only provides a brief respite from the rigors of combat, but, while not long enough, it is a treasured time for most soldiers. Some, unfortunately, have to deal with family problems and, in certain cases, a spouse who decides to leave. This can only add to the stress to a soldier returning to the combat zone.

3 March 2010

Today I got myself reoriented. Many changes since I was gone, including the fact that the ANA battery is gone. They were replaced by an ANA infantry company, which will help us in the AO greatly. HHB will partner with them, and my aim is to always have them with us and to push them to do their own independent ops as the means to assumption of full responsibility here.

Other changes:

IV. Sustaining and Making a Difference, 7 Dec. '09 to 3 Apr. '10

- MPs leave Monday; I knew this was coming, but it hurts.
- We are moving to J-bad first week of April to get ready for partnership role with ANA brigade.
- New PRT is here. Thank God for that.
- New Alingar CoP is on top of things.

IED found in Salaw (Valley) today. That makes 17 since 1 January. Up until 1 January we had 21 in seven months. The enemy is definitely trying to inflict casualties on us through IEDs because they have lost in all direct firefights. Plus we are winning the IO battle in the AO. All this adds up to providing us freedom of movement based on the success in fighting and trust we have built with the people. Further, we are embarrassing them (the Taliban), and IEDs are their preferred way to attack with any chance of success.

I confronted the Nurgaram CoP today about a cache found (while I was on leave) in one of his ANP officer's houses. I told him to fix it or I will find someone who can. I think that Abdullah Khan's incompetence is hurting the district.

I was surprised to discover all of the changes that had occurred in my absence. I was saddened to see the Afghan artillery battery leave, but receiving an infantry company represented an overall boost in our capacity for patrolling in the area. Losing the military police was certainly a letdown, but receiving our platoon back from Torkham Gate would more than compensate for the MPs moving to another location. I was not surprised to learn that we would not go to Gamberi. I had actually recommended moving to Jalalabad and Forward Operating Base Hughie before I left, and the recommendation was accepted. Overall, the shuffle was good for our future effort in Area of Operation Steel and for taking up our new mission. It would facilitate the success of the brigade by making better use of resources and concentrating on what would produce long-term success in Afghanistan.

Finally, while I was on leave our maneuver platoon with the Afghan National Army acted on a tip, capturing yet another cache that contained rockets and IED-making material. What made this find startling is the fact that it was confiscated from the home of an Afghan National Police officer. I had suspected for some time that the Nurgaram police had ties to the enemy, and now I had proof. I confronted the chief of police, who denied responsibility. To put pressure on him, I threatened to hold a shura of the elders for the purpose of determining whether they had confidence in him and, if not, drafting a petition as we did in Alingar. The Nurgaram chief, Abdullah Khan, was well aware of our success in removing the Alingar chief, and I used that as leverage against him. He claimed that "political" forces required him to employ certain individuals and this officer was among them. Regardless, I informed him that it was unacceptable and that he should clean up his department, or else I would take action against him.

4 March 2010

Today was a very quiet day. We focused on planning for our move to Jalalabad. A lot of work to be done in getting us ready to move logistically. Tomorrow I will go out on patrol with the maneuver platoon to Rajai on our southern boundary. On the way I am going to drop in and meet the new CoP from Alingar.

5 March 2010

I went with the maneuver platoon on their patrol today. On the way we stopped at the Alingar police station so I could meet the new chief. After the first meeting I had a favorable impression of him. He said his priorities are destroying the IED cell and combating corruption. If he sticks to this, then we will finally be moving in the right direction. I also provided him with info on the cell leader Haminullah Khan. We have a lot on him, and I want to get him off the streets before I leave.

Tonight he called to let me know that he confiscated 2 truckloads of smuggled timber this evening. Now we just have to make sure he retains his job. If he is too effective, the Afghan government will want to get rid of him because he is cutting in on their corruption rackets.

The new Alingar police chief quickly came under fire for his aggressiveness in fighting timber smuggling. Within days enormous pressure came down from the provincial governor and other high-ranking officials to release the confiscated lumber. The chief refused, and a battle ensued over the fate of lumber and the new man's job. I came to his defense and was successful in helping him keep his position, but political forces conspired against us with regard to the timber, as subsequent entries will show.

6 March 2010

We had a couple of patrols go into the Nuralam today, but nothing occurred. The Alingar CoP did well last night in confiscating the timber. It appears that the timber was moving on forged documents signed by someone in authority for kickbacks. So, it appears he has exposed a corruption ring with this action. He told me yesterday that he would take action against smuggling, and in fact he has.

We did battle drills with the new PRT today. I am encouraged that we might actually have a good incoming team, but I will save judgment for now. I had the same hope for the current one and it did not pan out.

7 March 2010

In a surprise to us, today a new SG for Nurgaram was appointed. Sakhi al-Nuralam (the interim district governor) will now revert back to being the deputy SG for the district. al-Nuralam did OK as acting SG, and although it is about time the district got a permanent SG, I am very wary of the change. You never know what you are going to get here. I just hope he isn't corrupt. I am so sick of dealing with corrupt officials. The new SG is Dr. Abdur Rahman. He is an actual medical doctor, so he has an education. We will see what he is made out of in the coming days.

The ANA Co Cdr finally arrived. He is a Tajik and had a fierce, determined look on his face. I hope that he is as determined as he looks. If so, he could make a big difference in the area.

The previous district governor for Nurgaram had left in October 2009 to take over in Barge Matal, his home district. It took the Afghan government more than five months to appoint a replacement. In the meantime, the deputy stepped in as the interim district governor, and he did a relatively competent job. I advocated for Sakhi al-Nuralam to receive the appointment to the permanent position, but political forces were at work in the appointment of Abdur Rahman. The previous several months in Afghanistan had tempered my willingness to immediately embrace this new official. Before I put full trust in him, I wanted to see if he had credibility and what motivated his actions.

The commander of the ANA infantry company, as noted above, was a Tajik. This could have serious ramifications on operations in our area if the people from other ethnic groups did not accept him. He was a Northern Alliance fighter against the Taliban, and with the formation of the army he received a commission as a captain. He had the look of a killer, and his appearance was that of a man who would let no obstacle stand in his way. While I was happy to have a partner who was a bona fide fighter, I worried that he might rub the local officials and elders the wrong way. As events will show, he was not readily accepted, and he had a disturbing habit of smoking hashish that led to serious issues with his leadership that we would have to deal with.

8 March 2010

We had a fairly busy day today. I was supposed to meet with NDS, but they could not attend because they were coordinating the release of a kidnapped engineer. While I was gone 2 Afghan engineers working for USAID were kidnapped by an insurgent leader named Amanullah Khan. Today one of the families paid a $30,000 ransom for him. The other family has not, and now the enemy is threatening to kill him. What bothers me is that the ransom could set a bad precedent. Obviously, the enemy will have money to finance themselves if they can pull off a couple of successful kidnappings. So, I would prefer that this was not the case, but since the local police are so weak it is probably the only way to get them back alive.

The new SG for Nurgaram did his first radio message today, and he said all the right things, but we will see if he has some action to back his words. I will reserve my assessment until then.

The new Alingar CoP called and said a local citizen reported an IED in the Nuralam Valley this evening. He went there and found two. We will meet him tomorrow with EOD to remove them. Just have to be careful of ambushes.

Finally, the new PRT is here and only 10 from the old one remain. I certainly hope this one is better than the last. The old team was such a letdown, uncooperative, and did little to make anything better in the area. In fact, they made things tougher for us. If this new one at least shows some interest and is willing to get out of the FOB, we might make some progress. Unfortunately, we only have 30 days before we pull out to move to J-bad for the partnership mission.

The enemy hit on a new tactic to accompany the uptick in IEDs while I was on leave. The Taliban from Dow Ab kidnapped two engineers working on the road project north of the FOB. The purpose was to extract money from the families in order to finance their operations. A real solution to the problem would have included the police actually engaging in some police work. However, this did not happen, and thus the enemy found a fresh source of financial support.

9 March 2010

Went out on patrol with the maneuver PLT to the IED site this morning, but it was gone when we got there. The locals had pulled the wires out to prevent it from detonating, and because it was discovered the enemy dug it up. The good news is that the locals acted to prevent the thing from working, which frustrated the intent of the enemy. The bad news is that we did not get the device. Oh, well, at least the locals are reporting and acting on what they see.

We think because of the size of the thing that it was a trigger for an ambush on us or on the ANP. Since Mohammed Gilani (the new Alingar

CoP) took over, the enemy knows they can't get away with the things they were doing with the previous guy around. So, they may be targeting the ANP to neutralize them for their own freedom of movement.

Intel coming in of the Dow Ab cell becoming active and looking to attack the FOB again. Their new Cdr is the brother of the commander we killed last November, so that explains what may be going on.

The local population once again provided us with information and intervened to prevent an IED attack. I would have preferred to recover the device for evidence, but the knowledge that the population was reporting to their own police and acting to prevent violence was certainly a positive development. It also demonstrated that the people were beginning to develop trust and confidence in their new police chief, and this was definitely a step in the right direction.

10 March 2010

The event of the day was the PRT changing over. I was so glad to see the old leadership leave. We had such a missed opportunity with the last crew in that they did so little to foster development and governance that could have led to strides in security. We had to fill the vacuum. Further, the uncooperative attitude was even worse. We would make the effort to do joint planning to leverage the capabilities of both organizations, and then their commander would change the plan at the last minute. It got to the point where I just had to do what I thought was best and execute. I think with the new team we may have an opportunity to achieve what I always wanted to. Unfortunately, we are leaving soon.

The entry above illustrates an issue of unity of command. The PRT and my battalion were considered equals because both were commanded by individuals of comparable rank. Unless one of the two units was placed in a subordinate status, the two had to form a partnership rather than a command relationship. Unity of command is a time-tested principle of war that states all military units operating together must fall under the command of single leader. Time and again throughout history there have been examples of units operating outside of this principle, which inevitably leads to friction and disagreements that are sometimes detrimental to the mission. Cooperation seems like a good concept, but it does not work in most circumstances. The best solution to ensure unity of command—from which flows common direction and singular focus of operations—is placing all units operating in a single battlespace, such as Area of Operation Steel, under one commander. Much of the friction that occurred between our battalion and the PRT arose from disagreement in the focus of operations. Since neither the PRT commander nor I had authority over one another, my team would often execute our own independent operations without the cooperation of the PRT. The issue of unity of command is a lingering problem in Afghanistan to date.

11 March 2010

Today I conducted the security shura with the local leaders. COL R. of the OCC-P led it, and before I went into the meeting I learned that the Nurgaram police had actually apprehended one of the kidnappers of the engineers. But they let him go on a technicality (lacking an interrogation questionnaire). This place kills me. Another incident to destroy my confidence in progress. They could have kept the guy and used him as a bartering tool to release the other engineer. Instead, they play by the rules, which they never do any other time, and release a guy because they don't have the proper questionnaire to interrogate him. What? The incompetence here is killing me. I confronted the police chief about the issue, and all he could do was say he can't do anything and he is doing his best. Meanwhile, the enemy sees this incompetence and takes advantage of it to paint the government as a bunch of stooges. And I have to sit there and look like a stooge by association with these clowns. I told them all at the security shura that I cared more about Afghanistan than any of them. And if they didn't start doing their jobs, all of them would lose. Also, I said if they didn't start doing their jobs, then I would push to get them fired. It is so frustrating trying to help people who won't do anything to help themselves.

I was extremely angered by the fact that the police released a kidnapper merely because they didn't have an interrogation questionnaire. This seemed like a contrived excuse to let the individual go. I believe that a bribe was paid for the kidnapper's release, but I could never prove it. At the time I remember thinking that the police should have detained him until they got the questionnaire from their higher headquarters. This would have been much better than releasing a suspected Taliban insurgent. However, even the things that are simple in Afghanistan are overwhelmingly difficult at times—hence my frustration.

12 March 2010

I flew to Asadabad today to visit B/3–321 for the first time. They replaced C Btry right before I went on leave, so I had not had a chance to go visit them. They are doing well and having no issues currently. We did a joint patrol with the new PRT, and when I got back this evening my staff gave them our O&I (operations and intelligence) brief. We should be able to develop a common operating picture of the AO and unity of effort. I am cautiously optimistic that this PRT is going to be more cooperative and much better than the last one. That would be a breath of fresh air. Tomorrow we are headed down to FOB Hughie to recon for our move. All the plans we made early on in the deployment are coming to fruition.

13 March 2010

Did the recon today, and we should be ready to move down to J-bad by 1 April. We will take on the mission of partnership with the ANA Bde and provide more focus on our fire support mission. I just wish I could get the maneuver PLT out of harm's way a little quicker. But until the infantry company arrives here in late April they will have to stay a little longer.

There was an IED found on the east side of the river. It was a small one, like the one on Wednesday in the Nuralam. I suspected on Wednesday that the small size meant that it was a trigger for an ambush by simply disabling the lead vehicle. Then we got an intel report this afternoon saying the exact same thing. The enemy might be trying to engage us directly to challenge us because they know there is a new PRT. Since they don't distinguish between the TF (our task force) and the PRT, the enemy probably thinks everyone here is new and that they have an opportunity to use direct attacks again. We will dispel that notion.

Since we were not turning over lead responsibility of the area to the Afghan leaders, we had to leave our maneuver platoon through April until an American infantry company could replace our security forces. This gave me cause to worry about them when we moved down to Jalalabad. We would transfer our other maneuver platoon from Torkham Gate to reinforce the headquarters maneuver platoon. Nevertheless, I was concerned for their wellbeing as long as they were separated from the main body of the battalion.

The enemy did believe that a new unit had replaced us following the departure of the old PRT. It is routine for the Taliban to challenge new units in an area to test their mettle. They would gauge the capabilities of that unit to determine what they could get away with in the presence of the new unit. The small IEDs were triggers meant to disable the lead vehicles of convoys. Once the convoy was halted, the enemy would launch an ambush on the rest of the group in hopes of cutting up the unit. This would lead to the new unit altering its patrol patterns, thus giving the enemy greater freedom of movement. We fed this intelligence to the new PRT so they could be aware of the threat.

In addition, we were beginning to receive information about another attempt to attack the FOB. The Taliban believed that since there was suppos-

edly a new unit on the base, they would test the defenses. Within a few days we would endure another attack on Kalagush. The enemy would receive the same reception that they had in November.

14 March 2010

I had several meetings today with the local Afghan officials. They exhaust me. First, the Nurgaram CoP, Abdullah Khan, came in with Hamid Osmani and Abdur Rahman to discuss the release of the second engineer. He told us the family paid a 1 million rupee ransom (about $12,000) for his release. The ANP then received him. Of course, they made no effort to arrest anyone. But Abdullah Khan then told us of his plan to apprehend the kidnappers. He is going to have 20 police dress in plain clothes and go to Pashagar village. He said they will work with the people to arrest those responsible. Might not be a bad plan, but then he wanted to put the cop who had the cache found in his house in charge of it. This is the very guy I told him was dirty two weeks ago. He just doesn't get it. That is the worst possible choice because this guy is a collaborator with the enemy. It is just like Abdullah Khan to put no thought into his ideas. We will see what happens, but I have little confidence that he will ever arrest anyone.

Then we talked about the "go green" program with Abdur Rahman and Mangal Abdullah. I am trying to mentor them on establishing a budgetary process and tying development to security. But this is a long uphill battle too. Finally, the good thing was the ANA In Co. went on their first patrol with us today. The Cdr took charge. It was nice to see a real leader doing something in Afghanistan.

This entry again demonstrates the incompetence of the Afghan National Police. The chief knowingly put a collaborator in charge of an important operation to arrest the kidnappers. The result was exactly what I expected when I wrote down my thoughts: nothing.

The "go green" program had nothing to do with environmental policy. It was a program through which we tied future development to villages' security situation. A "green" village is a secure village with no enemy activity, and one that will facilitate unfettered economic growth. A "red" village is one in which enemy activity is endemic. The idea behind the program was to place responsibility for security and cooperation with the government on the shoulders of the village elders. They could set up a sort of neighborhood watch program to identify and prevent the enemy from infiltrating their villages. The villages that did this successfully in cooperation with the government would receive priority for development projects. Those that did not would go to the bottom of the list. We believed that this program would create a competitive environment whereby a village that was expanding would be a model for stagnating villages, thus encouraging those that were behind to throw the enemy out in order to reap the benefits of economic development occurring in other areas. In beginning this program, we held up Sundawar and Paranieh as models. Both of these villages had forced the enemy out and were now enjoying a high rate of growth. We hoped the idea would catch on across our area.

15 March 2010

Very quiet day. The only thing of significance was the fact that the ANA did their own patrol down to Tupak. This company commander is pretty aggressive and willing to take initiative, and any Afghan willing to do that is impressive in my book. We are also now really beginning to focus on Jalalabad. That is going to consume our time. It is a Bn op, and the G Co Cdr is killing me. The Cdrs operate semi-independently over here and act on their own because they have to. In one sense they develop confidence in their own decision-making, which is good. But, on the other hand, it has taught a generation of officers to act on their own when they should focus on the Bn mission, such as for this move. I reeled her in today, and hopefully she will get a better grasp of what is needed after our talk. We have a combined patrol up to Shemgal and Gandalabuk tomorrow.

16 March 2010

I went out with the patrol to the Russian bridge at Gandalabuk and then into the Shemgal. The ANA company commander did very well out there and took charge, which was very good to see. He is really impressing me as a leader, and I hope it continues. The rest of the day was spent with planning the move and also packing up. We are well on our way to assuming the new mission and going home in a little over two months. Tomorrow I am going up to Monti (firebase) to visit B Btry and meet my new FDO up there.

17 March 2010

I flew up to Monti to meet my new FDO out there and gauge the morale/issues with B Btry. The BC has really let me down over the past few weeks, as he is not reporting issues and failing to set high standards so we can maintain the edge as we enter our last two months. I counseled the BC this evening on the issues and told him he has got to fix them for the good of the unit.

An IED detonated along the main road through the central valley today near the PRT. No injuries or damage, thank God. But they dug this one underneath the paved road, heavily damaging it. The enemy is continuing to try to hit us so that they can produce casualties and limit our movement. This tactic had the intended effect on the last PRT, as they basically took themselves out of the fight to huddle on the FOB. I hope this new crew doesn't do that.

Last thing, B/3-321 had an incident with a round today that flamed out the breech (of the howitzer). I wasn't there, so I don't know what happened, but I think the round wasn't seated right or there was a mechanical malfunction on the breech. I am sending up the Bn FDO to investigate it and report back.

The trend of increased IED usage in our area continued, and this time the enemy dug into the side of an embankment under the pavement of the main supply route. The purpose was to inflict casualties and deter our unit from utilizing the road. The tactic backfired because we continued with our normal rate of operations; in addition, this incident caused issues with the local population. The people needed this road for moving their goods to the south. By impeding this movement, the Taliban only succeeded in angering the people. Therefore, in the long run this incident worked to our advantage because we were able to contrast the negative activities of the enemy to the positive things that we were doing in partnership with the government.

The new battery that replaced C Battery started a trend of having firing incidents. In this case an improperly loaded round caused serious damage to a howitzer, but luckily there were no injuries. While we believed initially that a mechanical failure caused the incident, we learned later that human error was the culprit.

18 March 2010

I hosted a lunch to celebrate the Afghan New Year today with the local officials. It went well and I was not bombarded with requests, although I was still exhausted by the end of it. I did discuss the IED from yesterday with the SG of Nurgaram and Abdullah Khan. They will go down and meet the elders from Naylar in the next few days, and then we will jointly do it next week.

The gun at Bostick appears to have been a mechanical failure. The investigating officer will be done in a couple of days, and in the meantime we are moving a spare howitzer up there to make up the loss.

19 March 2010

Absolutely nothing today. It is almost Afghan New Year, so there are no officials or ANSF for that matter. So, it was quiet. We did host 1-102 IN today to go over bringing in their company to replace us in early May. We will be fine. Murray State beat Vandy in round 1 of the NCAA tournament 66–65. Hooah.

20 March 2010

It was Afghan New Year's Eve today and the first day of spring. We had a patrol go down to Tupak to see what we could find out about the IED from Wednesday. We didn't get much on that, but the patrol did get info about the cell leader from a source. Unbelievable what you can find out by just getting out and talking to the people. This guy has been on the FOB, knew the PRT had changed, and knows we are leaving. Where do they find this stuff out? It is from locals who work here. They overhear something and pass it on. It always amazes me how the locals find out information. I also know that there is an informant on the FOB. We have counter-intel coming next week to work the guy who I think is doing it. If he is, I want him arrested and taken to Bagram.

I had suspected for the past several days that we had an enemy informant working on the FOB. During our time out on patrol, we were able to pinpoint who the source was. As a result, we arranged for a counter-intelligence team to come and question select Afghan workers, including the suspected source. The team was able to positively identify the informant as the Afghan Army cook. The company commander was angry at learning this, and he had the man arrested through Afghan channels. For the time being we were able to deprive the enemy of additional information.

21 March 2010

Today was New Year's for Afghans. It was quiet here, but I guess there were some bombings in the cities. Our patrol is coming in now from a night op at "Gunny" mountain watching the Nuralam. They saw nothing. Tomorrow I have the radio address and meeting with the malik from Naylar to discuss the IED from the other day.

Gunny Mountain was a prominent hill on which our ANA unit and the Marine detachment set up an observation post during our operations connected to the election. We affectionately named it in honor of the Marine gunnery sergeant, who proved a great asset and friend of our battalion.

22 March 2010

I did the radio address today and later went on a patrol down to Naylar to talk to the malik about the IED last week. The SG met us there and we had the ANA, PRT, and some police with us. It is refreshing to do things jointly with the PRT. The last PRT generally left us on our own, and this one is really trying to do its job. Because of this, I think a lot of progress will be made now.

Of course, the villagers (in Naylar) have no idea who could have spent several days digging the IED under the paved road—they are so full of crap. But we did get the word out that without their involvement in security ops development will stagnate. The SG pushed this point hard, and we backed him up. The ANA Cdr gave his phone # to the people, and they eagerly wrote it down. We will see what happens.

More threats to the FOB tonight. There might actually be some credibility to it all. We will see. We will begin planning our actions to counter.

The new district governor took the lead role in scolding the village elders for allowing the insurgents to use their town as a base for IED activity. With our support, the district governor pointed out that there would be no further development assistance coming their way unless the elders cleaned up the security problem. The elders were very reluctant to volunteer any information, which told us that the enemy probably had great influence in the town. Further, they had probably threatened anyone who became too close to us. It would take some time to win the confidence of the people of this village, since it appeared that the enemy had a tight grip on them.

The reports of an impending attack were coming more frequently and indicators pointed to a coming assault. We would be ready.

23 March 2010

A lot of reporting today about the enemy moving down from Dow Ab to attack here. It is very similar to what we saw in November and again in December. The reporting in December came to nothing. I believe there is probably some enemy that came down to conduct ambushes and harass the FOB, but I don't know how far they will press it. We are ready regardless, and if the enemy does press an attack, they will lose heavily. Also, several reports of IEDs in multiple areas. The enemy is really starting to step things up against us. If only I had more assets to deal with it all. A platoon is just not enough. In Vietnam a company had a 5 × 5 Km area max to deal with. I have at least a 50 × 50 Km area with a platoon plus to secure it. The police absolutely suck, and we only 3 weeks ago got the ANA company (to help secure the area). I will be worried about the platoon until the day we leave. I wish we could get them out when the HQ leaves, but they have to stay another month.

With the advent of spring and warmer weather, the enemy always becomes more active in Afghanistan. Over the course of the 2009–2010 winter the enemy had primarily used IEDs, but the warmth was encouraging greater movement in the mountains, and the Taliban began to take advantage of it. We were fully prepared for the enemy when they did attempt their ground assault.

24 March 2010

The OP was attacked tonight by the enemy that came down from Dow Ab with a small element directed at the FOB to suppress our fire. They came out of the Shemgal just like in November, and once again they were driven back with casualties. The OP had none and the FOB had none. The ASG (Afghan Security Guards) with 4 ANP defended it, reinforced by our mortar and AASLT gun (a 105mm howitzer we designated to conduct all air assaults by helicopter). Once they were driven back the guns caught them regrouping. This caused the enemy to pull out, and I launched the ANA in pursuit with the maneuver platoon in a blocking position. They are still out right now clearing the area with no contact. Here are the highlights for tonight:

1. We were ready
2. Our intel reports are sound
3. ASG can hold the OP, so my decision to pull the Americans down was sound
4. Fires from artillery and mortars give us the distinct advantage in a fight
5. Pursuit is the key after a victory

Now we will see if this was simply a probing attack or if they are broken again. More to follow.

We learned the next day that we had killed three Taliban and wounded a few others. It was another clear-cut victory. The Afghans manning the observation post acquitted themselves very well, proving that they could handle the mission that we had performed for so long. The defeat of the enemy also demonstrated to the Taliban that the FOB was still well defended. We were able to retain our freedom of movement and continue our mission unmolested by the Taliban.

25 March 2010

It looks like most of the enemy pulled out after last night's attack. There are a few residuals left in Titin and a couple in Shemgal, but for the most part they pulled out. Intel says we got three. The ANA didn't find anything last night, and it looks like they just went back down into the valley where they came from. We will maintain our posture through Saturday and then refocus our effort to the south. The Torkham PLT should be back (with us) next week, so we will have two elements to conduct security ops.

I went down to Mehtar Lam today to the Laghman development meeting to continue our effort to unify development operations in Alingar. We will soon be handing the district back to Laghman, so it is good that we are giving them our full assessment before then.

Many things were beginning to come together for our move to Jalalabad and assumption of the new mission. Within days our platoon that had spent the deployment at the Torkham Gate border post would return to our control. This would give us two platoons to conduct security operations in our area and prepare for transferring responsibility to the incoming infantry company. Additionally, the Laghman PRT would soon take over full control of Alingar District for development, and my attendance at the development council meeting with the district governor smoothed the handoff of our efforts to the PRT. Finally, we were in the final stages of our planning for the move, and over the next couple of days we transitioned to the execution of the planned change of mission. We had just inflicted another defeat on the Taliban, and our time in Nuristan was coming to an end on some positive notes. I wished that we could have transferred the lead responsibility for the area to the Afghan leaders, but they were just not ready.

26 March 2010

I flew out to Torkham Gate today to talk directly to that platoon about their new mission when they get to Kalagush. They will do route security for the main paved road to enable us to better control our AO and retrograde all of our equipment. A second platoon in addition to our maneuver platoon will enhance our overall security and ability to disrupt the enemy so that when D/1-102 IN gets here, they can get off to a fast start without the enemy closing in on us. I just have to do everything I can to ensure that we do not hit IEDs and limit the ability of the enemy to place them. Nothing else happened today.

I flew out to the border post to personally brief our platoon leader out there on his change of mission. With the recent rash of IEDs in our area, I decided to give this platoon a very specific mission to conduct route security of the main road through the central valley. By varying the patrol timing and focusing the mission on this narrow task, this approach would ensure full mobility of the area for us as we began to move our equipment. Further, it would allow our other platoon, which had patrolled the region for a full ten months, to focus its patrols in the more dangerous areas east of the river to put pressure on the enemy. Finally, it would ease the transition of a new unit replacing us by knocking the enemy back on their heels, thus providing some breathing space for the new unit to get comfortable with the mission. As it turned out, we never had another IED on the main paved road for the rest of our time in Afghanistan and successfully retrograded all of our equipment with no losses.*

27 March 2010

We had the security shura down in the Nurgaram DC today. I confronted the Nurgaram police about the intel reports we have received stating that the police are cooperating with the enemy in the Mashpah Valley, enabling them under Mohammed al-Rahman to place IEDs there. Of course, I have known this for a while. The CoP, Abdullah Khan, was not there (he always seems to be gone when an attack is imminent), so it was his deputy. He became defensive, and the SG, seeing that I was angry, told the deputy to shut up. Then later the deputy said we should have had the ANA go into the Shemgal after the attack on Wednesday instead of asking the police. I lost it then. The Nurgaram police have only gotten worse over time since we have been here. This in spite of the efforts of the MPs to develop their skills. Rather than trying to work to make their country a better place, they play both sides for their own benefit. They act like they are our friends and then behind our backs help the people trying to blow us up. The galling thing is that they come back to us with their hands out. Screw that. Start doing something for yourselves.

Tomorrow we are going to dedicate the DFAC (dining facility) in memory of SGT Rao so that when we leave it will be a permanent reminder of his sacrifice.

We had received a series of reports stating that the IED cell operating in the Mashpah Valley was seeding the road with a series of IEDs. The reports also indicated that the police officer suspected of having the cache in his house was aiding the cell leader. Armed with this information, I intended to confront the police chief. However, he was not present at the meeting. Every time that our base was attacked or the enemy was planning an operation, the chief would leave his post. This left the deputy police chief in charge. So, I presented the information to him, and when he stated that there was no problem with the police or security in the area I exploded. At the ten-month mark of our deployment I had grown tired of the excuses for incompetence and the complicity of the police leaders in enemy operations. This incident illustrates the central issue with Afghanistan today: There is a crisis of leadership among the Afghans, and I believe that they are hedging their bets by playing both sides. This situation can never lead to victory. The Afghan leaders must commit themselves to winning and display some altruism for the sake of their people. Victory cannot be achieved by Americans for Afghans. We can set the conditions for success in Afghanistan, but until they make a commitment for themselves, their society and country will remain mired in insecurity and poverty. Until Afghan leaders begin to work for the benefit of their people, a stalemate is the best they can hope for. My outburst was meant to drive this point home to these leaders and demonstrate to them that they must step up and take charge in a meaningful way for their own good. The future of Afghanistan ultimately depends on the commitment of Afghans to their own success.

28 March 2010

Very quiet day. We named the mess hall the "SGT Rao DFAC" today. That was good. I just hope that we don't have any more losses. This one was too many. I am worried about these guys as I get ready to go down to FOB Hughie (in Jalalabad) for the partnership mission. I wish I was bringing them all out with me, but I have to leave the platoon here for security of AO Steel until the IN company arrives. I am getting the Torkham PLT back, but I just hope God will shield them from the enemy so they all come home.

Abdullah Khan apparently allowed a truck full of explosives to pass through his checkpoint in Nangaresh 3 days ago. He approved their passage. He is either incompetent or a collaborator. If an IED kills one of the troops in his district, I am going to hold him personally responsible. He has turned out to be nothing but a big turd since becoming CoP.

In exchange for a bribe, the Nurgaram chief of police allowed a shipment of explosives to move north for use by illegal gem miners in Nurgaram and Dow Ab. My concern was that these explosives could end up in the hands of the enemy for use in IEDs. This did not come to pass, but the actions of the chief again illustrate the endemic corruption of officials down to the lowest levels in Afghanistan.

29 March 2010

We had an early report about an IED where the last on detonated in Naylar, but this turned out to be a bogus report. Our platoon and the RCP found nothing. Also, we had a report that multiple enemy groups from Dow Ab, Konar, and Laghman want to conduct a major attack on the FOB. I don't believe at this point but must at least keep it in mind if we begin to see indicators.

Finally, I met with the NDS chief of Nuristan today with the district chiefs from Nurgaram and Dow Ab. The provincial chief was trained by the KGB during the Soviet era, and he appears to be a shady character whom the sub-governors told me behind closed doors that they are wary of. One of the chief's duties is to work the Afghan reintegration program, bringing TB individuals back from the arms of the enemy. But with the lack of trust in him, it begs the question, what would be the incentive for the TB to reintegrate? None. Just another example of the corrupt nature of things in W. Nuristan.

As hard as Hamid Osmani, the district governor in Dow Ab, was working to reintegrate the low-level Taliban members, he was doomed to failure. An untrusted government official like the NDS chief—who was trained by the hated Soviets—makes critical programs like the reintegration effort unworkable. When Osmani took over as district governor, he made a good-faith attempt to implement the program, but factors such as the shady NDS chief were working against him. Thus, we now understood the reasons behind the unsuccessful attempts to siphon some Taliban commanders away from the movement.

30 March 2010

We had our patrol go up into the Mashpah today, and specifically to Parisaw at Mohammed al-Rahman's and Malel, where the IED cell apparently hid after the detonation two weeks ago near Naylar. We wanted to disrupt the cell and put a scare into them. Well, they attempted to ambush the patrol, but the enemy got the worst of it, losing two people, including one of their leaders. al-Rahman planned the ambush. The ANA Cdr told al-Rahman's father that it was only a matter of time before we get him. I like this Cdr; he is aggressive and hates the TB.

I leave tomorrow from Kalagush for Hughie with B Btry CoC in between. I talked to the maneuver PLT and let them know they have done a good job and to keep it straight for 6 more weeks. Then I am getting them out of here. I will be worried about them until the new infantry unit arrives to take over.

I was very proud of the maneuver platoon on this day. Early on in our deployment I was disappointed with their reaction to direct firefights. But over time they became more proficient at their business. In this ambush the enemy attempted to cut off the platoon from the high ground on the side of the road, intending to destroy them by going down the line vehicle by vehicle. This was a classic tactic that the old Mujahideen had used in the Soviet-

Afghan war. However, it didn't work here. Our maneuver platoon, made up of cooks, mechanics, radiomen, and weathermen, broke the ambush and successfully attacked the enemy position. They dismounted the vehicles and used their heavy machine guns and grenade launchers to force the enemy back. As the enemy attempted to pull out, they got caught in a crossfire, killing one and wounding two. The leader of the ambush would later die from wounds suffered in the fight. Regardless of the situation, our soldiers handled themselves with great competence, and I was proud of their ability and what they were doing for their country.

The ANA company commander was certainly an aggressive individual and was competent most of the time. But, as we would discover in the coming weeks, he had a nasty habit that detracted from his ability. He was addicted to hashish and was a frequent user. When he was not high this man was a solid partner. But when he was using the drug his behavior was erratic and caused us credibility problems among the local people because of his overbearing behavior.

31 March 2010

We began to move down to FOB Hughie today, and G will arrive tomorrow, followed by HHB (less the maneuver platoon) the next day. The combined TOC we are constructing for our partnership mission is coming along, and within 3 days we will be 90% functional. The next goal will be to get the ANA working with us in the TOC that we have constructed for full partnership. They don't have the automation that we do, so they will be reluctant to leave their comfort zones, but we will work it. Final goal is to receive 2–320th FA, which starts in just 3 weeks. Hard to believe.

Tomorrow is the CoC up at Fortress for B Btry. It will be good to get a fresh guy in there. My current BC quit on me after the first of the year.

Finally, the two wounded guys from yesterday's firefight are in Sundawar apparently. We called the police under the new police chief to see if he will get them. He took off immediately. More to follow. One of the FOB workers apparently tried to steal some medical supplies today. Only later did we learn that he was from Sundawar. We should have nabbed him if we had known.

We sent our advance party down to the new FOB a week earlier under the supervision of the CSM and our operations sergeant. Their dual mission was to lay out the billeting and begin constructing our combined tactical operations center. It would take us a few days to make the new building operational for our communications architecture. In the meantime, my operations officer, who was staying behind at Kalagush to command the maneuver elements, would serve as the primary operation center until we were fully operational.

We had scheduled a change of command ceremony for Bravo Battery on this day, but weather intervened to prevent our flight from making it to Konar for the ceremony. We would conduct the change of command the following day and execute our move down to Jalalabad after the ceremony.

1 April 2010

Today was the CoC for B Btry up at Fortress. The ceremony at the gunline went very well, and now I feel confident that both firing battery commanders are very good. My last B Btry commander quit on me and his troops 3 months ago. Not a good thing in combat. If the new BC will listen and stay focused, he will do very well and has a good future in the Army.

G Co arrived at Hughie today and then the staff tomorrow. Then we can begin to make some more progress on building the combined TOC. B Btry's Torkham PLT finally comes back to us tomorrow at Kalagush. The extra platoon will really help us to better secure the area, and I am glad that the maneuver platoon will finally be getting some help.

Things were beginning to fall into place for our change of mission. After several months of planning and preparation, we were actually in execution mode. The change would keep us focused for the final two months in Afghanistan.

2–3 April 2010

I formally took over today (2 April) as the partner to the 2nd Brigade, 201st Afghan National Army Corps. COL Shir Mohammed (the Afghan brigade commander), whom I have met on several occasions previously on his visits to Kalagush, is our partner. I laid out what I would do and what the mission was and asked for his goals and objectives, plus what needed to be done in the immediate term. He will talk to me tomorrow about the goals and OBJs, but he did tell me that his most pressing need was housing for his soldiers here at J-bad. I will see what can be done because conditions are already tight and another Bn is coming here shortly.

Tomorrow I will go visit his companies in the Pech River Valley and see the guns from 3/321 up at FOB Blessing.

* * *

Assuming the new mission ushered in the final phase of our deployment to Afghanistan. When we arrived our mission was twofold and included providing artillery fires for our brigade and securing the population of western Nuristan and northern Laghman, as well as working with government leaders on development and administrative issues. These tasks absorbed the majority of our time and effort. The change of mission removed the battalion from the area and associated tasks, bringing us into a partnership with an Afghan Army brigade. After the frustrations we had endured in working with the Afghan government leaders, we had high hopes that the change in mission would usher in a more satisfactory environment. Unfortunately, we found that the new mission was not the refreshing change we had anticipated. Yet we were determined to make a difference with the remainder of our time in Afghanistan.

The maneuver mission probably required 90% of the battalion headquarters' time on a daily basis. Our fire direction center in the battalion headquarters was dedicated to providing daily oversight of our indirect mission. The partnership mission would allow our unit to focus more attention on the artillery mission, which we needed to do. Before we arrived in Afghanistan we found the security mission, with its associated tasks in governance and development, intriguing. With my previous experience in the country, I believed we could make an enormous difference in Afghanistan, opening up the door for the Afghans to assume full control. However, we were let down by the irresponsible and corrupt behavior of the Afghan officials. Given that eight years had passed since the fall of the Taliban, I had expected to see more progress made by the Afghans. As noted several times, this was not the reality on the ground. The new mission with the Afghan Army seemed like an opportunity for us to make a difference with an organization that was respected and clearly growing in capability.

The ANA has been the single institution in Afghanistan that enjoys widespread approval and has the confidence of the people. I had witnessed this in both of my previous tours in Afghanistan. Based on this knowledge, I entered into the new mission with very high expectations. In 2003 the ANA was formed, and by the end of that year the organization numbered about 5,000 soldiers. By 2006 it had expanded to over 40,000, and some units could operate competently at the battalion level. Upon my return in 2009 the ANA exceeded 100,000 soldiers. After two and a half years I believed it was plausible that the ANA could operate at the brigade level. Further, the army should have been approaching the point at which they could begin assuming control of areas from our forces throughout Afghanistan. Yet, as I soon discovered, this was not the case. For a number of reasons that I will discuss later, the ANA was simply not ready to take this step forward. This was quite a letdown, and yet there were many positives. For the next two months of our tour we would focus on the positives with regard to the ANA while providing mentorship to fix the problems.

IV. Sustaining and Making a Difference, 7 Dec. '09 to 3 Apr. '10

Regardless of the challenges, we were happy about taking on the new mission. It presented an opportunity to make a difference in a new arena and remain focused on the mission until the end of the tour. In spite of some remaining frustrations, I was determined to remain positive in order to have a lasting impact upon our partner ANA brigade. Yet with our new mission there was one thing more than any other that gave me pause. The maneuver platoon, along with the newly arrived B Battery platoon from Torkham Gate, had to remain at Kalagush for six more weeks. I found myself in a continuous state of worry for their well-being while we had moved on to the new mission. Until they were reunited with the battalion headquarters, this would remain my number one concern for the next several weeks.

V

Change of Mission: Pressing to the Finish Line, 4 April 2010 to 31 May 2010

As we entered the final two months of our deployment in Afghanistan, I had three primary concerns. First, our unit had to get off to a fast start in our partnership mission with the 2/201st Afghan National Army brigade. Yet several factors that we soon discovered would make a good beginning difficult. Second, our maneuver platoons remained at Kalagush in western Nuristan, and the threefold rise in use of IEDs was a source of constant worry. Finally, we were approaching the end of our tour, and this is always a dangerous time for a unit in combat. This trifecta of challenges would keep my leaders, staff, and myself busy until we flew home.

When we assumed the new mission in Jalalabad there were several things we had to do. Most important among our tasks was establishing a combined tactical operations center whereby the Afghan brigade and our battalion headquarters could work in an integrated manner. We built a functional operations center for both of our headquarters, and yet the Afghans were reluctant to occupy the workspace to integrate with us. Next, we learned that the ANA was overly dependent on American advisors and forces for transport, logistic support, planning, and technology. Further, the ANA wanted to model its forces after the U.S. Army instead of tailoring the army for its own needs and challenges. The Afghan Army therefore lacked the proper orientation and mindset for fighting and winning a counter-insurgency. This issue was a problem of our own creation, unfortunately, as the U.S. Army had played a central role in the development of the Afghan National Army. This begged the question: "What could be done?"

The first problem would require us to build a trust relationship with the Afghans combined with education and mentorship. Eventually, we were able to coax the Afghan staff into an integrated tactical operations center.

The second issue was more problematic, requiring a long-term approach that would extend beyond our time in Afghanistan. I settled on introducing a three-pronged approach to solving this problem. It included breaking the cycle of dependence on U.S. support, forcing the ANA to rely on its own resources, and convincing the Afghan soldiers that they held a significant advantage over U.S. forces in a counter-insurgency: they are Afghans. In order for this approach to work, our replacements had to buy into this philosophy to affect the change after we left.

Regrettably, the infantry company designated to replace our security forces would not arrive in time to allow all of our elements to make the move to Jalalabad. As a result, the maneuver platoon and the relocated platoon from Torkham Gate had to remain in Nuristan to continue the security mission. When I was with them at Kalagush I was always concerned, but my presence there allayed my fears. I would accompany the platoon on a patrol about once a week, and I became familiar with the fine soldiers in this unit. When Sergeant Rao was killed and Staff Sergeant McClintock severely wounded, it affected me very deeply because I used to sit next to Rao in the vehicle out on patrol. I didn't want any more losses, and my separation from these outstanding soldiers multiplied my worries.

To allay my own fears, I left my very competent operations officer at Kalagush with a small group of sharp staff officers and noncommissioned officers to provide command and control. These leaders would also maintain continuity between our forces and the local Afghan government leaders. This was a critical task, since the new PRT was still becoming familiar with the area. Our unit and the minimal staff element proved instrumental in maintaining security and easing the new PRT and infantry company into the mission in Nuristan.

Another cause for concern was the fact that we were nearing the end of our tour in Afghanistan. Historically, the last 60–90 days of a combat deployment are among the most dangerous of the tour. The reason for this is that the soldiers can see the light at the end of the tunnel and become complacent. Consequently, they fail to pay full attention to their jobs and have accidents, or else the enemy exploits mistakes made by forces in the field. I certainly did not want to suffer losses in the waning days of the deployment. Thus, I continuously admonished my battery commanders, platoon leaders, and staff to remain focused on the mission and safety. They collectively delivered, and we brought everyone safely home.

As we entered the home stretch there was still a great deal of work we had to get done. The key to winning in Afghanistan rests with Afghan institutions. Among these, arguably the most critical was the ANA. Once the ANA was capable of taking charge of securing its own people, U.S. forces could begin coming home confident that the Taliban would not rise again. Our battalion had the opportunity to make a solid contribution toward this end. Simultaneously, we had to keep everyone focused on the mission to fulfill our duty and reunite everyone with their families.

4 April 2010—Easter

Trip today got cancelled because someone at brigade over-manifested the aircraft, so I stayed here today. I spent several hours with Shir Mohammed (the ANA brigade commander) today, and he showed me his needs here on the base and he took me over to the OCC-P. I will try to help him with his legitimate needs, like soldier housing, but I won't do anything for his typical Afghan request of a house for him and his family.

Overall Easter was quiet, and that was good. Shir Mohammed went over his goals and OBJs (objectives) and they are:

- Conduct Kamdesh op to reintroduce government in the area
- Establish security on Hwy 1 to the west
- Maintain security along the road between Asmar and Naray
- Defeat the insurgents around Ghaki Pass on Pakistan border
- Brigade trained on NATO weapons in all Bns
- Increase housing capacity
- Finish range complex

I can do the Kamdesh and Hwy 1A op, assist with the range and NATO weapon training, and start the housing. The rest I will have to hand off to 2-320 (the field artillery unit that will replace us in two months).

I had originally planned to make a trip up to FOB Blessing in the Pech River Valley to visit with the platoon from our attached battery, but there were too many people manifested for the flight. Instead, I stayed in Jalalabad and spent the day with the Afghan brigade commander. He provided me with his goals and objectives so that I could align our effort with his guidance to his units. Many of his needs were absolutely legitimate, such as completing construction of a range complex on the Afghan Army base. But he also asked me to build him a house for his family. Building warfighting capacity was an appropriate request, but I could not help with personal requests.

There were several planned operations coming up that spring. Among them was a plan to drive the Taliban out of Kamdesh and reintroduce government control in the district. In October 2009 the Taliban launched the attack on Outpost Keating that killed eight Americans prior to the planned withdrawal from that post. The police and government summarily left the district following the fighting in the area. The Afghan brigade commander, in cooperation with the Nuristan governor, was planning to conduct an offensive in that district to regain control of the area. This was the first operation that I would assist my partner in planning upon my arrival in Jalalabad.

5 April 2010

I went to the ANA, ANP, ABP rehearsal today up in Naray. The whole operation is to reintroduce the government control in the Kamdesh District. If successful, it will be a major milestone following what happened after Keating last October. I have to go back up there tomorrow night with the ANA Cdr to set up a TAC in the ABP (Afghan Border Police) HQ in Bari Kowt.

The combined TOC is coming along, but I think our biggest issue with the ANA is their dependence upon us. We are their security blanket, and they need to become self-reliant. Or we can never leave. It is very frustrating that they (the Afghans) brag about their independence, defeating the Russians, British, etc., and yet are dependent on us and ask for everything without being embarrassed. I think it has come to the point after 9 years here that they are just taking advantage of us.

The operation in Kamdesh had already been in the planning stages for a few weeks before my arrival in Jalalabad. A rehearsal with all of the participants was conducted in Naray District of Konar on this day, and I accompanied the brigade commander to the rehearsal. We would kick off the operation within 48 hours, and I would spend the next several days with the Afghan commander at Naray near the Pakistani border.

6 April 2010

We arrived at Bostick with the ANA Cdr to C2 (command and control) the operation, which kicks off at 0400 tomorrow morning. I will spend two days up here with 3–61 Cav (the brigade's cavalry squadron), who is the battlespace owner here in Naray. I don't know how the op will go, but it is an all-Afghan show. Once the ANA with the ANP and ABP open up the route, they are supposed to link up with Mullah Agha, the local HiG commander. He has expressed the desire to reintegrate with the government, and if he comes through it could be a huge breakthrough in this area for the government. But we will see starting tomorrow. I have a small TAC element with me to shadow Shir Mohammed.

This all–Afghan operation had many elements to it, which made it unique among previous operations in Afghanistan. First, it was Afghan led and involved only Afghan forces from the army, police, and border police. Second, the operation involved a concerted reintegration effort with some former enemies of the government, primarily the Hezb-Islami-Gulbuddin (HiG) party commander in Kamdesh. (The HiG is an Afghan political party that has engaged in an insurgency against the Afghan government. It is a movement separate from the Taliban and is headed by former Mujahideen commander Gulbuddin Hekmatyar. This operation involved reintegrating local HiG leaders in alliance with the government against the Taliban.) Finally, success or failure rested on the efforts of the Afghans themselves. They could not point the finger of blame in our direction if the operation failed. Our battalion had embarked on its new partnership mission only three days before, and already we were involved in a major operation and I was personally shadowing the Afghan brigade commander to provide advice and support where needed. It was an interesting change from what we had done for the previous ten months.

7 April 2010

The ANSF launched their op this morning at around 0530, which was over an hour late, but then took their objective at the Gowardesh Bridge by 0700. So, everything has gone well so far. The ANA set up their ops center at the ABP HQ in Bari Kowt, which is a small town right on the Pakistan border leading into Nuristan and Chitral. I met with the leaders today in conjunction with the squadron Cdr here at FOB Bostick. They had done pretty well in taking their objective today. However, they did not plan to follow it up immediately by taking the Bazgal Bridge as originally planned. Instead, they want to do several shuras with the local elders to gain support before moving further. Then they will advance and link up with the Kamdesh HiG leader, who is willing to help the government against the TB. It is logical and they are working it. However, they also started asking for a lot of stuff. Nothing is ever just a success. The Afghans are not satisfied unless they are asking for things that will benefit them.

The operation did get off to a very good start and the idea of holding a series of shuras with the local leaders was a very sound plan of action. However, the Afghans would wait too long and cede the initiative to the enemy instead of following up their initial success. After several days of no action, it was irritating to watch the ANA still hunkered down on their initial objective rather than continuing to move forward.

8 April 2010

Contact around Gowardesh picked up today, as the enemy began taking pot shots at the ANSF there. However, it was mostly harassing fire, and the firebase here engaged with artillery from B Btry, 3–321 picking off several enemy fighters. I visited with the platoon from our battery that was attached to the battalion this morning, and, while motivated, they are far too young. All of the section chiefs are SGTs, and the FDC chief has only been in the Army 2½ years. The Gunny (gunnery sergeant) is a SSG in the Army with 6½ years' experience. The platoon sergeant is the only NCO of appropriate rank. This is a huge factor in their early mistakes like the howitzer that was destroyed following the misfire. Proper misfire procedures would have prevented the incident, but they are overmatched when a situation out of the ordinary comes up. The CSM and MG (master gunner) are going to come up here next week to check on them.

We visited the ABP HQ again today, and the first shura was conducted today, with more planned in the coming days. This is a good thing, but the begging started after that. The ABP and ANP claim they don't have the resources to start small projects to influence the populace and want more. It was painful. The Afghans always want more, but when asked to do something—like launch their own QRF to clear a ridge this morning—they have a hundred excuses. We have to really make an effort to start weaning them off of depending on us. I fly back to J-bad tomorrow with Shir Mohammed and his staff. The ANA Bn has the mission now.

While I was up in Naray I had the opportunity to visit with the platoon from B Battery, 3–321 FA. This battery had been attached to us for about two and a half months at this point, and it had a very highly motivated set of leaders. But as I surveyed the platoon I noted that most of the leaders were one to two ranks below what was appropriate for their duty positions. This inexperience contributed to the issue with the damaged howitzer and would lead to other incidents before we left Afghanistan. The war has placed a strain on our personnel systems to keep the right people in units in the field. We had experienced this phenomenon ourselves as we prepared for the deployment. In B Battery the issue was more acute and a contributing factor to some of the problems the unit had in Afghanistan.

The operation to reestablish control in Kamdesh still had promise. However, in our meeting with the Afghan security force leaders we heard a stream of requests for additional support. We had agreed before the start of the operation to assist the Afghans with a host of items to facilitate success. At the time they were happy with the promised support. Now, two days into the operation, the Afghans decided that it was not enough. It was incumbent upon us as Americans to make the Afghans learn to succeed with their own resources. Our forces had not done a good job in pushing this issue previously, but we had to change the dynamics of our relationship to force the Afghans to solve their problems.

9 April 2010

Returned to Hughie this afternoon. Not much happened up at Gowardesh today and everything is secure. At Kalagush there have been several reports of enemies coming down from Dow Ab again. It seems likely they will attack again, and they will also get hammered again. It is all utterly ridiculous. They are coming down to "liberate" Nuristan, and it only means that more of them are going to die. Hopefully if they come this time and get schwacked, they will finally get the message.

Mohammed al-Rahman, the IED cell leader in Mashpah Valley, is now in hiding. The family of one of our sources said that he was involved in a feud with another family and shot a young male he was arguing with. The family is committed to taking revenge. If they get him, then one of our targets is gone without us getting our hands dirty.

The incident with the IED cell leader is another example of how disputes are typically settled in Afghanistan. In the absence of the rule of law, tribes, clans, families, and individuals will seek their own brand of justice. This illustrates how important it is to have competent police forces and a civil court system that can dispense justice fairly. Developing such a system would go a long way toward stabilizing Afghanistan and taking away a lightning rod issue for the Taliban. With the departure of this cell leader into hiding, our incidents of IED activity in the valley dropped to nothing. The feud actually worked in our favor.

10 April 2010

Met with the ANA Bde CoS (chief of staff) today. I discussed with him the need for the ANA staff to get fully integrated into the TOC. He said they would on Monday, but this will remain a challenge.

Not much else happened today. There are more threats to Kalagush right now from the Dow Ab cell, but I don't know how much validity to give it. They might do something, and if they do, they will again get crushed. We reinforced OP Loyalty with ANA and ANP, so if they do come, the enemy will get a big surprise.

My old S2 takes command of the brigade MI (military intelligence) company tomorrow, so I will go to that on JAF (Jalalabad Airfield).

11 April 2010

Shir Mohammed traveled back up to Bari Kowt today to attend the Kamdesh jirga. Most villages had representatives at the event except for Kamdesh itself, but it still appeared to be a good event. The elders seemed very supportive, and there is confidence that the people will enable the government to come back in and deny support to the enemy. There were two ANA casualties at Gowardesh from sniper fire, but they are still securing their positions.

At Kalagush it appears the threats are not going to come about, but the enemy did come into the Nuralam. This is spillover from what is happening in the Korengal Valley. Tomorrow is four years to the day when I was here (with the 10th Mountain Division) for Operation Mountain Lion, when we established the outpost in the Korengal. Now in this brigade we are taking it down. The fighters in the Nuralam were hit by the op in the Korengal that is pushing them back to enable the retrograde. We have patrols going into the Nuralam this week and they could bump into the enemy.

Our brigade conducted an operation in the Korengal Valley to knock the enemy on their heels as a precursor to closing down the outpost in the valley. The Korengal is one of the most dangerous and violent places in Afghanistan, and it has served as the setting for popular books and the documentary Restrepo. I was the brigade fire support officer for 3rd Brigade, 10th Mountain Division, in 2006 and participated in the operation that established our presence in the valley. The 2010 operation brought things full circle. Our artillery provided support for the operation, and all went smoothly as the retrograde occurred, with no losses of soldiers or equipment. It was a great success and removed some fine Americans from a dangerous place, enabling them to conduct other missions elsewhere.

12 April 2010

The ANA (brigade headquarters) received a mission today to support poppy eradication in Nangarhar. They had initially balked at it, but the provincial governor called MoD (Ministry of Defense) and convinced them that he needed support for his op. This generated an order from corps headquarters that made its way down to the brigade. Shir Mohammed went to the palace and the governor told him he wanted to clear fields in three districts. The ANA will provide the outer cordon so the police can do the actual eradication. The governor does this mostly to drive up prices in Kandahar—where his poppy fields are located. Another example of self-interest at the forefront of government actions.

Enemy returned to Dow Ab, so no attack on Kalagush. Good. Also, no ANA in TOC yet. I addressed this with Shir Mohammed today, and he said tomorrow it would happen. No issues at Gowardesh today, and planning will commence tomorrow at the OCC with all ANSF for the poppy op. I will go to Kalagush with Mohammed for my first visit since moving down to Hughie.

The ANA did not want to become involved in poppy eradication missions. These operations tend to alienate the farmers from the government because it destroys their livelihood. While destroying the drug trade is certainly a high-priority need in Afghanistan in order to cut funding to the Taliban and stop the flow of drugs, it must be accompanied by alternatives for the farmers. At its heart, the farmers are only trying to make a living to feed their families, and poppy is a money-making crop. Any serious eradication efforts have to be part of an overarching strategy that also provides alternative, profitable crops to enable the farmers to survive. Eradication alone tends to create an issue that the Taliban can exploit and use to build their pool of recruits.

13 April 2010

I visited Kalagush with Shir Mohammed, and it went well. I went on patrol with the Torkham PLT and he visited the company (ANA company) and went to the DC. At the DC he wanted to talk to the CoP about security cooperation, but Abdullah Khan was not there. Big surprise. The Alingar CoP made a big drug bust in Sangar of 60 kilos of heroin. He is definitely making a difference in Alingar, and I am glad that I pushed so hard to fire his predecessor. It worked out well. The planning for the poppy eradication went nowhere because the ANP and ABP had no idea what they wanted to do, so now the ANA is just waiting for them. Don't know when it will kick off now. Nothing happened up at Kamdesh today, but the artillery platoon up there had yet another firing incident. They fired a smoke round that impacted short and hit a cow and a building. Luckily it wasn't HE (high explosive) or WP (white phosphorous). I think that platoon has some systemic problems; they are inexperienced and nonchalant. I called their battalion commander and told him that I thought it was time to start shifting some personnel. He agreed, and I will see what he intends to do. For now my FDO is doing the investigation.

Final thing today was a shooting out at Khogyani in which an enraged ANA soldier shot another before killing himself. The offending soldier was mad because the duty NCO kicked him out of the mess hall for not wearing boots. Unbelievable.

The platoon from Bravo Battery, 3–321 FAR, was continuing to have issues due to the soldiers' inexperience. Since the unit was only attached to my battalion I could not move personnel. This responsibility rests with the parent unit. Therefore, I called their colonel and informed him of the issues. He understood and took action to rotate some more experienced noncommissioned officers from his other batteries to Bravo. This helped bring some greater expertise to the unit to improve their precision in artillery gunnery.

The shooting at Khogyani was yet another example of Afghan fecklessness. Instead of settling an argument in a civil manner, the soldier in question took matters into his own hands and killed another soldier over wearing boots. When the duty NCO corrected him for not wearing boots, the offending soldier took this as an insult to his honor. The only way to rectify an assault on your honor is through violence. As a result, the ANA lost two soldiers. It is difficult for the American mind to understand, but it is a regular occurrence in Afghanistan.

14 April 2010

The ANA was able to finalize their plan to support the poppy eradication operation. They finally got some idea of what the ANP and ABP planned to do and were able to finish it today. The op will start on Saturday, and I will fly out with Shir Mohammed to Goshta District so he can see his people. The governor (of Nangarhar) is just making a show of this whole thing, plain and simple. It is all about him. Mohammed wants him to engage the local elders first to gain their buy-in (on eradicating the poppy), but the governor probably won't go for that.

The initial investigation is in from the ANA soldier shooting, and right now it is inconclusive if the soldier killed himself or if someone else did. The Corps sent down their own investigative team today. Tomorrow Mohammed is headed out there to get a look for himself.

We still don't have ANA officers in the TOC, and this frustrates me. They have complained about the fact that they have no computers and copiers, but if they integrated into the TOC, they would have full access to several devices. I told Mohammed to issue an order to get them in there, but we will see.

The ANA brigade commander did not want to participate in the poppy operation, as previously mentioned. However, he was going to do the best he could to make it a success. He suggested that, before starting the operation, the Nangarhar governor should hold a series of shuras with the elders to inform them of the situation. This would produce a level of understanding about the purpose of the operation and prevent any ill will from upsetting the plan. The governor refused to do this, and, as events will show, the eradication plan broke down with a great deal of animosity directed toward the government for the poor handling of the situation.

15 April 2010

Today Shir Mohammed went to visit his troops at Khogyani. He said they were very upset about the incident two days ago and the investigation could not determine if the soldier committed suicide or was shot in the deluge of bullets that came his way after he shot the NCO. Regardless, it was good that he went out there. The ANA did have five soldiers wounded yesterday in an ambush on their convoy north of Outpost Monti. Two are in critical condition at Bagram.

Up at Kalagush there was a great development today, as the ANA and ANP did a joint patrol without us. The new district governor, Abdur Rahman, met with the S3 today and stated that he wanted to work with the ANA and the police. We have wanted this since we got to Afghanistan. Finally, today, with Rahman's effort, they took the first step forward. Hopefully, this is the start of something good.

The new CoP in Alingar made a huge drug bust a couple of days ago. Getting rid of the old guy represents one of the most satisfying things we have accomplished in our time here. Hiring Najibullah as CoP is a big step forward for the area, and my folks at Kalagush tell me that it is making a difference with the people.

The twin developments at Kalagush were very encouraging. The Afghan National Security Forces of the ANA and ANP had finally combined their efforts to begin conducting their own patrols without our oversight. This represented an enormous step in the right direction for our piece of Afghanistan. In addition, the chief of police in Alingar was actually doing some important police work and not waiting for us or making excuses for failure. After all the frustrations we had experienced, these instances of positive action gave me hope that our effort from the previous several months was actually beginning to pay off.

16 April 2010

A very quiet day across the board. There was a big positive out of Kalagush today. When we first got here the village of Sundawar was an unfriendly place to us where we had several contacts and we had the ANA soldier die in the ambush. Then in September the heavy rains came that damaged the village. I visited there with Mangal Abdullah after the flood to see if we could make some headway toward friendly relations. The elders committed to security, and we agreed to help. We fixed the road, canal, cleared the farm fields of boulders, rebuilt the retaining wall, and gave them a greenhouse. Today the Torkham platoon visited and the elders expressed thanks to them for our effort, highlighting the retaining wall. A thunderstorm hit yesterday and the wall held back a rush of water coming down from the mountains. With all the frustrations, we have had this is a nice story of success.

The ANA moved to their assembly area in Goshta for the poppy mission today. They move at 0200 tomorrow to begin the op.

The gratitude of the villagers in Sundawar was yet another example of success in our counter-insurgency efforts. This village was vehemently anti-government when we first arrived. Yet ten months later these people were among our greatest friends and supportive of the government in Alingar District. The elders, in cooperation with the district governor and our unit, were able to rebuild the village while running the Taliban out of town. I had experienced so many irritating frustrations over the course of our ten months in Nuristan and Laghman. However, much of the effort that we had expended was finally beginning to pay dividends. Sundawar proved the premise that Afghanistan can stand on its own with the right effort and commitment from its leaders in cooperation with the people.

17 April 2010

The poppy mission kicked off this morning with no issues. They did take some fire today from long range and asked us to drop a bomb on the position. We asked what they (the ANA) were doing with the 300 people they have, which illustrates the next point. The ANA does not understand COIN (counter-insurgency operations). I took Shir Mohammed to meet the commander IJC (American Lieutenant General David Rodriguez, who is the commander of the International Security Assistance Force Joint Command). The LTG asked Mohammed what he thought would enable them (the ANA) to take over and win without us. He said air assets and engineers (meaning route clearance packages). Then he was asked what is the primary enemy. He said IEDs and complex attacks. Neither could be further from the truth.

First, to win they (all Afghan National Security Forces) need the support of the people, not technological solutions. Second, the corrupt government is the real enemy here, and if they don't get that under control, the people will never support the government. So, it boils down to winning over the people with security and a functioning government of which the ANA is a piece. Instead of offering that, Mohammed answered with an enemy-focused, technological answer. War is a contest of wills, and no amount of technology will win it unless the human dimension has been assessed and appropriately addressed. Unfortunately, the ANSF and government are only interested in what they can get. Their selfish outlook is killing their opportunity to make things better.

We had planned to fly out to Goshta on this day to be with the ANA troops involved in the poppy operation. At the last minute plans were changed, as the general requested a meeting with all the American and Afghan commanders in the region. We met with him in Asadabad in Konar Province. I was astounded by the answers that Shir Mohammed gave to General Rodriguez's questions. This conversation highlighted the real problem with the Afghan National Army: they did not understand counter-insurgency. The ANA would look at the American Army with envy for our technologically advanced equipment and capabilities. Their leaders believed that to become a good army, they had to model their force after ours. But this is not the case. Technology will not win the war in Afghanistan—people will. If the government can provide security, basic services, opportunities, and civil administration, including justice, then it will win the war. Therefore, the key to winning is the government's relationship with the people rather than helicopters and lasers on rifles. Further, the Taliban is a symptom of the real enemy—corruption in the government. A competent government would make the Taliban irrelevant because that government would be meeting the needs of the people, as noted above. This is the essence of counter-insurgency. It was at this point that I realized the most important thing I could do with the ANA was educate my partner on this point. It would be my number one task for the rest of my time in Afghanistan.

18 April 2010

Kalagush was attacked tonight, as indicators have been saying for the past several days. Two OPs were attacked simultaneously, and the enemy appears to have fired a couple of rockets to suppress the FOB. All has held so far except for the fact that the Afghans are running out of ammo on the OPs. That is because they won't control their fire. They just shoot full automatic and let it rip. I had a feeling that an attack would occur today because Abdullah Khan called (the S3 at Kalagush) and said he had an emergency to attend to. He was gone during the two previous attacks. He is such a coward and a poor excuse for a police chief. He is a poster boy for the reason Afghans will lose the war (if that happens). The most frustrating thing for me is the fact that I am down here in J-bad while all this is happening at Kalagush. I think there will be a serious attempt to attack the FOB and OPs at dawn, so we have lined up assets to support and defeat these people once and for all. Thank God we have the Torkham PLT back to help out up there. It was huge getting them.

I have a meeting with Shir Mohammed at 1400 with all the ANSF at Bde on JAF tomorrow.

The attack at Kalagush focused on the observation posts now manned by Afghan security guards. Again, the enemy failed and suffered defeat in the attack, which appeared to be more harassment than a full-fledged attempt to overrun the post, as on the previous occasions. I hated not being present during this round of fighting. Nevertheless, my mission took me to another location, and I had to trust the leaders whom I had at Kalagush. They did an outstanding job in carrying out their mission, and I should not have worried.

19 April 2010

The attack we thought would happen at Kalagush did not materialize. It is hard to know what the enemy wants to do because they don't follow a line of logic as we would. But these little pokes appear to be harassing in nature for now. If they could ever overrun one of the OPs, that would represent the most dangerous course of action because then they could place a heavy weapon and drop rounds on the FOB. This has yet to happen.

I went to the meeting today with Shir Mohammed, and there they met the Corps Cdr, CoP from Nuristan, ABP Cdr, governor of Nuristan, and a few others to discuss the way ahead for Kamdesh. A two-hour argument ensued over whose fault it was that the weapons for the new ANP had not arrived. The ANP tried to blame my brigade commander. Finally, the Corps Cdr of the ANA 201st Corps scolded them all and said that it was not the fault of the U.S. and that sooner or later Afghans would have to make do with their own resources. Finally, the CoP determined he could get the weapons, and a time for delivery was determined. The Corps Cdr was the only voice of reason through the whole meeting. The rest of them all had their hands out.

I was very impressed with this Afghan general. I accompanied Shir Mohammed to the meeting as his advisor and to participate in the discussion about future operations in Kamdesh. However, the meeting broke down early over the squabble about weapon delivery. Part of the original plan for the operation included equipping the new ANP recruits. The weapons were delivered to Naray via American aircraft. From there the ANP representatives were supposed to pick them up and move them forward on their own trucks for delivery to the district. However, they failed to do so. In order to divert blame the Nuristani officials attempted to say that it was our responsibility to move the weapons all the way forward instead of to the transfer point at Naray. However, having our forces deliver weapons directly to the police would make it appear that we were running the operation, and all planning had focused on making it an Afghan-led operation. The Nuristani officials had simply failed to carry out this part of the plan. The general had grown weary of the arguing and finally stepped in to say enough was enough. He admonished all the Afghan participants to stop trying to blame problems on U.S. forces. Further, he told the group that they had to start solving their own problems and begin leveraging their own resources. I was so happy to hear these words because, through his statements, it appeared that at least some of our effort to press the Afghans to begin taking responsibility was getting through to certain important players.

20 April 2010

Today there are more reports coming from Dow Ab that a big attack is imminent. The attack of the other night was apparently a probe, as we expected, and the big one with over 100 fighters is coming. They will attempt to breach the perimeter using a suicide bomber facilitated by an FOB worker. I think we can stop anything. The only advantage the enemy could possibly bring to bear is if they could achieve surprise.

The ANA are preparing for their poppy mission phase II. Shir Mohammed really does not want to do it but is being ordered to. He is frustrated right now because the CoS (chief of staff of the Afghan Army) raked him over the coals for stupid things. Rather than focusing on large strategy for winning the war, the Afghan CoS seems more interested in micro-tactics and soldier complaints. At his level he has to focus more on the big picture—i.e., operational and strategic matters. Instead, he jumps down to the lowest level, where company commanders are. Because he has not laid out a vision for how to win the war, the Bde and Bn Cdrs don't have focus. It is a matter of the highest levels of their military not understanding COIN (counter-insurgency). They need to implement a COIN strategy that can be translated into operations and executed at the tactical level. The failure to understand counter-insurgency is a serious flaw in the ANA.

In the aftermath of the latest stab at Kalagush, several reports had come in stating that the engagement was a probing attack to test the defenses of the observation posts. The enemy wanted to discover any weaknesses that they could exploit for a bigger attack later. The question that we had to answer was "Would the enemy actually attempt a large-scale attack?" Our assessment, based on our previous successes, was that, while it was possible that the enemy could make a large attack, they would in all likelihood not attempt one.

The Afghan Army chief of staff visited the Afghan battalion at Naray and was very agitated by what he believed he found. He immediately called

Shir Mohammed and admonished him for several things. Among them was the condition of the food and lack of leave for the soldiers. Mohammed conducted his own investigation and found that most of the complaints were erroneous. The chief had not sat down to have a meal with the soldiers and thus only heard the verbal diatribe. Further, leave was not an issue in the unit. In actuality, the problem was absenteeism, and the soldiers present thought they should be entitled to remain away from their units as long as those who were gaming the system. As a result of the reprimand, Mohammed was in a low state of morale. Yet he did rebound and he also made a concerted effort to address the absenteeism.

21 April 2010

I went up to Mehtar Lam today and all went well visiting A Btry. However, Kalagush had more action again tonight. They fired a 107mm rocket to suppress the FOB and then launched an attack on OP Loyalty. However, they got stopped again, and we had 25 ANA up there for a little surprise. It lasted about 5 minutes, and they broke contact after the mortar and howitzers hammered them with HE/VT (high explosives with fuses set for air bursts). Don't know yet if they got anybody, but we did learn today that they lost two killed from Sunday's attack. Every time they come down the enemy loses more people, and I don't know why they continue to do it. Oh, well.

The 1st Kandak (the Afghan word for battalion) S4 died of a heart attack at Naray. This is the same guy who got torched by the Afghan CoS on Saturday. Unbelievable. The ANA staff basically stopped all business today when word came in. Shir Mohammed went to Konar today to work on coordination between the ANA and provincial government up there. I will meet with him in the morning to discuss the details, and then I am hosting them for a lunch over here (in our mess hall on FOB Hughie) to build the relationship and get all his staff in one room to see exactly how many he has. Many of his staff are underemployed and we want to determine which ones are actually doing anything. If they are invited for food, you can bet that personnel will be coming out of the woodwork.

This was the final assault on FOB Kalagush during our time in Afghanistan. Once again the enemy lost. Following the attack of a few days before, my operations officer had reinforced the observation post with an entire platoon of the ANA. When the enemy made their concerted effort to overrun the post on this night they were stopped cold by the ANA platoon, and our howitzers and mortar system caught them in the open again. Further, we learned that the previous attack had resulted in two more fighters killed. The enemy was losing fighters in every engagement and we had lost none. While I was determined to defeat the enemy, I was still amazed at their ability to motivate their people to continue fighting in the face of continuous losses for seemingly little gain. I did not think they could sustain these losses for very long.

The Afghan brigade staff was very upset by the loss of one of their officers, and it was a coincidence that the man who died was the individual who bore the brunt of the Afghan chief of staff's wrath. All work virtually stopped in the unit following word of this loss.

During our short time working with the Afghan brigade we noted that on paper the staff encompassed more people than the personnel we actually worked with on a daily basis. In order to find out who was actually on the staff, we decided to host a meal to see who would show up. Those who came for the meal that we did not normally see were the malingerers. I knew that the Afghans would jump at the opportunity to eat in our mess hall, so it was the perfect way to determine who the offenders were. I intended to pass this information on to Shir Mohammed so that he could take appropriate action.

22 April 2010

Today the ANA 201st Corps Cdr made a visit, and we took the opportunity to cut the ribbon on the CTOC with him present. It is now complete and has full connectivity. It looks very good and is fully functional. Now we just need to get the Afghans in it and working, which is the bigger challenge.

This afternoon I had to go over to JAF for the Cdrs' Conference. We discussed the ways to get Afghanistan functioning independently. From my perspective we have got to get the ANA to stop using us as a crutch and thinking that technology will solve their problems. It will not. They have to execute counter-insurgency ops focused on their people. They need to work with the police, fight corruption, and leverage the cultural norms as only they can. When that happens, they can win.

23 April 2010

Nothing today at Kalagush except that the enemy rotated some personnel out. At the Cdrs' Conference we had a great deal of discussion about the redeployment. I have to keep everyone focused for a few more weeks before we will be able to let our guard down. I am concerned that as we move into the final 30 days accidents and stupid things will happen. So, I emphasized to the leadership that they have to focus on taking care of our people throughout.

24 April 2010

Kalagush had the first IED in almost a month on the east side of the river near Ja'laam. After a nice lull it looks like that threat has started up again. EOD got it out with no issue. The enemy threat to the FOB has not been active the past two days, but that doesn't mean it is not there. Apparently, one of the TB commanders suspects we have sources among them, and he knocked out the cell phone tower for a while today. Therefore, we did not get any reports. But it is back up tonight, so hopefully we will get some info. The platoons did a patrol with the ANA into the Shemgal to see if the enemy is in there, but they found none. It looks like the enemy has shifted over to Wadawu, so we are planning a big patrol with ANA in there for Wednesday. We will see what happens. Tomorrow I am headed up to Kalagush and will spend the night.

After the IED cell leader fled following his feud, our units had a nice reprieve from the threat of roadside bombs. This IED was reported through our hotline, and we had the explosive ordnance disposal team remove it safely. We continued to have reports of the enemy intending to attack the FOB. We also learned that the cell leaders suspected that we had sources who were keeping us informed of their movements. This, of course, was true. Our network of Afghan informants allowed us to anticipate enemy attacks and discover the IED locations. In retaliation, the enemy knocked out one of the local cell phone towers, ostensibly to prevent the sources from calling the hotline. Within hours the tower was back in operation, and the sources were able to let us know what was happening.

25 April 2010

Here at Kalagush tonight. There is a great deal of intel that the enemy wants to overrun the base, and apparently they are trying to bring in people from all over to do it. I don't think they can pull as many people as the intel says, but they can certainly attempt more attacks. The provincial leadership needs to pay more attention to the area and display some leadership with regard to planned attacks, but I am afraid that won't happen. If there is nothing to be gained, then the government won't do it, and so what was the most stable district in Nuristan, Nurgaram, could become volatile due to the lack of attention. I told the SGs, who came to visit when they found out I was here, that they would have to engage the people themselves rather than waiting for us to take the initiative. The leadership deficit is so palpable.

Meanwhile, the ANA are about the neediest army I have ever seen. They launched their poppy op today in Khogyani and mucked it up from the start. They had a firefight in the midst of the op and asked me for air support. They can't even establish good ground control, so what could they do with it? When I told them I could not get it, Shir Mohammed called the brigade commander over my head begging for it. Instead of worrying about techno solutions, they should have started the op with a series of leader engagements with the people. After all, they are Afghans and should connect with the people. They can make that connection so much better than we ever could. But they don't do things IAW (in accordance with) COIN strategy. So, that is the biggest issue. They want tech solutions instead of

Our partner Afghan National Army company patrolling in Nurgaram District of Nuristan. These soldiers are typical of the men found in the Afghan Army. Note the lush valley along the Alingar River in spring. The green zone in the background comprises terraced wheat fields that feed the local people (photograph by the 2-77th Field Artillery Public Affairs Officer, Captain Matthew Frye).

using their greatest advantage: the fact that they are Afghans. It will be tough to win here if the ANA doesn't start understanding this.

The entry above illustrates what I believe is the heart of the issue in Afghanistan. On the one hand, the local governments have got to clean up corruption and become engaged with the people. Further, they need to work with all Afghan security forces, including the army, to ensure the security of the people and foster economic growth. This is where caring leaders come into play. On the other hand, the ANA has to learn that they cannot model the organization after the American Army. Envy of our technological advantages and overreliance on logistical support from our forces made the ANA dependent upon us. This led to a situation in which the ANA found it difficult to implement sound counter-insurgency strategy. The Afghans had to change this dynamic for the good of their nation.

26 April 2010

Nothing happened while I was up at Kalagush, although there are a lot of reports of impending attacks. During the platoon's patrol today they set up a checkpoint at the mouth of the Wadawu while the ANA searched the village. Based on questioning of several of those coming through the checkpoint and in the village itself, the enemy is definitely using the Wadawu and intimidating the people. A large patrol is planned for Wednesday to see if there is any enemy there and to disrupt any plans if they are there.

I went to a meeting at JAF with Shir Mohammed today. My brigade commander brought everyone in to discuss what went wrong in the poppy op. Of course, the ANP tried to blame a lack of U.S. support for their casualties. This is bunk. All they want us for is assets, and our presence would allow them to escape blame for their half-baked plans and poor execution in the eyes of the people. The meeting got testy, but my COL put a stop to it and told them to start taking responsibility for their own security instead of passing the buck to us. Afghans will hide behind someone else to their advantage at every turn. They pass blame on to us to escape responsibility. It is getting old, and they have to start taking advantage of their own strengths that far outweigh any technological advantage we may have. Their strengths are:

1. Language
2. Culture
3. Religion

If they use this to their advantage to engage the populace, they can win using COIN strategy. If they continue to hide behind us, they lose.

Following the botched poppy operation, the Nangarhar police chief attempted to blame the fiasco on a lack of support from our brigade. Poppy eradication is not something we can become involved in because of the implication that we would be destroying the livelihood of the people. This operation was the idea of the governor of Nangarhar, and his refusal to engage the elders beforehand had a negative effect. My brigade commander had heard enough of the complaints and the Afghan police's failure to take responsibility. Therefore, he called a meeting with all those who were involved in the operation to clear the air and establish a line in the sand that would push the Afghans to step forward and assume responsibility. I was very happy to sit in the room that day and listen to my commander reiterate what I had been thinking for a long time.

27 April 2010

Nothing up at Kalagush, and that is good. There was a complaint about the ANA searching Nangaresh yesterday to the SG, but other than that little else.

Here in J-bad the ANA started the Liberation Day holiday, so they won't accomplish anything. I did go to a meeting with Shir Mohammed at the governor's palace. The ANP again tried to say that they did not get any support from us during their poppy op. And, again, we had to throw it right back at them. But the Khogyani elders came too, and the governor berated them for growing poppy and not supporting the government. He told them that all projects were off until they provided better support. An argument ensued, with the elders stating that they have always done what the government wanted. Bottom line is that if the governor had engaged the people before the op, all of this could have been avoided. The government doesn't seem to realize that the key to fixing the problems down at the district and village level lies with the people. If the government would get the people on board with security and development, it could be much more effective.

Afghan Liberation Day is a celebration of the withdrawal of the Soviet Union and the fall of the communist puppet government that the Soviets left in their wake.

28 April 2010

The advance party of 2–320 FA arrived today, so now we have 33 of their people in Afghanistan with us. Our first 6 hit the ground at Fort Carson today. Things are actually starting to come to a close on our tour here, but we still have about 4 weeks to go for the staff and less than that for the batteries. We just have to be vigilant to the end.

At Kalagush a report came in from two different sources that one of the elected officials in the parliament from the Kolotan Valley of W. Nuristan is tied to the TB. Also, we learned that a reason for the upswing in attacks recently is that the Dow Ab cell has been getting pressured by the Taliban shadow governor to step up attacks. Apparently, there is frustration in the TB that the attacks have failed, and so the shadow governor is ordering more. That answers the question as to why they keep coming. Their attacks have been ineffective and they have lost people in every engagement. I wonder how much longer the cell is going to keep following orders from the shadow governor and continue losing people. When will they decide they have had enough and just go back to Dow Ab?

The ANA were mostly gone today for Liberation Day, so nothing happened. Shir Mohammed gets promoted tomorrow, and we will open his new weapons range with a ribbon cutting.

On this day our replacements began arriving. The advance party would prepare to receive their unit and learn as much about our mission as possible so that there would be a smooth transition of authority when they took the mission.

The news from Kalagush about the elected official having ties to the Taliban was disturbing, and yet I was not surprised to hear this information. It is another example of my hypothesis that the biggest stumbling block to victory in Afghanistan is the crisis of leadership in the Afghan government. Where are the Washingtons and Jeffersons in this country? Selfless service from those serving in the government would go a long way toward securing victory over the Taliban.

29 April 2010

Today at J-bad we cut the ribbon on the new range and Shir Mohammed got promoted to BG (brigadier general).

At Kalagush we had the potential to accomplish some good in Wadawu Valley but missed the opportunity because the ANA company commander came out for the patrol as high as a kite. He smoked some hash before the start of the mission and made a fool of himself in front of the villagers in the Wadawu. There might have been enemies in there, but we were unable to find out for sure because of the disgusting display of their captain. Once again poor leadership undermines potential success. So, I talked to Mohammed today about relieving the company commander. We can't let dope smokers lead troops. They are then viewed as incompetent by the people, and they set the wrong example for their troops.

I was disheartened by the news that the ANA company commander at

Kalagush had behaved so foolishly. He had great leadership qualities to bring to the area. However, finding out that he was a drug user changed our opinion radically. He had to go, and I immediately engaged the newly promoted Brigadier General Mohammed to get the ball rolling on his removal. Drug use by any leader is unacceptable in any army.

30 April 2010

It was a quiet day here at Hughie, but Kalagush got a few interesting reports from sources. It seems that the reason for all the recent attacks is that the TB in Nuristan is placing a lot of pressure on the local TB in W. Nuristan to drive home a successful attack. The enemy's defeat in every previous attempt has irritated the TB at higher levels, so they are demanding success or suffer the consequences. The reports also said the enemy will make another attempt to attack in the next 48 hours. I don't know if it will happen, but it is interesting to hear of the frustration of the enemy. As far as I am concerned, they can break themselves against our defenses at any time. It is easier for us and we don't get branded as the aggressor among the people.

We were continuing to receive reports that the enemy wanted to drive home a successful attack. Apparently, the high-level Taliban leaders in sanctuaries in Pakistan were displeased that we still had a permanent presence in Nuristan. They believed that the local cells were not aggressive enough in their attacks and threatened to replace the local leaders unless they could win an engagement. I had no objection to the enemy's apparent desire to destroy themselves against our solid defenses. How much more could the enemy lose before they figured out that their tactics were not working and that it was not worth the effort?

1 May 2010

Today was interesting, to say the least. First, just after I went to bed last night, I got a call from the S3 saying that Kalagush came under rocket attack. They shot a couple of harassing rounds for the first time at a time other than dawn or dusk. We have never seen that before. The S3 thinks it was at that time because there was bad weather earlier in the evening. Could be. Patrols that went to the Shemgal and Wadawu saw nothing significant. Some elders from Dow Ab came in to ask for projects, and we flatly refused until security can be established. Then the Wadawu elders called to set up a meeting to ask for projects. They were told no until security improves. I can't believe that the Afghans have the audacity to ask for things when they do nothing to secure themselves, they don't report enemy activity, and do nothing to help themselves. It is amazing to me. I want to help them, but they have no gratitude for the things we have already done and will do nothing for peace. We have not done any offensive operations since we got here out of respect, and yet we get no respect in return. We have been attacked every time an engagement has occurred.

I did go up to ML (Mehtar Lam) today to plan an operation with the Afghans along Hwy 1A (the highway between Kabul and Jalalabad). Before I left, though, an interesting incident occurred. My driver and his wife—both my soldiers—were waiting to take us out to the airfield for the flight. While waiting in the vehicles an ANA soldier came up to her and started harassing her and yelling at her in Pashto two inches from her face. My driver kept his cool and got the XO, who in turn got the ANA CSM. They then went to find the guy so the ANA could punish him. They found him, and tomorrow he will apologize to her and her husband. Then he is going to jail. Good. I can't believe how some of these men (Afghans) act. When they see a woman they act like animals who can't control themselves. They think an uncovered woman causes them to sin. It never enters their minds that they have to exhibit self-control. Their solution to temptation is to cover up the woman. It isn't their fault if a woman is sexually assaulted if she isn't covered. What?

Before you go to a Muslim country you are told to treat them with dignity and respect; respect their culture, etc. But why doesn't anyone have to appreciate or respect us? We spend our treasure and give our lives for people who want our money and treat us with disrespect. And you have some arrogant and misinformed people back home who say we as soldiers are too heavy-handed and indiscriminate with our fires, etc. Well, the truth is no army in the history of warfare has been more discriminating or given more deference to the culture of the country (Afghanistan) than ours.

You would think the Afghans could reciprocate and the idiots in our country would find the truth about what we are doing here. But this will not be. The Afghans will continue to have their hands out and disrespect us, and some back home will cry that our imperial heavy-handedness is hurting the noble Afghans who just want to be left alone. Meanwhile, Joe over here tries his best to make a better world. I hope God will bless Joe's effort.

The entry above was indicative of blowing off steam after seeing a ridiculous incident. The Afghan called my female soldier a slut because her face was not covered and she had the audacity to drive a vehicle. Her young husband—who was armed with a 5.56mm M4 rifle—kept his cool and got our battalion executive officer. The XO broke up the incident and summoned the

Afghan command sergeant major. To the Afghan leader's credit, he handled the situation in a commendable manner.

I was so frustrated at this point of the deployment with the hypocrisy displayed by the Afghans. I vented into my diary. On the one hand, the Afghans were frequently irritating, as the entry above notes. On the other, there was a prevailing sense that some of our own people at home do not appreciate our efforts to do the right thing for the Afghans and our own country. The diary entry reflects my own sense from news media that our people did not really understand what we were doing in Afghanistan. I found it quite disconcerting.

2 May 2010

Today I went to Fortress to promote the gunnery sergeant out there to sergeant first class. That was the best part of the day. Then there was the ANA part of the day. Shir Mohammed held his Cdrs' Conference today and emphasized some good points and ideas like the need to operate independently and not rely on the coalition for everything; building his own RCPs (route clearance packages) in each Bn; and building better cooperation and coordination between the ANA and OCCs (provincial operation coordination centers). Very good points until we had a discussion about the Hwy mission set to begin tomorrow. He said that it would be hard for him to sustain security because of lack of air support. I told him to engage the villages so that they would deny sanctuary to the enemy; then there would be no attacks and thus no need for air support. He retorted that I have not helped him set up the meetings. So, I guess it is my fault. My frustration level hit a point today that I can't describe. He tells his officers to be more self-reliant and then whines to me later in the day that he has no air and I haven't set up any meetings for him. I might as well do everything for him because he is a child. But I won't do it. After 9 years in Afghanistan and 3 tours myself, it is sink or swim for the ANA.

This entry reflects yet more frustration on my part with the Afghans. Shir Mohammed conducted a conference with all his battalion and company commanders in the brigade, and during the meeting he made some very good points about what the ANA has to do to be a credible force. Then, within a couple of hours of making these statements, he said that we were not adequately supporting his mission to secure Highway 1A. I could not believe I was hearing this rant. Further, I was repositioning some of my own artillery to support the mission in order to provide additional fire support to the Afghan Army. I was beginning to reach a boiling point, and it was a very good thing that our deployment was coming to a close.

3 May 2010

It was a wild day today. A helicopter crashed at Kalagush, two IED makers blew themselves up in Tupak, and replacements began arriving today, including the Bn Cdr, CSM and S3 of 2–320 FA. Apparently, a resupply helicopter had its tail rotor malfunction, causing the helo, a MI-17 Russian aircraft, to lose control and crash on the LZ (landing zone) full of 120mm mortar ammo. The crew were all injured and the helo is completely wrecked. None of our people were hurt. Later in the evening the FOB heard an explosion, and it turned out that two guys making an IED in a house in Tupak south of Kalagush accidently blew themselves up. That is a blow to the enemy at no expense to us.

Finally, I went to JAF with Shir Mohammed to talk with the COL. The COL emphasized to him that he has to start taking the initiative and stop depending on us. He is getting the message pounded on him from several different directions, and I hope it is starting to sink in. Tomorrow is our final fires conference, and we have several of the replacements here for it so they can see how we have been doing business and how we use the con-

A Battery conducting an air assault from Forward Operating Base Mehtar Lam in support of the Afghan National Army operating along Highway 7 in April 2010. A Battery successfully engaged the enemy, enabling the ANA to drive them away from the road, thus ensuring freedom of movement between Jalalabad and Kabul (courtesy Major Chris Carpenter).

ference to help us change course to maintain the best possible fire support system.

One other note: We conducted our first AASLT (air assault) tonight of an M198 155mm howitzer platoon at ML (Mehtar Lam). No hitches and they are IPRTF (in position ready to fire). This was the first one by this battalion since the Vietnam War. This was the repositioning of our artillery to support the Afghan operation along Highway 1A. I sent our Assn. (the 77th Field Artillery Association) vets a note on it.

This was a very eventful day. The helicopter crash could have been catastrophic because the aircraft had several thousand pounds of explosives on board in the form of the mortar rounds. The quick action of some of our soldiers at Kalagush prevented a tragedy. They were able to remove the ammunition from the downed aircraft as fuel leaked from the hot engine to prevent an ignition. For this act, we awarded several participants commendation medals.

The IED cell at Kalagush suffered a serious blow with the loss of the makers. This was fortuitous indeed. IED activity had finally begun to drop off, and now the threat was seriously weakened by this event. I was very thankful.

Finally, I was proud of the troops in A Battery at Mehtar Lam. When I visited their location for planning of the operation along Highway 1A, the battery leadership presented me with a backbrief of the mission to confirm that they were ready. They were ready and executed flawlessly. An air assault operation with heavy equipment is a dangerous mission and involves moving the howitzers by aircraft slingload with all troops and ammunition on board. When they get to the next location they have to quickly put the guns in operation at night in order to provide support for the infantry—in this case, Afghan infantry units. The soldiers in the platoon from Mehtar Lam did it without error and were ready when the Afghans called for fire. In a week of frustrations, this operation was a gratifying event that reaffirmed my confidence in our leaders and soldiers.

4 May 2010

We conducted our fires conference at JAF, and I believe it gave the incoming unit a good overview of what the fires mission will look like. Plus, it should help them learn from our mistakes so that they don't make them like we did. While in the conference I got a tap on my shoulder and learned that nine soldiers from one gun section in B/3–321 were wounded by an 82mm recoilless rifle firing at them while they were in a fire mission. Even though they were apparently wounded, the section kept on firing. That sounds like stuff of valor—to stay at your piece even though you are hurt. Once we get the details we will work the awards. Also, may have some soldier medals from the downed helo at Kalagush. Two of our guys up there helped rescue the pilots. Our guys continue to do well. I just pray that the casualties will pull through, as there are two very seriously injured from today.

The casualties on this day brought our total up to 19 during the deployment, with one killed, four very seriously injured, six seriously injured, and eight with minor injuries who returned to duty within 72 hours. I wish there had been none, but I understand the reality of war. In this incident the gun crew was firing at a target when they were engaged in their gun pit by the recoilless rifle on a hill overlooking the firebase in the Pech River Valley. The howitzer crew remained at their posts, engaging their assigned target in the midst of the incoming rounds that had wounded the majority of the crew. An outstanding example of the dedication to duty and heroism of today's American soldier.

5 May 2010

Our guns that AASLTed (air assaulted) down to Zio Haq (along Highway 1A) fired last night and this morning in TICs (troops in contact with the enemy situations). The enemy tried to attack an OP overwatching the road and the PLT fired, driving the enemy back with losses. Excellent mission, and they returned (from the mission) by air this evening. I sent the pictures to the Vietnam veterans.

Took our replacements out to Firebase Garcia today and brought the Afghan Brigade CoS with us. Good visit, and they understand our firebase out there.

Kalagush started the RIP (relief in place) there today, as the first PLTs of the Infantry company arrived yesterday. Within 9 days I will have our platoons out of Kalagush. I will be happy to finally have them back and safe.

One of my CPTs' wife sent him a "dear John" email tonight. He is devastated. I can't believe she has done this to him within one week of coming home. There is a slew of them in the Bn right now. There is such a fickle lack of commitment to anything meaningful, like marriage, in our society. Everyone lives for the moment without regard for bigger things in life. It is pathetic. Thank God my wife has been there for me through every deployment and a year in Korea, four years away from home. I never had to worry about that.

We were making every effort to provide the unit replacing us with lessons learned and information about the environment in Afghanistan. The fires conference and the trips we made to other firebases were examples of working through a smooth transition so that the next unit would be able to hit the ground running. When a unit arrives in Afghanistan, there is a limited amount of time available to facilitate the transition, so we developed a step-by-step plan to make it as seamless as possible. Even when the outgoing unit does a good job in transition, there are still unanswered questions that the incoming unit will not be able to address in the short two to three weeks available to conduct the relief.

It was disheartening to learn that the marriage of one of my young staff officers was coming to an end. During the last few weeks of our deployment my command sergeant major and I were receiving many reports of marital issues as we began preparations to come home. This is, unfortunately, not an unusual occurrence. I had seen this dynamic many times in the course of my career, and it was part of the reason that I was so worried about our troops as the deployment came to a close. Not only will units suffer unnecessary losses from accidents in the last days deployed, but personal issues will also rise to the fore in that time. Soldiers react to such news differently based on their maturity level and inner strength. What we had to do as leaders was provide counseling and other services to these soldiers to ensure that they could cope with trying situations.

6 May 2010

Today's focus was on orienting the new unit's command on the way we see the problem with the unit-specific mission and offer the ways we would approach solving it were we to remain here. I certainly hope that we are giving our replacements a good boost to help them operate well during their time here. I hope they will be able to take what we started here with the ANA and take it to a level far beyond where we are. The key for the ANA is implementing a population-focused COIN strategy.

At Kalagush it was a quiet day, with little reporting and a lot of rain. I am glad it was quiet. The rest of D Co (the infantry company) arrived today minus the CP (command post with commander and first sergeant). The RIP there is well under way.

7 May 2010

It was another quiet day up at Kalagush, and with an entire infantry company and soon a full MP PLT there is going to be three times as much patrol capability as we ever had. That is good and should do a great deal to enhance security in old AO Steel. Here in Jalalabad the ANA actually did a very good thing today. They received an intel report about 5–10 suicide "fighters" planning to attack the garrison. So, they produced an order that reinforced the gates and established a QRF (quick reaction force). Then, shortly after they implemented it, the ANA detained 10 foreigners at the ECP (entry control point) without passports or ID. They claimed to be headed to Kabul looking for jobs, but if that were true, then why were they trying to enter an ANA base? We will see what happens with this. The incident does illustrate what the Bde staff is capable of with their own assets.

The detention of the ten foreign males was an outstanding example of the ANA's capabilities. Our task was to convince them of what they could do and instill the confidence they needed to start acting on their own to secure Afghanistan.

8 May 2010

Quiet at Kalagush. There were a couple of reports of night letters in Salaw being spread by the Alishang cell. This is the first that we have ever seen of folks from Alishang coming over to operate in our AO, although there are passes from Wadawu, Tag, and Salaw that connect that valley to the Alingar.

Here at Hughie I had an exhausting conversation with Shir Mohammed, who came back from back from Kabul today. After he gave my replacement and his S3 an overview of his brigade AO, he then asked for air to move 62 people up to Naray. I told him that they had to do an AMR (air movement request) for it and that the 62 probably could not be supported by our assets. We might be able to move a few. His S3, who was in the room, said that they had filled one out 15 days ago. I said that was impossible since we had only got it translated a week ago. Then he backpedaled. I used it as an opportunity to tell Shir Mohammed that if his officers were working in the TOC, we could avoid such friction. So, his S3 lied, and they tried to blame us for an unfilled "request." That was only half the frustration. After I left Mohammed, he called his corps commander and said we weren't supporting him, like some child. Then the DCG (deputy commanding general) of the 82nd Airborne Division called to ask why the brigade wasn't supporting them. The brigade in turn called us to see what was going on. After explaining it to the brigade, they provided the answer back to the DCG.

Once again the ANA demonstrates their fickle nature. They do no forecasting or planning, ask us for support for a mission the next day, and when we can't do it and try to teach them planning processes, they go whining. It is so irritating. My replacement is seeing the challenges of the partnership mission, as demonstrated today.

In order to obtain air support, American units have to forecast needs at least 72 hours from the required time and make an appropriate request. This allows the aviation units to prioritize those needs and service the requests. The Afghans were asking for American air support to move 62 Afghan troops up to Naray to support the mission in Kamdesh. Their request would have to go through the prioritization process just like any of our units. I tried to use this as a teaching moment to encourage the brigade staff to forecast their needs and then follow a logical process for requesting assets. When I did not give them the answer they wanted, the commander went to his superior to complain that I was not supporting him. In turn, the senior leaders of our Joint Task Force sent down a request for an explanation as to why we were not supporting the ANA. Once we explained the situation the incident cooled down. This incident is indicative of the challenges inherent in supporting the ANA in a partnership.

I had expected to assist the Afghan leaders with advice and technical support that they would enthusiastically soak up to become a better (and eventually independent) force. What I found was a force akin to a child that expected every need to be satisfied by our forces. If I fostered this behavior, then the ANA would never make progress toward becoming a credible and independent force for their nation. So, I had to break this mentality and force them to rely on their own assets while developing their own planning processes. Over the next few days, after our staff provided some close mentorship, the Afghans were able to accomplish the mission, and we had a very gratifying example of what they were able to do on their own.

9 May 2010

Went to FOB Joyce today so that the 2–320 Cdr could see the radar, MET (meteorological) station, and B Btry CP (command post). Good trip, and I did not have to wrestle with the ANA today. Our change out with this battalion is much smoother than the one when we came in. I have pressed our commanders and staff to make sure we did the right thing by our counterparts and not leave them hanging as we were. Everyone has met that guidance.

At Kalagush today there was nothing with regard to the enemy. However, the Corps Cdr visited there today with the DCG (deputy commanding general, 82nd Airborne Division). The 201st Corps Cdr stressed the independence and responsibility that his troops must display. Then the DCG asked my S3 why we are not doing more for them, such as logistical support for food and water, which was one of his specific comments. So, what is it? Independence or dependence? I find it irritating that an American general presses us to just do everything for the ANA, and yet we are supposed to be building a credible army. Again, this give, give, give has produced the ANA's current dependent mindset. If we don't force them to make their systems work, we will never have an ANA capable of defending its country. Some of our own leaders are the biggest offenders who have caused this overdependence on coalition forces for everything.

My operations officer at Kalagush was sternly admonished because the deputy commanding general perceived that we were not doing enough to provide material support to the ANA. However, we had just completed improvements to their housing, assisted in reinforcing their defensive positions, and did the initial contracting to provide the subsistence. This was meant to jumpstart the Afghans toward maintaining and providing for themselves after we established a baseline of logistical support. The Afghan general told his own people that they must become independent, and over his shoulder our own chain of command was reprimanding my operations officer for not doing enough. There are certain things we have to do to assist our Afghan partners. However, after nine years, was it unreasonable to expect the ANA to provide their own food and water without perpetual dependence on our forces, or their own housing, and so forth?

10 May 2010

At Kalagush today the RIP is continuing at a steady pace, and that is a good thing.

Within four days the PLTs will be here, and none too soon. The HHB maneuver platoon with D Co. found two IEDs and had a firefight in the Nuralam. This is the first contact in that valley in well over a month of any type. The enemy is definitely becoming more active in that area. I relinquish responsibility for AO Steel on the 14th, and 12 days I later turn over the fires and partnership missions to our replacements.

Did meet with Shir Mohammed today and went over several things. Tomorrow he is going to A-bad at the invitation of the OCC Cdr up there.

11 May 2010

At Kalagush there was a rocket attack this morning. It impacted outside the wire in the trash pit and the FOB counterfired (with artillery). This was said to be the work of the Alishang cell. They then apparently left the Wadawu and went back to Alishang.

We did move a lot of people and equipment around, as the RIP (relief-in-place) has now kicked into high gear. Half of HHB's maneuver platoon is out of Kalagush and all of Bravo's Torkham platoon arrived today. By Saturday all but the PL, PSG, and SLs (squad leaders) will be out, with them coming out on Monday. That will be great.

Here at J-bad the Corps CoS came and visited. He discussed basing two Afghan Air Force helos at JAF. If this happens, then maybe Shir Mohammed will stop bugging me to haul him around everywhere.

I was still worried about the platoons at Kalagush. The rocket attack reinforced that worry because I did not want to lose someone in the last 72 hours of their time in harm's way. Nevertheless, I would not hunker down and fail to accomplish our mission. At this point, we had to prepare the infantry company that was replacing us to assume full responsibility. That meant that the leaders had to continue to go on patrol with the new unit to help orient them, introduce them to the local leaders, and share the danger. As the reader can see, our process of conducting a relief-in-place is very systematic. Units will slowly integrate the soldiers and leaders of the incoming unit into operations until they can fully take charge. Then our leaders quietly assume a supporting role. Finally, when the assigned date for full assumption of responsibility arrives, our leaders—who are the last ones on location—formally turn over that responsibility and leave the firebase. This was the process we followed in order to prepare the replacement unit for full operations.

12 May 2010

Today we hosted the 1/101st (1st Brigade, 101st Airborne Division) Bde Cdr and gave him our viewpoint of the problem with partnership with the ANA. Bottom line: The ANA needs to focus on counter-insurgency and the population. Also, the biggest challenge for the incoming unit is weaning the ANA off of us as their resource provider and starting to depend on themselves. Which leads me to the next point.

The ANA actually has air assets of their own coming in tomorrow to lift their own guys out and push them up to Naray. When we learned about the ANA air force basing aircraft at JAF, we immediately pressed their staff to make the appropriate requests for support. They wanted us to move their troops, but we made them do the work and planning, and now they are actually getting it done themselves. The ANA can do a lot if they will just get down to business and stop depending on us. Once they do this and begin to work with the population, they will win.

A few days after my confrontation with Shir Mohammed and his operations officer over the issue of air movement support for his troops, we took advantage of the fact that the ANA would soon position helicopters at Jalalabad Airfield. The battalion staff coached the ANA brigade staff on the process of requesting air support from their own air force. The ANA staff sent the request forward to the corps through their chain of command, and the next day the request was approved. Afghan helicopters would now move their own troops and ideally build some confidence in their own abilities.

13 May 2010

A very successful day for the ANA. Today Afghan aircraft transported 62 of their soldiers up to Naray. It was outstanding and proves what I have been saying all along: Afghans can do things themselves if they will just try. It was a very good day from that standpoint.

At Kalagush the maneuver platoon finished their last patrol today. Now if we can just get them down here in the next two days, all will be well. However, we got a lot of intel that the enemy plans to attack once again within the next 72 hours. Unbelievable. Plus, it will probably happen because Abdullah Khan, the CoP, is gone again. Every time he has been gone an attack occurred. That guy is in bed with the enemy and a coward. I am making one last push to get him fired, but I probably will not be successful because there just isn't enough time. Andy's birthday today.

I was very pleased to have the maneuver platoon complete their final patrol. We had transportation planned for them to retrograde within the next two days. In the meantime, we were getting more reports that the enemy wanted to attack yet again. We would see what the future held.

14 May 2010

Almost nothing happened today. Only up at Kalagush was there any information. A report came in that said the enemy would attempt to initiate the attack on the FOB using suicide bombers at the ECP (entry control point) to spread confusion. Then, when everyone was preoccupied by the blast, the enemy would attack the FOB, having the element of surprise. With this information we can be ready for anything. If the enemy does attempt something tomorrow, they should get hammered. We still have the maneuver platoon leaders up there. They will all come out on Monday, leaving only the S3 as an overwatch for them until next Saturday. Finally we will be done at Kalagush.

Tomorrow is Maryellen's birthday.

15 May 2010

Quiet day at Kalagush after I had thought things would get interesting today. We quietly handed it off to D/1–102 today. Our TAC will remain there for a few more days, but there are only 6 of the maneuver platoon left up there. They will be here tomorrow, and our time in W. Nuristan is over.

I think we did some good things there, but I wish we could have accomplished more. Unfortunately, the deficit of good Afghan leadership in that region handicapped our efforts and made it difficult to accomplish our goals in governance and security. Without local leadership that is uncorrupted and somewhat competent, there is just no way we as Americans could tip the scale to victory. We can achieve a stalemate, but good Afghan leaders have to take it to victory. I hope the Afghan government will finally realize this and clear out the turds in favor of some people who care and can make a difference in tipping the scales.

In J-bad we had a meeting at JAF today with LTG Rodriguez, the Bde Cdr, Shir Mohammed, the ABP Cdr, Nangarhar CoP, and other hangers-on. The subject was the way ahead for the region and cooperation between the ANA, ANP, and ABP. Shir Mohammed discussed engaging the population and working with the others. My jaw dropped. He never discusses these things with me. I am the one always pressing him on them. He talks a good game, but when it comes time to implement this strategy he just asks me for air support, etc. Hopefully, his talk will turn into action in COIN so they can win the competition for the support of the people.

Maryellen's 45th birthday. Tried to call, but I think she is at Ashley's swim meet today.

I was very pleased to finally transition authority for our area in Nuristan and Laghman over to the next unit and know that all of our people were safe. I felt we had accomplished much, but, as noted, I was let down that we could not effect greater progress. However, a much of what had to be done required competent Afghan leadership, and this was the area of greatest concern. American forces could not win the war for the Afghans, nor govern the country. Only Afghans can do this. Our job is to create an environment where progress is protected from the enemy while the government builds the foundation for stability. If I had realized this before I arrived in Afghanistan for my third tour, perhaps my expectations would have been more appropriate to the situation.

It was surprising to hear Shir Mohammed speak so forcefully about things that I had been discussing with him since my arrival in Jalalabad. I realized that maybe I was not wasting my breath in continuing to emphasize the elements of a good counter-insurgency strategy. If the Afghan Army and other security agencies will engage in this strategy, then they can defeat the Taliban and enable the country to finally dig out of its 30 years of turmoil.

16 May 2010

Very quiet day. The Kalagush personnel minus the TAC will be here tomorrow, one day delayed. There was no attack last night or today, which surprised me. That is OK. As long as nothing happens in the morning, they will leave Kalagush with a quiet last few days.

At Hughie today we had lunch with the ANA, and they gave me another Karzai robe like what I got from the Afghan battery commander up at Kalagush. I will host a lunch for them next week and we will reciprocate the gifts.

Our time here is now rapidly coming to a close, only 9 days left. Over half the Bn will be moving home by tomorrow, and by this time next week there will only be 50 of us left. I am happy about that. I am ready to get home to see Maryellen and the kids. Afghanistan has had enough of me this third time around.

17 May 2010

B Btry is now moving home, followed in three days by A Btry. HHB and G remain in some strength, but even they are really starting to move quickly. In three days well over half the Bn will be gone. It is hard to believe the year is almost over, but I am certainly glad.

I took my counterpart up to Firebase Connolly today to see one of the A Btry PLTs. It was overcast and drizzling all day, so it was also cool for this time of year. When I was in J-bad four years ago I remember it being much hotter than right now. It has been hot, but not sustained like it was in April–May of 2006. The frequent rain we have had has kept it much cooler, and today it was nice. Tomorrow we head up to A-bad. Only a little more than a week left.

2010 was the year of the floods in Afghanistan and Pakistan. It was a wet spring while we were still in Afghanistan, but the real rains would come shortly after we left. The temperature in Jalalabad routinely hits 110 degrees Fahrenheit in May, but we did not see that in 2010. While it did get uncomfortable at times, it was not nearly what I had experienced in previous tours. During the summer of 2009 temperatures actually approached 130 degrees on the Jalalabad Airfield. As one can see, the environment of Afghanistan can be very harsh.

18 May 2010

The platoons are now out of Kalagush and the A Btry firing element comes out tomorrow. Other than the S3, Battle NCO, and radio operator, it is done. More people arrived home today in Colorado, and we now have less than half the Bn in position. I can't believe how quickly things are moving. Tomorrow is my last battlefield circulation to Monti. I will take our replacements to see the place. On Thursday they begin running things with our oversight, and then next Wednesday is the transition of authority ceremony. Hard to believe. I certainly hope we have made a difference here.

Just as when we arrived in Afghanistan, things moved very quickly toward the transition between the two units. I could not believe how fast our unit retrograded out of the respective firebases and back home. We remained in charge of the mission until the scheduled day of transition, but the incoming unit had a preponderance of people manning the bases. We provided leadership oversight until the day of transition, with their people performing the mission. The methodology of transition provides the incoming unit with the experience it needs to operate without the immediate responsibility.

19 May 2010

Today traveled up to Monti on my last battlefield circulation with our replacements. The firebase is completely manned by 101st people. Our folks from B Btry left yesterday and are at Bagram.

Well, at Bagram there was a heck of an event. The enemy attacked the place in multiple locations with suicide bombers, car bombs, mortars, rockets, and dismounts in U.S. Army uniforms. Although none breached the wire and ten were killed, I am sure they will achieve the goal of an IO (information operation) victory because the media is sure to spin it as "the enemy can attack at will, even at the major U.S. base in Afghanistan," blah, blah, blah. They just scrape the surface of the story and then fit it into the box that fits their agenda. Meanwhile, they miss the fact that the enemy uses young men, brainwashes them with radical Muslim ideology, and then sends them on missions where they are sure to die without caring about them one iota. Conversely, our forces will get cast in a negative light and it will be said that our mission is failing. Never any balance, and we as the U.S. are always portrayed as the villain. In actuality, if we didn't exist, who or what country in this world would stand for anything good? European countries? China? Iran? Exactly; nobody.

I am ready to get our people home and see my family.

20 May 2010

There were a couple of car bombs in J-bad today. We heard the explosions just down the road. The enemy appears to be making a concerted effort to make a statement that they can do anything they want, when they want. Of course, none of these attacks have amounted to much except dead enemies. It appears this is an effort to disrupt Karzai's upcoming peace jirga.

The jirga in Kabul will still happen regardless. It would seem that after 30 years of almost continuous war the Afghans would finally just get sick of it. Wishful thinking, I guess.

Here at Jalalabad we slid over to allow our replacements to start running things while we provided the overwatch. They took charge, and then I had to scuff up my staff because they vanished at a point when our replacements needed some assistance. It shouldn't happen again. Five more days left.

President Karzai conducted what became known as a peace jirga in May 2010. The gathering brought together Afghan leaders from throughout the country; even the Taliban was invited to participate. The purpose was initiating a process by which hostilities could eventually slow and come to an end. The series of bombings and high-profile attacks in the days leading up to the jirga were thought to be a statement by the Taliban rejecting the process. In spite of the Taliban's efforts, the jirga went on as scheduled and the spate of attacks amounted to little in the big scheme.

In the final five days of the transition process we relinquished day-to-day control of operations to the replacement staff and command. However, we were still responsible for what happened, requiring us to provide oversight of those operations. My staff was not providing that oversight, and I had to dress them down for failing to carry out their duties. As is common, my staff was becoming infected with what might euphemistically be called "get-homitis." I had to ensure that everyone was doing the right thing for our replacements and therefore had to rough them up a bit to keep them in the game for a few more days.

21 May 2010

2–320 FA ran everything today, and the staff did a very good job (after I scuffed them up yesterday) of taking care of our counterparts. Tomorrow everyone will be off all firebases and we will have only 50 people left here at Hughie.

I am hosting a lunch to give Shir Mohammed a gift from us to say bye. Then he goes to the ANA Corps Cdrs' Conference.

All remains quiet. There is a storm blowing in tonight.

22 May 2010

Nothing today. Everyone is off the firebases. I hosted the lunch with Shir Mohammed and staff and gave him and his CoS a farewell gift. Just ready to go now.

23 May 2010

Kalagush got rocketed this morning. This is the first attack since everyone left. Apparently, the reaction was not too good in spite of the fact that we drilled them constantly. Also, the company commander is a dud. Arrogant and yet does little outside the wire, so his company does not respect him. Oh, well, I don't own it anymore. We only have 35 people left here at Hughie, and 27 of them leave in the morning. 2–320 has it now, and we are just getting ready for the ceremony. I sure will be glad when Wednesday gets here.

24 May 2010

36 hours left before I start moving home. It is just me and the primary staff left now. We did our final conditions check this evening and everything is on track. All of our people are somewhere between JAF and Manas, Kyrgyzstan. All people on JAF will be in Bagram tomorrow morning. I can't believe this year, which saw so many things happen, is finally coming to an end. I just hope that the Bn has had a positive impact with its efforts.

25 May 2010

We did a rehearsal today for the TOA (transition of authority) ceremony. Everything is ready. I think it will go very well. There are more Afghans coming than we originally thought, as several elders and leaders from Nuristan are coming down. They heard about the ceremony and wanted to come.

The incoming Cdr went to a Nangarhar security shura with the ANA Bde CoS, and apparently all that took place was arguing about the ineffectiveness of each ANSF entity as each threw barbs at the other. Glad I wasn't there. I have had enough of bickering and finger pointing.

Tomorrow at this time I will be in Bagram with our last few troops waiting to fly out.

26 May 2010

The TOA ceremony was well done. The Afghan Btry from Kalagush participated in the ceremony at my invitation and did very well. They had their howitzers—the D30—on display and looked great. A huge weight came off my shoulders today, and I am happy that we are headed home. Several of the Afghans whom I worked with at Kalagush came to the ceremony, including the district governors, one of the CoPs, and one elder who is said to be in the running to replace the Nuristan governor. Hamid Osmani from Dow Ab was the best one that I worked with in Nuristan; it is just too bad we could not have done more to assist him because he was the one guy who could make things happen. All the rest were all talk and asking for handouts. Oh, well, it is over now, and we are working our way back home from here. I just hope we made a difference.

I was quite relieved to turn over responsibility for the mission to the next unit. I was mentally and physically spent, as were all of our soldiers and leaders. I know that we did many good things to help the Afghan people while pressing forward with progress so that the Afghans could have a better life. We worked hard to build security, develop the economy, mentor the district leaders, and advise our Afghan Army counterparts, as pointed out in numerous journal entries. However, we also experienced a great deal of frustration as we observed Afghans acting in a self-serving manner. But if our influence could help just a few Afghans take heart and seize control of their future, then we certainly did make a difference. I believe that we had a positive effect, regardless of the frustrations.

27–30 May 2010

It was painful trying to get back home. Our flight got canceled twice, and a third time we could only get the soldiers of one unit on a plane to Kyrgyzstan. That left two other elements at Bagram and I stayed with them. At the last minute some additional seats came open, and I made the decision to maintain unit integrity and push what was left of one battery out intact. The Cdr of the remaining battery pitched a fit because not all of that unit could leave, and the soldiers started grumbling. That pissed me off because the attitude of the commander rubbed off on the whole unit. It can't be said enough: the Cdr sets the tone. If the Cdr has a bad outlook, so will everyone else in the command, including the families. It is amazing the influence that a Cdr has. I gave the Cdr a butt chewing and said "execute what I say, like it or not, and keep the attitude to yourself."

Finally arrived in Kyrgyzstan on 29 May.

Flew out of Manas on 30 May, and it was a horrible flight. The stupid plane did not have air conditioning, so it was over 100 degrees on the plane every time the thing landed and took off. You would think for a returning flight after a year at war we could get a better ride. Oh, well, we are on our way.

Our flights out of Afghanistan kept getting canceled for various reasons. As we were trying to push out the last soldiers of each unit, I made the decision to keep the units together so that the leaders of the batteries could maintain accountability for their people. I could have taken the available seats and spread them among the remaining units, but then it would have been difficult to keep track of the soldiers scattered in several locations. So, I opted to maintain unit integrity. This meant that one unit would have to be last. The battery that ended up last began to grumble, and it was because the leaders complained about my decision. Whatever attitude the leaders of a unit take on, the soldiers in the unit will reflect that disposition. Of course, I did not want to make any unit be the last one out, but the bottom line is that one battery would have to do this. When I heard of the grumbling I immediately called the leaders in and told them to fix it quickly. Once the decision was made, it was time to execute, personal feelings notwithstanding.

31 May 2010

It is Memorial Day, and we landed in Colorado Springs around midnight. The welcome home ceremony was at 0230 in the post gym. The 77th Assn members were there, and so were Birr and his mother. I can't believe that he survived a shot through the head, but there he was. God really performed a miracle for him. I am so glad he made it. If only Rao had survived. I was the Cdr of troops for the ceremony, and after it was over Maryellen, Andy, and Ashley were there and our next-door neighbors came as well. It was all very good. It was so good to see everyone's friendly faces. I am so glad I can walk around without body armor in 100+ degree heat. It is nice to be home in America. If only Americans could realize how great our country is in government, freedom, wealth (even our poor are well off compared to Afghans), and beauty. We have the best of everything, and going to a place like Afghanistan makes you realize it.

As noted above, I was very happy to be home. I was amazed that PFC Birr was doing so well in his recovery, and yet I regretted that we had not been able to bring everyone home. So, while I was very pleased to have returned, there was a part of me that was saddened by the fact that everyone did not make it back. Every American should realize how blessed we are to live in the United States. We have the best of everything, and ultimately the reason for this good fortune is the sacrifices made by soldiers, including those who made the supreme sacrifice like Sergeant Rao.

* * *

Our arrival home in Colorado ended the deployment. I had about two months left to command the battalion. In that time my duty was to guide the recovery of the personnel and set the conditions for the battalion to begin preparations for the next deployment under a new commander. The last few entries cover this period, and they demonstrate how the cycle we went through at the beginning of my command began yet again. The final journal entries are weekly notations, as at the start of the book.

1–4 June 2010

Had a 3-day pass and didn't do anything but spend time with Maryellen and kids. It is nice to be home.

5–14 June 2010

Went through the reintegration process, which includes medical checks, classes on relationships, suicide prevention, PTSD (post-traumatic stress disorder), etc. This stuff is so much more extensive than when I came home from Desert Storm or even the first time I got home from Afghanistan. While I think some of it is beneficial, I also think that many soldiers use the things they learn to beat the system. For others we create a dependent class of soldiers who never take responsibility for their actions and instead blame PTSD for bad behavior.

The good news is that in the first few weeks home the Bn has had no instances of soldier misconduct. We will see how block leave goes.

The first weeks home from a combat deployment are always a critical period. It is when accidents occur, substance abuse is possible, and relationships collapse. The process of reintegration training seeks to raise soldiers' awareness of these issues so they can recognize the warning signs and prevent escalation of problems. Reintegration training has come a long way from my early days in the Army, when such focus was unheard of. I had virtually no reintegration training in returning from Iraq in 1991 and very little following my first tour in Afghanistan. The Army expends a great deal of energy in helping soldiers have a smooth and safe transition home. As I noted in this journal entry, I had concerns that some underhanded soldiers would use what they learned in the training to take advantage of the system for their own benefit.

15 June–14 July 2010—Block Leave

Block leave was very good. We took trips to Rocky Mountain National Park, Leadville, climbing Mt. Elbert, and Chicago. In Chicago we finally put Nana to rest beside Armand (my grandfather). It is still a shock to me that she died while I was in Afghanistan. I guess I never really thought she would pass on. But at least now she is at rest.

At the end of block leave I attended the faculty orientation at the AF Academy for my new job teaching strategic studies and military theory. They did a very good two-week program to help prepare the new instructors. I am very much looking forward to teaching.

During block leave there were three soldier incidents: 1 DUI, 1 domestic, one drug use. Not too bad considering what I walked into as I took command in 2008.

Every returning unit receives 30 days of leave following the deployment. This is the time for the troops and leaders to recover and recharge before beginning the whole preparation cycle over again. It is also a time when some soldiers will make some poor decisions. When I took command of the battalion there was a rash of driving under the influence and drug use. Bearing this in mind, we implemented a series of measures to mitigate issues with substance abuse. With only three incidents in our first 45–60 days home, it represented a 50% drop in issues from 2008. It is critical for unit commanders and leaders to establish programs to help soldiers, not only for the sake of the individual but also to preserve the force. The Army is not a nebulous instrument. Instead, it is an organization made up of individual American citizens (and, in some cases, immigrants). Taking care of these people ensures that the Army has the soldiers needed to accomplish the mission at hand. For this reason, unit commanders have a great deal of power and influence over their soldiers.

15–23 July 2010

Received the incoming Bn Cdr and began orienting him to the unit. With the staff, we laid out a calendar to enable the new Cdr to visit all agencies on post, tour the back 40, and meet with each Btry and staff section, in order to get a good awareness and feel for unit and post. I think we will help him feel very comfortable with what he has moving forward.

On the 22nd G Co. changed command. Their commander is the longest-serving Cdr during my command, and she did a good job. As the new Bn Cdr comes in he will have 4 fairly new Cdrs, with the longest serving one having a year in command.

I believe that the FA Bns require reorganization based on my time as a commander. First, we must bring back SVC (service) batteries vs. FSCs (forward support companies). These units lack an understanding of FA operations because there are no FA MOSs (military occupational specialties). The new Co Cdr is one of my FA officers vs. a logistics officer. Plus, the FSCs are full of people with non-combat specialties and therefore require an inordinate amount of time to train for FA missions. Also, we need a third firing battery. With only two, it is difficult to cover the brigade

AO with adequate fires. We lose coverage and flexibility to support. In fact, during our combat deployment to Afghanistan we had to have a third battery attached to our organization in order to fully cover the brigade area of operation. These are two immediate changes I would make to improve our field artillery organizations.

Military units have to constantly evaluate their effectiveness in terms of training, manning, and organization. This frequent review of efficiency enables the Army to maintain its edge in warfighting capability. Contrary to what people may believe, debate within the military occurs all the time. This is an integral part of our ability to keep our place as the best Army in the world. Following our tour in Afghanistan, I believed that there were a few things our Army needed to change in order to improve our performance and efficiency.

24–29 July 2010—Visit to Portland

This week I continued to help bring the new commander on board. All went smooth and I am confident that he will be able to hit the ground running when he takes command on 11 August.

On the 27th I flew up to Portland, OR, to see Ash swim in the W. Sectional swim meet and also visit the family of my fallen soldier from Afghanistan, SGT Rao. I had never met them, although I had spoken with them several times. It was very tough when we lost Rao, and what made it worse is the fact that Rao was the only one we lost. I still feel very bad because I wish we had brought them all home. As the commander, it is on me that he did not make it home. I wish I had never given in to the PRT Cdr and approved any mission to clear culverts. I disagreed with this stupid TTP (tactics, techniques, and procedures) in the first place, but I needed them to patrol and they were refusing to do it unless we cleared culverts. After Rao died I refused to do it ever again. Anyway, the PRT didn't patrol with us even when we were clearing them.

Rao's mother Sharon is a strong and gracious woman. It just broke my heart that I didn't get her son home. I did my best to answer all her questions, but I did not live with him and work with him on a daily basis. So, she will need to talk to the PLT members next week when she and her husband come down for the memorial. (We will dedicate our Regimental Room in his name as a part of the itinerary.) It was good for me to make this trip because it helped me in seeing his final resting place and being able to talk to the family. I only hope that my trip to see the family was helpful to them as well. I will always live with this loss as the commander who made the decision to conduct the patrol.

Ashley medaled in the mile at 6th place.

30 July 2010—Organization Day

We did our final Bn Run with me as the commander before Organization Day. The day went very well, with my presenting awards to our ladies, a BBQ, and the Bn softball tournament. A Btry won. I was with HHB, and we were horrible. Birr attended the event. It is an absolute miracle that he survived that wound to his head. Overall the Organization Day was a great event before the CoC and beginning of reset and retraining.

Organization Days, as noted at the start of the journal, are social events through which units celebrate their history and conduct competitions. This facilitates camaraderie while providing the opportunity to relax with families. At this particular Organization Day I recognized several of the volunteers—all spouses of the soldiers in the unit—who performed great service in supporting us during the deployment. Without the contributions of these ladies, the deployment would have been a difficult experience for those remaining behind as well as the soldiers who deployed to Afghanistan. Just as it is important to reward soldiers for outstanding performance, it is also critical to recognize family members who go above and beyond for their loved ones and others.

I continued to be amazed at PFC Birr's recovery. It was nothing short of a miracle that he survived. However, even though he made this strong recovery, he is not without issues. Birr suffers from seizures that are the direct result of the damage to the brain. Further, while he retains his cognitive skills, he is challenged at times with fine motor skills and dexterity. As a result, he will soon be medically retired from the Army. This is very unfortunate because this young man wanted nothing more than to continue serving the nation. His motivation and dedication made me very proud to have served with him and saddened that he cannot continue on in service.

2–6 August 2010—Memorial Week

We made some very detailed preparations for the Bde Memorial on 6 August. The Rao family came to the series of events, which included dedicating the 77th Regimental Room, print signing, memorial dedication at Fort Carson's walk of the Fallen, and uncasing the colors. The family arrived on 4 August, and Maryellen and selected soldiers received them at the airport. I designated the maneuver PLT as the honor PLT for the events and to take care of the family. It would be their last duty together as a PLT after forming in August 2008. The first thing we did was have a simple but formal ceremony to dedicate our Regimental Room in Rao's name. The PLT was there with the family, Assn. members, Bn leaders, Bde Cdr and CSM. The

CSM and I unveiled the name and collage of pictures honoring Rao. Then we did a reception. The BC and PLT members went out to dinner with the family that evening so that Rao's mother could talk with them about her son. This is important for her to fill in gaps that she has. On the evening of the 5th the Bde unveiled the deployment print by Dietz (the painter). Each family member got a print.

On the 6th we uncased our colors symbolizing our arrival back home, and the stone with names of the Fallen was dedicated by the post, and the family attended that. This was also helpful for the mother and wife, but I know that they still have a long road to go down before they can truly move forward. It still bothers me that I could not get every soldier home. Knowing that a mother lost a son and a spouse has no husband is a horrible reality. Worse, Rao's young daughter will grow up with no father. This is the most stinging aspect of command. The responsibility for the lives of others is the greatest of all. And when you lose one you feel that you have failed regardless of the mission successes. The empty chair of a fallen comrade brings the true cost of war home to the participants. While I will always feel and know that what we are doing in Afghanistan is for the best, the loss also reminds me that the decision for war must always be a last resort because the cost is permanent and wrenching. SGT Rao was a fine man who volunteered to do his duty for the country in a time of war. He is the best of the best and deserves honor and respect from the nation he sacrificed for. His family does as well for giving him to us.

Our brigade held a series of events to honor the families of the Fallen. Our battalion added to the list of events by specifically planning the ceremony to designate our regimental room as the "Sergeant Elijah J. Rao 77th Field Artillery Regimental Room." The purpose of all the events was twofold: first, to honor the Fallen, and second, to show their families that they are not forgotten. Hopefully, it helped bring about a sense of closure for the families as well. It was certainly tough for all concerned, but important so that the families could understand more about the events that occurred and their loved ones who served selflessly in Afghanistan.

9–13 August 2010—CoC (Change of Command) Week

This is my last week of command following a weekend with one domestic issue, a DUI, and a suicide ideation. As a commander, there is never really a moment in time when you get a break from caring for soldiers regardless of what they do. The call comes in and you have to act, first to get all the information, and then to implement controls. Luckily, we have had far fewer issues with off-duty misbehavior returning from Afghanistan vs. when I took command. I think it is because of some of the measures we took before return and during reintegration. However, whatever the case, you have to solve the problem. That involves getting them help and discipline when appropriate. The Cdr has to decide based on the info and then act.

On Monday we did a Bde run, my last with the Bn. I spent the day doing some of my final admin tasks. Admin is a pain, but necessary to take care of people and maintain morale. Evaluations, awards, property has to be processed and cared for to keep the unit running.

On Tuesday the BSTB (brigade special troops battalion) and 2–12 IN changed out, then we rehearsed our change of command for the next morning. Following the rehearsal, I promoted the G Co. first sergeant to sergeant major, which is always a good thing to do. Then I gave my final talk to the Bn about how proud I am of them and to keep doing the right thing. I also told them to be proud of what they did in Afghanistan. After that I asked those who would like to come by and shake my hand for one last time. All of the soldiers did, and some even had tears in their eyes, which surprised me greatly. I guess over 28 months I made an impression and connection with them. They certainly did with me. With that we went into the CoC on Wednesday morning.

Thoughts on Command

On 11 August 2010 I gave up command to a good friend of mine who had followed me in several jobs in the 10th Mountain Division. The ceremony went very well and soldiers looked good. I cannot believe that it is over. Of course, my wife and kids were at the ceremony, along with many friends of mine and the Bn. The ceremony was a fitting culmination for me and a good start for my buddy, the new Cdr of 2–77th FA.

My whole career preceding April 2008 had prepared me for the responsibility of being a Bn Cdr, and while I believe I handled it well and the unit more than accomplished the mission in combat, I still had much growth to go through to become a mature leader at that level. Regardless of how much you think you know going in, you quickly find out how little you actually know. Command was a learning experience, growth opportunity, humbling, rewarding, frustrating, exhilarating, and a big letdown at times. Yet I would not trade the experience for anything.

All that said, command at its heart is about three things: serving the nation by taking responsibility, taking care of people, and, when called upon, exercising that responsibility in a combat zone and employing these people in a place where they can be killed. All the while you must accomplish the mission the nation asked you to do and preserve lives in the process. Our Bn trained for the mission for a year and knocked every task out of the ballpark. This was not because of me; instead, it was because these young Americans are made of tough stuff and determined to do their duty. All Americans should be proud of the .5% who serve in harm's way. All I did was give a little guidance and they did the job.

Along the way we had 18 WIA (wounded in action) and 1 KIA (killed in action), SGT Rao. These are the ones who hallow the ground and the mission, giving it meaning. The loss of these humbles the commander so that he understands the cost of the decisions and responsibility. And while I desired that responsibility and was blessed to have it, I would give anything if I could have been wise enough to have prevented the losses. But I couldn't. Therefore, as I think about the GWOT (global war on terror), a war we can't lose, we must always consider the cost. In considering it, political and military leaders must apply the human resource judiciously to win through thoughtful reflection while minimizing the loss. When the cost exceeds the benefits, it is time to do something else.

Finally, I am thankful to God for his faithfulness to me and to my family for their continued love and support as they endured my command and my fourth combat deployment.

12 August 2010

I took up my new duties as instructor of military and strategic studies at the AF Academy. Great transition job. I have time with family. Thank God.

VI

Possibilities

Based on two previous tours to Afghanistan and my faith in our nation's Army, I believed that what we did as Americans leading the coalition of nations was the key to victory. Therefore, as the commander of our battalion, I focused our training on what we could do to bring that result about in our own area. The battalion worked hard in its year at home to prepare for the mission to Afghanistan. Our military had spent several years there already, and I had come to believe that the Afghans were ready to step forward to assert their own will. Shortly after our arrival, however, I began to observe things that would change my belief that Afghanistan was close to the point of taking charge of its own affairs. Over the course of the year I witnessed Afghan incompetence permeating the government, overcentralization of the government apparatus, and rampant corruption. This wore down my preconceived notions, tempering them to the point that I developed a different perspective on the issue.

As I recorded my thoughts in the journal, my tone and expectations changed over time as I identified the issues associated with our effort in Afghanistan that I had naively discounted before the deployment. Even though I left Afghanistan frustrated, I still believe there is great promise for success. So, what would bring about a successful conclusion to the war in Afghanistan? I have given much thought to this question and offer several points that may facilitate accomplishing the mission. First, the central government of Afghanistan—known as the Government of the Islamic Republic of Afghanistan (GIRoA)—must push power away from Kabul and vest more responsibility in the provinces and districts to better reflect traditional power structures in the country. Second, the Afghan government, with international oversight, must clean up corrupt practices. Third, we must make a concerted diplomatic effort to find a regional solution to Afghanistan. Fourth, the people at the village level have to become involved in their own security through a militia or neighborhood watch–type arrangement. Finally, all development projects for infrastructure improvement

VI. Possibilities

must have Afghan investment so that projects benefit the community and the villages take ownership of them. None of these elements can be implemented in isolation. Rather, each point should be part of an integrated, simultaneous approach that all players agree to execute. Here is how it would work.

The first of the five pillars identified above is to divert some of the power of the Afghan central government away from Kabul and push it down to the provinces. Historically, successful governments in Kabul have instituted very loose control of the country while retaining the support of the tribal leaders in the provinces. This confederation-like arrangement has worked relatively well in Afghanistan, particularly during the time of King Zahir Shah (1933–1973). The current form of government created by the Bonn Conference of 2001 centralized nearly all decision-making in Kabul. I personally witnessed Afghan government leaders at the district level, as well as military leaders in the brigade, who were handcuffed in their ability to act on even minor issues. Because of this arrangement, the people in rural Afghanistan feel that they have little influence in government affairs and are at the mercy of leaders in Kabul who have no connection to the people.

The people derive their connection to the government from the village and tribal elders. All males can participate in shuras and jirgas and have a say in local affairs by leveraging village and tribal leadership. If the central government developed a partnership with the elder hierarchy and reassigned some of the power to make decisions to the districts and villages, then the people would have a greater stake in their government. This could lead to a greater sense of ownership and less apathy about the success of Afghanistan. As a result, the people might invest more of their energy in helping their country succeed. Changing the Afghan constitution to reflect a more traditional Afghan power structure would represent a step in the right direction.[1]

To complement the reform of power structures, the GIRoA must make a concerted effort to stamp out corruption. In my opinion, out of all the problems facing Afghanistan that could facilitate victory by the Taliban, this is the number one issue. Throughout my third tour in Afghanistan nearly every Afghan leader I encountered was involved in some corrupt enterprise. Provincial and district leaders were involved in everything from smuggling to skimming payrolls. The people are well aware of this activity and frown upon its practice.

The dissatisfaction with corruption provides the Taliban with influence and opportunity. The Taliban came into power in the late 1990s with a pledge to provide security and eliminate the corrupt activities of warlords who controlled much of the country during the civil war of 1992–1996. The current levels of corruption hearken back to the unsettled days of the civil war, when rogue parties extorted money in the form of "tolls" levied on ordinary travelers. As before, the Taliban continues to offer its own brand of security and justice, capitalizing on GIRoA failures. As long as the government fails to crack down on corruption, it will continue to leave the door of opportunity open to the Taliban.

To stop this, the GIRoA must form an anti-corruption task force. The purpose of the task force would be to identify corrupt schemes and individuals, assigning responsibility. The judiciary must then prosecute offenders and publicly punish offenders to make an example of them. Further, lawmakers should examine existing laws to close loopholes and modify them to prevent lucrative activities such as smuggling. An example of a law that only serves to facilitate corruption is the one pertaining to timber. It is currently illegal to cut a tree in Afghanistan. The law was initially passed in order to stop deforestation. However, it fosters smuggling because the price of timber skyrocketed with passage of the law. Modifying such laws—combined with cracking down on people engaged in corrupt activities—could help eliminate rampant corruption that plays into insurgent hands. Finally, the effort of the government to stamp out corruption must have independent oversight in order to maintain transparency and credibility. One way to bring this about might be setting up a United Nations or NATO commission to observe the anti-corruption task force. The pressure emanating from such a commission would keep the Afghans honest in their pursuit of corrupt individuals while providing mentorship to lawmakers engaged in revamping unworkable laws.[2]

The problems within Afghanistan are not limited to its own borders. Afghanistan is a regional problem, requiring Central Asian states to play a role in solving the issues. Therefore, the third pillar of success is a concerted diplomatic effort led by the coalition with participation from regional players. The two biggest players in the region with influence on Afghan affairs are India and Pakistan. The Taliban is to some extent a creation of the Pakistani Inter-Services Intelligence (ISI) agency. The reason for this is the long-running rivalry between India and Pakistan. Since the two nations were formed in the late 1940s, they have fought a series of border wars. Pakistan is much smaller in terms of population and territory when compared to India and thus at a great disadvantage in military strength. In light of these facts, it is in Pakistan's best interest to have a friendly and weak neighbor to the west, at its back door.[3]

In the mid-1990s the ISI was instrumental in facilitating the creation of the Taliban movement. The Pakistanis needed a stable and friendly government in Afghanistan so that they would not have to divert their attention away from what they deem their primary threat: India.

By supporting the fundamentalist movement, the Pakistanis were able to secure strategic space. Afghanistan stabilized under the iron hand of the Taliban government, which was subservient to its Pakistani ally. Thus, Pakistan was able to focus on India. The Pakistanis believe it is in their national interest to maintain a weak neighbor to the west, and this is a big reason why the ISI still supports the Taliban and meddles in Afghan affairs. Diplomacy could potentially change this dynamic.[4]

The key to eliminating Pakistani covert support of the Taliban is reducing the tensions between India and Pakistan. The atmosphere of distrust convinces both nations that they must do whatever is necessary to maintain military and political advantages over the other—including, for Pakistan, supporting the Taliban. Therefore, diplomacy must focus on reducing these tensions with the ultimate goal of a rapprochement between India and Pakistan. This is a difficult proposition, but we have to make the effort. The diplomatic effort must find common ground between the two sides in order to lower tensions so that the long-standing problems between them do not further spill over into Afghanistan, creating an intractable problem for the entire world. If Pakistan does not feel threatened by its larger neighbor, then perhaps it will not believe that it must support the Taliban to maintain strategic space to its rear.[5]

The fourth pillar of success is the people's involvement in maintaining their own security at the local level. The Afghan government has been very reluctant to underwrite or support organizations such as the successful Sons of Iraq, which helped reverse fortunes in that nation. This is understandable based on Afghanistan's recent experience with "warlordism" and considering Afghan cultural norms. During the Afghan civil war (1992–1996) there were many militias formed, ostensibly for security purposes, across the country. However, these organizations degenerated into the personal armies of various warlords vying for power. These rogue forces did nothing to enhance security and instead resembled a crime syndicate. With this in mind, the Karzai administration is wary of giving support to any security organization other than national institutions such as the ANA, ANP, and ABP. Further, there are cultural considerations that rail against community policing. Traditionally, tribal and familial ties are so strong that even when an individual within a village is known to engage in criminal activity, the village will turn a blind eye out of considerations of honor. However, the time to reconsider support for community policing may have arrived, since the Taliban continues as the source of instability in the country and warlords have largely disappeared.

The Taliban has an innate ability to infiltrate villages in the hinterland. Its members use a combination of carrot and stick to gain the support or acquiescence of the people for their activities. Conventional forces, including Afghan national security forces, have a difficult time identifying these penetrations at the village level. The local people, however, know exactly when someone new has entered their village. If a militia or neighborhood watch following the rough model of the Sons of Iraq were formed, they could prevent the Taliban from extending its tentacles in a village. The locals could act immediately upon an attempted infiltration and stop the enemy from extending its influence. By contrast, conventional forces are often too late in identifying the infiltration, providing the Taliban with precious time to become entrenched in an area. When forces do clear it, the cost is much greater than preventing the infiltration in the first place. Therefore, the Karzai administration must consider organizing local security to enhance the national security organizations. The added benefit to this approach is that the local people will then have a stake in their own security and future.

The final pillar of the strategy is Afghan investment in development. The trajectory of development in Afghanistan heretofore has focused on the military coalition's use of foreign investment and contractors in a top-down approach. This has led to a lack of buy-in from the local population and opened the door to corrupt practices. Until recently, the people at the village and district levels had little input regarding where money was spent and who benefited from the largesse. Decision-making was consolidated in the hands of the coalition and a select few Afghans who were sometimes of questionable character. This is another source of dissatisfaction among the people, giving the Taliban more material to exploit for its own purposes. This dynamic began to change in 2009, but it still has a long way to go.

A better way to use development funds would be to build Afghan consensus first and bind local Afghans in contracts to invest in the agreed-upon projects. The investment could come in the way of labor, resources, or funds, but the Afghans have to invest from their own resources in order to establish ownership. The Afghan Ministry of Rural Rehabilitation and Development is a model that we can build upon to bring about the local buy-in. Here is what this nascent ministry has implemented to date: Its approach to development is bottom-up and involves the people at the village level in decision-making. Locally formed councils set priorities for development and then provide at least 50% of the resources for these projects. Through use of localized councils, the people have influence in their affairs and own the projects decided upon. Therefore, they will protect these endeavors from enemy attempts to disrupt or destroy them, as the Taliban has frequently done with other projects around the country. This approach is in line with traditional Afghan tribal affairs.[6]

Rather than the international community pouring money into projects using a top-down method, it should provide support to programs such as those run by the Ministry of Rural Rehabilitation and Development. In addition to allowing Afghans to participate in setting the priorities and taking ownership, it saves money. Contractors used by our forces tend to charge exorbitant prices for the work they perform. Further, since the projects are generally conceived without local input, the people do not have a connection to them. When the Taliban targets and destroys the projects, such as schools, the money is wasted. By utilizing the Ministry of Rural Rehabilitation and Development model, costs would be cut by half or more in most cases. Also, the people contractually tied to the project will then secure it to protect it from the enemy. In the long run this bottom-up approach will save the coalition money while remaining true to traditional Afghan cultural norms.[7]

The five-pillar strategy that I have outlined could provide a path to enable Afghans to win the war for themselves with our assistance. Previously, the way we prosecuted the counter-insurgency in Afghanistan placed our forces—military and civil—in the lead in every facet of operations. As a result, we have unwittingly usurped responsibility for Afghanistan away from the Afghans. Now, Afghans are only too willing to let us have this responsibility while casting blame on us for things that go wrong and demanding resources for their personal benefit. This has to stop if Afghanistan is to succeed as a nation.

What I witnessed in Afghanistan in 2009–2010 convinced me that we had to change tack, and I believe that we have begun to do so. Before I arrived in June 2009 I had expected that we were entering a transition phase in our involvement with Afghanistan. I believed that the time and resources expended in the previous eight years had brought things to the point where Afghans were on the cusp of taking over their own affairs. What I found and noted along the way in my journal was that Afghanistan was still crawling as an infant rather than taking steps as a young adult. The Afghan dependence upon us for everything made me realize that we had for too long held the hand of the Afghans rather than walking behind them.

Afghanistan is a beautiful country with great potential for a bright future. I still believe that victory is in sight in Afghanistan and that we as Americans must assist the Afghans in winning so they can achieve that potential. It would be wrong to walk away from these downtrodden people who have suffered so much over the past three decades. However, we cannot do everything for the Afghans. They must do things for themselves, and we have to resist the urge to just do things for the Afghans because it is easier than mentoring them to act on their own. The path to victory in Afghanistan will be blazed by Afghans with our support assisting them along the way.

What Happened to Some of the People in the Battalion?

Within 90 days of returning from Afghanistan almost half of our battalion scattered to the four winds. Some soldiers left the Army, returning to civilian life. Others went to Army schools to improve their professional skills, and still others moved on to new units across the Army. Those choosing to remain in the Army were also opting for another deployment to Afghanistan. Such is the life of an American soldier in the twenty-first century. Our wounded soldiers are in various stages of rehabilitation and recovery. As for myself, I left command and began my new job teaching at the Air Force Academy the day after the change of command ceremony. Here is what happened to some of the folks mentioned—both named and unnamed—throughout the journal.

As I stated early on, I used very few names for a number of reasons. Those I did name were generally outstanding performers and heroes during the deployment. Sergeant Rao was laid to rest in Willamette National Military Cemetery in Portland, Oregon. I had the privilege of meeting his family and visiting his gravesite after returning from Afghanistan. It was a difficult time for me, since I know that as Rao's commander I was ultimately responsible for not bringing him home. He represented everything that is good about America, and he made the ultimate sacrifice to ensure that our nation would not have to endure another 9/11.

Staff Sergeant McClintock, who was severely wounded in the IED attack that killed Rao, spent several months recovering at Brooke Army Medical Center in San Antonio, Texas. I visited him in the hospital during my mid-tour leave. He had made a great recovery, although he still had fragments from the explosion embedded throughout the right side of his body. This would have forced him out of the combat arms into a desk job in the Army. McClintock is a warrior and leader who could not have stood for such an assignment; therefore, he decided to accept medical retirement and return to civilian life. The perpetrator of the IED attack—whom I identify as the IED cell leader, or Haminullah Khan, in the journal—that killed Rao and wounded McClintock was recently captured on the battlefield in Afghanistan.

Specialist Birr made a miraculous recovery from the gunshot he received to his head. However, seizures that he continues to experience as a result of the wound are forcing him into medical retirement. He wanted to remain in service, but the physically debilitating seizures prevent his return to active duty. He lives with his mother in the Colorado Springs area.

Lieutenant Mazella, who was wounded in the Korengal shortly after I moved him to an infantry company, spent many months recovering from lacerations to his face and a fractured lower leg resulting from the rocket fragments embedded there. He has done great service in helping other wounded soldiers and is able to continue in Army service, having returned to the unit. He and his wife had their first child in March 2011. He is no longer the baby-faced lieutenant who arrived in the battalion only a month before the deployment. Mazella is now a seasoned veteran who is still stepping forward to lead troops in America's Army.

The reader may recall that a young soldier named Forester suffered a severely broken foot early on in my command (prior to our deployment). We were worried at one point that one or more of his toes might require amputation. Happily, this did not come to pass. Specialist Forester's foot healed and he deployed to Afghanistan with the unit. He is a jack of all trades and served with distinction in his year there. He has since separated from the Army and returned to college in Kentucky to complete a degree in criminal justice.

Others who were unnamed and yet played an enormous role in our success require a note about what they are engaged in now. My battalion XO became the brigade deputy commanding officer after my departure. He is now the executive officer to a general in Third Army. He is an immensely talented serviceman who is on a path toward higher command in the Army. Our battalion S3 had some family issues that required his immediate attention when we returned from Afghanistan. Within two weeks of returning he had transferred to the Army Human Resources Command to be closer to his family. Had he remained, he would have become our executive officer. This man was quietly competent, and his arrival in Afghanistan filled a void that allowed me to stabilize the senior staff of the battalion for the first time in my command. His early departure was a loss to the unit, and he was sorely missed.

The battery commanders who served with me in Afghanistan have all moved on to new assignments. My HHB commander who did such a fine job in Afghanistan is now a fire support instructor at the infantry school in Fort Benning, Georgia. Probably my most talented captain, he has since been promoted early to major and is on track to command a battalion in the future. My A Battery commander debated leaving the Army for a time. I am happy to say that he decided to stay in and make the Army a career.

Losing him to the civilian world would have been a tremendous loss; he has three combat deployments as a young captain, and his experience is vital to the Army. He was promoted to major and is now stationed in Hawaii, where he trains National Guard troops for deployment to Afghanistan. My B Battery commander also decided to remain in the Army after serving three combat tours. He is now at Fort Sill, Oklahoma, teaching fire support to young artillery lieutenants at the field artillery school. Finally, my competent logistic company commander decided to change her career field within the Army. She currently works in training simulations, which prepares Army units for deployment by placing them in realistic, simulated situations. She is now a major and stationed in Hawaii with her husband—who served as my A Battery commander.

Finally, I will add a few words about my CSM. The senior enlisted man in any unit represents the heart and soul of the organization. My CSM gave everything he had for the good of the battalion. He typified the crusty, hard-nosed noncommissioned officer. While he came across as a mean, hard-charging leader who never gave any slack, deep down he had a heart of gold. He was, and still is, committed to the welfare of soldiers, their development as individuals, and their performance in service to the nation. This requires the ability to impose discipline, teach others, and counsel to improve individual performance. We didn't agree on everything, but he always gave me complete loyalty. He was the perfect counterpoint to my personality, providing the right balance of leadership for our unit. As a result, our battalion was an outstanding unit, and it accomplished every mission, including in combat, with competence. The CSM is the one senior leader who remained with the battalion after I left. He is providing the continuity needed to get the unit ready for another deployment to Afghanistan, and that is exactly what they need, whether the troops realize it or not.

The troops of the 2nd Battalion, 77th Field Artillery Regiment, are representative of the soldiers who serve in America's Army. They are dedicated to the mission and capable of accomplishing anything they set their minds to do. Those serving in the military today represent less than 1% of the American population, which puts them in a special category of American citizen. They are the best of the best that our country has to offer, and America should take great pride in their service.

Chapter Notes

Introduction

1. Troop level information is available to the public via numerous websites. This information is taken from a CBS News tracker at http://www.cbsnews.com/8301-503544_162-5855314-503544.html.

2. The Asia Foundation and the United Nations have commissioned a series of annual opinion polls to canvass the sentiments of the Afghan population. Each year's results can be found online at http://asiafoundation.org/country/afghanistan or http://www.acsor-surveys.com/. Also, the Associated Press provided feedback on Afghan attitudes in 2010, revealing that an overwhelming majority of Afghans—81% of respondents—have little to no sympathy for the insurgency. This article, titled "Poll Says Most Afghans Back Talks with Taliban," headlined the front page of *The Gazette* (Colorado Springs) for 10 November 2010.

3. A *jirga* is an assembly of male elders who meet to decide matters of importance to the community. This is a Pashto word from the dominant ethnic group in the country. In this case, the jirga was an assembly of respected elders from across Afghanistan meeting to formulate and ratify their constitution.

4. See the CBS News troop tracker mentioned in note 1.

5. The brigade effects officer coordinates all artillery and air support for the brigade to assist infantry operations. Additionally, the effects officer synchronizes nonlethal operations with brigade operations such as information and media engagements, civil support, and co-ordination with government officials.

Chapter 1

1. The term *organic* means that the unit is an integral part of the organization to which it belongs. For example, every infantry brigade in the Army has an artillery battalion that is permanently assigned in that command, and it provides fire for that brigade and all of the assigned units in the brigade.

2. As noted, I generally refrain from referring to people by name in the journal in order to not show favoritism or animosity. However, I do mention some individuals who were outstanding performers or involved in extraordinary circumstances, such as becoming wounded. Treating all people with dignity and respect is something I continuously preached, and I maintain that practice here by maintaining anonymity in most cases. Some of my original misspellings and errors in the daily entries to the journal have since been corrected, but the majority of the original language remains intact.

3. The Army physical fitness test consists of three events—the push-up, sit-up, and two-mile run—each scored on a 100-point scale for a total of 300 points. Achieving a score of 270 or above for an individual is considered excellent.

4. I wrote two books about the Red River Campaign in the Civil War. Central to the thesis of both books is the need for teamwork among leaders and units within an army. Learning that my unit had a reputation for whining was unbearable to me, and much of my effort as a commander for the next two years revolved around establishing a reputation for competence, cooperation, and dependability.

5. Rounds within 50 meters of the target are considered within the acceptable radius to have material effects in the object. The reason for this rule is that the burst radius of artillery is 35–80 meters, depending on the caliber. Anything standing on a football field with artillery raining in that area would be incapacitated.

6. When an individual is "fired" in the Army, it does not necessarily mean that the individual

must leave the Army. In many cases it means that the individual leaves his current job and accepts a position of lesser or no responsibility. It does mean that future advancement in rank is limited, thus stunting the individual's career.

7. "Moving" someone gets the individual out of a position of responsibility and into a job with lesser or no responsibility.

8. In popular opinion, the "surge" in Iraq was simply an infusion of more American troops into Iraq. However, this was only one component of what became a successful counterinsurgency strategy in Iraq. The additional troops enabled the success of the strategy, which focused on increasing population security, building Iraq security force capacity, and facilitating the sound functioning of an Iraqi government capable of solving its own problems. The simplistic application of the term "surge" provides a misleading glimpse into what was actually required to achieve success in Iraq. The bulk of the success was only partially attributable to what we Americans did. Much credit must be given to the Iraqis themselves for doing their part to achieve victory. This commitment on the part of Afghan officials is what has been missing for so long in Afghanistan.

Chapter 2

1. See Lester Grau and Ali Jalali, *The Other Side of the Mountain: Mujahideen Tactics in the Soviet-Afghan War* (Quantico, VA: United States Marine Corps Studies and Analysis Division, 1995), 100–103 and 118–21. I also had the privilege of speaking with some of the Mujahideen fighters who participated in these battles. They spoke with great pride of their accomplishments in driving out the Soviets from this area.

2. I must note that this is the only reference that I ever make to the days of the week other than in passing in journal entries. The reason for this omission is that during a deployment the days of the week do not matter, and they seem to run together until a soldier does not know what day it is. In keeping with what we experienced in Afghanistan, I purposely will not refer to days of the week so that the reader will somewhat understand how the soldier interprets time. Time organizes around events in a deployment as opposed to arbitrary days of the week.

3. An abbreviation for an individual based on the need to protect either the person or the intelligence source.

4. An individual declared by a soldier as their primary next of kin in place of a parent or blood relative.

Chapter 6

1. Nathaniel C. Fick, Dave J. Kilcullen, John A. Nagl, and Vikram J. Singh, "Tell Me Why We're There: Enduring Interests in Afghanistan (and Pakistan)," Center for a New American Security, http://www .cnas.org/node/4776, 2, and Richard de VillaFranca, "Reconsidering Afghanistan: Time for an 'Azimuth Check,'" *Parameters* (Winter 2008–2009), 90.

2. United Nations Statistics and Surveys Section, *Corruption in Afghanistan* (New York: United Nations, 2010), 3; United Nations, "Fighting Corruption in Afghanistan: A Roadmap for Strategy and Action," unpublished discussion paper drafted in 2007, 10; and Julius Cavendish, "In Afghanistan War, Government Corruption Bigger Threat than Taliban," *Christian Science Monitor* (April 12, 2010), http://www.csmonitor.com/World/2010/0412/In-Afghanistan-war-government-corruption-bigger-threat-than-Taliban. See also David J. Kilcullen, "Perspectives on Reconciliation Options in Afghanistan," from testimony before the Senate Foreign Relations Committee on July 28, 2010, found online at http://www.cnas.org/files/documents/publications/Kilcullen_SenateTestimony.pdf. There are literally hundreds of articles, studies, and testimony produced in reference to Afghan corruption. A Google search of key words "corruption in Afghanistan" will result in over 25 million hits.

3. De VillaFranca, "Reconsidering Afghanistan," 91–92.

4. Ibid.

5. De VillaFranca, "Reconsidering Afghanistan," 93–94; and Fick, Kilcullen, Nagl, and Singh, "Tell Me Why We're There," 2–3.

6. Patrick H. Donley, "Bottom Up and Outside In: Why Community Development Councils Deserve International Support," Kabul, Afghanistan: Ministry of Rural Rehabilitation and Development, 1. This is an unpublished paper written in 2009 by Lieutenant Colonel Donley when he worked as a military advisor to the Afghan minister of rural rehabilitation and development.

7. Ibid., 2.

Index

Numbers in **_bold italics_** refer to pages with photographs.

Abdullah Abdullah (presidential candidate) 152, 200-1
"accidental guerrilla" 84-85
Afghan Border Police (ABP) 88, 151, 159, 289-91, 294, 299, 320
Afghan National Army (ANA) 5, 21, 60-61, 92, 103, 121, 126, 131, 133-34, 136, 145, 150, 154-55, 174, 179-80, 184, 191, 206, 215, 255, 304-5, 318; artillery battery 87, 110 116, 118, 128, 135, 157, 166, 172, 176, 190, 193, 234, 255, 261-62, 264, 294, 324 (battery commander issues 193-94; new commander 194, 200, 209-10, 234, 237, 256, 284; training 87, 110, 116, 118, 128, 157, 166, 172, 234-35, 251-52); Chief of Staff 300-1; infantry company 264, 267, 272-73, 276-77, 294, 301, ***304*** (commander 267, 272-73, 275, 281-82, 307-8); liaison officer 183, 270; 2nd Brigade, 201st Corps 135, 223, 226, 258-59, 262, 265, 271, 283-86, 289, 293, 302, 314, 316, 318-19 (assessment 286; Chief of Staff 292, 313, 318, 323-24; Command Sergeant Major (CSM) 309-10; commander's conference 310; 201st Corps 299, 302, 316, 323
Afghan National Police (ANP) 5, 55, 61, 87, 131, 144-45, 164, 169, 179, 186, 190, 231, 238-39, 299, 305; assessment 44-46, 123, 150-51; pay issue 164-65, 169-70, 229-30
Afghan National Security Forces (ANSF) 5, 20, 59, 103, 108, 121, 151, 186, 252, 274, 290, 296-97, 299, 324
Afghan Security Guards (ASG) 5, 105, 277
Afghanistan (AFG) 5, 54; Liberation Day 306-307
after action review (AAR) 5, 61-63, 67, 96, 146, 156
agricultural projects 228, 235-236, 242
air assault (AASLT) 5, 40, 120, 123-124, ***311***, 312-13; training 47-48, 63
Alingar District 79, 84, 108-9, 115-16, 120, 129-30, 132, 139, 144, 149, 154, 160-61, 163-65, 171, 176-77, 179, 184-85, 203, 210-11, 225, 229, 239, 245, 248, 266, 278; Chief of Police (also known as AM) 242, 247-48; governor 108, 112-113, 128, 132-33, 160-62, 197
Alingar River 79, ***80***, 84, 120, 135, 179, 187, ***304***, 315
Alishang Valley 120, 212, 256-57, 315, 317
Al Jazeera 124-25
Alkozai tribe 79
Al Qaeda 17-19
alternate supply route (ASR) 172
ambushes 133-135, 158, 183, 203-5, 250, 271, 281-82, 296
area of operation (AO) 5
Area of Operation Steel 16, 78, 81, 83, 92, 146, 151-52, 157, 176-77, 185, 188, 190, 225, 232, 265, 269, 280, 314, 317
Army Commendation Medal (ARCOM) 186, 226; with valor device 226
Army, Department of the 1
artillery gunnery 27, 295; combat readiness 86-87, 178; importance of 30-31, 46-47; M198 howitzer training 47-49; necessity of 22-23; testing 43-44, 46, 48-49; training 35-36, 40, 42-43, 51
artillery registrations 171
Asadabad city 90, 114, 172, 270, 298, 317, 321

Baba Kala village 261
Badakshan Province 195
Bagram airbase 219-20, 222, 275, 296, 324-25; attack on 322
Barge Matal village 111, 121, 168-69, 171, 175, 177, 179, 196
Bari Kowt village 289-90, 292
Barno, Lt. Gen. David 20
battalion 6, 29
battery 6

345

battery commander (BC) 6, 23, 86–87, 164–65, 172, 174–75, 222; assessment 31, 47, 51, 69, 273, 282–83; conferences 174–75, 251–52
battle damage assessment (BDA) 6, 94
battle drills 98–99, 142, 170–71
Bazgal bridge 280
"big 3" 44
"big 5" 22, 41
Birr, PFC Mathew *134*–36, 138, 146–47, 153–54, 186, 211, 217, 326, 330, 340–41
Blessing (forward operating base; FOB) 288
bomb making 174–75
Bonn Conference 335
Bostick (forward operating base; FOB) 258–59, 274, 289–90
brigade 6
brigade combat team (BCT) 6, 26, 51, 140
brigade combat team commander 40–41, 45, 52, 64–65, 68, 91–92, 100, 102, 108–9, 113, 118, 120–22, 125, 138, 140, 142, 165, 172, 175, 193–94, 201, 226, 257–58, 305; Afghan counterpart 193–94, 201; commander conferences 120–22, 195, 257–59, 302
brigade support battalion (BSB) 233
Brooke Army Medical Center (BAMC) 264
Brunner, Capt. Anthony "Tony" (A Battery commander) *216*, 341–42
Brunner, Capt. Carrie (G Company commander) 137, 180–81

captain (CPT) 7
Carpenter, Capt. Chris (commander of HHB and A Battery) 226, 260, 341
casualties 180, 182–83, 201, 221, 254, 256, 264–65, 293, 312–13, 320, 339; enemy 207–8, 212, 277, 281, 301–2; training 42
centralization of power 335
change of command (CoC) 6, 26, 29, 328, 331–32
change of mission 225–26
Chapa Dara Valley 155, 197, 239
chaplain 46, 202
charge of quarters (CQ) 7
chief of police (CoP) 104, 139, 176, 178–79, 184–85, 194–95, 97, 212, 215, 225, 229, 231, 233, 242, 244, 247–48, 253, 255–57, 265–66, 268, 299
Chitral, Pakistan 290
Civil Affairs (CA) 6, 59–61, 163
Clark, Mandy (CBS News reporter) 132
close air support (CAS) 207, *208*
colonel (COL) 6; *see also* brigade combat team commander
combat action badge (CAB) 211, 217
combat lifesavers 44
combat logistics patrol (CLP) 233
combat observation lasing team (COLT) 233
combined joint task force (CJTF) 6, 21, 121–22, 134, 180, 233

command 6
command and control (C2) 6, 58–59, 60
Command and General Staff College 17–18, 141
command and staff (C&S) 6
command issues and decisions 43, 45, 47, 51–52, 57, 59, 84, 178, 222–23
command post exercise (CPX) 7, 158
command sergeant major (CSM) 7, 23, 39–40, 68, 83, 114, 222, 237, 330–31; forming maneuver platoon 45; impressions of 29, 64–65, 103, 342; managing people 51, 53–54, 58, 64; role in training 46, 48–49, 70, 291; security of Kalagush 84–85, 98; supervises move to FOB Hughie 282
commanding general (CG) 6, 135, 217
communications exercise (COMEX) 6, 52
Connelly (forward operating base; FOB) 216, 242, 321
consequence management 91
corruption 76–78, 91, 93, 95–97, 100, 108, 136–39, 143, 145, 148–51, 156–57, 160, 165–68, 173–75, 179, 183, 187–88, 193–96, 215, 219, 225–26, 230, 234, 243, 247, 253, 261, 266, 284, 297–98, 305, 334–36
counterfire 105–6, 142, 171, 205, 317
counterinsurgency (COIN) 6, 20, 55, 61, 83–84, 90–91, 116–17, 143, 161–65, 175, 196, 199, 230, 233, 239, 297, 300, 304–5, 314, 318
counterintelligence (CI) 6, 84
course of action (COA) 6
crater analysis 142
crew served 7
"crisis of leadership" 24–25, 143–44, 160, 218–19, 223–24, 230, 236, 254, 279, 304, 307, 320

D30 howitzer 7, 110, 116, 324
daily prayer 27–28
Dareng village 237
Daud Mohammed (interpreter) 125, 172, 213, 219–20, 251
Dear "John" letters 313–14
Dearman, Lieutenant 66
Demagal village 129
Democratic Republic of Afganistan Army (DRA) 79
demographics of area 77–79, 88–89
Department of Defense 1–3, 24
Department of State representative in provincial reconstruction team (PRT) 93–94, 100, 125, 147–48, 163, 185, 233–34, 238, 243
deployment begins 73–75, 81–82; arrival 77, 81–82, 84–87; priorities 86–87
deployment tasks and preparation 67–69, 71–73
deputy commanding general (DCG) 315–17
Dinnen, Lt. Eric 71
diplomatic solutions 336–37
Directorate of Logistics (DOL) 7

disciplinary actions and problems 66–69, 84–87, 93, 114, 200, 211, 328, 331–32
district center (DC) 7, 108, 114, 139, 145, 212, 214, 253
district field coordinator (DFC) 7, 127, 129–30, 141, 144–45, 156
"distro" distribution platoon 7, 58
Dow Ab District 55, 83–84, 120, 127, 139–40, 144–45, 147, 154, 156, 167, 176–77, 186, 188, 190, 204–5, 208, 212, 232, 251, 269, 276–77, 300; sub-governor 109–10, 132, 139, 157, 178, 196, 263, 281 (*see also* Osmani, Hamid); Taliban shadow governor 210, 307–8
drug and alcohol issues 31, 38, 66–68, 85, 201–3, 232, 328, 331–32

economy of area 79, 84–85, 88, 109, 112–13, 117, 124, 166, 183, 215–16, 236
education system 231–32
Eid (post-Ramadan celebration) 166, 170–71, 176
18th Field Artillery Brigade 114
85/15 Rule 47
election for president 77, 80, 93–94, 100, 102, 104, 111–12, 114, 118–19, 124–31, 133, 135–36, 139–41, 143–54, 156, 193, 198; disruption operations 126–27, 130–33, 135, 158, 176, 201–2; fraud 148, 196; runoff 195–96, 200–2
embedded training team (ETT) 7; Marine trainers 87, 92, 110, 118–19, 191, 237, 275
explosive ordnance disposal (EOD) 7, 102, 168, 190, 215, 221, 230, 241, 245, 268, 303

family readiness group (FRG) 8, 29, 52, 72
family readiness support assistant (FRSA) 8, 38, 40
field artillery (FA) 7, 178; ammunition 48, 58–59
field artillery regiment (FAR) 7
fire and effects coordination cell (FECC) 8, 43, 49, 113
fire direction center (FDC) 8; training 30, 44, 86–87, 284
fire direction non-commissioned officer (FDNCO) 8, 30, 42
fire direction officer 8, 30, 42, 81, 208, 211, 217, 273, 294
fire support coordination exercise (FSCX) 8, 39, 62, 64
fire support element (FSE) 8
fire support officer (FSO) 8, 164–65, 217
fire support team (FIST) 8, 49, 50
fire support training 39, 66; issues 62–63; lessons 66–67
firebase (FB) 7
Firebase Fortress 88–89, 96, **98**, 110, 123, 134–35, 159–60, 211, *212*, 254, 282–83, 310
fires conference 161–62, 164–65, 175, 233, 311–13

1st Battalion, 12th Infantry Regiment 50, 62, 64
1st Battalion, 32nd Infantry Regiment 87, 89–90, 184; Delta Company 211
1st Battalion, 39th Field Artillery Regiment (Airborne) 68
1st Battalion, 102nd Infantry Regiment 259, 274, 317, 319; Delta Company 278, 314
1st Battalion, 321st Airborne Field Artillery Regiment, Charlie Battery 87, 90, 100, 108, 114, 172–73, 185, 211, 274
1st Brigade, 101st Airborne Division (AASLT) 318
1st Kandak, 2nd Brigade, 201st Corps, Afghan National Army 301
first sergeant (1SG) 5, 53, 58, 174, 211
Forrester, PFC Daniel 32–33, 35, 341
Fort Bragg 18, 68
Fort Campbell 18
Fort Carson 1, 29, 57, 60, 64, 74, 83, 114, 209, 306, 331–32
Fort Drum 18–19, 21, 29, 34, 39
Fort Leavenworth 17–18, 28, 52, 141
Fort Polk 18, 39, 51–52, 56–57
Fort Sill 18, 39, 48
forward observer (FO) 8, 49
forward operating base (FOB) 8, 54, 61, 109, 121, 139, 157, 207–8, 215, 221, 231, 271, 275, 277, 303
4th Battalion, 25th Field Artillery Regiment 34, 38
4th Brigade, 4th Infantry Division 22, 26, 80 (change of command 40; training priorities 41; vision for action 84)
4th Infantry Division 106
4th Kandak, 2nd Brigade, 201st Corps, Afghan National Army 234
fragmentary order (FRAGO) 8
frustrations with Afghan government officials 78–80, 169–171, 173–74, 180–81, 192–194, 199, 220, 223–24, 226, 230, 241, 259, 261, 270, 279, 295, 310, 325, 334

Gajour, Jamaluddin (Taliban commander) 203–204
Gajour tribe 79, 128–29, 149, 156, 167–68, 187, 190, 192, 212–13, 252
Galula, David 60–61
Gamberi (forward operating base; FOB) 257, 259, 262–63, 265
Gandalabuk village 186, 206, 220, 273
Garcia, firebase 163, 188, 249, 313
gem mining 182
general (GEN) 9, 56
Ghaki Pass 288
Gilani, Mohammed (new Alingar chief of police) 268–69
Global War on Terror (GWOT) 26, 333
"go green" program 272–73

Index

Goshta District 85–86, 163, 249, 295–98
government of Afghanistan (GoA) 9, 77, 93, 122, 142; in AO Steel 78, 103; assessment of 75–76, 80, 103, 109, 135–36, 141–43, 150, 195
Gowardesh Bridge 290–93
Great, Lt. Tony 71, **95**
"Gunny" Mountain 275

Hafizullah, Captain (ANA battery commander) 201
harassment of women 309
Headquarters and Headquarters Battery (HHB) 9, 59, 97, 173, 239–40, 260, 264, 282, 321, 341; change of command 64, 69, 226; issues with 64–65, 68
Headquarters and Headquarters Company (HHC) 9
Hekmatyar, Gulbuddin (HiG leader) 290
helicopter crash 311–12
Hezb-Islami-Gulbuddin (HiG) 188, 289–90
high explosive 9, 113, 181, 207–208, 294, 301
Highway 1A 288; operation 309–10, 312–13
Hindu Kush Mountains 82
Hughie (FOB) 259, 265, 271, 280–82, 292, 294, 301, 308, 315, 321, 323–24
human intelligence collection team (HCT) 9, 93
humanitarian assistance 203
Hussein, Saddam 18

Iftar (breaking of Ramadan) 160–61, 166
illumination shells 9, 119, 145, 169, 187, 202
improvised explosive device (IED) 9, 60, 78, 85, 100–2, 104–5, 107–9, 112, 116, 119–20, 123–24, 126, 131–32, 137–38, 151, 164, 167–70, 174, 182, 185, 190, 194, 197, 200, 203–4, 206, 210–12, 215, 218–21, 225, 232, 236–38, 241, 254, 258, 261, 263, 265, 268, 271, 273–74, 302, 317; bombmaker 311–12; cell leader 22, 99, 232, 235, 255–256, 259, 261–63, 266, 275–76, 279–80; schoolgirl incident 244–46, 340 (*see also* Khan, Haminullah)
indirect fire incidents 108, 274, 291, 294–95
infantry (IN) 9
infiltrators 91, 106, 116, 155, 197–98, 202, 257
information operations (IO) 92, 99–100, 102, 107, 113–14, 120, 122, 125, 147, 151, 155, 178, 210, 246, 251, 265, 322
intelligence, surveillance, and reconnaissance (ISR) 206
Inter-Services Intelligence (Pakistani intelligence agency) 336

Ja'alam village 101, 203, 218, 262, 303
Jalalabad (J-bad) 9, 54, 113, 120–21, 133–34, 142, 145, 147, 161, 164–65, 195, 233, 259, 265–66, 268, 271, 278, 289, 298, 306–7, 314, 318, 320–22; move of battalion to 283, 286
jingle trucks 88

Jirga 20; constitutional 122, 230; Kamdesh 292; note 343; peace 322–23; tribal 168, 192, 213
joint fires observer (JFO) 9
Joint Readiness Training Center (JRTC) 9, 39–40, 49, 52, 55, 57–59, 62–64, 72
Joyce (FOB) 110, 199, 237, 316
junior leader performance 86

Kabir, Mullah (Nuristan governor) 108–110, 129–30, 132, 136, 138–39, 148, 177
Kabul 145–146, 164, 172, 248, 252
Kabul River 199
"Kafirs" 204
Kafiristan 90
Kalagush 77, 81, 83–84, 86, 96, 99, 121–22, 152–53, 158, 160, 173–74, 185, 224, 237, 259, 278, 281, 283, 285–286, 292–94, 296, 300, 303, 306–8, 311, 313–15, 317, 319–21, 324; attacks on 271–72, 276, 298–99, 301; battle 184, 186, 204, 206–10, 237, 250; description 54–55, 120–21; initial impression 84–85, 87, 99, 101
Kamdesh District 121, 179, 182, 186, 196, 206, 299, 316
Kamdesh Valley 21, 288–91
Karzai, Hamid (president of Afghanistan) 20–21, 25, 144, 146, 148, 152–53, 156, 193, 195–96, 199, 201, 213, 226, 230, 248, 321–23, 337
"Karzai 12" 199, 234
Keating (combat outpost; COP) 121, 179, 182, 184, 221, 243; battle of 179–83, 220, 249–50, 288–89
Kellogg, Brown, and Root (KBR) 87
Khan, Abdullah (Nurgaram chief of police) 265, 272, 274, 279–80, 294, 298, 319
Khan, Aminullah (insurgent leader) 268
Khan, Mohammed 95–96, 239
Khogyani District 85–86, 179, 294–96, 304, 306
Khyber Pass 88, 117, 151, 158
kidnapping incident 267–68, 270, 272
Kilcullen, David 85
Kolotan Valley 307
Konar Province 96, 116, 155, 176, 202, 237, 280, 289, 298, 301
Korengal Valley 21, 142, 155, 293
Kowlak village 144–45

Laghman Province 55, 84, 87, 116, 121, 149, 152, 163, 202, 212, 226, 240, 248, 257, 259, 278, 280; description 78–80, 86, 113; governor 160–61, 247–48, 253–54, 266
Laghmani, Sikander (Nurgaram sub-governor; later Barge Matal sub-governor) 100, 108, 111–113, 123–24, 128–32, 134, 147, 152–53, 163–64, 166, 168–69, 174–77
Lashkar-e-Tayibba (LeT) 10

leadership development program (LPD) 10
lessons of command 40, 65, 67–68, 71, 91–92, 94, 193, 255, 325, 328–29, 332–33
lieutenant (LT) 10, 23, 118, 179
live fire exercise (LFX) 10, 46, 48, 50, 53, 57–59
Lowell (combat outpost; COP) 249–50
Lowkar village 229, 236–38, 245–46, 255, 257, 261

M203 grenade launcher 10
Ma'in village 120, 142
Malel village 238, 281
Manas, Kyrgyzstan 19, 54, 81–82, 324–25
Mandol District 115, 139, 143, 156, 175; description 115; election incident 144–45; sub-governor 115, 143, 175
maneuver platoon 77, 97, 144, 172, 188, 190, 218, 221, 226, 230, 262, 266, 268, 271, 281–83, 286, 330; first contact 94–96; formation 44–45; operations 132, 169, 176, 194, 203, 239–40, 249, 255, 263, 265, 317; redeployment 317, 319; training 50, 58, 60–61, 70–71
maneuver units 10, 57, 165
Mangal Abdullah (Alingar sub-governor) 112–13, 128, 132–34, 161–66, 183, 198, 205–6, 213, 240, 244, 246–47, 252, 255–57, 259, 261, 272, 296
Mangow Afghan National Army checkpoint and village 187, 190, 251
marksmanship 48, 68–70, 72
marriage retreat 46
Mashpah Valley 99, 101, 104, 119–20, 122, 124, 128–29, 142, 190, 238, 243, 279, 281, 292
Mawlawi Mohammed 189
Mazella, 1Lt. Jason *216*–17, 341
McChrystal, Gen. Stanley 196, 219–20
McClintock, Staff Sgt. Jimmy D. 221, 223, 264, 287, 340
media visits 116–117
medical civil assistance program (MEDCAP) 10, 61, 138
medical evacuation (MEDEVAC) 173
medical training 44, 72
Mehtar Lam city 85–87, 158, 163–64, 184, 211–12, 217–18, 228, 240, 242, 255–57, 259–60, 278, 301, 309, 312
meteorological (MET) 10, 50, 66, 316
military police platoon 92, 112, 176, 179, 190, 203, 211, 218, 220–21, 238–40, 243, 246, 249, 252, 254, 265, 279, 314
mine resistant ambush protected vehicle (MRAP) 11, *137*, 258
Ministry of Defense (MoD) 191, 293
Ministry of Interior (MoI) 10, 132, 191, 233
Ministry of Rural Rehabilitation and Development 338–39, note 344
mission essential task list (METL) 10
mission rehearsal exercise (MRE) 11, 61

Monti (forward operating base; FOB) 167, 184, 220, 273, 296, 321–22
Mullah Agha (HiG commander) 289
Murray State University 18, 275

N2KL (Nangahar, Nuristan, Konar, and Laghman) 11, 77–78, 85, 142, 220; map 15–16
Nagil (combat outpost; COP) 256
Najibullah (new Alingar chief of police) 296
Nana 110–16, 119, 121–22, 126–27, 147, 156–57, 327
Nangarhar Province 85–86, 135, 199, 216, 293, 295, 306, 324
Nangaresh village 79, 166, 234–35, 241–42, 280; agriculture center 143; protest 253
Naray (forward operating base; FOB) 181, 184, 288–89, 299, 301, 315–16, 319
National Directorate of Security (NDS) 92, 104, 145, 186, 203, 205–6, 210, 219–20, 241, 248, 261, 267, 281
Naylar village 274–76, 280–81
negligent discharge 93
Nerdalen, Lieutenant 71
night letters 246
night vision goggles (NVG) 172
9/11 events 17–18, 26, 48, 228
non-commissioned officer (NCO) 11, 23, 30, 37
non-deployable 69
non-governmental organization (NGO) 11
al-Nuralam, Sakhi (deputy Nurgaram sub-governor) 177, 249, 266
Nuralam Valley 116, 138, 144, 155–56, 167, 172, 174–75, 178, 196–97, 203, 205, 213, 218, 231, 235, 244–46, 249, 266, 275, 293; operations in 176–77, 182, 185–87, 202, 239, 317
Nurgaram District 96, 99, 112, 114–15, 122, 128, 130, 138–39, 141, 144–45, 147, 149, 160, 164, 166, 169, 175, 178, 184–86, 194–95, 197–98, 206, 210, 218, 233, 248, 265, 270, 303; deputy sub-governor 204, 214–15, 232, 234, 239, 242, 249, 267 (*see also* al-Nuralam, Sakhi); new sub-governor 267, 274, 276, 279, 281; sub-governor 99–100, 108, 111–13, 123–24, 128–30, 132, 136, 138–39
Nuristan chief of police 97, 109
Nuristan Province 54–55, 83–84, 86, 121, 124, 131, 133, 138, 141–42, 148–49, 152, 156, 182, 187, 233, 324; description 78–80, 90, 93, 112–13, 115, 182; governor 90–91, 108–10, 129–30, 136, 138, 143–44, 148, 164, 173–75, 178, 180, 188, 190, 196–97, 212–14, 229–30, 234, 243–44, 247–48, 253, 299 (*see also* Kabir, Mullah); "liberation" of 182, 204, 206, 208, 221, 292; needs of 90, 111

observation post (OP) 11, 154; OP Loyalty 84, 94, 98, 206–9, 217, 221, 229, 237–38, 243, 249–52, 277, 292, 299, 301

observer controller (O/C) 11, 57
officer-in-charge (OIC) 11
officer professional development (OPD) 11
100 days of wind 19
173rd Airborne Brigade 203
Operation Enduring Freedom 29; IV 22; VII 23–25; X 11, 23–25
Operation Freedom's Sentinel 3
Operation Gunsmoke 64–66
Operation Mountain Lion 21
operations coordination center-provincial (OCC-P) 11, 176, 140, 146, 184, 262, 270, 288, 294, 310, 317
operations sergeant 11, 46, 81
organization day 47–48, 330
organization of journal 23–24, 27
Osmani, Hamid (Dow Ab sub-governor) 109–10, 132, 136, 139–40, 147–48, 152, 174, 177–78, 188–89, 196–98, 203–4, 212–14, 219, 232, 236, 238, 240, 246, 249, 251, 261–62, 272, 281, 324
out of traverse fire mission 11, 60

Pakistan 19
Pamir Mountains 81–82
Panjshir Province 183
Paranieh village 187, 194, 197, 218, 225, 244, 273
Parisaw village 236, 254, 281
partnership with government and ANA 78, 110; partnership mission 283–86, 290
Parun (Nuristan capital) 164, 169, 173–74, 185, 231
Parwai village 102, 107, 116, 185, 211, 238, 258
Pashagar village/valley 146, 272
Pashai tribe 79, 128–29, 149, 156, 167–68, 187, 192, 212–13, 253
Pashtun 20
patch ceremony 106–7
Pech Valley 176, 283, 288, 313
Pentagon Papers 3
Persian Gulf War 18
petition to remove Alingar chief of police 252–54
Petraeus, Gen. David 85
physical training (PT) 12, 31, 40, 72
plan of action in AO 83–84, 93–94, 99, 102, 107–9, 112, 121–22, 134–35, 151–52, 158, 223–24, 233, 258, 287; assessment of 122–23, 220, 223–24, 245, 256, 260, 265
plane crash in AO 188–92
platoon (PLT) 12, 53
platoon leader (PL) 12, 117
police pay issue 164–64, 169–70, 173–74, 185–86, 229–30, 234
poppy eradication 293–98, 300, 304–6
pre-command course (PCC) 12, 28
Predator unmanned aerial vehicle (UAV) 208, 250

pre-deployment site survey (PDSS) 12, 54–55, 83, 157, 159
Presidential Unit Citation 48, 56
professional development program 23, 32–33, 37–38, 44, 47, 51–52, 65–66, 141
proposed way ahead for Afghanistan 334–40
provincial election officer (PEO) 12, 147
provincial reconstruction team (PRT) 12, 77, 92–93, 100–2, 107, 113, 118, 137–38, 153, 155, 161, 163, 167, 171–73, 176, , 179, 211, 229, 245, 249, 265, 268–71, 273–76, 287; change of command 118, 269; relationship with 171–73, 240, 242–43, 252, 267, 269, 271
public affairs officer (PAO) 123
purple heart medal 186

Qargyhee District 257
quarterly training brief (QTB) 45
quick reaction force (QRF) 12, 107, 215, 291, 315

radar 199–200, 316
radio addresses 107, 112–13, 118, 123, 128, 130, 133–34, 136, 143, 152, 156, 161, 164, 171–72, 183, 191–92, 204, 210, 239, 244, 248, 261, 268, 275
radio station at Kalagush 90, 105, 123, 132, 134, 140, 154, 213, 251–52
Rahman, Abdur (new Nurgaram sub-governor) 267, 272, 296
al-Rahman, Mohammed (bombmaker) 121, 131, 238, 254, 279, 281, 292
Rajai village 266
Ramadan 12, 146–47, 152–53, 160–61, 163–64, 166–67, 170
ramp ceremony 134, 222
Rao, Sgt. Elijah John-Miles 221, **222**–23, 225–26, 228–30, 244, 258, 279–80, 287, 326, 330–31, 340; visit to Portland 329
rear detachment 12, 69, 71–72, 114, 140, 178, 207, 217
Rechalam Valley 176
recognition-primed decision making (RPD) 52, 58–59
reconciliation program (also known as reintegration) 80, 106–7, 109, 119–20, 148, 177–78, 196–97, 232, 236, 246–47, 280
reconnaissance 12
recovery operations 172
recovery period/reintegration training 326–331
redeployment 325–26; preparation 252, 302, 306, 313–14
Regional Command East (RC-E) 178
regional coordination center (OCC-P) 114, 116
relationship building 87–88, 92–93, 112, 114, 116–17, 124, 127, 136, 152–54, 158, 160–61, 177, 205, 225, 230, 245–46, 261, 286

Index

relief in place 77–97, 313–14, 317–18; process 82–87
remembrance ceremony 202–3
report hotline program 105, 107–8, 112, 155, 245, 256, 261, 263, 303
"resetting" 26
Riley, SFC Kyle **96**
ring road 20
rocket attacks 99, 105–6, 142, 45, 170, 205, 218, 308, 317–18; launch sites 94, 100, 106–7, 170–71, 206–7, 221
rocket propelled grenade (RPG) 12, 115, 130, 134–35, 208, 231
Rodriguez, Lt. Gen. David 297–98, 320
route clearance package (RCP) 194, 215–16, 254, 258, 260, 263, 280, 310
rules of engagement 234
Russian Bridge 91, 273

S1 (personnel officer) 12, 81, 200
S2 (intelligence officer) 13, 81, 232, 292
S3 (operations officer) 13, 42, 81, 86, 107, 140, 202, 282–83, 287, 296, 298, 301, 308, 316–17, 321, 341
S4 (logistics officer) 13
S6 (signal officer) 140
Sadr City 26
St. Barbara's Day Ball 52, 55–56
Sakhi, Wakil 122, 166, 230–31
Salaw Valley 229, 265, 315
School of Advanced Military Studies (SAMS) 18–19, 243
2nd Battalion, 12th Infantry Regiment 62, 332
2nd Battalion, 77th Field Artillery Regiment 22–23, 28, 80; assessment of 29–32, 34, 36–37, 39, 51–54, 57–58, 75–76, 332–33, 341–42; assumption of command 26, 30; character of soldiers 24, 75; outside perceptions of 45, 52–53, 58–59, 63, 178, 220; personnel available 68; preparations for combat 25, 27, 56, 61–62, 67–70, 72, 73, 76; situation in Afghanistan 74–75, 84–87, 91–92, 97–98, 101, 108, 150–51; vision for unit 27, 35, 55 (Alpha Battery 32, 34, 36, 47–49, 51, 53–54, 59, 70, 158, 163, 179, 184, **209**, 211, **260**, 301, **311–12**, **321**, **341**; Bravo Battery 43–44, 48–49, 51, 58–59, 62, 70, 88, **89**, 94, 96, **98**, 110, 118, 158–59, 201, 211, 273, 281–83, 285, 316, 321–22; Golf Company 40, 50, **137–**38, 158, **180–81**, 184, **198**, 200, 217, 241, 273, 282–83, 321, 328, 332)
2nd Battalion, 320th Field Artillery Regiment 282, 288, 306, 311, 316, 323–24
2nd Squadron, 221st Cavalry Regiment 259
sergeant (SGT) 13, 200
sergeant first class (SFC) 13
servant-leader 28, 30
Shemgal Valley 169, 203–4, 243, 249–51, 273, 277, 279, 308

Shir Mohammed (commander 2nd Brigade, 201st Corps, Afghan National Army) 283, 288–90, 292–93, 295–301, 304–8, 310–11, 315, 318, 320, 323
Shirzai, Gul Agha (Nangarhar governor) 55, 295, 306
Showk Valley 188, 190, 192
Shrobe, Lieutenant 66
Shrode, Lt. Cason 66, 220
shura 13, 72, 111–12, 146, 161–62, 176, 204, 215–16, 295; budget 214–15; development 246–49; education 231–32; Eid 177; election 104, 125, 127, 129–31, 138, 156, 198; friendship 114, 116–17, 122, 127; Mullah 147, 152–57; "pine nut" 168; reintegration 246, 261–63; security 92–93, 104, 114–15, 125, 139, 144, 153, 165, 173–74, 184, 205, 213–14, 233, 241–42, 250, 258, 279, 324
6th Battalion, 37th Field Artillery Regiment 36
6400 mils 5, 60, 63–64
small rewards program (weapon buyback) 13, 105–6, 110, 112, 117, 119–20, 122, 124–25, 130, 135–36, 142, 147, 154–55, 198
smuggling 78; gems 187, 235–36, 280; timber 187, 192, 220, 230, 235–36, 238–39, 248, 261, 266
Sons of Iraq 146, 337–38
Soui Tre, battle of 48
Soviet-Afghan War 79, 116, 136
specialist (SPC) 13
staff ride 43–44, 64
staff sergeant (SSG) 13
Steel Challenge 70
Steel Victory, operation 151
Sundawar village 116, 135, 144, **159**, 183, 185, 187, 205, 211, 225, 238, 244, 273, 282, 296; disaster 158–64, 168–69
"the surge" 3, 26, 54, 75–76, 81, 196, 219–20, 236, 344n

tactical command post (TAC) 13, 60, 289, 319–20
tactical operations center (TOC) 14, 61, 142, 170–71, 202, 207, 282, 289, 295, 302, 315
Tag Valley 220, 249, 315
Taliban (TB) 14, 19–20, 91, 111, 120, 128–29, 138, 251; in area of operation 77–78, 91, 100, 102, 128–29, 148, 155, 183; attacks 167, 179–80, 184, 207–10, 220–21, 262–63, 277, 302–3, 308; change in tactics 254, 256, 274; creation of 336; desire for revenge 210–11, 220, 237; election day 145–46, 198; loss of support 122, 133, 138; opportunity for victory 335–38; pay system 214, 220, 268; plans 121, 129; propaganda 127, 157, 165, 182–83, 188, 192, 236–37, 246; staying power 25; tests our mettle 99, 101–2, 106, 116, 271, 274; threats 213–14, 218; wedges 141, 152–53, 158, 162–63, 166, 191, 214

Index

target (TGT) 14, 60–61, 205, 215
targeting process 59, 91, 93–94, 158, 170–71, 179, 198, 228–29
Tatford, Flt. Reagan 62, 71
teacher pay issue 166, 231–32
10th Mountain Division 19–21, 54, 57, 142, 332
3rd Battalion, 321st Field Artillery Regiment: Bravo Battery 270, 274, 283, 291, 294, 312
3rd Brigade, 10th Mountain Division 19–21, 54, 57, 142, 332
3rd Squadron, 61st Cavalry Regiment 62, 100, 180, 289
13B (cannoneer) 5, 34
Titin Valley 99, 100, 122, 153, 169, 182, 196, 205, 215–16, 220, 238, 277, 283, 285
Torkham Gate 88, 117–18, 151, 158–59, 182, 201–2, 232, 262, 265, 271, 278, 280, 296, 298, 317
training (TNG) 14; issues 22, 49–51
transition of authority (TOA) 14, 90, 94, 97, 103, 108-, 120–21, 135, 160, 314, 320, 322–25; brigade 101
tribal culture 101–2, 167–68, 172, 195, 205, 219, 23334, 292, 334–35, 337
tribal dispute 128–31, 149, 156, 167–68, 187, 190–92, 212–13
troop leading procedures 45
troops in contact (TIC) 14, 94–95, 313
Tupak village 155, 198, 237–38, 273, 275, 311

UH (Taliban leader) 110
Under-Secretary of the Army 217
United Nations (UN) 336
US Army Corps of Engineers 166–67
unity of command 240, 269
USO tour 115

Vessey, Gen. John W. 56, 97, 186
Vietnam veteran support 47–48, 56, 312, 326

Wadawu Valley 106, 132, 161, 169–70, 189, 191, 215–16, 230, 250, 305, 307–8, 315, 317
Waigul Valley 21, 176
Wakil (member of parliament) 122, 166
Wamai tribe 79
"warlordism" 337
"warrior 12" tasks 70
Warrior Strike exercise 50–52
Wasilewski, Lieutenant 66
Wat-e-Jabbarkheyl 245
Waterman, Amanda 38
weapon cache 105, 110–13, 115, 117, 120, 123, 136, 215, 229–30, 236, 243, 245, 261–62, 265
white phosphorus 14, 294; use of 113–14
women in Afghanistan 162
World Food Program (WFP) 231
World Trade Center 17

XO (executive officer) 14, 45, 81, 140–41, 173, 262, 309–10, 341; issues with 63, 65, 140–41

Zahir Shah (former king of Afghanistan) 335
Zakat (gift offering) 152
Zio Haq (COP) 313
Zirat village 132
Zuma (German news service) 138

www.ingramcontent.com/pod-product-compliance
Ingram Content Group UK Ltd.
Pitfield, Milton Keynes, MK11 3LW, UK
UKHW021843140426
5217IPUK00022B/1570

www.ingramcontent.com/pod-product-compliance
Ingram Content Group UK Ltd.
Pitfield, Milton Keynes, MK11 3LW, UK
UKHW021842140426
5217IPUK00022B/1560